Engaging with Irish Vernacular Worldview
Narrative and Ritual Expression of Native Cultural Tradition

Engaging with Irish Vernacular Worldview

Narrative and Ritual Expression of Native Cultural Tradition

GEARÓID Ó CRUALAOICH

CORK **cup** UNIVERSITY PRESS

First published in 2022 by
Cork University Press
Boole Library
University College Cork
CORK
T12 ND89
Ireland

Library of Congress Control Number: 2022936350
Distribution in the USA: Longleaf Services, Chapel Hill, NC, USA

British Library Cataloguing in Publication Data
A CIP record for this book is available from the British Library.

ISBN: 978-1-78205-543-3

Printed in Poland by BZ Graf
Print origination & design by Carrigboy Typesetting Services
www.carrigboy.co.uk

COVER IMAGE – Tarot card 'Joker' woodcut circa 1750. Bavarian National Museum, Munich. Sourced from Alamy agency. Vide references to 'borekeen'/joker figure in the Part 1 article entitled 'The "Merry Wake" and Popular Resistance to Domination'.

www.corkuniversitypress.com

For Gay

Contents

PART 4: HISTORY AND POLITICS

Acknowledgements

I am very grateful to many people for encouragement and assistance during the very long time it has taken for this book to be completed.

Initially, Dr Stiofán Ó Cadhla was generous in his endorsement of the idea of my republishing essays and articles along with new writings. Bláthnaid Ní Bheaglaoich went to considerable trouble to prepare a fresh version of existing and new texts.

At a later stage, Dr Aoife Granville helped me to recover, re-edit and re-type large sections of the work when ill-health and the inadvertent in-office destruction of some of my books and papers rendered me unable to continue working.

Maria O'Donovan of Cork University Press afforded me forbearance and cooperation throughout the long delays to which the preparation of the book has been subject. I am extremely thankful to her for her patience and kindness.

I am grateful to the press' external readers for their observations and suggestions regarding improvement of the initial draft. Their guidance and ideas led to a re-organisation of the work that has been to its very considerable advantage.

Such re-organisation benefited very significantly from the insights and help – technical and editorial – of my wife Gay and my daughter Sorcha. Their love and their belief in the enterprise made it possible for me to persevere in the face of vicissitude.

Cúlra agus comhthéacs dátheangach atá leis an saothar so, mar is léir, agus táim an-bhuíoch dem chairde go léir a choimeád uchtach ionam in am an ghátair nuair a bhíodh caidreamh eadrainn – as Gaeilge nó Béarla – ar a raibh ar siúl agam.

Ní oraibhse ná ar éinne seachas mé féin amháin atá locht le cur maidir le fabhtanna agus easnaimh an leabhair.

Any errors, flaws and shortcomings in this work are mine alone.

I wish to express special acknowledgment to the first publishers for generous permission to republish, as noted, those essays previously in print and – in some cases – to other publishers, also noted, who subsequently acquired the initial copyrights and equally generously granted permission to republish.

Preface

The articles and essays of the four parts of this anthology present a treatment of aspects of the field of Irish studies in its many domains. The anthology is intended as a contribution to the teaching of Irish studies itself and to the formation of students of the several disciplines that are constituents of its essentially interdisciplinary nature.

Part 1 – 'Ethnology' – aims at providing a holistic introduction to topics of the field that is grounded in an anthropological perspective that can frame the treatment given in later sections to specific issues.

The second part – 'Poetics of Oral Literary Tradition' – concentrates on a central strength of Irish cultural tradition and a central concern of the scholarship of that tradition, namely the artistic richness of traditional narrative and vernacular storytelling. The significance of the relationship of such narrative richness to modern issues of literary excellence, language pedagogy and the representation of gender relations is touched on.

Part 3 – 'The Otherworld Feminine' – engages with an enduring topic within Irish cultural and religious tradition whose roots are prehistoric and whose relevance survives into modern times. Facets of medieval literature and society concern the otherworld feminine, and the evidence of the significance of such a figure in modern Irish literary imagination and in the intimate coping mechanisms of pre-modern and modern Irish mentality at times of life-crisis can be found in popular ritual practice and in legends of human females who are perceived as avatars of the otherworld feminine.

The final section – 'History and Politics' – deals with the interrelationship of folklore and history in the study and scholarship of Irish cultural tradition. The presence and the power of myth and mythological legend is touched on in relation to social history and to iconic historical events. Returning to an ethnological/anthropological perspective, treatment is made of the processes whereby the heritage of vernacular historical tradition and identity is constructed and the popular representation of these in folklore and folk life can be located 'in the field', collected and archived.

The essays and articles in this book issue from more than four decades of academic engagement on their author's part with the teaching of Irish studies in both Irish and English to students of a variety of institutions in Ireland and without. They exhibit a variety of styles from the occasional and discursive to the sustained and scholarly. They also exhibit a degree of overlapping and circularity – bordering on traces of repetition in places – that reflect both pedagogical choices and the ongoing development of the author's engagement with and understanding and interpretation of the matters involved.

A deal of the material here will have been previously encountered by some. A deal of it is new and unpublished. All of it is presented here in a fresh framework that attempts to be conscious of recent developments and recent publications.

It is to be hoped that the anthology will prove of interest and of academic use to students at all levels of Irish studies, from first year up to postgraduate level.

It is also intended that the anthology should be of use – as supplementary, elective reading – to students whose work on Irish language and literature, on Irish literature in the English language, on Irish history, on the sociology or anthropology of Irish communities past and present, brings them into contact with issues of culture and tradition relevant to the topics explored here.

It is the author's hope that readers of the anthology will regard it as both accessible and instructive and will derive from it some benefit in respect of their own work.

GEARÓID Ó CRUALAOICH

Ethnology

Introduction

While the articles in each of the four parts of this book can be seen to treat different aspects and topics within an Irish ethnology overall, the use of the term 'ethnology' itself as a title for this first part can be taken to indicate that the articles it contains are in some sense indicative of a generic sense of ethnology that informs the other parts with their own specific emphases on the poetics, the cosmology and the external history and politics of Irish vernacular culture and tradition.

It may be useful to consider briefly the actual term 'ethnology' in conjunction with its disciplinary sister terms 'folklore' and 'anthropology' as names for streams or divisions of scholarly study applied to the lives and cultural heritages of various groups and communities of people in modern times.

Discussing 'ethnicity' in the introduction to *History and Ethnicity*, Monograph 27 of the Association of Social Anthropologists, the editors suggest that it is a term that only makes sense in a context of relativities and of processes of identification.[1] 'Ethnicity' derives from the Greek term *ethnos*. This originally referred to large, mobile and seemingly disorganised groupings – akin to a swarm of bees or a routed army fleeing the battlefield – and had therefore a negative connotation. Over time the term *ethnos* underwent a long process of semantic and political inversions, coming in the nineteenth century to be adopted by scholarship as denoting something like 'a group of people of shared characteristics'.[2]

Ethnology, the study of *ethnos* and ethnicity today, is concerned not with some static, essentialist notion of group or national identity but rather with the dynamic processes of the cultural construction, contestation, transformation and ongoing representation/externalisation of local and community self-understanding and self-realisation in the face of the historical movements of modernisation and globalisation.

A recently published book entitled *Irish Ethnologies*[3] deals comprehensively with the origins and development of the subject in

Ireland and presents ethnographic detail and analysis of a wide range of topics within the overlapping foci of ethnology and anthropology. The concepts of locality and local tradition loom large in the study of Irish ethnology (including folklore) and Irish anthropology. As a comparative and analytic study of cultures, alongside its sister disciplines, it focuses especially on the everyday life of peoples and on the transformation and resurgence of vernacular cultural heritages.

Hastings Donnan shows that while this remains the case, it is also true that nowadays fieldwork can encompass a site where the local and the global are 'mutually constituted in a single research location'.[4] Writing elsewhere in the same book, on the sociocultural construction of 'folk history', Guy Beiner sees local tradition – a concept he locates at the heart of Irish ethnology – as proving to be 'a continuous process in the making, through which the extent and nature of its localness is constantly redefined'.[5]

Given an emphasis on constant redefinition and dynamic processes in respect of ethnology taken as the study of *ethnos* and ethnicity today, it may be useful to review the origins of the present author's understanding and use of the term together with a discussion of the terms 'ethnography' and 'worldview' as used here.

An initial undergraduate formation in both the linguistic and literary dimensions of Irish and English language provided an acquaintance with both vernacular and elite expression and representation of local, regional and national Irish identity in the manuscript traditions and literary texts engaged with. Subsequent postgraduate study in the history of the English language and an introduction to the methodology of fieldwork in folklore broadened into formal study within the disciplines of linguistics and anthropology focusing on the diversity and dynamic creativity of vernacular cultural lifestyle and worldview.

Such study illustrated how the history and development of linguistics and anthropology since the mid-nineteenth century in both America and Britain can be seen to share an aim to document and analyse materials that derive from the indigenous and non-western traditions of pre-modern *native* communities whether in non-metropolitan or colonial settings.

While western engagement with such communities had historically involved the unheeding ignorance and incomprehension of conquest and colonisation, the rise of Enlightenment philosophy resulted in the gradual pursuit and accumulation of knowledge of non-western pre-modern cultures from the point of view of the bearers of those cultures themselves.

Ethnography – the fruit of a gradual systematic and respectful documentation of the utterances and behaviours of the communities and individuals with whom fieldworkers in linguistics, folklore and anthropology interacted – yielded cultural materials for scholarly study according to the theories and methodologies of these disciplines.

The present author was encouraged by American scholarly mentoring to distinguish the matter of such ethnographic material from its necessary subsequent analysis and interpretation in the form of an ethnology that was the disciplinary sequel to fieldwork.

In modern European scholarly tradition, ethnology was widely regarded on the British side as just another name for social anthropology while Scandinavian, French and eastern European scholarship saw the development of concepts of ethnology as deriving from an appreciation of localised and national expressions of cultural identity. Particularly in a folklore and ethnology perspective this reflects the embracing of regional and local vernacular cultural traditions as enduring and nationally significant expressions of identity in the face of modernity and globalisation.

In Ireland, as in many other small new nation-states emerging in the early twentieth century from the European empires, the identification and privileging of various native vernacular traditions was seen to be a way of asserting national identity and the claim to nationhood. The customary and the traditional in the realms of verbal art, music, costume, calendrical festivals, life-cycle ritual, food production and cooking, craft-work decoration and adornment was recorded as folklore and documented into archives and museums – leading to academic analysis and publication under the name ethnology.

With industrialisation and the development of town life and urbanisation, the vernacular traditions of the mill, the factory, the shipyard began to be seen as folklore in their own right even as, in Ireland, the main focus of folkloric and ethnological scholarship remained until recently focused for the most part on traditional material of a rural ambience.

Nowadays, however, in Ireland as elsewhere the study of folklore and ethnology is concerned with the dynamic processes of community identity and self-expression, both as these once operated in terms of the creativity of vernacular, rural, cultural tradition *(béaloideas)* and as they operate in the contemporary creativity and imaginative vernacular popular art and craft of what has been styled 'the wonderful world of the everyday'.

This is a largely urbanised, cosmopolitan, globalised, post-modern and continually dislocated world where – in Guy Beiner's words – local tradition is constantly transformed and redefined in cultural performance and re-enactment that continually enlivens and enriches what might be mistaken as the mundane and the banal.

The dynamic creativity of vernacular verbal art and popular lifestyle, whether in a former largely rural setting, in the setting of the crafts and trades of town and urban life or in a contemporary setting of post-industrial, globalised modernity and digital post-modernity, can, in each instance, be envisaged as issuing from and being constitutive of a cultural self-identity possessed by its bearers and amounting to a vision of the world – a *worldview*. Where such self-identity – such worldview – might once have been understood as shared by a local community, the changes undergone by society in the course of modernisation and globalisation have rendered any such essentialist concept of worldview outmoded and inappropriate in relation to the ethnological and anthropological reality of cultural life in the contemporary world.

In modern theoretical perspective then, any idea of a discrete quantum of shared worldview is dead. But for the folklorist, the ethnologist, the anthropologist, the goal remains of understanding the world from the perspective of the performer of whatever culture is in question; the culture of which the performer is native and potential informant. The presentations of the various aspects of Irish tradition and vernacular culture dealt with in the articles of the different parts of this book are intended to offer insight, or at least entry, to representations of a worldview of Irish communities and Irish individuals as manifested and creatively expressed in customary narrative and ritual form.

Such manifestations and representations of worldview were a primary concern for Bronislaw Malinowski who is seen as a founding father of the craft of ethnography that remains at the heart of the practice of anthropology and ethnology. He understood every human culture to give its members a definite vision of the world.[6]

Such definite vision of the world – worldview, *Weltanschauung* – can be understood as being grounded in and issuing from some such fundamental ecological reaction and adaptation to environment touched on in the early part of the treatment of Irish culture in perspective proffered in the first article of Part 1 and which pertains to all living organisms. In the human instance, reaction and adaptation is to environments of a terrestrial, a social and a symbolic/imaginative order within which life is lived. Such human reaction and adaptation and the worldview(s) to which it gives rise is the stuff of culture.

The term 'culture' can be understood then, in a generic sense, as referring to the specific and characteristic adaptation to environment(s) which all living creatures employ in the course of their existence and the phases of their life. We may speak of the sense in which all sentient creatures can be said to have – within their culture – knowledge of their environment(s) and can be said to be capable of knowing the world(s) in which they live. Such knowledge and such knowing – such worldview – underlies and creatively informs their reactions to environment(s) in a continually changing and modulated way that is their response to the continually changing demands of living their life. For other creatures apart from humans, cultural knowledge may perhaps be thought of as instinctual, for the most part, and not consciously known and creatively reflected on as it is in the case of humans.

Knowing in human culture, the knowing underlying human reactions and adaptations to human environment(s), can be analysed into cognitive, affective and operant kinds of knowing.

The human cultural knowing arising from such responses and adaptations is capable of being envisaged as knowing/knowledge of landscape, knowing/knowledge of social relationships and knowing/ knowledge of the domains of memory and imagination to which, in the case of humans, speech and language give rise and give access.

Understood in this way, worldview could be taken, in a somewhat passive sense, to consist of the sum of what is known, seen or *viewed* in these domains from the point of view of the individual or group of individuals. But worldview is better understood – in the case of the human individual and the human group – not as what is seen or viewed but as a *viewing*, a *seeing*, an active, conscious engagement with and categorisation of the environments wherein their lives are lived. Such relationships of engagement and categorisation, consciously imagined, reflected on and *known* within a universe of symbolic/linguistic discourse, constitute, as it were, a grammar of cultural articulation whereby expression is given to the relationships and their out-working in the course of daily life. In this perspective, worldview is somewhat akin to human language itself in its symbolic categorisation and manipulation of perceived reality – something understood by Wilhelm von Humboldt, who held that language and worldview were inextricable.[7]

Accordingly, we can understand how worldview, like language, can filter, as it were, the cultural perception of individuals and of the communities of which they are members. Worldview thus channels cultural expression by individuals and community of that perception – in terms of the evaluations, the narrations, the ritual behaviours and institutions, the social customs, the technology and the material culture that goes to make up the individual's and the community's heritage of tradition, identity and self-realisation.

In filtering and channelling cultural perception and cultural expression in this fashion, worldview can be taken to mirror, to a degree, the linguistic filtering and channelling stance associated with the Sapir-Whorf linguistic relativity hypothesis – a hypothesis envisaging continual intersection between language and perception and positing the existence and endurance of specific modalities of expression characteristic of specific *linguistic* traditions.[8]

Going on these lines, Irish folklore and Irish vernacular tradition can be seen as giving cultural expression to the worldview creatively and continually constructed out of the historical and cultural experience of Irish communities by individuals in community. Such creative cultural construction is part of and contributes to an enduring and continually modulated communal creativity that issues in the form of narrative, custom, ritual and lifestyle and that channels Irish vernacular worldview and self-realisation and gives vernacular expression to specific modalities of *cultural* identity and tradition.

One of the aims of the author in presenting the various treatments of Irish folklore and tradition that are contained in the sections of this work is to suggest and indicate, in different ways, how the various aspects of Irish tradition discussed in the articles each instances that individual and community creativity residing at the core of the worldviews of the individuals and the communities with whose culture and traditions the articles deal.

Reference can be made to three works of scholarship where such individual creativity in the outworking of *worldview* is exemplified to a noteworthy degree in the narrative domain of cultural tradition in the case of three informants whose narrative repertoires and performances have been recorded and analysed by three folklore scholars.

Leabhar Sheáin Í Chonaill, published in 1948 by Séamus Ó Duilearga, consists of a comprehensive scholarly edition of the stories and traditions of Iveragh collected from a single celebrated informant over a period of years.[9] The material was, for the most part, written by hand verbatim, with particular attention on the collector's part to recording the phonetic and stylistic characteristics of the narrator in the performances that gave rise to the texts published. The degree to which this collector succeeded in capturing to a significant extent the creative interplay between the worldview of the narrator, that of his sparse audience and the communal worldview embedded in the traditional material recounted can be demonstrated to some extent in the article entitled *An Bhean Mhíreáireach* in Part 2 below.

Such creative engagement with local worldview by the master storyteller drawing on the repertoire of narrative heritage and communal tradition can readily be understood as the basis of this informant's local pre-eminence as a bearer and narrator of tradition.

Another such scholarly anthology of the extensive repertoire of traditional material written down from the narrative performance of a single informant is *Gort Broc: Scéalta agus Seanchas ó Bhéarra* edited and published by Máirtín Verling in 1996.[10] The editor's research into the biography of the informant, Pádraig Ó Murchú, and into the setting and operation of storytelling in the local community in which he lived during the early years of the last century, makes clear the extent to which Ó Murchú was able to utilise worldview as a resource with which to assert and establish for himself in his community a social and artistic identity. This he achieved despite personal circumstances of handicap, poverty and isolation. It was his personal prowess as tradition-bearer and narrative performer that gained for him the communal identity and recognition he enjoyed in the later part of his life. *Gort Broc* demonstrates the creative, dynamic nature of worldview as it can be invoked and put to work in the construction of the cultural reality of an informant's life and social status.

A third and comprehensive scholarly exposition of this dynamic, creative and constructivist nature of worldview in the achievement and maintenance by an individual informant of a sustained and sustaining sense of self is *Packy Jim: Folklore and worldview on the Irish border* published in 2016 by Ray Cashman.[11] The author entitles his introduction to the work 'Using Tradition, Constructing a Self', and succeeds in a pioneering way in showing how this informant's dynamic knowledge of a rich local narrative tradition combines with his own creative talent and his astute sense of history and identity to locate himself – in the words of one commentator – 'both in the technological consumerist future and in the primordial self-sufficient past'.

In considering ethnology, folklore and anthropology as sisterly disciplines engaged in the study of Irish tradition and worldview we can regard *Irish Ethnologies* (2017) – already referenced in note 3 above – as providing an overview of scholarship in the perspective of that particular discipline. In regard to anthropology, on the other hand, a comprehensive treatment of anthropologically oriented study of Ireland and Irish culture is contained in *The Anthropology of Ireland* (2006).[12] Similarly, in regard to folklore, a comprehensive account of the origin and development of that discipline in Ireland is given in *Locating Irish Folklore* (2000)[13] and in the chapter 'Folkloristic-Ethnological Studies in Ireland' in *Irish Ethnologies.*[14]

The essays of Part 1 – following this introduction – aim to introduce and engage with the study in ethnological and anthropological perspective of certain prominent features of Irish local tradition. One of these has been the presence in worldview of an ambiguity or duality of allegiance in respect of the nature and location of an otherworld and of the supernatural agencies that control it and that can be encountered in the ordinary course of human life in ways involving alternative mediators.

A specific instance of that ambiguity – showing an accommodation to Christian orthodoxy of a heterodox aspect of vernacular religious practice – is illustrated in the case of a medieval charm enduring in folklore and in modern creative literary narrative.

Another feature has been the perception and recognition of links between the supernatural agency of native otherworld and the hermeneutic and therapeutic functioning at times of life crisis accredited to certain women who perform valuable services for individuals and for community.

A further feature has been the ethnographically striking sacred and social centring of community life in the rituals and behaviours of funerary custom. Here both the duality of cosmological allegiance and the relationship of female social function to native otherworld agency is manifested in ways that have been shown to continue to colour contemporary funerals in Ireland today.[15]

CHAPTER I

Cultural Ambivalence and Clerical Authority

[A paper read to the Merriman Summer School, County Clare in August 1984]

C lergy are the professional, full-time practitioners who operate in that dimension of culture frequently characterised as symbolic and consisting, in large part, of Ritual and Belief. Another way of describing the ambit in which clergy operate is to call it the magico-religious domain of life. In Irish tradition there is relatively little magic to be encountered centrally in this domain but in Ireland, as everywhere else, magical beliefs and magical acts are to be found – operating not only in the field of religion and ritual but also in the fields of the economy, law and justice, medicine and therapy. So, too, notions of witchcraft and sorcery are definitely peripheral in Irish tradition when we focus on the central, mainstream continuity of Christianity as the main morality cult of the Irish. Nevertheless, in the conception and characterisation of the worlds of physical phenomena and social structure, Irish tradition, in company with that of other traditional societies, shows plenty evidence of the operation in popular culture of beliefs and practices that are not congruent with a strictly orthodox adherence to the tenets and observances of the Christian faith. In so far as popular Christianity in Ireland is concerned, we need not be surprised to find such a mixture of the orthodox and an unorthodoxy consisting of both remnants of earlier religion and outgrowths of the popular imagination that develop, as it were, around the edges of the central orthodoxy.

Belief in some kind of supernatural power would appear central to all religion. What is important to realise is that the emotional content of such belief is equally important with its intellectual content. Thus religion can operate as a medium for the achievement of people's keenest experiences and serve as means of coping with fundamental personal problems at the level of the individual as well as the group. Traditional religious beliefs are deeply infused with and based on emotional attitudes of great strength and practical relevance so that when conversion of a traditional society to Christianity takes place it is generally the case that the old gods continue to exist and are popularly regarded as being capable still of interfering in human life. Religion, like art and language, while being individually interpreted and supported, is shared socially and transmitted socially in ways that give rise to elaborations and transformations of its formally authorised orthodoxy. Thus the description of the actual religious beliefs and practices of a Christian society, and especially a traditional Christian society, will – in regard to both the conception of the supernatural and the modes of ritual action – show a mixture of a sort that is well exemplified in Seán Ó Súilleabháin's *Handbook of Irish Folklore*.[1]

Chapters 4 and 12 of the Ó Súilleabháin *Handbook*, headed 'The Community' and 'Religious Tradition' respectively, deal with the practice of religion in Irish popular tradition, with the faith, the priest and the folklore of priests. Chapter 10, on the other hand, is headed 'Mythological Tradition' and deals with the characters and other aspects of Irish folk culture that can be considered as retentions from a magico-religious world that preceded and, to a considerably limited degree, managed to survive the domination by Christianity of the religious domain of Irish popular tradition. Chapters 5, 8 and 9 of the *Handbook* deal with further aspects of popular belief and practice that exemplify that kind of intermingling of the orthodox and the unorthodox in the area of religion and the supernatural that is the basis of the cultural ambivalence which I wish to examine. I believe that we have good evidence of the conflict of such ambivalence with Irish clerical authority in regard to questions such as the location and nature of the otherworld, divination in regard to the true causes of things, arbitration between differing conceptions of the otherworld and arbitration between the clergy as champions of Christian orthodoxy and the ordinary people whose popular culture contained unorthodox items of both practice and belief to which they had profound emotional attachment. I emphasise again that such a state of affairs is very commonly encountered in the study of traditional culture elsewhere in the world. Naturally such study is best approached on the basis of broad comparison, since religion, as a universal corollary of human social existence, presents a bewildering tapestry of ethnographic detail on the ground.

I would like to refer here to an approach to the study of religion that is global in the comprehensiveness of its scope and that yet can be utilised to provide a model very useful for the analysis of material in relation to ritual and symbolic aspects of Irish popular tradition. The originator of the approach is Anthony Wallace, a professor of both anthropology and psychiatry.[2] Wallace's starting point is a list of thirteen categories of what he describes as 'minimal religious behaviour'. The categories are those of Prayer, Music, Physiological Exercise, Exhortation, Recitation of Code, Imitating Things, Touching Things, Avoidance of Touch, Feasts, Sacrifice, Congregations, Inspiration and the use of Symbolic Objects. From these minimal behavioural categories Wallace goes on to establish levels of both Ritual, which he defines as patterned sequences of behaviour, and Belief, which he sees as the rationalisation of ritual in terms of myth, legend, value system and cosmology. At a higher level again in the Wallace system of looking at religion such rituals and beliefs become integrated as cults. These cults constitute for Wallace the characteristic religious institution. Anthropologists in general differentiate what they call the main morality cult of a culture from peripheral morality cults, highlighting in this way a central aspect of religion whereby it constitutes the moral basis in society for all human action. While Christianity has afforded the main morality cult of the Irish for something approaching a millennium and a half, we need not be surprised to see evidence in Irish tradition of peripheral cults too.

Regarding ritual, Wallace insists on its universality and on the universality of the oral narrative repertoire that, in every society, justifies it. However, he makes an important distinction between the ritual and narrative of the religions of civilisation as opposed to those of the religions of the traditional society, whether peasant or tribal. In the case of the ritual and narrative of the religions of civilisation, the ritual and narrative of, say, the so-called world religions, we find, as a rule, an intellectual elaboration and a central authority that serve to codify both ritual and narrative into logically integrated, closed systems of thought. In traditional religions, on the other hand, it is far more common to encounter low levels of integration together with an accompanying degree of inconsistency in the interpretation of ritual and narrative orthodoxy. Any model for use in connection with religion in Irish tradition should allow for both an integrated, formally transmitted orthodoxy and an informally transmitted body of belief and practice that includes popular versions of formal orthodoxy as well as items of ritual and narrative that ultimately hail from outside the Christian tradition – no matter how well adapted and integrated with that tradition they may have become over the years.

The following is intended to be an indication of the way such a model might be set down in schematic form.

Figure 1.1 The magico-religious domain

The Magico-Religious Domain			
era	*archaic/early medieval*	*early/late medieval: early modern*	*late modern*
cult	Celtic rituals	Christian rituals/ beliefs: popular Christianity	formal/vernacular Christianity neo-pagan/wicca- practice
transmission	Druidic tradition	clerical orthodoxy: popular/vernacular tradition	formal/vernacular Christianity/neo- pagan traditions
Ongoing accommodation/reinterpretation			

The distinction between formal and vernacular relates to the mode of transmission of the material in question. Examples of popular prayers and practices that exemplify the relationships involved would be: 1) the observance of Reek Sunday on Croagh Patrick, and 2) the observance of pattern days, for example St Gobnait's Day in Baile Bhúirne. In both cases there is an input into the observance from the learned, formal, clerical world of orthodox, mainstream Christianity but also from the popular, vernacular unorthodox periphery where continuity of contact is maintained with ancient tradition originating independently of Christianity in Irish culture. St Patrick replaces Lugh, on the one hand, and Gobnait, the female euhemerisation of Goibniu, a Celtic god of craft, becomes an exemplary Christian holy woman and the patron saint of orthodox Catholic observance. Many more examples are readily adduced to support such a model.

I have spoken of the location and nature of the otherworld as an issue on which cultural ambiguity and clerical authority come into a sort of opposition. In general such opposition cannot be seen to have given rise to any very dramatic or very serious conflict on a large scale. At the same time the portrayal of the relative powerlessness of priests in the face of manifestations of the fairy Otherworld is evidence that in the popular mind the whole ritual, symbolic, religious domain is not entirely within the field of authority of the Christian clergy. Many examples of such portrayals can be found in the texts collected and published by Seán Ó hEochaigh and Séamus Ó Catháin in *Síscéalta ó Thír Chonaill/ Fairy Legends from Donegal³* and *Scéalta Cois Cladaigh/Stories from Sea and Shore*, the latter deriving from the repertoire of north-west Mayo.⁴ One particularly interesting example was told by Amhlaoibh Ó Luínse of Cúil Aodha to Seán Ó Cróinín.⁵ The piece is entitled 'Bean ón Saol Eile' and tells the story of a young girl troubled day and night by a phantom woman who follows her from place to place and who is more than a match for the *sagart*. The phantom woman is finally mollified only when the girl performs on her behalf the ritual observances of the 'rounds' at St Gobnait's cemetery. It is to the Christian afterlife that the phantom woman seeks and ultimately gains admission in this narrative; but in its mixing of Christian and Celtic-peripheral material the tale well exemplifies the kind of cultural ambiguity I have in mind. Incidentally, one incident in this narrative points to the skilful invocation by Amhlaoibh of people's fear of the otherworld in a manner that tells as much of the power of popular tradition as it does of the narrative prowess of the storyteller. The relevant passages of the narrative are as follows:

1. The powerlessness of the priest:

> *Do dhin a muintir gach ní fhéadadar. Thógadar tig istig i gCill Áirne, agus bhíodh na buachaillí istig acu a' scuraíocht agus ag imirt chártaí, mar chuideachtain.*
>
> *Tráthnóna éigint, do chonaic an gearráchaille an bhean, nú an sprid, mar adeirims, a' teacht isteach agus a' dul fén leabaig. Nuair a thit an oíche, do thosna sí arís ar an gcailín beag. Bhí na buachaillí istig, agus do ritheadar amach a' d'iarraig an tsagairt. Tháini sé, agus isteach sa tseomra mar a raibh an cailín.*
>
> *'A' bhficeann tú anois í?' ar sisean.*
>
> *'Chím', aduairt an gearráchaille.*
>
> *Thosnaig sé ar léitheoireacht, agus t'réis tamaill d'fhiafraig an sagart: 'A' bhficeann tú anois í?'*
>
> *'Chím', arsan gearráchaille: 'sidí ansan í!'*
>
> *'Ach theipeadh ar éinne eile í fhiscint. Ansan, thug sé scian choise duí 'na láimh dhi agus sheasaimh agá drom'.*

'Sáig anois é', aduairt sé, 'leis a' sciain sin!'
'Chó luath agus bheadh an scian curtha i láimh an ghearráchaille ag an
sagart bheadh an scian sciubaithe agus curtha 'na seasamh i gclár an úrláir.
B'sheo mar fhan an scéal.

Her people did everything they possibly could. They built a house
inside in Killarney and they had 'the lads' in storytelling and card-
playing for company.
One evening, the little girl saw the woman, or the spirit, as we'd say,
coming in and going under the bed. When night came she started
troubling the girl again. The 'lads' were in the house and they ran out
to get the priest. He came, and down with him into the room where
the girl was.
'Do you see her now?' he says
'I see her,' said the little girl.
He began to read [his holy book] and after a while he enquired
again, 'Do you see her now?'
'I see her,' said the little girl, 'look at her there.'
But everyone else failed to see her. Then the priest gave her a black-
handled knife into her hand and stood behind her back himself.
'Stab her now,' he said, 'with that knife.'
As soon as ever the priest used to put the knife into the girl's hand it
used to be whipped away and put sticking into the floor. And that's
how things remained.

2. The preferred vision of the otherworld:

   Nuair a bhí na t'ruis túrtha aici, d'inis sí don chailín mar gheall ar an
   oíche do bhíodar i gCill Áirne, nuair a tháinig an sagart isteach.
   'Dhin sé a dhíthal orm', aduairt sí, 'ach ní raibh baol ormsa uaig, nuair
   ná rabhas damanta. Agus anois', ar sise, 'más maith leat seasamh anso ar
   mo chois agus féachaint siar do dhruím mo gualann, tá radharc muar le
   fiscint agat'.
   Ach do dhiúlthaig an cailín don rud so a dhéanamh.

When [the girl] had the 'rounds' completed [the woman] told her
about the night they were in Killarney, when the priest came in. 'He
did his level best on me,' she said, 'but there was no danger to me
from him since I wasn't damned. And now,' said she, 'if you would
care to stand here on my foot and look back over my shoulder you
could see a wonderful thing.' But the girl declined to do this.

In *Scéalta Cois Cladaigh/Stories from Sea and Shore* we find many such examples of the mixture of Christian and peripheral items of lore that indicate an ambivalence in traditional culture regarding the question of the otherworld. We also find incidents recording the powerlessness of clergy in the face of peripheral Otherworld characters. Séamus Ó Catháin, in his introduction to the texts, describes the contexts of their recording and gives us to understand that the local people gave general sympathetic approval to the work whereby community traditions and lore regarding the otherworld – among other topics – were being documented. This approval was not without its ironic side. A chorus of mock warnings would be directed against Séamus' elderly informants concerning the dire consequences of telling too many 'lies', and the prophecy made that '*Á, bo, ní fhicfidh sibh flaitheas choích.*' / 'Well, indeed, ye will never see heaven'. In cultural reality, it has not always been entirely clear which of two heavens Irish tradition envisaged as the one we could all look forward to seeing. Allegiance appears to be given at one and the same time to the notion of the heaven of orthodox Christian teaching: an afterlife, entirely separate from this human world, in which the soul enjoys for eternity the vision of the Christian Godhead, and also to the notion of a version of *Mag Mel* or of *Tír na nÓg*. This alternative Otherworld is envisaged as existing under the same sky as our human world, as being inhabited by a society of goddesses, gods, heroes, fairies and ancestors whose lives impinge, on occasion, on human society.

The many legends concerning the human midwife carried off to the hill to assist at a fairy birth or the sickly fairy changeling left in place of the healthy human infant often typify this ambivalence in a very vivid way. There is evidence too that such ambivalence could have tragic consequences in the human world for real people. The Bridget Cleary affair in south Tipperary in 1895 is one such case.[6] Bridget Cleary was thought by her husband and others to be a fairy changeling and she died as a result of maltreatment administered to her in an effort to reverse the changeling process. Clerical authority, in the person of the parish priest, a Fr Ryan, visited the house twice during the days of Bridget's ordeal but claimed later in court not to have seen anything improper or unusual going on in the house. It is illustrative of the relationship between cultural ambivalence and clerical authority that Fr Ryan should be quoted as saying, 'The priest is very often the last to hear of things like this.'

I want to mention aspects of the merry wake and the legend of Biddy Early as bearing on the question of cultural ambiguity and clerical control; but first let me point to something relating to the same question in the work of the eponymous ancestor of the Merriman School. I have commented elsewhere on ways in which *Cúirt an Mheán Oíche* operated in the lives of the ordinary people as a solace and a source of imaginative regeneration.[7] To an extent, this power in the poem is based on Aoibheall's status as a female sacerdotal figure who mediates between human society and the supernatural world. She is thus an alternative to the clergy in their role as mediators and ministers of the Lord. Around line 120 of the poem she is represented thus:

Líne 115 *Duine don buíon so líonta i gcomhachta*

> *Cara na Muimhneach, síbhean Léithchraig,*
> *Scaradh le saoithibh sí na slua so,*
> *Scaitheamh ag scaoileadh daoirse i dTuamhain seo.*

One of that company so filled with power

> The friend of all Munster, Craglee's Otherworld woman
> Parted a while from the knowledgeable ones of that company
> To release Thomond's bonds of misery.

The clerical image the poem projects seems to me to contain an ambivalence in the priestly role between the priest as minister of the Lord and the priest as himself a kind of worldly 'lord' – wielding great power in the social arenas of justice and morality but outshone by Aoibheall when it comes to the sacred unction of mediating with the divine. When the elderly plaintiff at Aoibheall's court describes how he brought his wife to the priest for marriage, such ambivalence in the priestly role, between worldly potentate and man of God, is put at its crudest. The priest, we are told, was excessively approving of the marriage in a manner that casts doubt on the clarity of his own role in the affair. The line (*líne 506*) in question is:

> *An sagart ró-bhaoch is b'fhéidir fáth leis*

> The priest was exceedingly thankful – and
> Maybe not without good cause.

This degree of complicity on the part of the clergy in worldly matters is one ground of the general complaint in the poem regarding the non-

availability of priests for conjugal business. In a sense we are given a vision
of the clergy as prime human stock and, as such, ridiculous aspirants
to the status of divine mediators. This vision also, I think, is an element
behind the call in the poem for the abolition of institutionalised marriage:

Líne 593 *Cá bhfuil an gá le gáir na bainise*
    Cartadh biotáille is pá lucht sainte,
    Sumaigh ar bord go fóiseach taibhseach,
    Gliogar is gleo acu is ól dá shaighdeadh
    Ó d'aibigh an t-abhar do bhronn Mac Dé
    Gan sagart ar domhan dá dtabhairt dá chéile?

What need for the shouts of the wedding-feast,
The waste of drink and the remuneration of the greedy,
The plump at table ostentatiously pampered,
With noisy din and drink to incite them
Since the child which the Son of God bestowed
Ripened without any priest at all giving them to each other?

Thus, the anti-clerical streak noted in *Cúirt an Mheán Oíche* can be rooted,
to a degree, in the ancestral perception of an Otherworld alternative to
that represented in the orthodox notion of the Christian afterlife, an
alternative Otherworld that is not mediated by Christian clergy.

Next, if we examine the legend of Biddy Early, we learn that she is
alleged to have married at least three times and that on the third occasion
it is reported that she was obliged to go down to Limerick in order to
marry, having been, as it were, excommunicated locally by the clergy
of Feakle where she lived during the latter part of her career.[8] She is
portrayed in the stories relating to her as having been always at odds with
the clergy but as having had no difficulty in renouncing her powers and
being fully reconciled with the Christian faith when the time came for
her to die. One gets the strange impression in these stories that the clergy
are portrayed as having consistently misunderstood the nature and origin
of her gifts – regarding her, mistakenly, as someone having contractual
obligations with evil otherworld powers whose ultimate service was
diabolical. The ordinary people, among whom she lived and who came
to her to engage her services, are portrayed as having an understanding
of her that is free of any contact with diabolic power and that regards
her as enjoying a morally and spiritually innocent status. Certainly she
is understood as someone who has had access to and who has developed

psychic power. The origin of this power, however, is understood to be located in the fairy regions where Aoibheall reigns and the commonest account of her acquisition of her powers tells us how her son stepped into the *lios* (fairy fort) to come to the aid of the local fairies who were being hard-pressed in the course of a hurling match with a rival team. As a reward he received the famous 'black bottle' which he was to carry home to his mother and which was to be the symbol of those powers which she is henceforth to enjoy and to operate for the benefit of those seeking her aid. Thus, Biddy Early, in oral tradition, is clearly to be understood as a *bean feasa*, a wise woman, and not as any kind of practitioner of witchcraft or sorcery. Neither is she portrayed in any primary way as a healer or herbalist though there is a therapeutic aspect to her ministrations. What she traded in was knowledge, the real – if hidden – causes of things, and she inherits, in her legend, a status deriving from this that is well known in medieval and in early Irish literature and tradition. She is a kind of mediator on the people's behalf with the peripheral Otherworld of ancestral tradition and is to be regarded in her legend as being on a par in her mediatorship with clerical mediators between the people and the Christian supernatural.

She herself is shown as respectful of the priests and their powers but confident and masterful in the exercise of her own similar powers in the domain that the people understand and allow to be properly hers. Clerics are sometimes portrayed in stories about Biddy Early as trying to outwit her or demonstrate the superiority of their brand of power, but here again, as in stories of the type of 'Bean ón Saol Eile', we are shown the superior efficacy, in its proper domain, of the power operating on the Celtic periphery of Christian orthodoxy. Biddy mediated for the people between human society in the natural world and the fragmentary remnant of the Celtic otherworld that has been retained in the periphery of Irish Christianity in popular tradition. The oral narrative that codifies and manifests that tradition is not to be understood as implying any clash or opposition of hostility between that peripheral supernatural (and its mediatrix) and the dominant, mainstream, orthodox, Christian supernatural that is mediated to the people through Christ and his clerical ministers. There is ambivalence and co-existence rather than open hostility but there is not the same Christianisation of the old and the peripheral as took place in the case of, say, the festival of Lughnasa or the feast of St Bridget. Biddy Early operated in tradition in a separate domain that resists integration with mainstream orthodoxy. She is shown to be capable of 'standing out' to the priests on occasion as the poet-heroes of tradition also do, since she, like them, has independent access to the supernatural. Biddy Early is a shamanic figure in Wallace's terms, neutralising and mediating supernatural and psychic power on behalf of the community in which she lived and practised. She is one of a long line of such practitioners who, in Irish tradition, avail of a general access to the ancestral supernatural realm through spells, charms, fairy contact and poetic prowess. The social cost of such contact and such powers is marginalisation and, in tradition, Biddy is portrayed as being marginalised in both the civil and the ecclesiastical order of things. She cannot be regarded as a witch, however, in the general European or the general anthropological use of the term. That she should be portrayed as having been so misunderstood as a witch – by a least some clerics who are shown as regarding her as an opponent – is a direct and interesting outcome of that cultural ambivalence regarding the supernatural and the otherworld that is so untroublesome a part of Irish popular tradition.

Finally, we can look at the customs of the merry wake and the specific wake amusements that are a feature of it in order to illustrate further aspects of the tension between clerical authority and popular allegiance to peripheral areas of our model of the magico-religious domain that Irish tradition records.[9] Here we have a documented history of serious ecclesiastical opposition at all levels of hierarchy to what the church saw as pagan excess and impropriety. From the Synod of Armagh in 1614 to an episcopal pronouncement in the diocese of Ardagh and Clonmacnoise in 1903 we see the behaviour of the people to be, to a degree, in defiance of the authority of their clergy. Actual excommunication is prescribed in regulations for the archdiocese of Cashel in the year 1782, but it is generally acknowledged that the abandonment of the customs of the merry wake came about more through the rise of a form of Victorian respectability in the countryside than through the belated success of the clergy in imposing standards of behaviour in this matter that accorded more closely with orthodox Christianity. Many people who remembered the more full-blown version of the merry wake from their youth may well, of course, have believed that it *was* clerical influence that had effected the change. Certainly we can suppose that as the power of tradition weakened throughout rural Ireland in the nineteenth century – that is, as the repertoire of traditional knowledge, custom and belief was radically transformed and reduced – the ability of the emergent and socially enhanced clergy to dominate increased. This is probably especially true in areas where the decline of the Irish language was a significant element in a general socio-economic transformation. Wood-Martin reports as follows the comment of an informant who was questioned about that part of the wake game 'the building of the ship' that was known as 'erecting the mast': 'Lord, how did you know that? It's nearly sixty years since I saw it and sure the priests won't let it be acted now.'[10]

Seán Ó Súilleabháin touches on another aspect of the wake amusements that is germane to this discussion.[11] He reports that certain games and customs were 'filled with sarcasms on various Christian rites and customs' and that the church's teaching was 'ridiculed to her face' in the case, for example, of the enacting of mock marriages and mock confessions. He emphasises, however, that there was in these traditions no idea of 'outraging propriety or religion' and that the people had an unquestioning faith that such behaviour, allowed on the occasion of the merry wake, was otherwise very wrong. Dr Connolly takes this view also.[12] While he sees that the satire 'directed at the Catholic clergy and at aspects of Catholic teaching and practice' is suggestive of more than 'a general lack of reverence', he thinks that the main reasons for clerical opposition to the traditions of the merry wake were practical rather than ideological. While it may be granted that the stated clerical objective was to control and to manage manifestations of peripheral cult remnants in the religious domain, it may still be argued, given the fact that the clergy and the bishops can have been in no doubt whatsoever of the nature and antiquity of the tradition from which such customs sprang, that we have here evidence pointing to an ecclesiastical acknowledgement of how unlikely was their eradication. Thus, the seeming lack of ideological opposition does not mean the absence of ideological and cultural ambivalence. Rather it is further support for the notion that such cultural/ideological ambivalence has been continuously deep-seated in Irish popular tradition. Again, as in the Biddy Early case, where – by contrast – clerical opposition is expressed in substantial and ideological rather than in managerial terms, there is the tendency to view wake games and the like as diabolical rather than as spiritually innocent manifestations of ancestral peripheral cults. And of course it is not surprising – in the historical context of the spread of Catholic popular devotion and mythology – that in some accounts of the mock marriage the false bridegroom to whom the girl is wed is fitted out with *crúibíní an áirseora*/the hooves of satan. This can be regarded as an early equivalent to Catholic Truth Society pamphlets of later times with titles like 'The Devil at Dances'.

Drawing on the thinking of Scandinavian scholars, Seán Ó Súilleabháin has suggested that wake amusements and the merry wake itself can be seen as a form of *rite de passage* whereby the wound of death is healed in the community and the ancient, universal fear of the dead is assuaged. Dr Connolly sees much to commend this point of view and adds that in such rites the continued vitality of the community is asserted in the face of death. The festive wake, he writes, served for the community in general to handle the emotional and psychological stress of death. One must point out, however, that it was in precisely these instances of death where the emotional and psychological stress would be felt most keenly – the death of a young person, the death of the mother of a young family, the sudden death of an adult man in his prime – that the festive wake was strictly precluded in Irish tradition. Rather was it the case that the deaths of the very elderly, the unmarried and other socially marginal individuals were the occasion of the greatest merriment and the greatest festivity. In its truly tragic and sorrowful losses the community gave full and respectful preference to the prayers and observances of mainstream Christian orthodoxy. In the case of marginal deaths, however, room was found for the expression of values somewhat oblique to Christian orthodoxy but traditionally respectable and revered. The ancient notions of the feasting and hunting that occupied the time of the inhabitants of the kingdom of *donn* and the land of the *sí* cannot be seen in any simplistic way as lying under the surface of the customs of the merry wake. Nevertheless, they do, I believe, exert, at very long range, a residual influence. The customs of the merry wake in their character as manifestations of peripheral values also serve as a vehicle for the signalling in popular tradition of perceptions of the new clerical presence that emerges in penal and post-penal Ireland. On this point I would simply note that the character of the priest portrayed in the mock marriage, the mock confession and the other clerical mimes and representations in question is that of the priest as a civil authority regulating the social order rather than as a charismatic or shamanic figure respected and feared because of his sacred status as a mediator of supernatural power.[13] This conflict in the role of the clergy in Irish life is one that has perhaps continued to exist into the present day where a role as community leader and indeed as politician has seemed to come easily to many priests in social contexts where a residual popular ambivalence regarding the supernatural and its human mediation has persisted.

CHAPTER 2

An Leabhar Eoin: The In Principio charm in oral and literary tradition

[Published in Ilona Tuomie et al. (eds), *Charms, Charmers and Charming in Ireland* (Cardiff: University of Wales Press, 2019), pp. 177–87]

Leabhar Eoin ('The Book of John') is the Irish-language name of a Christian textual amulet consisting of the opening passage of the fourth gospel. Such textual amulets were widespread in medieval and early modern Christian tradition. While other gospel passages were held to be powerful and holy in their own right, the most frequently encountered scriptural quotation in textual amulets was John 1:1–14 – known as the *In Principio* and described by Eamon Duffy as one of the most numinous texts used in the late medieval church.[1] Written on a scrap of parchment or paper, folded, covered and hung around the neck, it was widely used as a charm against all evils. Its provision by clergy for payment features in the list of charges brought by reformers against greedy ecclesiastics, and in particular against mendicant friars;[2] such a friar, perhaps, as is portrayed by Geoffrey Chaucer in the General Prologue to the *Canterbury Tales*, of whom we are told: 'So plesant was his *In Principio* / Yit wolde he have a farthing er he went'.[3]

Thomas Aquinas took a nuanced view of the use of textual amulets, condemning all ritual practices that the church deemed 'superstitious', but accepting such amulets as legitimate if they were understood as the visible signs of Christian devotion.[4] According to Don C. Skemer, in his study of textual amulets in the Middle Ages, the Inquisition was inclined to take the use of Jewish or Muslim amulets as evidence of sorcery, while the Protestant reformers broadly condemned all such ritual practices associated with the Church of Rome (pp. 231, 237 note 8). Martin Luther preached to the effect that it was 'a frightful misuse and a piece of witchery to write the words *In Principio erat Verbum* on a slip of paper ... and hang it around one's neck or somewhere else ... as a protective charm against thunder and storm, as was customary in the papacy' (pp. 66–7). William Tyndale, the English translator of scripture, condemned amulets, charms and blessings based on John 1 and also condemned the itinerant friars who 'served them up to the laity' (p. 89).[5] Skemer, however, questions whether 'subtle theological critiques of amulet use had much impact on rank-and-file Christians' (p. 68).

A comprehensive account of the history of the use of the *In Principio* in Catholic rubric and as a charm in Irish tradition has been provided by Pádraig Ó Héalaí.[6] Noting that the earliest Irish reference to the use of the *Leabhar Eoin* appears to be a jocose reference in the late-eleventh-century tale *Aislinge Meic Conglinne*, he points to the specific defence of the practice in Irish counter-reformation sources such as *Parrthas an Anama* (*The Cloister-Paradise of the Soul*), published at Louvain in 1645, and *Lóchrann na gCreideamhach* (*The Guidelight of the Faithful*), published at Rome in 1676 – both of which emphasise that its non-superstitious nature derives from its approval and blessing by the church (p. 369).[7] Even though the so-called devotional or tridentine evolution in vernacular Catholic practice brought about, in Ó Héalaí's view, the disintegration of both the name and the form of *Leabhar Eoin* tradition in the course of the nineteenth century,[8] vernacular Catholic practice featured the widespread use of the *Leabhar Eoin* down into the late nineteenth century in the Irish-speaking parts of the country, and the Irish Folklore Commission's collections show it to have survived in those areas well into the twentieth.

Ó Héalaí deals in detail with the history and status of the *Leabhar Eoin* as a devotional practice that shades, on occasion, into superstition – its use to locate a drowned body at sea, for instance. The present contribution explores the use of the *topos* in oral and literary narrative sources, the latter ranging from nineteenth-century manuscripts to twentieth-century creative fiction.

THE *LEABHAR EOIN* IN FOLK LEGEND

As a Christian devotion, the *Leabhar Eoin* is restricted to channelling communication and influence between human life and the realm of the

Christian supernatural. Its occurrence in folk legend, however, brings it into the domain of the native or ancestral supernatural of Irish tradition, where female agencies of mediation and power serve as alternatives to the agency of male divinity and male clerics and where, on occasion, the two agencies come into oppositional contact. In folk narrative the *Leabhar Eoin* is regarded as being charged in itself with a power that is capable of doing harm as well as good if not managed properly. Either the sick person for whom the remedy is sought actually worsens, or the priest himself is afflicted. In extreme cases, death is said to result from the improper use or administration of the *Leabhar Eoin*.

In the folk narratives, the *Leabhar Eoin* must be written out carefully and in full by the priest if it is to be effective. On occasion, there is tension between the parish priest and the more junior 'curate' with regard to which of them provides the 'better' *Leabhar Eoin*. A west Kerry legend tells of a poor woman who seeks a *Leabhar Eoin* from a parish priest at the end of a 'station' gathering (i.e. a community assembly for the purposes of administering confession and celebrating mass). While the parish priest is writing it out for her, the curate tells him to make sure that he does it correctly. The parish priest immediately throws down his pen and tells the curate to write it out for the woman himself. When the curate starts to do this, the table on which he is writing begins to tremble and shake. The curate requests of the people of the station house a sop from the shakedown straw that is kept on the house-loft for charitable provision to wayfarers. Throwing the sop under the table, he is able to complete writing the *Leabhar Eoin*, thus defeating, as it were, the authority of his superior.[9]

Another legend from west Kerry features the parish priest and the curate as brothers in the same parish. The younger brother, the curate, cures, by means of a *Leabhar Eoin*, a man who was sick because of having had contact with 'the good people', the fairy host from the otherworld. Shortly afterwards, the curate becomes disoriented and is lost crossing the strand on the way back from celebrating mass so that his brother, the parish priest, is sent for. The local people advise the parish priest to go to the man who had been cured of his sickness and to get back the *Leabhar Eoin* from him. It is now given to the curate and it restores him to health. The other man now in turn becomes sick again: this confirms the locals in their belief that the sickness has indeed been caused by the fairies, and teaches the parish priest a lesson, as it were, about the existence and power of the native otherworld.[10]

A legend from Connemara recounts another instance of this lesson given to the priest of the power of the native otherworld – this time in the person of the wise woman (*cailleach feasa*) whose knowledge and healing power is widely attested in popular tradition.[11] The father of a sick boy goes to the priest and gets a *Leabhar Eoin* in the hope of curing him. When it proves of no use, however, the father consults with a wise woman, who tells him that the priest has omitted certain words from the *Leabhar Eoin*. The father reports this back to the priest, who then says, 'Well, whether it was God or the Devil who gave her the knowledge of it, she has it right. I did leave out a part of it.' Then the priest writes it out again correctly and the son is cured.[12]

While the ability to write a *Leabhar Eoin* is usually portrayed as the prerogative of the priest, the ability can sometimes be acquired by laymen. Narratives from the west of Ireland tell of how only three words out of the complete *Leabhar Eoin* have efficacy, and how these were revealed one time by a priest to a layman who was thus able to write the *Leabhar Eoin* himself in the aftermath of the priest's death.

The most sustained account of the operation of the *Leabhar Eoin* by a layman comes from a County Galway legend about a schoolmaster who had been dismissed from his post on account of drunkenness but who was, nevertheless, on friendly terms with the priest. One day while the priest lay sick in bed an old woman came to him for a *Leabhar Eoin* to cure her husband. The priest asked the schoolmaster to write out the *Leabhar Eoin* for him, saying that he would tell him what to write. When the schoolmaster handed it to the priest there were three more special words to be added. The priest told him these three words and they were inserted. The schoolmaster, an educated man, remembered these three extra words, meaning that thereafter he could draw up the *Leabhar Eoin* himself. The priest and he subsequently fell out because of the words that now appeared to have been given away by the priest. A trial-by-fire took place and it was the *Leabhar Eoin* of the schoolmaster that survived the flames. Afterwards, the schoolmaster acquired the status of a wonder-working hero in the parish, seemingly able to accomplish marvellous deeds.[13]

The text or written matter of the *Leabhar Eoin* in these accounts appears to be not necessarily identical with the essential John 1:1–14 of Catholic devotion – nor is this surprising, given that the stories were told by narrators who were often illiterate, and who often had no Latin. The curative and other powers of sacred text – and, specifically, of the gospels – were already well established in medieval Irish tradition. Professor Seán

Ó Coileáin has kindly drawn my attention to an instance referred to by Charles Plummer, in which some letters and text from the manuscript of the Long Book of Leighlin were scraped onto water which was then given to an accused man to drink as a kind of oracle to establish his guilt or innocence; if the accused sickened he was guilty.[14]

A similarly fluid view of the *In Principio* text is envisaged in narratives where the *Leabhar Eoin* has to be made especially powerful in order to enable the person – who has come to the priest to have it written out – to survive the journey back to the sick party, a journey that will involve an encounter with a *sprid* ('spirit' or 'ghost'). A bilingual version from Uíbh Ráthach tells of how a man of the Dennehys comes to the priest to invoke his help in curing his sick child.[15] '*Dhera*, what way can I cure him?' asks the priest. '*Á b'é do thoil é, Athair … tabhair dom leabhrán do, pé scéal é*' ('Please, Father … give me a *leabhrán* for him in any case').[16] The priest replies, 'All right, *a Sheáin, tabharfad*' ('All right, Seán, I will'). On receiving the *Leabhar Eoin*, Seán tells the priest of meeting with a hostile spirit called *Sprid na Bearnan* on his way to him and of how he will have to face her again on his return journey. The priest asks for the return of the *leabhrán*, opens it and goes 'down to the room' to write it again. He then assures Seán that, kept safely in his vest pocket, it will protect him against *Sprid na Bearnan* and be of help to his sick son. It can be suggested on the basis of this and other accounts of 'stronger' and 'better' versions of *Leabhar Eoin* being provided, that other texts, apart from the *In Principio* verses, functioned as the written matter that the priest provided for amuletic use. Further instances of this wider range of written matter being regarded as constituting the *Leabhar Eoin* follow in the examples of poetic usage.

THE *LEABHAR EOIN* IN FOLK POETRY

Mention has already been made of what appears to be the earliest-known Irish reference to the *Leabhar Eoin*, in the eleventh-century tale of *Aislinge Meic Conglinne*: here there is a humorous reference to a gospel (*soscéla*) being placed 'around' the speaker for protection.[17] A similar mocking use of the idea of the *Leabhar Eoin* is found in the last quarter of the eighteenth century, in the verse composition of the County Clare poet and schoolmaster Tomás Ó Míocháin.[18] A fellow poet, Donncha Ó Mathúna, had criticised Ó Míocháin's work; and Ó Míocháin wrote derisively, in English, of Ó Mathúna's 'desperate present state' of being afflicted in body and mind by 'some red fairy witch or fallen demon' and 'wholly robbed of all human sense'. Since, as Ó Míocháin writes, 'No physic can this grievous case address', the only remedy left is 'to contrive a Gospel ... the power of which will free him from all evil'. There follows a long poem entitled *Leabhar Eoin*, written by Ó Míocháin and another of his friends, the scholar Séon Lloyd, in which the resources of County Clare tradition, natural and spiritual, are invoked in the cause of restoring Ó Mathúna to full health. The poem consists of twelve stanzas of eight lines, each followed by a coda of three quatrains of verse. Significantly, the poem contains no trace of the *In Principio* text in the gospel of John other than what is implied by the title '*Leabhar Eoin*'.

Another instance of the term *Leabhar Eoin* being used for a verse composition not involving the *In Principio* verses is a charm of twenty-eight lines to drive out rats, entitled '*Ag seo* Notice, Summons *is Fógra*'. At the end of the lines of verse the following is written:

> *Críoch leis an leabhar-eoin sin mur do ceapadh le Donnchadh Ó Céirín chum na bhfranncach do dhíbirt agus do choimeád as dhá stáca coirce Sheáin Mac Diarmada.*

> An end here to that *leabhar-eoin* that Donnchadh Ó Céirín composed to drive out the rats and keep them out from Seán Mac Diarmada's two cornstacks.[19]

The Donnchadh Ó Céirín to whom this composition is attributed was an itinerant weaver-poet from north Kerry; the text dates from around 1840. It was published by Tadhg Ó Donnchadha ('Tórna') from a manuscript owned by a Liam de Nógla of Buttevant in north Cork.[20]

A cante-fable that tells of a verse composed *ex tempore* by a priest as a *Leabhar Eoin* to cure illness was collected in Coomhola, near Bantry, County Cork in 1935.[21] It tells of a priest staying overnight in the house of a local poet where a 'station' is to take place. The priest is also a poet, and he and the man of the house spend the evening in rivalry, quoting verses to and fro in a contest of wits. After mass is said on the following day, the woman of the house requests a *Leabhar Eoin* from the priest for her sick child, saying that she has been told that if she got one, her child would be well again. In this Coomhola instance, the priest's *ex tempore* verse is as follows:

Go mairir do leanbh, a bhanaltra chaoin-cháile,
Gan mhasla, gan mharta, ná cealg ag snaoidhe an chnámha leis,
I gcomhluadar na n-Apsal agus a mbeannacht go síor-ghnáth leis,
Agus beidh cara de shagart id aice go dtí an táin-rith.

May you live to have joy of your child, nurse-mother of kind repute,
May he live free of insult or crippling injury and may no treachery
waste his frame
May he have the constant company and blessing of the Apostle,
And you will have the priest's patronage until he is fully recovered.

When the man of the house, the poet-rival, heard the priest say this,
he said 'Wisha, Father, for the love of God, will you read a *Leabhar Eoin*
for me too!' Then the priest said:

Leabhar Eoin do scríbhim duit mar dhíon ar na hAspalaibh,
Samhlacha agus síofraí síorraidhe ag gabhailt greadadh dhuit,
Sprid agus gósta romhat i ngach aon bhall,
Agus púca led thóin nuair is dóigh leat nach baol duit.

A *Leabhar Eoin* I write for you to seal you off from the Apostles,
To have spectres and sprites trouncing and thrashing you,
To have phantoms and apparitions before you on all sides,
And the púca under your backside – just when you think you are safe!

We are told that the man of the house said no more.

It is interesting to note here the use of the verbs 'to read' and 'to write'
in the context of the apparently entirely oral, *ex tempore* composition of
the verses styled *Leabhar Eoin* in the story. This juxtaposition of the oral
and the literate is a fundamental feature of vernacular narrative and poetic
tradition, in Ireland and elsewhere.[22]

THE *LEABHAR EOIN* IN MODERN LITERATURE

Reference to the *Leabhar Eoin* and its use occurs extensively throughout
the modern Irish-language novel *Cré na Cille* by Máirtín Ó Cadhain, of
which two separate English translations have recently been published.[23]
Ó Héalaí makes mention of the novel in connection with the belief that
the administration of the *Leabhar Eoin* always involves a health cost to the
priest providing it, or a third party onto whom the illness in question is

transferred. This, he says, is an example of the kind of zero-sum thinking associated with magical curing practice in peasant society – something which he would, no doubt, locate at the superstition end of the range of meaning pertaining to the *Leabhar Eoin*.[24] The attribution at one point in the novel of the power of the 'evil eye' both to Caitríona, the main character, and to her sister Neil might be regarded as further evidence of such superstition.[25]

The novel consists entirely of dialogue in which an intensified variety of the usual acrimonious and derogatory village gossip of a small, close-knit, rural community is carried on *post mortem* in a highly loquacious and combative fashion by the inhabitants of the local graveyard, whose number gradually increases as further deaths occur above ground and news arrives of the doings of still-living relatives and neighbours. Matters of inheritance, land ownership and marriage are central to the concerns of the subterranean world and especially to the central character, Caitríona Pháidín.

When Caitríona Pháidín learns that her sister Neil's son, Peadar, who had suffered a smashed hip in an accident involving a lorry, is fully recovered and back working the land, she refuses to countenance the attribution of the cure to a visit he made to the holy well of Cill Íne. Instead, she insists that it was a *Leabhar Eoin* that his mother, her sister, extracted from the priest that has effected the cure of her nephew and the subsequent death of her brother-in-law, his father. She says of her sister, '*Tá an smuitín sin ina dhá chuid déag leis an sagart*' ('That pussface and the priest are thick as thieves'), and she dismisses any notion of cures being available through the making of pilgrimages to the holy well.[26]

Caitríona Pháidín has a similar way of explaining a variety of other happenings which she has heard about, and she continues to attribute these to the *Leabhar Eoin* machinations of her sister. Such misfortunes range from death down to the badly smoking chimney that threatens the health of another of Neil's 'victims' (p. 305).

In the chatter of the gossip someone suggests that Caitríona's own death might be God's punishment for all the bad things she had done to her neighbours – cheating them and stealing from them. But it is also suggested that her death came about due to the provision – through Neil – of a *Leabhar Eoin* to Caitríona's sickly daughter-in-law. Caitríona Pháidín latches on to this idea, since she is convinced that her son's wife should surely have died in childbirth much earlier than herself. She further accuses Neil of causing another death in place of her own at a time when she, Neil, was mortally sick for a month – again all through the operation of the *Leabhar Eoin* with the connivance of the priest (pp. 281, 291–2).

Caitríona Pháidín's constant reiteration of this explanation of her own and other deaths brings her into conversation with a character called *Billeachaí an Phosta* ('Billy the Post'), who had been postman in the village up above. He contradicts her and tells her that what she says is only an old wives' tale, old-fashioned nonsense. He admits that he himself once believed it too, but that a learned priest had told him that all the *Leabhar Eoin* in the world wouldn't keep you alive when God wished to send for you. He also says that his wife, a schoolteacher, who had gone on pilgrimages for him when *he* was sick, had been told the same by another very holy priest (pp. 355–6).

Here we see the traditional, 'superstitious' belief of the pre-modern village world challenged by the fictional representatives of modernity in the persons of a schoolteacher and an employee of the state-run postal system – formal education and postal systems being to the fore among the cultural and social mechanisms whereby the pre-modern world is disenchanted.

Máirtín Ó Cadhain, the author of the novel *Cré na Cille*, grew up in this world which had folklore tradition at its heart. It is striking how he puts the refutation of an item of that tradition – the malign unorthodox use of the *Leabhar Eoin*, the *In Principio* amulet – into the mouths of characters who represent the social order that replaces the village 'peasant' society and who bear witness to a more orthodox theology. The postman clinches his case with a memorable simile in which the magical, oracular use of the *Leabhar Eoin* is seen as a kind of mindless formality. Referring to God, he asks, '*Ar ndó, a Chaitríona, a chomharsa, ní shíleann tú go bhfuil an oiread téip dhearg Aige Siúd is atá ag Oifig an Phosta?*' ('Surely, you don't think, Caitríona, neighbour, that He (God) is as full of red tape as the Post Office?') (p. 356).

We see here, I think, a notably sophisticated handling of the concept of the *Leabhar Eoin*. It is, initially, portrayed as operating in the minds of the novel's characters – and in their discourse – as a procedure that constitutes an explanation of why certain events happen; and why, when they happen, they happen to certain individuals rather than to others. I would characterise this portrayal of the understanding of the nature and use of the *Leabhar Eoin* as something analogous to the nature and operation of witchcraft belief among the Azande people of South Sudan as described by E.E. Evans-Pritchard in his classic study of 1937.[27] Billy the

Post's attempt at countering this traditional view of Caitríona Pháidín's concerning the etiology of misfortune is aimed at undermining any such understanding of the magical operation of the *Leabhar Eoin* in people's lives and sets it in a modern frame as an item of orthodox theology.

Cré na Cille was published in 1949 and is set in a context where Christianity is the religion which has been practised by the novel's characters and which represents the official orthodoxy in the society in which they had lived their lives. Their vernacular religious beliefs and practices, however, diverge from Christian orthodoxy in ways that are similar to the unorthodox ancestral beliefs and practices of vernacular religion collected by the fieldworkers of the Irish Folklore Commission. Such elements of tradition, regarded officially as being of a suspect and magical nature, include those traditions of the *Leabhar Eoin* that Pádraig Ó Héalaí situates at the 'superstition' rather than the 'piety' end of the range of material covered in his article.[28] Máirtín Ó Cadhain, for his part, as creative author, also allocates such traditions to the realms of superstition and magical thinking – in the words and person of the fictional postman/state employee who tries to disabuse Caitríona Pháidín of her conviction that her misfortunes have all resulted from the magical operation against her of the *Leabhar Eoin*. Crucially here, however, it can be argued that it is not on the grounds of deviation from Christian orthodoxy that *Leabhar Eoin* belief is being found wanting, but from the point of view of developments in modern Catholicism.

As a traditional charm, the *Leabhar Eoin* is clearly capable of having an afterlife – or a meta-life – in both legend and literature that will repay further investigation.

CHAPTER 3

Reading the *Bean Feasa*

[Published in *Folklore*, vol. 16, no. 1, April 2005, pp. 37–50]

INTRODUCTION

There was this girl on Sherkin Island who was an only child and she lost her speech. She went to bed in her health and in the morning she was unable to speak. There was a woman east in Béal Átha an Fhíona who used to be giving out knowledge – she used to be going with the good people. The girl was brought to visit her to see if she could cure her. When she saw her, she couldn't do anything for her and she told her to come back again after a fortnight.

She came back and the woman asked her father why he built his house so close to a *port* (bank, or raised passage) and she said that while they would never thrive there, neither would they ever want for anything there. She took a basin off the dresser and asked the girl did she recognise it. She said she did and that she had missed it. 'I was at your house since,' said the woman, 'and I took the basin.' 'Weren't you,' she said, 'driving a horse down the hillside when you met an angry, red-haired woman of the Harnedys and she had a woollen cloak around her and she struck you a blow on each side of you and the third blow down on top of your head? There was poison in that.'

She cured the girl then, but the loss of speech used to return, at the same time, regularly, until the day she died.[1]

[CBÉ/IFC, vol. 49, pp. 143–4]

Legends about the *bean feasa* are a part of the repertoire of traditional or ancestral Irish lore. A *bean feasa*, literally 'woman of knowledge, wisdom; a wise-woman', is credited with having a gift of prophecy and second-sight, the taghairm of Scottish Gaelic tradition. Legends of the *bean feasa* are numerous in the manuscripts of the Irish Folklore Commission, though there has not yet been any comprehensive work done on their distribution patterns. Neither has much attention been given to the categories into which legends of the *bean feasa* might be classified: ones in which she travels with the *slua sí*, the otherworld/fairy host, ones in which herbal cures and healing is involved, one where she makes prophetic diagnosis, and so forth. Since *bean feasa* or wise-woman legends are not to be regarded as migratory legend, they were not dealt with in the Symposium on the Supernatural in Irish and Scottish Migratory Legends (1988) nor in the Nordic-Celtic Legend Symposium (1991). Consequently, the *bean feasa*, the wise-woman, does not feature in the legend sampler 'Crossing the Border' published in conjunction with the 1988 symposium[2] nor in the papers from the Nordic-Celtic Symposium that have been published in two issues of *Béaloideas*, the journal of the Folklore of Ireland Society and that deal with Scottish and Welsh legends as well as Irish ones and with legend-aspects of Irish literature, medieval and modern.[3] Similarly, apart from Biddy Early, in Lady Gregory's account of her,[4] there is no mention of a wise-woman in the very comprehensive Field Day anthology of women's writing and traditions.[5] Nevertheless, the *bean feasa* is a central, prominent personage in Irish oral tradition whose characteristics are well worthy of study as part of any initial consideration of the significance, in cultural terms, of the lore concerning her and her powers.

I am emphasising the legendary status of the lore in *seanchas* concerning the wise-woman. Thus we are attempting to 'read', literally and metaphorically, a corpus of legends written down from oral performance, in our efforts to understand the cultural significance of the wise-woman and the cultural functioning of the traditions associated with her. As ever with legend, the lore of the wise-woman presents itself in the guise of history and truth. We have here, it seems, accounts of events that really took place and that are known in reliable ways to those who tell of them – with such knowledge being based on their own experience and that of their relatives and neighbours. In particular, these legends portray the wise-women as real, human females who have lived in communities within human memory, whose houses are still there and whose presence in everyday living is still remembered. Against this we sense that Nancy Schmitz[6] failed to locate the historical Biddy Early despite sustained research on the historical background to the Thomond and north Munster traditions of the famous wise-woman of that name. In like fashion, Máirtín Verling has registered his failure to identify and locate any historical Máire Ní Mhurchú in the censuses and genealogies of the Eyeries community of Beara, a community and a district with both an extensive tradition of a wise-woman of that name and a well-developed knowledge of the history of the parish and its families.[7]

It appears as if the lore and legends concerning the wise-woman, in Irish ancestral tradition, are possessed of the truth, not of history, but of another order of knowledge, to which assent is readily, if ambiguously, given in oral narrative performance. In this other order of knowledge, truth has a character nearer to religious faith than to historical fact, it seems, and we can count the legends of the wise-woman as expressions of popular religious tradition and place them together with the exempla of Christian piety, on the one hand, and the *síscéalta* or fairy legends, on the other, as sub-genres of the religious folk-narrative. It was C.W. von Sydow, three quarters of a century ago, who urged caution in respect of any attempt to study legends *in vacuo*.[8] He believed that they should always be regarded as developing on the basis of beliefs that constitute elements of systems of cosmology or elements of worldview that cannot, ultimately, be reduced to the affairs and circumstances of a historical order. In keeping with this understanding of the belief-based nature of legend, other aspects of traditional Irish lore have already been studied and illuminated, for example traditions of the *iarlais*/changeling,[9] the banshee,[10] the *lucharachán*/leprechaun,[11] the *bean chabhartha*/midwife,[12] the child-murderess,[13] the old woman as hare,[14] and the *bean chaointe*/keener.[15]

There is another level again, apart from that of belief – religious or non-religious – on which legends can be said to operate and to have significance: the level of the psychological. Bo Almqvist has already asserted as much in regard to Irish migratory legends of the supernatural. We are able to obtain from such legends, he claims, 'keener understanding and deeper psychological insight into the fears and hopes of the people who tell them and listen to them'.[16] I am reckoning this to be the case, to be true also in respect of legends of the wise-woman, and my interest and emphasis hereafter is directed towards the way in which such legends represent and give effect to the workings of a psychodynamic aspect of popular cultural tradition – at least, as I see it, in the instance in question: that of the traditions of the *bean feasa*/wise-woman.

SOURCES AND METHOD

In the same article in which Bo Almqvist refers to the way in which migratory legends of the supernatural can yield psychological insights, he urges that empirical study rather than speculative assertion is required if progress is to be made in our understanding of the significance and operation of such legends in this and in other respects. I have attempted such empirical study, in initial fashion, on the texts of a small corpus of largely Munster legends of the wise-woman, together with a few legends from western and northern Ireland. With the exception of nine texts that are not of *Gaeltacht* provenance, they are all in the Irish language.

The corpus of legend in question here derives from a search through the subject index to the manuscripts of the main collection of the Irish Folklore Commission archive under the key-word '*Bean Feasa*', noting especially texts of a Munster provenance but omitting those relating to Biddy Early, the best-known and best-studied Munster wise-woman. The search yielded forty-six texts and these, while certainly not exhausting the possibility of the archive to yield many more wise-woman references and texts, can, I believe, constitute a satisfactorily adequate sample for analysis and commentary (see Appendix, 1–40).

Almost half of the texts in the corpus came from County Cork – twenty-two legends. Seven more are from County Kerry, three from County Clare, two from County Tipperary and one from County Waterford. Outside Munster, eight legends came from County Galway and three from County Donegal. The majority of them were written down from oral narration in the 1930s though a small number were recorded up to a decade later than that. Among the recorders of this material – practically all of them male – who wrote it down in the field, from oral tradition, are well-known, experienced and full-time collectors with the Irish Folklore Commission such as Nioclás Breathnach, Proinsias de Búrca, Liam Mac Coisdealbha, Liam Mac Meanman, Tomás Ó Ciardha, Seán Ó Dubhda, Seán Ó Flannagáin and Tadhg Ó Murchú. Also, it is from male informants and tradition-bearers that practically all of this material has been collected, although eight items come from a single female informant, Máiréad Ní Mhionachain, the Beara woman of the anthology of traditional material – lore and story – taken down by the collector Tadhg Ó Murchú and edited and published, in both the original Irish and in an English translation, by the folklore scholar Máirtín Verling.[17]

Overall, one can say that these legends concerning the wise-woman involve resort to her, as a possible source of help, by those afflicted with a misfortune that cannot be alleviated otherwise and that is obscure, perhaps even mysterious, in its origin. Despite variation in form and narrative style from district to district and from one textual version to another, a basic patterning presents itself that is worthy of study. In this regard the following aspects of these wise-woman legends suggest themselves as being of significance:

- by what title or term is such a person known?
- what is her name (first; family) in the story?
- what is her age and her social standing in the community?
- is travelling with the fairy host attributed to her?
- what affliction or sorrow is involved in the story?
- in what manner is the wise-woman engaged in the face of affliction?
- what explanation (if any) of the affliction does the wise-woman provide?
- what kind of treatment or healing does she provide?
- what affirmation is proffered of the powers of the wise-woman and the veracity of the story?

TITLE

The term *bean feasa* (lit. 'woman of knowledge') is one of the most frequently encountered. Other terms used are *bean leighis* ('woman of healing'), *bean siubhail* ('travelling woman'), *seanbhean* ('old woman'), *cailleach* ('old woman', 'hag'), *bean chumhachtach* ('powerful woman, woman of supernatural power'), *bean chrosach* ('fortune-telling woman'), *a strange woman*, and *old woman*. In one third of the stories, no particular title or term is used and the female in question is called by her own name(s) with a clear implication of her acceptance on all sides as a wise-woman. In the case of the title *bean feasa* ('woman of knowledge'), its use can be taken to indicate both knowledge and power, extraordinary knowledge and power, that are mysterious.

THE NAME OF THE WISE-WOMAN

In the case of three wise-women we are given both a first and a family name: Eibhlín Ní Ghuinníola from Baile Bhoithín, Dingle, County Kerry (see Appendix, no. 3); Máire Ní Chearbhaill from West Carbery, County Cork (ibid., no. 25); Máire Ní Mhurchú from Beara, County Cork (ibid., nos. 26–40).

A first name, only, is given in the case of a further five wise-women, as follows: Máire Liam on the border of Cork and Waterford between Mitchelstown and Lismore (ibid., no. 10); Nóirín na Sprideanna ('N of the Sprites') from the Déise of west Waterford (ibid., no. 20); Brighdín Cuileann from Tiaquin, County Galway (ibid., no 17); Lizzie Scott from Golladuff, County Donegal (ibid., no. 14) of whom it is remarked that she was an *Albanach* (lit. 'Scottish'), that is, a Presbyterian. One other female in this material is given a first and family name with the suggestion that she is indeed a wise-woman (ibid., no. 4); she is from Tuosist, County Kerry, and it is related of her that she used to bring 'knowledge' *(fios)* out of the trance-like states that regularly befell her during attendance at wakes. We can take it that this is a real individual. There is no evidence of anyone having ever had to resort to her, however, in the face of affliction, and she cannot be considered as an equivalent to Eibhlín Ní Ghuinníola or Máire Ní Mhurchú or Máire Ní Chearbhaill, despite being a very interesting instance, in her own right, of the interface of life and lore.

AGE AND STATUS OF THE WISE-WOMAN

She is obviously aged, as a rule. She is frequently referred to as a *seanbhean*, an 'old woman'. She appears to be unmarried or at least there is no mention of marriage or spouse in relation to her. This contrasts, interestingly, with the case of Biddy Early, whose stories I have excluded from consideration. The wise-woman of this corpus has a status as itinerant, shifting, multi-locational presence that is attested to in at least three ways:

1. She is a 'travelling woman', an itinerant who, in one instance, is engaged in the business of having goods for sale.
2. Even though a settled resident of the community, she frequently travels with the fairy host so that she is present in various locations at various times and she has detailed local knowledge in different settings.
3. She is regularly present, in a usual and normal way, in different locations distant from each other, so that she takes on something of the multi-locational omni-presence of the territorial sovereignty queen who, in medieval literature and tradition, personifies territories and

kingdoms. The figure of *Cailleach Bhéarra*, the tutelary goddess of landscape, is a powerful articulation of this tradition and has powerful associations with much of the territory from which these stories of the wise-woman derive. The question of the relationship in cultural logic between the personages of the wise-woman and the *cailleach* is discussed in detail in my previous book.[18]

Another aspect of the wise-woman's status is that she is regarded as an oracular authority for her community in relation to the meaning and significance of experiences they fail to understand – accidents, misfortunes, mysterious illness. Because of this, she is regarded with a certain respectful awe mingled with anxiety in respect of her extraordinary and supernatural endowments of knowledge and power.

TRAVEL WITH THE FAIRY HOST: OTHER AVENUES OF KNOWLEDGE

In eight of the County Cork stories it is unequivocally stated that travel with the fairy host is the means whereby the wise-woman comes by her extraordinary knowledge:

> *bhíodh sí ag dul leis na daoine maithe* ('she used to travel with the good people');
> *bhíodh sí ag imeacht leis an tslua* ('she used to travel with the host');
> "twas said she used to go with the good people';
> *bhí sé ráite go mbíodh sí in éineacht le dream an uabhair* ('it was said that she used to go along with the proud set [Angels of Pride]');
> 'it is many a night she spent out in the company of the good people, the poor woman'.

Such travel with the fairy host is attributed to the wise-woman not only in County Cork sources, but in sources from all over, in the present corpus.

In stories from Galway and Kerry, the wise-woman has her powers not as a result of fairy host travel but on the basis of 'cup-tossing', the 'reading' of bowls and cups that are mixed and shuffled about on a table or dresser for the purposes of divination. In another story, from Galway, the wise-woman is said to shape-shift into the form of a hare, on occasion, and to acquire her knowledge in this way. In a Tipperary story, she has her knowledge from being 'fasting, in bed, for seven years, without food or drink'. In one of the Kerry stories in which the local priest is obliged to resort to the wise-woman when his horse is mysteriously lamed, we are told that many people believed that it was from the devil that she had her powers. As the story proceeds, however, it is made clear that these powers do not derive from a demonic source. As a kind of corollary, or reinforcement, even, of this clarification, the story tells of how, in this instance, the wise-woman was able to teach the priest a lesson in Christian piety when she reveals to him that the cause of his horse's injury is his own neglectfulness in not uttering a prophylactic blessing on the animal when he was praising it extravagantly.

THE CRISIS THAT CAUSES PEOPLE TO SEND FOR THE WISE-WOMAN

There are two kinds of crisis to be identified here:

1. a small crisis, as it were – an animal stolen or strayed; the shortage or absence of a substance like butter or tobacco; a non-mysterious physical injury or illness; the misfortune or danger arising from certain behaviours, for example returning at nightfall from tilling a field without bringing one's spade along or building one's house on a fairy fort.
2. a mysterious illness striking down an individual or an animal, for example:
   - the priest's horse;
   - two young men in the course of robbing the landlord's orchard;
   - someone returning from an evening's storytelling;
   - the young girl who was struck dumb (see text of story at head of this article).

THE ENCOUNTER WITH THE WISE-WOMAN

At least two kinds of encounter are to be distinguished:

1. She is intentionally sent for or visited at her home, since either she is well-known and her power appreciated or else those who would not normally credit her with such power are advised, in affliction, to resort to her, and do so, for example the priest in Dingle with the lamed horse, the sceptical husband in Béara whose wife is abducted across the waters of the bay by the fairy host.
2. The local wise-woman happens on the scene of the affliction, by chance or by fate. Both Eibhlín Ní Ghuinníola and Máire Ní Mhurchú are

related as having called in, unexpectedly, to the house of a victim of unexplained illness. A wise-woman from another district can, likewise, make a similarly timely appearance – as in the case of the travelling wise-woman from County Clare who calls in to the Bantry, County Cork household just as they are mysteriously failing to churn their cream to butter.

THE WISE-WOMAN'S EXPLANATION OF THE MISFORTUNE

On occasion she extracts the meaning of the occurrence by means of a divinatory ritual involving the 'tossing' or other handling of bowls or cups. This seems to occur mainly in connection with the location and recovery of animals that have been stolen or have strayed – though we have noted its occurrence in the story of the girl who was struck dumb.

On other occasions, the wise-woman already knows the nature and cause of the misfortune, before anyone comes to visit her. In these cases she has foreknowledge, as it were, either because she has acquired it in the course of her travels in the company of the fairy host or else she has herself been mysteriously present when the misfortune happened. A story of Máire Ní Chearbhaill and the blow her 'client' received from the otherworld red-haired woman he met late at night is an example of this (see Appendix, no. 25).

Sometimes, too, the wise-woman will offer no explanation at all but pronounce and prophecy that even greater misfortune will befall the afflicted party. For example, Nóirín na Sprideanna foretells the death of the husband of the woman who meets her (ibid., no. 12); Brighdín Cuileann foretells further the catastrophe for the mother of the drowned/abducted child – that the whole family will die of the plague in a little while (ibid., no. 17).

THE HEALING THE WISE-WOMAN PROVIDES

The simplest kind of healing she effects is in terms of the knowledge she has out of which the missing animal or object is recovered. Sometimes the information she communicates is coded or covert – where exactly the missing animal may be found, for instance. Having found out by means of cup-tossing that the heifer that was lost for several days is still alive, Máire Ní Chearbhaill says to its owner, in relation to finding it, no more than '*d'imighis thairsti trí uaire ar maidin inniu*' ('you have passed by her three times this morning') (ibid., no. 25).

In other instances definite, specific advice is available from the wise-woman in order to set things right. The travelling wise-woman instructed the Bantry family as to how they might prevent their butter being magically stolen: they were to make a bottleful of butter on a Sunday morning before sunrise and to put portions of this butter into three successive churnings (ibid., no. 7). Máire Ní Mhurchú directed that a specific herbal ointment be used to relieve the suffering of a young girl afflicted since passing water into a kitchen utensil within the house (ibid., no. 37).

Another wise-woman story, from Duhallow in north Cork in this case, has highly specific instructions being given to the man whose wife has been abducted by the fairy host, with a male changeling substituted in her place (ibid., no. 13). The instructions include detailing the use by him of holy water to wrest his wife back from the *lios* (the 'fairy fort', ring fort) and one is reminded of aspects of the tragic and notorious case of Bridget Cleary, of Tipperary, whose death, in the late nineteenth century, resulted from attempts by her husband and other family to combat what was believed to be a fairy abduction.[19]

Herbs – or a liquid prepared by boiling herbs – sometimes feature in the healing the wise-woman effects. Such herbal use, however, is seen to involve mysterious healing power that goes beyond the range of herbal and folk medicine. For instance, in one story, Eibhlín Ní Ghuinníola is reported as having a *leannán sí* ('fairy suitor') accompanying her as she picks and gathers herbs (see Appendix, no. 3). In other cases, the herb that is required to effect healing has to be obtained from a distant graveyard under cover of darkness (ibid., no. 37). Even when the healing itself involved no more, apparently, that the rubbing on of a herb or the drinking of a herbal infusion, there are still circumstances of a mysterious nature that pertain. For example, Máire Ní Chearbhaill happens to bring along the exact and specific requirements to the house of the sick individual when she chances in unexpectedly (ibid., no. 25); Máire Ní Mhurchú pointedly forbids anyone to be present with her when the herbal potion is administered (ibid., no. 27); Eibhlín Ní Ghuinníola dispenses the herbal remedy to her visitors only on condition that they obey a taboo in regard to looking behind them on the journey home to their sick relative (ibid., no. 3).

Stories where the wise-woman is using herbs as part of healing treatment in the case of fairy-abduction show most clearly that more than the 'normal' folk pharmacopoeia is involved, for example the stories featuring Máire Ní Mhurchú's journeying on horseback or by boar, along with the relatives of the abducted individual, in order to acquire, in a distant graveyard, the necessary herb with which to treat the affliction (ibid., nos. 26–8). The struggle and race to avoid fairy pursuers confirm beyond doubt that supernatural healing, beyond herbal medicine, is involved in these instances.

AFFIRMATION OF THE TRUTH OF THE STORY

Sometimes, we are given to understand that what happened, in the story, befell the family of the narrator – her or himself: it was from one narrator's grandfather that a colt was stolen; it was to another narrator's own mother that the woman came in seeking the loan of a saucepan and flour; another narrator again says, 'all that happened within this house' (the stealing away of butter and its redress).

Other times we are told that the house of the wise-woman is still in existence and that her descendants are known to members of the narrator's own family. 'Her children are alive today; they are old, of course.' In some cases it's the ruin of the wise-woman's house that still stands – near the informant's own home. In other cases, we are told by the narrator that his own parents were well acquainted with the wise-woman – in their day.

Of particular interest are those instances where features of the wise-woman and her activities are affirmed that are, in reality, beyond any human scale of things. Máire Ní Chearbhaill is affirmed from the evidence of relatives of the different narrators to have been present daily in two far-flung locations. She is said, on the one hand, to have visited a house in Gallans every day 'where my mother's aunt was serving' (ibid., no. 25). On the other hand we have it vouched for by someone whose 'wife's people were living over beyond Reenascreena' that 'Máire Ní Chearbhaill used to come in visiting them every day' (ibid., no. 25). The location of Gallans and Reenascreena is unlikely to allow for their both being visited on a daily basis by the same woman. Similarly it is related how there were daily sightings of and dealings with Máire Ní Mhurchú in places as far apart from each other in Beara as Dursey Island and Adrigole, a distance of twenty-two miles.

Nevertheless, the narrators strive to affirm the authenticity of their stories of the wise-woman. An account may end with the words, 'This is a true story' or 'But I am absolutely certain that this story is no make-up' or 'and there is hardly anyone today who could believe that things were like that long ago, and they were like that'.

A separate study of such affirmations could be made in respect of the narrator Pádraig Ó Murchú, of Gort Broc in Beara, who tries continually to impress on his listeners (and on his collector) the veracity of the incidents he relates concerning Máire Ní Mhurchú, the Beara wise-woman. He invokes his own father and mother together with his parish priest as witnesses to the truth of the stories he narrates about Máire and he proclaims the truth of his lore again and again. 'There's no lie in that,' he says, at the end of one story, 'or any old make-up.' '*Bhí san chomh fíor agus tá an ghrian ag taitneamh ar an aer*' ('That was as true and as real as the sun shining in the sky') (ibid., no. 26).

It is difficult to think of any other metaphor of affirmation that could go so directly to the heart of things and to the centre of existence – the sun shining in the sky. It brings us back to a consideration of the function which such lore and legends of the wise-woman had – and has – in the oral narrative tradition of Ireland and of the Gaelic-speaking world.

READING THE *BEAN FEASA*

We are today increasingly aware of how aspects of folklore relating to women and the feminine have to be understood as a kind of code in which metaphorical expression is given to matters that would, otherwise, normally prove impossible of expression in the public arena (Bourke, 1993). Such matters include, for example, marital difficulties, anorexia, post-natal depression, physical and sexual abuse and other injuries, afflictions and misfortunes of an intimate and private nature. I would like to suggest that the finite, closed set of complaints and troubles and disasters that cause people in Irish legend tradition to resort to the powers of the wise-woman represent the open, unlimited order of just such troubles and afflictions as all women and all men are prone to experience in the course of their lives. I would argue that these stories deal imaginatively – if at a symbolic remove – with the troubles and afflictions that arise for people in respect of the psychodynamic aspect of their personal lives, especially at the emotional level. In these stories from tradition people fail to comprehend sickness or loss or disaster. It is related how the wise-woman is able to elucidate the cause of such affliction – even if she sometimes omits to communicate her knowledge fully. It is to be seen that such understanding of what is happening, or what has happened, to the victims of affliction and their families is something that they could themselves have known had it not been for a kind of denial, and rejection of the truth about their lives and their relationships. Such denial results in the suppression of their access to the truth – and the true causes of things – to a level lower than that of everyday social consciousness. In the stories they are made to submit to the truth – about themselves and about life – by means of the diagnostic explanations and the authoritative pronouncements of the wise-woman; they are obliged, in general, to recognise their failings and shortcomings in respect of their relationships to family members, to neighbours, to their communities, to their environment and to their cultural heritage of cosmology and worldview. The inevitable transgressions of fallible, fearful mortals as well as the darker transgressions arising from pathology and personality disorder are what are being processed imaginatively and narratively in the legend tradition of the wise-woman. In so far as these stories relate – and propose to their audience – that relief from the affliction that arises from situations where there is denial of human reality is available for those who can submit to the honesties of the deeper levels of heart and conscience, these stories represent understanding of psychic life. They represent that implicit knowledge of cultural psychodynamics that exists for communities in the vernacular imagination of communal discourse – in the telling of stories out of the common repertoire of local narrative tradition.

Such simple stories told in the public domain about the knowledge and power of the wise-woman – stories telling of a limited and repeating range of afflictions and of the healing of such afflictions in time-honoured, traditional fashion – engage, in vernacular narrative and cultural tradition, with the private psychic lives of their listeners. In doing so they constitute a public and communal reflex of that private, complex, individual and highly personal process through which people cope with, and come to terms with, the vicissitudes of life. Such coping and coming to terms may be understood as being achieved, within the psyche, on grounds that involve deep symbolism and the operation of archetypes of human living. In regularly listening to and identifying with the figures and the events of wise-woman legends in the arena of the public discourse, individual consciousness is able, on occasion, to attain to the archetypal levels of the psychic life of the individual and to benefit from the psychodynamic processes that enable imagination and creative imaginative energies to somewhat assuage the troubles and pain of living.

Writing of a different sub-genre of legend than that of the wise-woman, Éilís Ní Dhuibhne states, 'I suggest that it is because it has a structure that carries … archetypal meaning that it exists in tradition.'[20] She is referring here to the migratory legend of the elderly female in the form of the hare. What she says can, I believe, also be referred to the legend of the wise-woman. They possess a structure that enables the listener, hearing them with the 'ears of tradition' and in the framework of a traditional worldview, to open his or her imagination to the healing and remedial energies of psychic creativity and thereby contain and even transcend life's current difficulties.

Regarded in this way, the lore and legends of the wise-woman constitute a limited set of accounts – regarding the dealing with, and the healing of, afflictions – that operate in the arena of public communal discourse to the benefit of the individual members of the community in their personal achievement of a sense of meaningfulness and a sense of hope in their lives.

In the face of life's troubles, those that manifest themselves in physical, bodily affliction and those that arise in emotional life and in the psyche, oral narrative tradition can here be said to be providing a cultural mechanism whereby the redemptive powers of the psyche itself and of the creative imagination are made available in the course of community life. Thus one of the functions of the recounting of legends and lore of the wise-woman is to make whole, as it were, that sense of oneself that resides in the individual and in the communal group. Consequently, the bearers and narrators of such *seanchas* ('lore and legendary') can be seen to play a very significant role in the cultural life of the community in terms that are creative and therapeutic along with being commemorative. It is surely this understanding of the powerful and vital contribution to life and tradition of the *seanchaí*, the narrator of lore, that underlies the invocation of the Aran Island *seanchaí* Darach Ó Direáin in a poem by the Aran-born Máirtín Ó Direáin, long resident in Dublin.[21] Remembering back to his early life on Aran, the poet calls on the now-dead *seanchaí*, Darach, to come to the assistance of the living. Out of the stressful, lonely, threatening circumstances of urban life in a modern city, the poet turns to his remembered experience of the imaginative riches of the *seanchaí's* repertoire and performance. Everything could be right again if only Darach would let loose his stories and his storytelling, narrating each item and event of lore exactly as tradition had it … Alas, this cannot be and the reality of loss and death, personal and communal, infuses itself quietly into the last two lines of the piece:

Cén scéal, a Dharaigh, ón tír úd thall?
Ar casadh Seáinín ort nó Séamus fós?
An bhfuil Mac Rí Éireann féin san áit?
An bhfuil Fionn Mac Cumhaill ná Conán ann?
An raibh an Chailleach Bhéarra rót sa ród?
Scaoil chugainn do scéal, a Dharaigh chóir!

Chuireas do thuairisc uair ar Cháit
Ach d'fhágais ise féin gan tásc;
Fóir orainn a Dharaigh, go beo
Is aithris dúinn gach eachtra i gceart.
Ach b'áil liom a rá cén mhaith bheith leat,
Tá an fód, mo léan, i do bhéal go beacht

[What news, Darach, from the land beyond?
Did you meet Seáinín yet, or Séamus?
Is the King of Ireland's Son himself there?
Is Fionn Mac Cumhaill or Conán there?
Was *Cailleach Bhéarra* out in front of you on the road?
Let us have your story (i.e. news), Darach, my honest man!

I enquired after you one time from Cáit
But you had left even her without tidings;
Come quickly to our aid, Darach,
And narrate every adventure correctly for us,
But, I would want to say, what's the use of going on about you,
Since, to my great sorrow, the sod sits trimly in your mouth [author's translation]

We may consider that the figure of the wise-woman and the repertoire of legends about her in oral narrative tradition constitute a significant native resource in the imaginative and cultural life of the Gaelic world.

ABBREVIATIONS

IFC: Irish Folklore Collection, Department of Irish Folklore, University College Dublin, Ireland
ML: Migratory Legend
MLSIT: Migratory Legend Suggested Irish Type

APPENDIX

IFC Manuscripts, The Department of Irish Folklore, University College Dublin, Ireland

1. IFC 4: 262–3, Baile an tSlé, Ventry, County Kerry, July 1931
2. IFC 20: 95–102, Dingle, County Kerry, July 1928
3. IFC 22: (i) 305–6, (ii) 306–8, (iii) 308–10, Baile Bhoithín, Ballyferriter, County Kerry, October 1932
4. IFC 30: 131, Doire Locha, Tuosist, County Kerry, July 1932
5. IFC 32: 209–12, Tuosist, County Kerry, December 1933
6. IFC 33: 267–70, Kilcommon, Upperchurch, County Tipperary, November 1934
7. IFC 44: 406–7, Cum Sheola, Bantry, County Cork, June 1934
8. IFC 49: 143–4, Baile Iartach, Cape Clear, County Cork, December 1933
9. IFC 54: 49–51, Kilworth, County Cork, November 1934
10. IFC 54: 72–4, Kilworth, County Cork, December 1934
11. IFC 74: 264, Clochán, Connemara, County Galway, December 1937
12. IFC 84: 214–15, Béal na Molt, Clonmel, County Tipperary, July 1934
13. IFC 132: 134–5, Kanturk, County Cork, June 1935
14. IFC 171: 410–12, Golladubh, County Donegal, January 1936
15. IFC 185: 89, Clochán Mór, County Donegal, March 1936
16. IFC 188: 306–10, Baile an Tobair, Ros, County Galway, April 1936
17. IFC 257: (i) 535–41, (ii) 542–3, Baile Nua, Mainistir, County Galway, October 1936
18. IFC 257: 696–8, Gleann-a-Mhíl, Mainistir, County Galway, November 1936
19. IFC 257: 699–700, Gleann-a-Mhíl, Mainistir, County Galway, November 1936
20. IFC 259: 650, Dungarvan, County Waterford, November 1936
21. IFC 305: 10–11, Seanbhóthar, Mainistir, County Galway, November 1936
22. IFC 354: (i) 351–2, (ii) 352, (iii) 352–3, Dubh Ros, Cill an Aonaigh, County Clare, May 1937
23. IFC 389: 404–23, Tóin Raithnighe, County Galway, August 1937
24. IFC 435: 217–25, An Mín Doire, Clochcheannfhaolaidh, County Donegal, November 1937
25. IFC 437: (i) 392, (ii) 393, Cnoc an Lích, West Carbery, County Cork, December 1937

26. IFC 612: 245–51, Na hAoraí (Eyeries), Beara, County Cork, April 1939
27. IFC 612: 251–7, Na hAoraí, Beara, County Cork, April 1939
28. IFC 612: 257–61, Na hAoraí, Beara, County Cork, April 1939
29. IFC 612: 262–8, Na hAoraí, Beara, County Cork, April 1939
30. IFC 623: 117–21, Na hAoraí, Beara, County Cork, May 1939
31. IFC 623: 122–3, Na hAoraí, Beara, County Cork, May 1939
32. IFC 842: 60–3, Na hAoraí, Beara, County Cork, March 1942
33. IFC 1224: 159–62, Dhá Dhrom (Ardgroom), Beara, County Cork, September 1951
34. IFC 1224: 215–17, Dhá Dhrom, Beara, County Cork, September 1951
35. IFC 1224: 247–8, Dhá Dhrom, Beara, County Cork, September 1951
36. IFC 1224: 248–51, Dhá Dhrom, Beara, County Cork, September 1951
37. IFC 1224: 274, Dhá Dhrom, Beara, County Cork, September 1951
38. IFC 1224: 275, Dhá Dhrom, Beara, County Cork, September 1951
39. IFC 1224: 282, Dhá Dhrom, Beara, County Cork, September 1951
40. IFC 1224: 294, Dhá Dhrom, Beara, County Cork, September 1951

CHAPTER 4

The 'Merry Wake' and Popular
Resistance to Domination

[Published in James S. Donnelly Jr and Kerby A. Miller (eds), *Irish Popular Culture 1650–1850* (Dublin: Irish Academic Press, 1998), pp. 173–200]

Writing on the ecclesiastical organisation of Ireland in the mid-eighteenth century, J.L. McCracken notes that Roman Catholic bishops 'had to contend with the ignorance and superstition of their flocks and the excesses which attended traditional gatherings'.[1] Pilgrimages, pattern-festivities and wakes are identified as phenomena especially incurring ecclesiastical disapproval because they manifested in officially unacceptable ways a religious sensibility on the part of the rural masses that derives as much from a Celtic or pagan cosmological tradition as from a Christian one. This native or ancestral religious sensibility, at once alternative to and co-existent with orthodox Christian values, beliefs and ritual, should not be seen, in the eighteenth and nineteenth centuries, as an ever feebler and more marginalised vestige of archaic Irish culture. The evidence suggests that as a part of the worldview and lifestyle of the majority, non-élite population which experienced both immense demographic growth and radical socio-economic transformation in the period in question, ancestral Irish religious belief and practice responded to and reflected prevailing social and historical circumstances in a way that made them in that age very much a 'going concern'. That the 'excessive' mortuary ritual characteristic of the rural Irish population in the early modern period should have proved resistant to official ecclesiastical exhortation and command until the early decades of the twentieth century suggests that the ritual in question was highly significant in the symbolic culture of the population that practised it. It also suggests that the ritual was functionally significant in relation to the structure and organisation of social relationships in the Irish eighteenth- and nineteenth-century worlds. It is a part of the aim of this essay to suggest that the merry wake was in fact a central social mechanism for the articulation of resistance – or at least reaction – on the part of the Irish peasantry to new forms of civil and clerical control in Irish society in early modern and modern times.

Seán Ó Súilleabháin's study of the games played at wakes includes a transcription of some of the edicts whereby Roman Catholic ecclesiastical authorities attempted to suppress the 'excesses' of the merry wake over a period of at least three hundred years.[2] The changing nature of the terms in which these edicts were expressed is evidence of the dynamic nature of the wake as a social institution. This evidence bears out my view that the practices of the wake and funeral in Irish popular culture that gave offence to eighteenth- and nineteenth-century Catholic Church authorities are very far from being vestigial remnants clinging to the fringes of orthodoxy.

The earliest edict noted by Ó Súilleabháin was issued by the Synod of Armagh in 1614. We should note that the primary complaint of that synod in relation to contemporary popular mortuary rites was that the common people were, inappropriately it is claimed, imitating their social and financial betters in both the matter of wearing black clothing to express their grief and in the provision of a feast to those attending the wake and the funeral. These things were objectionable in the eyes of the bishops because the expenditure of money which they entailed was thought excessive and was said to impoverish the succeeding generation of the family indulging in it.[3] While the custom of dressing in fashionable and expensive black mourning clothes does not seem to have persisted into the eighteenth and nineteenth centuries among the common people, the question of the costs of the wake and funeral feasts remained an issue. The amateur antiquarian and folklorist Thomas Crofton Croker reported more than two hundred years later that it was usual for the peasantry to provide shroud and burial dress for themselves many years before they were wanted and not to resort to wearing any of these articles in life 'despite wretchedness and rags'.[4] He also claimed that it was not unusual 'to see even the tombstone in readiness and leaning against the cabin wall'.[5] If the practice of holding a feast involving conspicuous consumption by family, neighbours and friends of the deceased began to establish itself in the ranks of the common people in the early modern period, as the evidence from the Synod of Armagh suggests, then such a practice was certainly firmly established by the time Crofton Croker described the popular culture of the south of Ireland in the early 1820s. He depicted the peasantry as 'looking forward to their death as a gala given by them', and even in the case of the 'destitute and friendless', seeking to 'hoard for the expenses of their wake and funeral'.[6]

A second ground on which the Synod of Armagh spoke out against customary wake practice in the early seventeenth century was that wakes were an occasion for the performance of 'obscene songs and suggestive games' that would be inappropriate even in legitimately merry contexts.[7] This is a charge that is constantly repeated across three hundred years, with the Maynooth Synod of 1927 still specifically outlawing the practice of engaging in immodest behaviour in the presence of the corpse.[8] Here again I believe that the symbolic significance and the important social function of such practices must be emphasised.

The problem of excessive expenditure on wake feasting and the problem of merriment, gaming and misbehaviour are again alluded to in Statute 20 of the Synod of Tuam in 1660. Here it was suggested that such money as was involved would be better spent as mass offerings for the clergy or given as alms. In this statute censure was also expressed against those females who engaged in excessive keening and lamentation at wakes, something which had already been deplored a generation earlier in Statute 3 of the Tuam Synod of 1631. Merriment in the forms of music and dance were also deplored in 1660 in the edicts of the Synod of Armagh, where excommunication was prescribed for those indulging in such musical merriment, just as it was for those indulging in the provision or consumption of *poitín* ('aqua composita') during matchmaking.[9] Such direct, specific and punitive opposition to the characteristic practices of the merry wake was repeated in the edicts of synods and in the pastoral letters of bishops through the later seventeenth and all of the eighteenth century in various parts of Ireland –Armagh, Meath, Dublin, Leighlin, Cashel and Emly, Waterford and Lismore, and so on.[10] Nevertheless, we find recorded from the diocese of Cashel and Emly for the years around 1800 a pastoral letter, which the archbishop there directed to be read each year before Christmas in every chapel of the archdiocese, and in which he solemnly warned his flock against the shameful and obscene behaviours at wakes which, he reported, are 'growing in strength daily', to the disadvantage of the faith.[11] Specifically identified as being most shameful and injurious were those games in which the officers and offices of the church were mimed and mocked – especially the sacrament of marriage. Those guilty of partaking in such games were to be excommunicated and were subjected to heavy penalties before being readmitted to the sacraments, including having to obtain written absolution from the archbishop himself or from the vicar general of the diocese. Such solemn prohibition from the wake house of the mimicry of the sacraments, especially marriage, and of sexual gratification in the festive access of young women and men to each other was kept up by hierarchy and clergy in official pronouncements throughout the nineteenth century. In places – Dublin in 1831, Monaghan in 1832, Ardagh in 1834 – virtual curfew was imposed on young people, especially the unmarried, in an attempt to combat what the church considered the shameful and irreligious behaviours in which those attending the wake house indulged.[12]

Besides their opposition to the merriment and games of the wake house, clerical hostility to the activities of keening women at both wakes and funerals was a further continuous element in the response of the ecclesiastical authorities to manifestations of popular ancestral religious feeling from the seventeenth century to the beginning of the twentieth. Ó Súilleabháin lists edicts against the practice of employing the services of keening women at wakes and funerals from Tuam (1631), Armagh (1660), Dublin (1670), Armagh (1670), Meath (1686), Kildare and Leighlin (1748), and Cashel and Emly (1800). He quotes oral traditions from the nineteenth century in the same sense.[13] Thus the two characteristic elements of mortuary ritual in the ancestral common culture of the Irish rural population in early modern times that were most severely opposed by the officers of orthodox Roman Christianity were (a) ritual public mourning and (b) merriment and licence, especially of a sexual nature. These are of course the two elements of mortuary passage rites that Van Gennep identified on a comparative basis as being the universally present elements of funerary ritual in traditional cultures. While there is no mention of Ireland or Irish mortuary tradition in Van Gennep's work, the rituals of the Irish merry wake and funeral are nevertheless consonant with his theories, not least in respect of his comment regarding the situation where, as in Ireland, more than one cosmological system informs the worldview of a population: 'Funeral rites are further complicated when within a single people there are several contradictory or different conceptions of the afterworld which may become intermingled with one another, so that their confusion is reflected in the rites.'[14]

In the merry wake and funeral of eighteenth- and nineteenth-century popular Irish culture an ostensibly Christian ritual marking the translation of the soul of the deceased to the Christian afterlife was very strongly marked by a vivid native and localised apprehension of the otherworld and of death that drew on a cosmology and a religious sensibility deriving from a native, or pagan, or Celtic worldview alternative to the Christian one. Such ambiguity of worldview in the popular culture of early modern and modern Ireland was a central characteristic of the products and manifestations of the culture – ritual, literature and political life. The merry wake was an institution embodying that ambiguity in a specially marked way.

A general sampling of the practices and beliefs surrounding death and burial in the popular culture of rural Ireland in the later nineteenth century, as reflected in the archival materials accumulated by the Irish Folklore Commission fieldworkers in the early and middle years of the twentieth century, will, I hope, support what has been so far claimed for the symbolic and social significance of the merry wake and provide a basis for further interpretation.[15]

For reasons of space I confine the data presented here to those of informants from two counties only, Galway and Cork. I am aware of the extensive discussion required as to the representativeness of this selection of material in the context of the considerable regional and historical variation to be found throughout the archival folklore evidence of wake ritual. The data selected derive, for the most part, from fieldwork carried out in the 1930s with elderly informants. Typically, we find there material recorded in, say, 1935 from someone aged about seventy-five who was allegedly relating what he or she recalled of what parents or grandparents related of their own young days. Thus the material can easily take us back to the middle of the previous century, to a time when the merry wake was still practised or enacted in both counties in the case of certain communities or families.

There is of course very little direct contemporary insider evidence for the functioning and significance of the Irish merry wake at the time when it appears to have flourished at non-élite levels during the later eighteenth and early nineteenth centuries. Among fictional accounts of wake ritual in nineteenth-century Anglo-Irish literature, the story 'Larry McFarland's Wake' included by William Carleton in his *Traits and Stories of the Irish Peasantry* (1830) is perhaps the most prominent. What direct evidence we do have from Folklore Commission informants in the 1930s is a mixture of personal memory and recalled anecdote, with little possibility of cross-checking or other verification, and it has been subject to a variety of collecting and editing variables. Nevertheless, it yields authentic data for examination.

The County Cork data used here is from at least seven communities ranging from Beara and Bantry in the west to Araglen and Kilworth in the east; from Glandore on the south coast to Charleville near the Limerick border to the north, and including mid-county communities in the baronies of West Muskerry and Kinalmeaky. The County Galway data used is from both the western coastal communities of Cois Fharraige and Connemara, viz. the parishes of Knock, Ros Muc, Carna, Baile na Cille, etc., and from such inland communities as Menlough, Moycullen, Craughwell and Kiltartan. The data are, for the sake of coherence, presented in the ethnographic present tense under four headings: (1) the laying out of the corpse; (2) keening and keening women; (3) tricks, games and play; (4) funeral and burial.

1. *The laying out of the corpse*

(a) *County Cork* After a certain period of time has elapsed after death during which the corpse has been left undisturbed, it is washed and dressed and laid out by some local female who specialises in this work. On no account must any member of the family of the deceased handle the corpse or touch it while it is being thus readied for the wake. A male neighbour is got to shave a male corpse if this is considered necessary. When washed, the corpse is dressed and laid out on the kitchen table or perhaps on a bed where the corpse house is large enough to have sizable bedrooms. The face of the corpse should always look to the east.

The corpse is dressed in either the deceased's best clothes (the last worn to mass) or else in a black or brown 'habit', a dress-like garment often associated with lay membership of a religious order. A rosary is twined around the deceased's hands, which are folded and joined on his or her breast, and a prayer book may be placed on the breast or under the deceased's chin.

Some corpses are not dressed in a habit because of the belief that the person whose corpse wears a habit will not meet with his or her 'own' relatives or ancestors in the next life.

While the feet of a corpse are usually fastened together during the wake either with a cord or a sock-pin (where socks are put on the feet), there is a great fear of coffining the corpse with such a foot-fastening still in place. Were such fastening to be left undone, it would prove to be a severe impediment to the deceased's activities in the next life of the otherworld. Also for this reason no pin or clip is left in the habit or other corpse garment, even though a number of these have been used in the dressing and laying-out procedure. The woman who lays out the corpse must undo the room when the corpse is taken away. The tented linen sheets that stand or hang about the corpse during the wake must be taken down before the body is coffined. These sheets, together with every scrap stripped off the table or bed on which the corpse was waked, must be bundled up into a heap in the centre of the room while the corpse is being coffined. The person who brings the loan of clothes or sheets to the wake house has to be the person who takes these back again to wherever they came from. In the case of loaned sheets the woman who washed the corpse must afterwards wet the four corners of the bundled sheets before they can be sent away again.

These 'waking sheets' are five in number. They are kept at one house in every ploughland and may never be used for anything else. One of them goes under the corpse on the wake bed or on the kitchen table; one goes overhead, fastened to the ceiling; one goes to one side of the corpse and one each goes to its head and feet, with these also being fastened to the ceiling so that the corpse lies within a sort of linen tent.

Brass candlesticks are kept for wakes at the same house as the sheets. Five candles are lit in them and kept lighted for a corpse dressed in a shroud or habit. Three candles are lit and kept lighted in the case of a corpse dressed in its own clothes.

The pillows and bolster on which the corpse rested, the mattress of the bed, and even the kitchen table on which the corpse was waked must be turned over after the corpse is coffined. The two sides of the deceased's family will compete with each other to be the first to do these turnings in an attempt to turn away from themselves the next succeeding death that is to occur. The length of time to such next succeeding death can be gauged by the relative stiffness or limpness of the deceased's corpse during the wake. A limp corpse is regarded as a sure sign of impending further death in the family.

The little stumps of the first candles lit during the wake are kept in the house for a very long time and used as a *leigheas* (cure) for both people and animals. The water in which the corpse was washed is also regarded as having a 'cure' in it and is kept for this purpose by some people, who will rub it on sores subsequently, saying at the same time, 'In the name of the Father and of the Son and of the Holy Ghost'. Where it is not kept in this way, it is at least carefully retained until the end of the wake and then, when the funeral leaves the house, 'thrown after the corpse' in the direction in which the coffin has moved off. To throw out the corpse water before the corpse has been buried is regarded as a very dangerous thing to do, and such instances have been followed by a lot of trouble and misfortune for a long time afterwards.

(b) *County Galway* It is not right to say a prayer for the soul of the deceased until the body is laid out *ós cionn cláir* (literally, 'on top of a board'). Immediately after death occurs, two or three persons are picked to lay out the corpse. The first task is to wash it. The oldest woman in the townland is properly the one to wash the corpse and wrap it in a white sheet on the table, with a pillow under its head and perhaps a sod of turf under its chin to complement the *marbh-fháisg* ('the binding of the hands, feet and chin of a corpse'). The two big toes are tied together until the body goes cold.

If the deceased was the 'man or woman of the house', i.e. the male or female head of household, then they have to be laid out in the kitchen. Invariably, the feet of every corpse must lie to the east. Those who have washed and laid out the corpse are the ones who eventually coffin it. Whoever puts up the *cábán* ('tent') of white sheets around and above the corpse is the one who has to take it down again.

A male corpse is dressed in home-made stockings, a *báinín* (homespun white-flannel vest) and white-flannel drawers. A female corpse wears a homemade white- or red-flannel 'coat', a grey-flannel jacket, and a little shawl on the head. The corpse of a young girl wears a dark dress with a white shawl on the shoulders. The *aiséadach* ('gravecloth') made from five yards of 'union cloth' is put on the corpse before coffining. It has a hole cut for the head of the corpse at its mid-point and is put on so that half is under and half over the corpse. The sides of the *aiséadach* are cut off in three-cornered sections to be kept as a *leigheas* ('cure') against lumps and swellings. The triangular sections are most often made up by the old woman who has washed and laid out the corpse. The hand of the corpse at a wake is rubbed over a wound, lump, or ulcer as a 'cure'. People are brought up to the corpse for this purpose at various stages of the wake in order to have the deceased's hand rubbed over the affected part.

Any clothes or cloths hanging on the walls of a house in which a person dies are taken down and left in a bundle in a corner of the house until the funeral is over. The deceased's own clothes and bedclothes are washed and hung out on bushes after the burial. Any neighbour who wishes to rid his own or a relative's family of illness can cut an *ascallán* ('a four-cornered section') out of the clothes and take and use this as something having a *leigheas* ('cure') in it.

2. *Keening and keening women*

(a) *County Cork* It is not right for any member of the family to touch the corpse or go near it to express grief until it is laid out properly. Then the whole family assembles around the corpse and cries over it, talking to it and calling back the deceased. Later, when the corpse is coffined and just before the lid is put on, every member of the family must again come and cry over the corpse and kiss it. The final family crying is done outside the house just before the coffin moves off. When the family have finished their initial crying over the corpse, the neighbours cry over it in turn as they arrive at the wake house during the course of the night. The special 'keeners' also cry over the corpse from time to time during the wake. These are old women who are especially good at crying and composing extempore verses in praise of the deceased, for which they are rewarded with drink and money. They are like poets in the wake house, and their performance makes people very 'lonesome'. It also elates the whole assembly when they 'open up' in the middle of the night after the rosary has been said. Such 'keeners' were summoned from miles away to come and perform at wakes, and it is disrespectful to the deceased not to arrange to have keening at the wake and funeral.

The keening women walk with the coffin during the funeral or ride with it in the horse-cart, often sitting on the coffin itself if the journey to the graveyard is a long one.

(b) *County Galway* When the corpse is first laid out, the household members come together over it and 'keen'. When other 'family' arrive, they do likewise and are joined at these times by the available household members. A final, very loud keening by members of the deceased's family takes place on the day of the funeral, when, after coffining, the deceased is taken out of the house and placed for a short while on two or four chairs in the *sráid* ('roadway') outside the house.

Apart from the family, the keen is also performed by old women with shawls on their heads who stand around the corpse, cry over it, and praise the deceased in verse. Tension is generated by the attempts of such keeners to outdo one another. Sometimes the keening old women will 'turn on each other', attacking each other in verse and heaping up verbal abuse. This gives rise to great amusement and merriment at the wake.

There is twice as much keening when it is a young woman or a young man who has died, and in such cases especially (though it is the common practice anyway), the keen is kept up on the day of the funeral all the way to the graveyard. The keeners will walk with the coffin, regardless of whether it is shouldered or horse-drawn on a cart. When the latter is the case, then one old keening woman walks in front, two others sit with the coffin on the cart, and the remaining women keeners walk alongside the cart, while holding onto the cart by one hand and keeping up the keen.

3. *Tricks, games and play*

(a) *County Cork* When people are waked on the kitchen table, there is great sport at wakes, with flutes, music and dancing. Sometimes there will be mummers sent during the night, with everyone dressed up in different clothes. A wake can be like a wedding, with all the fun and laughter. If there is no one to keep the 'fine boys' in check – say, at the wake of an old woman who has few relatives and who is 'no loss' – then they get up to a great deal of 'devilment' as the night passes, tying to their chairs people who doze off to sleep or to the hen-coop on which they are stretched, or shaving, in their sleep, bearded old men who have dozed off near the fire.

Once the rosary has been said after nightfall at a wake, then horseplay and rough tricks can be expected. 'Croosting' occurs with no objection or interference from the family of an elderly deceased person. This involves the pelting of various individuals at the wake with little pieces of turf brought along specially in their pockets by the 'fine boys' to create mischief. Those 'prime lads' have great fun annoying some cranky man, knocking the clay pipe out of his mouth, for instance, by firing a *caorán* ('piece of hard turf') at him unawares.

The general horseplay of this type can amount to 'the devil's own kip-of-the-reel' – all sport and blackguarding and every fellow trying to be better (i.e. more outrageous) than the next.

It is known for the corpse to be secretly roped by tricksters during the wake so that it can be hoisted into an upright position in the middle of the night, striking terror and panic into the assembly, especially the women, who then attempt to flee the house. Sometimes the people of the house are extremely angry at this, and there is very nearly 'a real fight'. At other times a family will not mind, as such behaviour is half-expected and, if given a chance, they would play the same tricks themselves. There is generally some old man in each district who is well known for organising and directing such 'devilment' at wakes, and the 'prime boys' will send up to five miles for such a person to come to a local wake so as to indulge in sport and tricks.

Some of these gaming activities are organised set pieces. The young men will start to erect a pyramid of themselves and ask some innocent or inexperienced fellow to top it off for them, telling him to catch the cross-beam of the roof for a moment and then all running away so as to leave him hanging. Occasionally, a not-so-innocent individual will allow himself to be duped like this but will extract revenge by suddenly flinging down ashes or soot into the eyes of those gazing up.

Sometimes an unsuspecting individual will be pounced on and made to crouch in the centre of the floor as an anvil. Two or three others will start sledging him with their fists. The cry will be taken up, '*Buail é, buail é, buail é trina chéile, buail é, buail é, buail é go léir*' ('Beat him, beat him, beat him all over, beat him, beat him, beat him entire') and perhaps ten or twelve fellows in all will be pounding him. Someone will suddenly shout, '*Tá sé ag dóigheadh*' ('He is burning'), whereupon the 'anvil' will be picked up and rushed either to a bucket of water or outside to a mud puddle to be doused. Another version of this game involves having a patient, lying on the floor, visited and examined by all the 'doctors' at the wake and thus subjected to rough handling. In this game too, the victim sometimes turns the tables by suddenly throwing a concealed fistful of ashes or soot in the face of his visitor.

On one occasion a group of five or six 'lads' going to a wake could not decide which of them should lead their party into the wake house to go and stand over the corpse and cry a little, as it was customary for everyone attending a wake to do. They drew lots for the honour and it fell to a 'hardy boyo'. As they went in the door of the house, one of them struck their leader a terrible blow on the earhole with his fist so that his crying over the corpse was remarkably authentic. The others had to back out of the door again because of their need to burst out laughing.

'Brogue about' is regarded as the best and most popular game of all. For this all the men sit around on the kitchen floor in a circle with their legs pulled up to them. An old shoe is passed around the circle under the raised knees, and someone is prevailed on to stand in the middle of the circle and to try to intercept the shoe in its passage. As he turns to scan the circle of knees, he may be struck with a crack of the shoe on the poll while his back is turned to whomever happens to have it. If a 'slow fellow' is sitting in the middle, he may be a very long time looking for the shoe and will have to endure a great deal of punishment. In general, this is regarded as a 'great' game.

(b) *County Galway* It is the custom for some piece of clothing belonging to each individual at a wake to be collected into a shawl and brought to the centre of the room. Each item is held up in turn and its owner identified. Unless the owner can perform with either a story or a song, the item of clothing is first threatened with a lighted candle and is finally burned with the candle flame so that a hole is left in it, should its owner absolutely refuse to perform.

It sometimes happens that people assembled in a house for storytelling or recreational purposes organise a false wake so as to provide themselves with entertainment of greater scope and intensity. A stranger in the community, usually a beggar man or woman, can be prevailed on to act the part of the corpse, and word will be sent out to neighbours and friends to gather at the house. Special provision of food and drink will be made, and the merriment will last through the whole night until morning.

The boisterousness of the horseplay and gaming at wakes is well illustrated in the account of a Galway informant, who says that once, in about 1868, not having previously seen '*Cleas na mBullán*' ('The bull-calf game'), he was pressed into playing the part of a bull-calf along with several other young men. In the course of the game, which mimicked buying and selling, the 'calves' were hemmed in and pressed against the wall of the kitchen with such vigour that the wall collapsed on to three or four children who were in bed in the room on the other side of it. All at the wake ran out of the house in terror, expecting that there would be three or four extra corpses at this wake now. But the children were brought out unharmed, and the crowd returned to resume the wake, except for four or five boatmen from Connemara, who, having fled in terror like the rest, never stopped until they boarded their boats and made off from the land.

Boisterous behaviour at wakes begins when people – always men in these accounts – begin to fire small objects at each other and at certain targeted persons at the wake in order to cause merriment and disruption. Pieces of hard turf are used in this way, as are bits broken off the ten-inch shanks of the chalk pipes that are being smoked on all sides – pipes known as 'Lord ha' mercies' from the response required on being presented with one on arrival at the wake house. These bits of chalk clay are extremely hard and sharp-edged, and the way in which they are fired hard is extremely dangerous, especially to people's eyes.

Once they have prayed at the side of the corpse, parties of young men arriving at a wake by night will straightaway fall to playing such group games as 'Hurry the brogue', 'Hunt the slipper', and 'Who has the marble?' To be caught out in these games means to suffer the lash of a stick on the hand or a blow on the head. Regarding the most commonly played game of all, called '*Faic*' (another name for 'Hurry the brogue'), it is said that at the wake of an elderly deceased it was commonly the case that the roughness and horseplay was such as almost to dislodge the corpse from the table on which it lay. Legend tells of a local rogue who actually stole the corpse from a wake house where the only people present were a handful of elderly people who had all fallen asleep. He later won a reward of £5 from the priest of the parish for 'finding' the corpse again.

4. *Funeral and burial*

(a) *County Cork* When coffined, the deceased is brought out of the house feet-first, and the coffin is placed for a little while on two or four chairs in the open air. The family engage in their last crying over the deceased before the funeral moves off. When it does so, the chairs on which the coffin last rested will be knocked over, together with other chairs and seating brought out of the house after the coffin itself. All of these, together with the table inside the house on which the corpse was laid out and which will have been knocked over at the time of coffining the corpse, will be allowed to remain in the fallen position until after the burial has taken place.

Four male relatives of the deceased, if possible with the same surname, should be the ones who 'go under' the coffin when it comes out of the house, when it goes into the chapel, again when it leaves the chapel (that is, when the corpse is brought to the chapel at all), and finally, when it enters the graveyard.

There are memories of bodies being buried uncoffined, carried to the graveyard either on a stretcher or else in a coffin merely borrowed for the occasion and later returned to its owner; this was the 'hinge' coffin, so called from the hinged-end board that swung open to allow the body to slide out into the grave.

The coffin is preferably shouldered all the way to the graveyard, especially if the deceased was well liked. Relays of men 'go under' the coffin as required. If the journey to the graveyard is very long, then after a mile or so, the coffin can be placed in a horse-cart and drawn the rest of the way to the gate of the graveyard, where it is again shouldered by close relatives.

The funeral procession takes the longest traditional route to the graveyard, with no shortcut whatsoever, in accordance with the customary injunction, '*an timpeall chun an teampaill*' ('the long way round to the churchyard'). Once brought into the graveyard on the shoulders of four close relatives, the coffin is carried all around the perimeter path in a sunwise (*deiseal*) direction before being brought to the grave. At the graveside, before the earth is piled on top of the coffin, the screws on the lid are either loosened or withdrawn altogether and placed on the lid in the form of a cross. This is done to ensure that deceased persons have *cead a gcos* ('footroom', 'liberty') in the otherworld.

It is reported as 'usual enough' not to have any priest in the funeral procession or at the grave, though in some places it has become the custom for two priests to attend every funeral. When no priest is present, the funeral will halt at any crossroads, the coffin will be let down, and the people will all gather around it. Someone will then recite the *De profundis* and other prayers for the soul of the deceased.

A 'bog sod' should be carried at the end of every funeral. This is a 'blanket' of turf or top sod, about eight feet by four, which is cut in a local bog or field and rolled in one piece onto a stick and tied with rope. This 'blanket' is unrolled after the burial and laid carefully in one piece over the filled grave.

The grave itself should always be aligned on an east–west axis and should be opened or dug, not by any relative of the deceased, but by a 'gravedigger' or else by a neighbour not having the same surname as the deceased. The grave is usually 'reddened' (i.e. opened by removing the top sod and turning the earth) on the day after the death occurs. On no account, however, can a grave be 'reddened' on a Monday, so that the grave of someone dying on Sunday is either opened that same day or else on the following Tuesday. A grave is usually opened by two men working together. When it is made, the two who made it cross their shovels over it, and these are left in position until the burial time as a protection against interference with the grave by spirits or fairies. For both people making a grave and people at a burial it is wrong to clean boots or shoes afterwards on graveyard grass and wrong to spit while in the graveyard.

Some people will open a grave but will on no account close it again themselves, even if it has been opened in error. Having been opened, a grave must receive something before being closed again, even if it is only half-opened. If nothing is put into a grave, even a partly opened one, before closing it again, then it is sure to claim one of the family whose grave it is within a very short time.

Just as all those meeting a funeral – even a fairy funeral – on the road should turn and travel *trí choischéim na trócaire* ('the three merciful steps') with it, so those closest to the deceased, and to the grave at burial, should throw in three shovelfuls or three fistfuls of earth onto the coffin before the business of closing the grave begins in earnest. The noise of these first few shovelfuls of earth thudding onto the coffin causes the bereaved family to cry again in unison, a cry taken up once more and for the final time by any keening women present.

When a person has died and been buried, his or her clothes are given away to someone else to wear as something that will benefit the soul of the deceased. The deceased's best suit of clothes, for instance, will be given 'in the name of God' to his best friend to wear to mass on the next three Sundays. These clothes may not be altered in size to suit the recipient, and after the three Sundays on which they are worn to mass, they are often kept hanging up in the recipient's house until they melt away in moth-holes, just as it is believed that the body of the deceased melts and withers away in similar fashion in the grave.

(b) *County Galway* Certain rules apply to bringing a coffin into and out of a house. It must be brought in through a southern door and out again through the same (or through a back door), as normal practice. When, however, a 'stranger' is being buried from a house, his or her coffin goes out a northern door so as to take the bad luck and the harm of death with it out of the house and out of the family. An attempt is often made by a man's own family to enforce this same rule of 'stranger brings and takes bad luck' in the case of the death of a new wife, as in childbirth, for instance. In such cases the woman's death is regarded as being due to 'ill-luck' and as ultimately attributable to fairy intervention. The woman's own family may oppose this practice, and the result is often dissension and fighting. Once brought out of the house, the coffin is put down on two or more chairs to rest briefly. When the coffin is taken up again, to be placed on a stretcher or hearse, these chairs are tumbled upside down.

There are accounts of corpses buried without coffins in the 1880s. These were brought to the graveyard in a hinged coffin, from the opened side of which they were slid into the grave. One hinged coffin is said to have served all the townlands connected to the one burial ground. On the coast the coffin, shouldered by four men to the graveyard, rests on two oars and is covered with a white sheet which is knotted and pinned in its corners and afterwards brought home again.

Four men of the same surname as the deceased should shoulder the coffin out of the house and later from the gate of the burial ground to the graveside. No two brothers should ever be among the bearers for fear that the death of one of them within the year will result. Everyone 'going under' the coffin in a funeral should do so three times in all to avoid subsequent bad luck. Bad luck or the fairies themselves will reside in any spot where a coffined corpse rested during a funeral procession, and so the coffin is never 'let down' anywhere between the house and the graveyard. Funerals stop, however, at places where a roadside cairn of stones marks the spot where another, previous death has taken place. Prayers are said at such stops and small stones added to the cairn.

Anyone meeting a funeral on the road should turn and accompany it for three steps, and not to do so is to show lack of respect for the deceased and lack of sympathy in the bereavement.

Where a horse is used to draw a coffin in a funeral going a long distance, people never like to use a mare that is in foal for this purpose. Nobody on the way to or from a funeral should make any purchase, as this will surely lead to misfortune. *'Bail ó Dhia air an obair'* ('God bless the work') is never said to someone at work making a coffin or a grave. Those who dig a grave should be the ones to fill it in again. Anyone with any contact with a grave should wash their hands on returning home, even if their hands are 'crystal-clean'. The loy and the shovel are left crossed over the open grave from the digging of it until the arrival of the coffin at the graveside. No grave will be dug on a Monday if the top sod has not already been removed on the previous day; since it is very bad luck to turn the sod on a Monday.

Every family has its own grave into which the generations go, except that no grave can be reopened until seven half-years have passed since the last interment. If a second death occurs sooner than that, then a new grave must be dug next to the old. When, after at least seven half-years, an old grave is opened, the old boards and any bones found are taken up and replaced on top of the new coffin, which must always go to the bottom of the grave. Conflict has been known to arise in the case of elderly brothers, one of whom is married and makes clear his intention of burying his deceased wife in his parents' grave. The unmarried brother in this instance runs the risk of being excluded from his parents' grave should his own death occur within the seven half-years required before the grave may be opened a second time. Potential conflict is also present in the instance where the family of a young woman who dies early in marriage will want to 'bring her home' to the family grave. The reason given for her family's wanting this is that the bereaved husband is likely to marry again, and that his first wife really has no business being buried in his family grave.

At the graveside the pins of the sheet that covered the coffin during the funeral journey are thrown into the open grave. A bottle of 'holy' (i.e. blessed) water brought from the chapel will also be put into the grave. People at the graveside, along with the family and relatives of the deceased, catch up three handfuls of earth each and fling them down onto the coffin at the bottom of the grave. A man from County Clare introduced the practice of putting a *scraith* ('sod') down on the coffin before the grave is filled so as to reduce the stark sound of earth and stones falling onto the coffin.

Finally, before people move away from the graveyard and the funeral ends, 'close mourners', i.e. a spouse, parent, child or sibling of the deceased, may be taken by the arms and swung by neighbours three times over the filled grave. This is done in order to 'take away' the close mourners' grief for the deceased.

5. Commentary

The above material, taken as a whole, makes clear that the merry wake and funeral, the characteristic mortuary ritual of Irish popular custom, involve a centring of the life of the community into a traditional assembly with both sacred and social significance. A structural principle of traditional cosmology in Ireland has always been the centring of community life into occasional sacred assemblies that 'serve to renew social order as well as to acknowledge and venerate supernatural forces'.[16] The ancient royal assemblies at burial sites, for example Tailtiu, Carmun, etc., which featured horse-racing, board games and athletic contests, are early examples of such centrings occurring as events of an annual or triennial community calendar. The merry wake and funeral are a later and more proletarian manifestation of the same structural principle, occurring not in calendrical sequences but in accordance with the arrival of crisis points in the life cycles of individual members of the community. Assembly custom is especially prominent in the Irish cultural tradition, at both learned and popular levels, at *Samhain*/Halloween, when the otherworld is closest to the human social order and when otherworld powers, ancestral and fairy, present the greatest danger to human life. Play and performance in assembly, whether in the royal banqueting hall or around the peasant fireside, have always had at *Samhain* prophylactic significance in relation to the threat of otherworld contact. The merry wake can be seen as a kind of movable *Samhain* assembly, playing its protective and expressive role at the liminal interface of life and death in the community and constituting a prominent part of the means by which the community effects the re-establishment of social order in the face of the disruptive power of death, which requires the deceased to pass into an afterlife ambiguously ancestral/fairy and Christian. If the 'old man' or 'borekeen',[17] who is said to have been well known in each district as an organiser and director of the pranks and games of the wake assembly, is the agent of that socially cathartic chaos out of which a renewed social order can emerge, then the keening woman, the *bean chaointe*, is the agent of the transition to the next life of the individual whose corpse lies at the heart of the wake assembly, and whose passing is ritually mourned all the way to the grave in the highly charged performance of the female practitioners of the *caoin*.[18]

Figure 4.1 Wake as functional centring

OTHER WORLD

Individual transition/incorporation

SACRED

WAKE ASSEMBLY

SOCIAL

Communal reversal/regeneration

HUMAN SOCIAL REALM

The structural outline of what occurs in the merry wake is suggested in schematic form in Figure 4.1. The role of the *bean chaointe* as the female agent of the mournful transition of the deceased individual to the afterlife of an ambiguously Christian/fairy otherworld should be viewed in relation to other female roles which in Irish cultural tradition also associate the female with the sovereignty of the supernatural in human affairs. At the supernatural level itself there is the pre-eminent figure of the sovereignty queen, the intimate spouse and divine legimatrix of the rightful ruler,[19] but also a terrifying figure of war and death,[20] who alternates between the poles of this fundamental hag/spouse opposition in Irish ancestral cosmology and mythology. The 'banshee', who in Irish tradition is the supernatural messenger portending death to the family and community about to be bereaved, and who is heard crying and keening in the vicinity of the wake-house-to-be, is a reflex in popular culture of the aristocratic figures of the great sovereignty queens associated in medieval Gaelic literature with royal and ruling lineages.[21] I suggest that we view the *bean chaointe* at the wake as a flesh-and-blood reflex of the supernatural female sovereign who rules over the otherworld and into whose domain the deceased is now to be translated. In this light the *bean chaointe* is the (human) structural adjunct of the 'banshee', and the *bean bhán*, the female corpse-washer, is another being who must be seen as having symbolic and structural status that insulates her against the common plight of other mortals at risk of pollution and misfortune by virtue of their contact with death and the corpse of the deceased.

The figure of the male 'borekeen', the trickster-master of ceremonies at the merry wake, is free of such supernatural associations. Rather, his role is that of the social order itself personified.

In the person of the 'borekeen' and of his willing helpers and henchmen (the 'hardy boys' and 'prime lads'), the community displays its vitality and continuity in the face of mortally threatening contact with the supernatural realm. In this regard especially, the merry wake became a focus in eighteenth- and nineteenth-century Irish popular culture for the carnivalesque element of social life, which was increasingly denied expression in those other domains subject to those wielding new civil and clerical forms of social control, as the forces of modernisation impinged economically and politically on the Irish peasant population. In the imitative and mocking games played at wakes, the matter of culture and the matter of history mingled in ways which articulated in traditional symbolic language both a commentary on and a resistance to social forces threatening the continuance of old ways and old mentalities.[22] This was not, of course, a unique development and was akin to similar articulations in peasant communities elsewhere.[23]

The degree to which such wake rowdiness and play-acting was offensive to contemporary Christian religious sensibility is well illustrated by the remarks of the County Kilkenny antiquarian John Prim, who wrote in 1852:

> These wake games are never performed in the houses of persons who felt really afflicted by the bereavement which they might be supposed to have endured in the demise of a member of their family. They are reserved for the deaths of old people who had survived the ordinary span of life, or young children who cannot be looked upon as an irreparable loss. They are placed under the conduct of some peasant of the district who excelled in rustic wit and humour, and this person, under the title of 'borekeen', may be termed the hierophant of the observances, whose orders are carried into force by subordinate

officers, all arrayed in fantastic habiliments. The 'game' usually first performed is termed 'Bout' and is joined in by men and women, who all act a very obscene part which cannot be described. The next scene generally is termed 'Making the ship', with its several parts of 'laying the keel', forming the 'stem and stern', and erecting 'the mast', the latter of which is done by a female using a gesture and expression proving beyond doubt that it is a relic of pagan rites. The 'Bull and the cow' is another game strongly indicative of a pagan origin, from circumstances too indelicate to be particularised. The game called 'Hold the light', in which a man is blindfolded and flogged, has been looked upon as a profane travestie of the passion of our Lord; and religion might also be considered as brought into contempt by another of the series, in which a person caricaturing a priest and wearing a rosary composed of small potatoes strung together enters into conflict with the 'borekeen' and is put down and expelled from the room by direction of the latter. If the former games be deemed remnants of pagan rites and of ante-Christian origin, these latter may be looked upon as anti-Christian, and devised with a view to making religion religious at a time when the masses had a lingering predilection for paganism. 'Turning the spit' and 'Selling the pig' are the names of two other of those games. In the game that was called 'Drawing the ship out of the mud' the men engaged actually presented themselves before the rest of the assembly, females as well as males, in a state of nudity, whilst in another game the female performers attired themselves in men's clothes and conducted themselves in a very strange manner. Brief as are these particulars, they will give sufficient idea of the obscene and demoralising tendency of the wake orgies and show the necessity which existed for their total suppression.[24]

We can assume a corresponding outrage on the part of the practitioners of the civil professions – doctors, lawyers, merchants – whose activities and image were mercilessly pilloried in the games described so thoroughly in Ó Súilleabháin's account. Ó Súilleabháin, of course, makes it clear that there was a marked regional distribution in the practice of indulging in games at wakes, and he asserts that the excesses and improprieties of the merry wakes of the other three provinces were unknown in the funerary traditions of south-west Munster, his native region.[25] He offers no explanation for this marked regionalism in the content of the prophylactic-assembly performance that constitutes the licensed revelry of Irish traditional mortuary rites. It would appear, however, that there is a correspondence between the distribution of carnival-type games at wakes and other indicators (in the market place or at the holy-well pattern) of the acculturation in Ireland during early modern times of European-derived popular pastimes and recreations. The way in which such carnivalesque games and performances, redolent of the street culture of early modern Europe, became quite specifically focused on the Irish wake house, whose traditional performances were hitherto of a more verbal nature (storytelling, riddling, etc.), is a matter needing further research. What is clear, however, is that all such performance at wakes of story, song, trick, game or mime is a manifestation at group level of a social solidarity and continuity that contrast with the matter of the deceased's transition and incorporation into an otherworld – a matter that is, at the level of the individual, the other and equal concern of the wake and funeral ritual and those participating in it.

The extent to which ancestral otherworld incorporation is a joint primary function of the wake has perhaps not been sufficiently emphasised in previous commentary on the significance of the merry wake. In the wake and funeral as Christian ritual, however unorthodox, the function of delivering the soul of the deceased into the afterlife of the communion of saints in the Christian heaven is clear. The perception, however, that any non-Christian meanings in the ancestral rites of wake and funeral were simply vestiges of archaic and primitive custom has not done justice to the way in which structures and values of ancestral cosmology (i.e. concerning the location of and access to the otherworld) could still inform the worldview and lifestyle of Irish peasant communities until at least the mid-nineteenth century.

Ó Súilleabháin does refer to mortuary rites in contemporary traditional societies elsewhere, but his own understanding of the theoretical and functional significance of the merry wake – mourning and merriment – extends no further than to say, following the ideas of the Scandinavian scholar Christiansen whom he openly acknowledges, that the merry wake was a vestigial survival in Irish tradition of a set of rites from ancient pre-Christian times designed to effect two things: (a) to protect the community by means of a communal feast against the anger of the deceased at dying and to pacify the deceased by having him or her as the guest of honour at the valedictory assembly, and (b) to heal in a ceremonial fashion the wound in the social fabric which the deceased's departure has occasioned.[26]

In his treatment of the native supernatural, S.J. Connolly accepts the Ó Súilleabháin-Christiansen explanations for the origin and significance of the practices of the merry wake, and he adds a further pair of assertions connected with what he calls 'the important psychological function' of the merry wake. It attests, he claims, the vitality of community even in the presence of death, and the continuity of social life in the face of the sudden social rupture of an individual's demise.[27]

I consider this explanatory theory of the merry wake to be too general and too static, if not actually ahistorical. Certainly, it is hampered by one major flaw from the outset. It is claimed that the merry wake existed to assuage the anger of the deceased individual, to heal the social wound of death, and to manifest the continuing vitality of social life in the face of sudden rupture. Why, then, is it the ethnographic reality that merriment, vitality and excess were minimal, if not entirely absent, at precisely those wakes where anger, social wounding and sudden rupture were likely to have been at their most acute, as in the sudden and calamitous death of young, healthy adults (by accident or misfortune, including female death in childbirth), or in the kind of death traditionally attributed to fairy abduction and so well exemplified in the Donegal legends collected by Ó hEochaidh.[28]

In the case of such deaths our evidence suggests that the wake at least was a subdued affair, with too much genuine grief to allow for the levity and revelry of the full-blown merry assembly. The funeral, on the other hand, in the case of deaths attributed to fairy abduction – certainly, when the death was that of a young married woman – appears to have been regularly marked by inter-family rivalry. This tallies with Richard Jenkins' idea that explanations of death as fairy abduction are tied to the incorporation process in Irish tradition.[29] Clearly, a young wife dying in childbirth and subsequently regarded as the victim of fairy abduction had not been fully or finally incorporated into her husband's family life. Thus her own family were especially concerned to bury her body in their own graveyard with their own ancestors as the nearest they could come to reincorporation and recovery from the otherworld of the *sí*. There was even a known way, reported in the oral narrative tradition of Coolea in the Cork barony of West Muskerry, whereby the changeling corpse could be disposed of so as to restore the abducted deceased to her human family again. This involved opening the coffin three times on each of three bridges over which the funeral procession passed on its way to the woman's ancestral graveyard. On the third bridge, if the bereaved family were certain that the body was not that of their kinswoman but rather a changeling who lay in the coffin, then they should fling the corpse out into the running stream and their own kinswoman would be at home before they arrived there![30] Beliefs such as these lay behind the ritualised struggle to carry off the corpse to the graveyard of one's own side during funerals, a practice which was widely reported.

Deaths of the sort attributed in Irish traditional culture to fairy abduction were regarded as 'untimely' in contrast with the 'timely' deaths at advanced ages of elderly community members who had lived a full life and whose demise was understood as the will of God. This distinction between timely and untimely death determined the extent to which merriment coincided with mourning in each specific instance of individual demise, and thus it determined the overall character of the ritual occasion within which various lesser rituals occurred.

Basically, what is at issue in the distinction between timely and untimely death in Irish tradition is the recognition of two separate cosmological mechanisms or agencies of death, the one ancestral or Celtic, the other Christian. A distinction between the 'natural' and the 'magical' is also involved here, with untimely death, attributed to the agency of the powers and personages of the contingent ancestral/Celtic otherworld, being regarded as 'magical', while timely death, attributed to the agency of the Christian divinity and his ordinances, is held to be 'natural'. Thus an elderly deceased, deemed to have lived out an entire life-span and to have enjoyed the full range of human fulfilment in the course of that life, was thought to have undergone a natural death that was timely and offered no very sudden or serious challenge to the social order. On the other hand, unforeseen or accidental sudden death, especially in those who were young or in the fullness of life, was judged as untimely and attributed to the magical agency of the fairies. Fairy abduction was thus commonly said to have been the cause of such sudden or accidental deaths as those of the young mother who died in childbirth, the young man who, collecting firing, fell over a cliff-edge, the cowherd who perished on the home mountain, the fisherman drowned in calm weather, or the child who grew sickly and then wasted away.

The fairy abduction that explained such untimely deaths was considered not only a grievous rupture of the social order but also a serious challenge to the whole social realm and its continuing vitality. Revelry and merriment were subdued in the waking of the untimely dead by comparison with the behaviours exhibited during the wakes of the elderly and timely deceased (see Fig. 4.2).

Figure 4.2 Hermeneutic framing

	Untimely Death	**Timely Death**
Origin	magical	natural
Agency	fairy	God's will
Reaction	restraint	excess
Performer	*bean chaointe*	borekeen
Outcome	incorporation	dissolution

This reduction of emphasis on the function of the 'borekeen' – mirroring the way in which untimely death was perceived as seriously impairing society's 'natural' ability to restore social order in the face of 'natural' death – placed increased emphasis on the function of the *bean chaointe*, whose role was chiefly concerned with effecting the transition of the deceased to the afterlife and with ensuring his or her incorporation with the family ancestors, as these were perceived to co-exist dualistically, both in a Christian heaven and in the fairy realm. Such special concern with the proper incorporation of the deceased was justified in the sense that fairy abduction, the attributed cause of the deaths in question, had disrupted and impaired the process of incorporation in both the social realm of this life and the afterlife of the otherworld.

As previously noted, Richard Jenkins has suggested that explanations of death as fairy abduction were tied to the process of kinship – group incorporation in Irish tradition.[31] Faulty incorporation denied the individual access to the benefits of membership in his or her kin group in both this life and the next. This is particularly relevant to the deaths of young married women. Clearly, such victims of fairy interference in human affairs were not fully or finally incorporated into the husband's family, and their incorporation into an appropriate ancestor group in the otherworld was now problematic because of their abduction. The extensive archive of oral tradition collected by the fieldworkers of the Irish Folklore Commission from 1935 on suggests that in such cases a struggle or contest frequently took place between the original family of the deceased and the family of her husband, with each side seeking to bury the body in their own ancestral graveyard with their own ancestors.

A revealing late-eighteenth-century account exists of one such struggle that took place at a funeral in Killarney and was witnessed by a

French traveller, the Chevalier de Latocnaye. Even though he described the events of the funeral rather than the wake, de Latocnaye captured essential features of the effectively unified mortuary ritual of the popular Irish culture of his day:

I was witness here, a few days after, of a somewhat strange scene. Hearing the funeral bell, I went out to observe the procedure. It was the funeral of a poor woman who was being carried to her last resting-place, the coffin surrounded by a prodigious number of females who wept and chanted their '*hu lu lu*' in chorus, the men looking on rather indifferently. When the funeral arrived at the head of the 'T', that is, at the end of the principal street of the town, a singular dispute occurred between the husband and the brother of the deceased. One of the parting ways led to the abbey of Muckross, where it was the custom for the family of the husband to bury their dead; the other led to Aghadoe, where are buried the family of the brother. The latter assumed the right to direct the funeral toward Aghadoe, while the husband wished to go in the other direction to Muckross. The friends of the two parties took hold in turn of the remains of the poor woman, each wishing them to be carried to the side they favoured; but each finding themselves unable to succeed, by common accord they deposited the bier on the street and commenced a vigorous fight to determine by blows of sticks to which side the remains should be carried. I was at the time with the minister of the parish, Mr Herbert, who is also a justice of the peace. With great courage he threw himself into the middle of the fight, seized the collars of the two principal combatants, and after some explanation he decided that the husband had the right to decide where his wife should be buried. He allowed the husband then to go without letting go hold of the brother-in-law, and the funeral moved in the direction of Muckross. I remarked that neither fight nor controversy which followed arrested the cries of the wailing women, who continued to beat their breasts, tear their hair, and cry '*hu lu lu*' as if neither fight nor controversy proceeded.[32]

The chevalier and the clergyman -cum- legal officer thought that they had witnessed a senseless outrage, a breakdown of law and order bordering on the obscene. To the anonymous actors in the event, however, its meaning was very different. In terms of both robust assembly and ritual mourning, honour and respect had been shown publicly to the individual deceased and to both sides of her family. Her radical transition to a new order was mirrored and marked in the public drama of the transfer of her mortal remains, a drama that also represented the re-establishment of a renewed social order in the aftermath of her demise. De Latocnaye found it especially remarkable that the keening should have continued throughout the fracas. But this was of the very essence of the merry wake and funeral that they should simultaneously serve a dual function, mourning a transition and also resolving and removing social tension. He was also surprised when, he said, 'the peasants showed the greatest respect to the magistrate and submitted promptly to his decision'. They did so presumably because this was not a real battle and because they had already shown in their mounting of such a public ritual – in this case in the actual physical presence of their legal masters and social betters – their claim to independence of a resented civil authority and their allegiance to ancestral ways.

In the eighteenth and early nineteenth centuries the merry wake and funeral together constituted a central institution of popular Irish rural culture which had both great symbolic and behavioural significance in people's lives. This institution articulated for them, in powerful ways which they long continued to value highly, their collective response to their life experience. It performed this function as a sophisticated amalgamation of the symbolic resources of both the magico-religious and the socio-political universes of discourse. Along with other aspects of the popular culture of pre-Famine Irish tradition, it succumbed to the immense transformation of the society of the 'lower Irish' that overtook Ireland and Irish popular culture in the mid-nineteenth century.

CHAPTER 5

The Production and Consumption of Sacred Substances in Irish Funerary Tradition

[Published in Hannu-Pekka Huttunen and Ritta Latvio (eds), *Entering the Arena: Presenting Celtic studies in Finland* (*Etiainen* series, no. 2) (Turku: Finnish Society for Celtic Studies, 1993), pp. 39–51]

Funerary ritual in traditional culture in early modern Ireland may be regarded as a topic of Celtic studies since (a) there are significant continuities in later traditional cosmology and ritual from prehistoric and early medieval times, and (b) the majority of the bearers and participants in early modern traditional culture are Irish-speakers.

Students of early Irish narrative tradition have recently begun to decipher the codes that carry the cultural significance of tales at a level that underlies the surface texture of plot and incident. We can hope to arrive at a similar exposition of the significance of the ritual behaviours of Irish wake practices by means of an analysis of the narrative evidence of the Irish Folklore Commission's archive of field transcriptions regarding this topic.

Our approach to the interpretation of early modern wake ritual is founded on an appreciation of a symbolic logic that characterises both early and late forms of traditional culture in Ireland and that continues to manifest the archetypal sensibilities of native ancestral tradition. Two matters in particular may be mentioned as framing the significance of much wake ritual. Firstly, the sense in which there is symbolic congruence between *Samhain* – the major turning point of the traditional calendar –

and death in the life cycle of the individual. It can be argued that the wake house is a kind of liminal arena where otherworld intrusion is likely to be encountered as in the *bruíon* (fairy palace). Secondly, the sense in which the festive aspect of the early modern wake can be seen not only as an Irish reflex of early modern European carnivalesque, but as an articulation at popular/commoner level of ancient Celtic funeral feasting.

The wake is best regarded as both a sacred and a social assembly that serves to perform important cultural functions in regard to the incorporation of the deceased into the otherworld and the renewal of society in the aftermath of the death it has suffered. Important female and male agencies are at work in the wake ritual to act out and ensure the efficacy of these functions. The liminal boundedness of the wake assembly exists in time as well as space and is marked also by the creative/playful qualities of the behaviours associated with participants. A fundamental part of the process of bringing this liminal space into existence is the work of the female corpse-washer who 'lays out' the body of the deceased.

The process of 'laying out the corpse' gives rise to the production of sacred substances, i.e. material objects that are now charged with supernatural power. Much evidence exists in the Irish Folklore Commission archive regarding the charged, sacred and, most often, curative nature of the corpse's clothing, the water that has washed it, the stumps of the candles that have burned about it, the straw or other bedding on which it has lain. The ashes of the fire in the wake house and even the sweepings of the floor are also envisaged as being charged with sacred magical power in this fashion. Some of this evidence is discussed here.

Such sacred, magic power, centred on the sacred quality of the corpse itself, can take the simple form of a prediction based on the physical condition of the corpse. While it is held by a Foulksmills, County Wexford informant that a corpse will change in appearance every twenty-four hours,[1] what is crucial is whether the body remains soft and limber or whether it stiffens into complete rigidity. If the former is the case, or even if the body remains warm or limber for 'longer than usual', this is a sure sign that another death will occur in the household before very long. Evidence for this kind of divination from the condition of the corpse is widespread from Wexford, Longford, Galway, Cork, Kerry and Donegal.[2]

Such sacred, magic power is also reported as being used in terms of bringing the hand of the corpse to bear on people or things for magic effect. In the parish of Baile na Cille, Connemara, County Galway, it is reported that at wakes, the hand of the corpse was rubbed over the affected part of anyone afflicted with a wound, an ulcer or any similar lesion, and that people were brought up to the corpse for this purpose.[3] It was claimed by an informant in the parish of Waterville, County Kerry that there was knowledge in the district of Bord Eoghan Fhinn of a woman who used to keep the arm and hand from a corpse under her milk tub as a charm to protect the milk and enhance the churning of butter.[4]

A cure for physical ailments was widely reported as residing in the water with which the corpse had been washed. A County Cork source, Kilworth parish, speaks of this corpse-water as being kept to be rubbed on sores while also invoking the name of the Christian Trinity.[5] Another County Cork informant, from the Glandore district, reports the curative property of the water but is unable to recall the specific ailment for which it is efficacious. A Donegal source, from Clocha'n Liath, speaks of the corpse-water, and especially the water that has washed the head of the corpse, as being kept in a keg and rubbed as a 'cure' onto injured animals, cripples and people with broken limbs and with *pian na gcnámh* (arthritis, 'rheumatics') in the hope of giving them relief.[6] Whether regarded as having curative properties or not, water in which a corpse was washed could not ever be disposed of ('for love nor money') until after the funeral had taken place. In some areas such water is thrown after the corpse in the direction in which the funeral has departed, as reported from Charleville, County Cork.[7] In other areas, the parish of Killimer, County Clare, and in Achill and in Ceathrú na gCloch in Erris, County Mayo, for instance, the corpse-water is carefully disposed of by spilling it onto a clean, sheltered spot outside the house, where neither person nor animal will walk over it.[8] This is so that the spirit of the deceased, which is believed to retain an association with the place where the corpse-water is spilled, will have peace there at any time when it returns. In the County Clare case it is reported that the corpse-water might be spilled within the house, in a corner near the fire, 'as a kindness' to a parent by a son or daughter of the deceased.[9] Where this is done for both parents the informant reports that a quarrelsome couple might, in this instance, 'get a corner each' so as to avoid quarrels in the next life.

In both Achill and Erris in County Mayo there are reports that the soap, the washing cloth and the comb that have been used in the washing and arranging of the corpse are all disposed of in this way also 'in a sheltered corner of the garden'.[10]

Where the deceased's bed was a straw-pallet, as in accounts from Rann na Feirste, County Donegal,[11] or Achill, County Mayo,[12] or where, after death, the deceased's body was placed on a 'wisp', a spread sheaf of hay or straw, for the purposes of washing, dressing and arranging it for the wake,[13] then this too is disposed of carefully in some secluded place. The magic power adhering to this material which has been in contact with the corpse is illustrated in the Curlisheen, County Sligo report that calves penned on ground where a 'wisp' has been formerly disposed of have been known to sicken and die.[14] Where straw was laid under the corpse for the duration of the wake, the same care was taken in its eventual disposal.[15]

Even the dirt sweepings of the floor of a wake house are imbued with something of the magic charge of the corpse. They are best not swept up at all and may not be thrown out until after the funeral when the corpse is gone from the house.[16] If swept up during the wake they are kept under the bed. This custom obviously emphasises the special boundedness of the wake house but it also testifies to the danger to the community and the environment of projecting or carrying out of the insulated protection of the wake house any substance that has been contaminated through contact with the corpse and with the 'laying-out' process.

From west Kerry we have an account of how even the ashes of the fire, that chief symbol in the house of its social life and the normal agency in the household for the regular transformation of nature (in the processes of burning fuel, cooking food, purifying iron), are better kept piled up on the back and sides of the hearth or stored there in a bucket until after the funeral, rather than being disposed of outside the house as is usual. As well as showing the necessity for care in not contaminating the world outside the wake house, this custom again has the added sense of a closing up of the boundaries of the wake house in liminal time where the daily round of life, symbolised in the kindling, cleaning and banking of the fire, is, as it were, symbolically suspended.[17]

There is widespread evidence – from informants in Kealkill and Enniskeane, County Cork,[18] in Annascaul, County Kerry,[19] in Ceathrú na gCloch, Erris, County Mayo,[20] for instance – that the stumps of the candles burned by the side of the corpse during the wake have a 'cure' in them for various ailments such as swellings and burns, in the case of both human and animal sufferers. In the Kerry evidence we also learn of the value of such candle stumps to those wishing to procure a neighbour's butter by magical means.

From Erris, County Mayo we learn that the pins, nails and fastening on the cloths around the corpse during the wake are buried with it.[21] From Wexford, Cork, Galway and Donegal evidence we learn that the cloths themselves together with the sheets, blankets, pillowcases and quilts from the wake bed or table, and indeed that bed or table itself too, are ritually cleansed in the aftermath of the wake and funeral. All cloth is bundled up in a heap before the corpse leaves the wake house and water is sprinkled on the four corners of sheets and blankets before bundling. All are later left steeping in water for some time before being hung outside to dry and air for an extended period.[22] From a Cois Fharraige, County Galway informant we learn that any neighbour who wanted to rid his own or a relative's family of an illness would cut an *asclán* (a four-cornered piece of cloth) out of some cloth or clothing left out in this fashion, in the belief that there would be a cure in it.[23]

There is widespread evidence of belief in the curative properties of pieces of the *aiséadach* or burial sheet which is placed around the corpse in the coffin. A Connemara, County Galway description of the *taiséadach* has it made from five yards of 'union cloth' with a hole cut in it for the head of the corpse at mid-point so that half of it was under, half over the body in the coffin. The sides were not sewn up.[24] In other areas the *aiséadach* is simply a white sheet spread over the coffined corpse. In either case we learn that corners of the *aiséadach* were regularly cut off and taken away as a 'cure'. People liked to get a triangular piece of the *aiséadach* for this purpose and it is as a cure for various lumps and swellings that these pieces of the burial sheet were mainly used.[25] In some areas, it was the old woman who had washed and laid out the corpse who cut and distributed those magic triangles of cloth.[26] A Mayo informant relates how in her district a *sean-chailleach* (an old, hag-like female) cured a young girl of an ailment of this kind through the use of a corner of corpse-sheet when medical doctors had failed to do so.[27]

The next section will deal with the consumption of tobacco and snuff at wakes. We may note here, in passing, that a Granard, County Longford informant tells how, in her experience, snuff left over after a wake should be kept carefully for future use since it has in it a cure for headache.[28]

Finally, in this section, we can note the sense in which the deceased's ordinary clothes are rendered special after death to the extent that they can be described by an Upper Creggan, County Tyrone informant as 'precious things'.[29] In this district it was the common practice that a woman who washed and dressed a female corpse was given some of the deceased's clothes in remembrance. These were not worn again but kept as relics. In Kilworth, County Cork an informant reports that the clothing of a dead person is kept by a friend until it 'goes in moth-holes and melts away'. This is understood to mirror the process in which the body of the deceased is 'melting and withering away too' in the grave.[30] A Craosloch, County Donegal informant tells how his own brother's suit of clothes has been hanging up in their mother's house for over thirty-five years.[31]

If everything that has been in contact with the corpse is somehow charged with a magic that can work for the good of the community, as in curing, or for the harm of the community through drawing misfortune on it, then we can see the point of the disengaging and purification of the last handlers of the corpse as reported by an informant from Killimer, County Clare, who speaks of whiskey being poured from a bottle in the church yard over the hands of the undertaker and of those who have coffined and shouldered the deceased for the funeral.[32]

Conversely, other material substances, in being ritually consumed in the course of the wake, also take on a sacred character. These fall into three main categories: tobacco, 'tea', alcohol. These wake provisions are not ordinary food and drink and have to be bought and brought to the wake house quite apart from any mundane goods. This 'tea', drink and tobacco have the ritual nature of sacred substances to be conspicuously and communally consumed in the course of the wake. Funeral feasting is a widespread ritual practice in very many cultural traditions and we know that the Celtic peoples of iron-age central Europe both practised funeral feasting and interred evidence of the consumption of substantial quantities of food and drink along with the body of the deceased in the royal burial chambers. At Hochdorf, for instance, modern excavation has uncovered in the tomb of a fifth-century BC Celtic chieftain a mead cauldron of 400 litres' capacity (104 gallons) and nine large plates and three platters of bronze together with tools for butchering and carving.[33]

The kind of funeral feasting reported from the wake as practised in the non-elite popular culture of late nineteenth- and early twentieth-century Ireland is at a much humbler level but it too represents a ritual intensification of experience in the liminal domain of the laid-out corpse by means of the communal ingestion of tobacco and alcohol on the one hand and of festive forms of subsistence food on the other. Those in the wake assembly are, as we shall see as we discuss the different kinds of communal consumption, under an obligation to partake of the substances offered and thus to participate in what is a kind of sacred communion that expresses the heightened sense of community that exists in the liminal wake house, and that physically produces some degree of the carnivalesque mood-elevation that underlies much of the festivity and the licence of the wake house that are described in such detail in Seán Ó Súilleabháin's *Irish Wake Amusements*.[34]

The central significance in the wake of the act of smoking – or otherwise ingesting – tobacco is caught in the comment of an informant in Na Cruacha, County Donegal, who says that there is nothing in the world as lonesome as a church without a priest or a wake without tobacco.[35] Taking nicotine – in the form of pipe-tobacco, tobacco-snuff or cigarettes – is a primary duty of those assembled to wake the laid-out corpse, and a male neighbour or neighbours of the deceased play the role of tobacco-priest, as it were, in the sacred location of the wake house, administering nicotine in one of its forms to all who are present.

The sacred/symbolic significance of tobacco-smoking at the wake is clearly signalled in another account, from Aughintemple, County Longford, which tells how tobacco smoke was blown onto the corpse by some people and how this was regarded as a mark of respect to the dead person, and as a counterpart to the more common Christian rite of sprinkling holy water on the corpse.[36] The two substances are mentioned in the same breath by an informant from the Meath/Cavan border district who describes how, on arrival at a wake, you removed your headgear and said a prayer by the side of the corpse. You then sprinkled the corpse with holy water and were handed a clay pipe filled with tobacco which you sat with and smoked.[37] Another Longford account speaks of going directly to the corpse on arrival at the wake house where one sympathised with relatives and knelt to pray. 'Before going down again to the kitchen each visitor was given a filled pipe …'[38] From Tuosist in County Kerry we hear that when the wake provisions arrived from town, in this case Neidín (Kenmare), everyone in the wake house, without exception, took a pinch of snuff and everyone was also expected to smoke a clay pipe.[39] Non-smokers, we are told, could decline this offer of a pipe-full of tobacco but we are also told that the family of the deceased would certainly have preferred them to smoke.

To be properly and fully present at a wake was to take nicotine in some form, and the significance of this is shown by the locating of the tobacco in there with the corpse at the heart of the wake assembly. A very common report is of the tobacco and snuff being on the table near the head of the corpse that also carried the candles and the crucifix, and in some cases a saucer of snuff rested on the breast of the corpse itself.[40]

Another indication of the central significance of tobacco consumption in the wake house is the account from Cushendall, County Antrim of the man who attended his own 'wake' which was being held without a corpse, as sometimes happened when, as on this occasion, word was received in a community of the death abroad of one of its members.[41] In this case word had been sent by 'gay boys' (fun-loving, boisterous youth) that a local man, due to return from working at the Scottish harvest, was, in fact, dead. 'All the neighbours gathered when me bold John walks in ...' As if to emphasise that he is one of the living assembly and not the corpse for which it has come together he then does the one thing that is essential to the attender at a wake: 'he asked for a pipe, was reached one and smoked it'.

Tobacco and its use, in any of its forms, became known in Ireland only in the course of the seventeenth century, so its universal incorporation into the wake is a remarkable adaptation of new knowledge and new material to the functioning of an existing ritual. Like other cultural borrowing in early modern Irish popular culture we can assume that the consumption of tobacco was something spread among the ordinary population by imitation of the ways of the better off, as the goods of the commercial market penetrated throughout all of Ireland and at levels of society that had hitherto been, in large part, outside the cash economy. As in all such cultural borrowing, innovative use was made of the item borrowed and the popular Irish innovative use of tobacco-smoking as a central part of wake ritual gives rise in Irish popular tradition to accounts of how the practice had an origin in events central to the Christian religion, thereby legitimating it and blending it with the Christian significance of the wake and the funeral.

Accounts from both Galway[42] and Mayo[43] tell that tobacco is the plant that grew over Christ's tomb when Christ had risen – the Ballyhaunis, County Mayo informant relating that St Thomas the Apostle, who was absent from Christ's funeral, subsequently visited the tomb and, sitting absentmindedly on it, plucked some of the plant and put it in his pipe to smoke. Other informants, from Longford and from Swinford, County Mayo, for instance, speak of the origin of tobacco at wakes as being associated with the Blessed Virgin Mary. In the Granard, County Longford version,[44] Christ's mother, weeping beside his tomb, sees pipe and tobacco and says, 'If we had pipes and tobacco it'd aise our minds.' From that day on pipes and tobacco have been at wakes. In the Mayo version Mary herself is the first to smoke a pipe at a wake. She did so for comfort the day Christ was crucified and thus it is not right, ever since, and not even for 'young ladies', to refuse 'a draw of a pipe' at a wake.

An informant from Kealkill in County Cork says that most of one's time at a wake is spent in either smoking, if you are a man, or taking snuff, if you are a woman.[45] While there is considerable regional variation in this, the general pattern is that tobacco and snuff circulate pretty continuously throughout the night and that everyone at the wake has every encouragement to consume as much tobacco as they may wish. This also applies to wakes that are held not in the dwelling house but in an outside barn or shed.[46]

The business of cutting up the tobacco, filling the pipes and handing out pipes to visitors as they arrive at the wake falls to one or two male neighbours of the deceased.[47] From informants from Upper Greggan in County Tyrone to Beara in County Cork we have it emphasised that the male neighbour in charge of tobacco consumption must see to it 'that every smoker at the wake got plenty to smoke' and that people were free to fill their own regular pipe with the cut tobacco as it went around.[48] As one Ballycastle, County Antrim informant has it, clay pipes, tobacco and cigarettes 'are left out on a help-yourself basis'.[49] From County Kerry we hear that it was considered an insult not to take the proffered pipe and 'at least redden it', even at the cost of being sick if one was not in fact a smoker.[50] From Kilgevin parish, County Roscommon we hear that 'pipes at wakes made smokers of a great number of young lads' as they brought the pipes home with them afterwards.

The pipes were long-stemmed, made from clay or chalk and shop-bought. A Dromard, County Longford informant says they cost two shillings and sixpence a dozen in the 1930s.[51] An earlier account from west Cork speaks of clay pipes costing one halfpenny each and that plates of filled pipes were constantly going around through the crowd at the wake so that a smoker would smoke several different pipes and put them all in his pocket after finishing them.

In County Wexford, by contrast, pipes and tobacco were available to smokers but not offered generally. People here never smoked their own pipes at the wake and never brought home with them the ones provided there.[52]

The general obligation was to take a pipe and light it or to take a pinch of snuff; in either case accompanying the ingestion with a prayer for the deceased and for the dead in general. From County Longford we hear that the prayer inevitably was 'Lord have mercy on X' (name of the deceased).[53] From Kilworth, County Cork we get the phrasing 'The Lord have mercy on the dead' and its Irish equivalent '*Beannacht Dé le hanam na marbh*', literally 'The blessing of God on the souls of the dead'.[54]

Pipe-smoking is also reported as part of the ritual of the funeral day from a variety of areas. To some extent this is to give people attending the funeral who may not have been at the wake the opportunity of performing one of the general acts of the wake ritual. From Beara, County Cork we learn of a basket of clay pipes being carried out from the wake house a little before the funeral leaves. The man carrying this basket gives a filled pipe from it to those he meets who are on their way to join the funeral.[55] From the parish of Spiddal, County Galway we learn that, there, a stocking specially filled with tobacco is carried into the graveyard with the funeral and the tobacco distributed by a specially chosen man who gives it out freely to anyone who wishes to smoke it.[56] From the townland of *Tóin Raithige* in east County Galway we hear of a *bodhrán* (a circular winnowing pan made from an animal (e.g. goat) tightly stretched over a timber frame; used also as a drum-type musical instrument) – full of clay pipes – being left on the ditch at the side of every road leading to the wake house on the day of the funeral.[57] People coming to the funeral each took a pipe for themselves. In Priracht parish in Iveragh, County Kerry we have an account of a *bean bhán*, a corpse-washerwoman (lit. 'a white woman'), who used to distribute filled pipes to mourners at a funeral from a box carried along with the coffin in the funeral cart.[58] There are various accounts of the surplus pipes and tobacco being left, after the funeral is over, in the graveyard, perhaps on the fresh grave itself, available for taking away by anyone at all.[59]

'Tea' can range from literally a cup of tea to a substantial meal, prepared and served by female neighbours of the bereaved family and, again, a kind of ritual imperative applies to its provision and consumption.

The Irish Folklore Commission archive does not support the stereotype of the Irish wake as an inevitably drunken and alcohol-derived event. The evidence suggests that 'strong drink', while a very normal part of the wake and funeral, is an incidental variable, depending on the resources and generosity of the bereaved family. It does not play a crucial structural role in the wake proceedings.

Another powerful, sacred commodity is, of course, produced and consumed in the wake assembly. That commodity is poetry, in the form of the verbal compositions and histrionic recitative of the *bean chaointe*, the keening woman, a semi-professional elderly female retained by the bereaved family for the service she can crucially render in crying the deceased into incorporation with their ancestral kin-group in the otherworld and thus also crying death out of this life. An analysis of the production and consumption of these sacred laments must await another occasion.

PART 2

Poetics of Oral Literary Tradition

Introduction

The study of legends, wonder tales, hero tales and other genres of oral narrative tradition has proceeded from an initial concern to classify texts in historical and geographic frameworks on the basis of motifs and types of content.[1] Other approaches have concentrated on the structural characteristics of narratives[2] and have attempted to connect these with the cultural context in which they operate and with the psychological realities of individual and community life.[3] Another approach again has concentrated on the performance of narratives in terms of the social situations in which they occur – and the social functions which they fulfil.[4] An understanding of what is termed the ethnopoetics of oral narrative has developed out of a concern to render texts of narrative performance on the printed page in a way that acknowledges the 'poetic' qualities of the spoken word of which they are constituted.[5]

Discussion of oral narrative, its linguistic nature and the literary or poetic qualities it embodies can, initially, usefully consider the general notion of discourse and the way that discourse analysis can contribute to the study and understanding of the folklore text. A fundamental consideration is that such texts, as examples of discourse, consist of speech that has been rendered into writing and that the spoken voice is the primary underlying medium through which the story – tale or legend – is realised. An 'ethnography of speaking' approach has highlighted the linguistic 'performance' of the narrator and been concerned with the stylistics and poetic artistry that the text issuing from the performance embodies.[6]

Following an overview of Irish storytelling tradition, some characteristic modalities of that tradition are proposed – including gender modality – and the continuing prominence of orality in the study of modern culture is touched on. The oral/literary duality of traditional narration is exemplified in the texts of a story told twice by a single narrator where the potential for narrative performance to embody both traditional genre-type 'tale' and modern creative short story is achieved through a sophisticated differential employment of plot and character.

Finally in this part, possible pedagogic applications of folklore are considered.[7] The relevance, in certain instances, of the dynamics of the folklore text to some of the requirements of the language teacher for the rich, idiomatic passages of native-speaker speech is suggested in the context of linguistic and educational developments in Ireland.

CHAPTER 6

The Concept of Discourse in Relation to Narrative Literary Tradition

The term 'discourse' carries a range of meanings within the domains of language study, literature, philosophy and cultural studies. Ruth Finnegan speaks of it as 'an umbrella term' to cover *all* forms of verbal communication in society.[1] In the Irish language, as a loan-word from Latin or English, *dioscúrs* has the earliest meaning of 'argument' or 'proof' in the usage of Froinsias Ó Maolmhuaidh in *Lucerna Fidelium (Lóchrann na gCreidmheach)*, printed at Rome in 1676 as a devotional text.[2] In its late modern Irish form *dioscúrsa*, it is given a strict philosophical definition by another Franciscan scholar, Colmán Ó Huallacháin, in his *Foclóir Fealsaimh*: '*gníomhaíocht intleachta a thugtar i gcrích trí chéimeanna idirmheánacha (m.sh. réasúnadh; contr. imfhios, rinnfheitheamh)*' ('intellectual activity that accomplishes its purpose by means of intermediate stages (e.g. reasoning; by contrast with intuition or contemplation)'.[3] This technical sense of the word is maintained in Niall Ó Dónaill's *Foclóir Gaeilge–Béarla*, where *dioscúrsa* is styled as a term of logic. On the other hand, Tomás de Bhaldraithe's *English–Irish Dictionary*, while noting its occurrence also in the register of logic, translates 'discourse' as *tráchtas, aitheasc, caint* and *comhrá*. These words cover a semantic range – outside of the strictly logical or philosophical – that encompass both Ó Maolmhuaidh's 'argument' and Finnegan's general 'verbal communication'. In relation to Irish manuscript literature, it is to the literary and cultural significance of the term 'discourse'/*dioscúrsa* that our interest turns. In either case the starting point is modern developments in the study of language that have focused on the communication of meaning. Drawing on such developments in both descriptive linguistics and cultural studies, the study and analysis of verbal art has made use of the concept of discourse – along with the concepts of narrative, performance and popular culture – to pursue the comparative study of local communication processes and specifically the communicative processes of verbal art and 'oral' literature. In this it has attempted to go beyond the dichotomies of oral/written and traditional/ modern debates and to concentrate instead on the processes of linguistic interaction across forms and modes.[4]

The discussion of discourse by Lindstrom in Barnard and Spenser notes that discursive analysis comprises various methodologies as a consequence of the multiple meanings that the term can encompass. It very usefully distinguishes the discursive concerns of linguistics, on the one hand, from those of anthropology, folklore and cultural studies.[5] Within the strictly linguistic field, 'discourse' was formerly understood as referring to the range of the utterance above or beyond the structural verities established for language use from the level of phonetics to that of the sentence. Following on from the rise of an 'ethnography of speaking' approach, the concept of the 'speech event' has drawn attention to the structural elements of discourse 'beyond the sentence' – how talk and verbal art is subject to interaction and control on the part of speakers and listeners, performers and audience. Features of the speech event such as conversational speed, silences, degrees of overlapping, loudness, intonation and so forth are examined both for the patterning they display and for the ways in which they constitute control and creativity on the part of participants and, furthermore, constitute modes of producing, experiencing and reinforcing their culture for the participants and for the community at large.

Within the cultural studies field the act of talking or writing in itself, as a behaviour that communicates meaning, is distinguished both from the body-of-knowledge 'contained' in the act and from the protocols and procedures that regulate the communication of the body-of-knowledge in question and the function it serves. Patterned cultural discourses, centred on acts of speaking and writing, are thus seen to be communal ways of knowing the world. More than knowing the world, however, such cultural discourse is understood also as being a way of manipulating and controlling the (social) world through the network of power relations established in the participation by individuals and groups in the speech acts and writing activities that can be taken to constitute a patterned universe of discourse. Influenced in this regard by the writings and analyses of Michel Foucault, some postmodernist anthropologists regard all culture as discourse with implicit connotations of power and potential contestation at its heart.

Rapport and Overing offer further insights into contemporary understanding of the concept of discourse and its application to the topic of the literary text.[6] Taking the literary text as an instance of discourse, one can regard it as exemplifying ways of 'speaking' that are commonly practised to the extent that the text's audience or readership is capable of evaluating it in terms of its merits by comparison with other texts, other literary acts of 'speaking'. The audience or readership for literature, then, especially in the pre-modern context in which Irish manuscript literature was produced and performed, constitutes a 'speech community' which is familiar with the generation and evaluation of literary texts comprising speech acts associated with certain speech situations and involving certain speech styles. Such familiarity will encompass the qualities of regularity, conventionality, propriety and diversity among others, and amounts to a kind of rules-of-the-game concept with some similarity to the language-game concept promoted by Wittgenstein. If all speech is embedded in routine social behaviour and in social relationships, those speech acts which are evaluated as literary – and give rise to literary texts – emerge from some degree of common literary worldview and some degree of a common set of literature-related social structures. The work of Dell Hymes in developing an ethnography of speaking and an ethnopoetics of creativity in verbal art is particularly valuable in attempting to bring discourse analysis to bear on literary tradition.[7] In this perspective the channels and setting of the speech act, its addressors, addressees and audience, its goal and outcome, its history and development together with its relationship to the social structure of the group and the community in which it operates are all highlighted along with its rhetorical and ethnopoetic features.

In such a context, we might look at how literature comes into question in respect of institutionalised – or at least customary – traditional Irish storytelling. Here customary narrative performance arises in the context of the everyday participatory linguistic processes whereby everyone plays a role in the social communication and cultural creativity that marks Irish as well as every other society. Writing and written literature in the modern sense has, of course, a very different modus of production and reception but nevertheless shares with oral literature (so called) the primary rhetorical nature of narration as a cultural phenomenon – shares with it its linguistic nature as speech act. At the 'sites' within Irish vernacular or popular culture where storytelling happened, it arose naturally as an integral aspect of people's daily social intercourse. At such 'sites' – the winter evening hearth, the summer bog, the knitting bee, the local well, the childminding, the wake house – there was the regular expectation that the talk and the chatter of the assembled company would develop towards a rhetorical and artistic discourse within which storytelling and other forms of narrative performance – of a standard judged locally to be excellent – would be likely to occur in due course. The 'literary' plane would, step by step, be attained out of the midst of ordinary talk. One recalls Tomás Ó Criomhthainn exclaiming at the public house in the aftermath of the pig fair, '*Tá an ceol sí ar siúl* /'The fairy music has begun', as a fine rendition of a song began.[8] Henry Glassie's detailed micro-account of the process by which the 'literary' level of excellence in narrative was attained in the west Fermanagh of his fieldwork is especially instructive of how 'literature' can be understood as being essentially both the process and the product of a form of linguistic communication.[9] When, under local, oral narrative protocols, linguistic performance acquires sufficient intensity, it achieves a plane of verbal art that merits at least local recognition and privileging as 'oral literature' – a plane on which the imaginative engagement of the narrator with the listener is creative in a transforming way.

While it is not at all as easily characterised – or even envisaged – I believe we can argue for a similar dynamic process of linguistic performance and reception in the case of written literature, involving a similar kind and degree of intensification and uplift. Writer and reader are, of course, in this case, likely to be widely separated in space and time. Nevertheless, the process of intensified linguistic communication (a function of verbal competence on the part of both writer and reader just as in the case of narrator and listener) can result in the creative, transformative engagement of minds and imaginations that is widely held to pertain to the experience of 'literature' in either medium.

Literature, in this estimation, is spoken language, whether it is fashioned from the raw materials of phonetic articulation or of hieroglyphic inscription. Its fundamental characteristics are rhetorical and poetical in the case of both 'prose' and 'verse' convention. The speech act is always at the heart of the production of literature, and its 'literary' quality, its *literaturnost*, is located in the context both of a rhetorical excellence in the case of the writer/narrator and an attentive and imaginative openness of response on the part of the reader/listener. In this light we can acknowledge that literature is not a stable, permanent fixture but rather an occasional phenomenon potentially 'present' during the listening of an audience and during the reading activity of individuals in the case of written narrative. We can see how it is not necessarily the case that 'literature' is present for every reader/listener at the same times or on all occasions of reading/listening since it is always – when/where it *happens* – the result of a dynamic, subjective inter-relation between a stimulus of symbolic enactment in words and a response of individual consciousness involving a creative co-engagement. Such inter-relation and that to which it gives rise – the 'spark', as it were, of identification, desire, disgust, transference, transformation, or other such psychic effects – can never be predictable. Instead it inevitably has the nature of being a gift, a grace – for whose capacity to delight, to enlighten, to repel, to enthral, to shock, to inspire us, we must simply be grateful.

In attempting to bring some insights from this theory – and praxis-rich field of discourse analysis – to bear on examples of Irish manuscript literature, one is very conscious that one is engaging with speech acts that simultaneously inhabit the worlds of orality and literacy in complex ways. The culturally rich ambiguities inherent in Séamus Ó Duilearga's reference to Seán Ó Conaill as 'a conscious literary artist'[10] – in the case of an individual speaker/performer who was illiterate (never having been to school) and who was a lifelong bearer of, and participant in, an overwhelmingly oral culture – can be paralleled, *pari passu*, to varying degrees in the cases of other 'authors' – known and unknown of Irish manuscript literature from the beginning. If Michelle O'Riordan[11] can characterise Irish bardic poetry as an expression of medieval European high literary culture, with the poets participating consciously and creatively in a scholarly-cum-literary enterprise, we can still agree with Walter Ong regarding the essential speech-act nature of even the most refined and sophisticated literary productions:

> … in all the wonderful worlds that writing opens, the spoken word still resides and lives. Written texts all have to be related, somehow, directly or indirectly, to the world of sound, the natural habitat of language, to yield their meanings … Writing can never dispense with orality.[12]

The speech-act nature of the literary artefact is again being emphasised in a recent book by the literary critic Terry Eagleton entitled *How to Read a Poem*.[13] Eagleton deplores the fact that students of poetry today are not sufficiently taught how to be sensitive to language – that raw material of which the poem is made. Given that the words 'poetry' and 'poem' derive, etymologically, from the Greek *poieein*, 'to make' (cf. Scots *makar*, 'a poet'), reading a poem, for Eagleton, requires that due attention be paid to tone, mood, pitch, pace, rhythm and texture as well as 'content'.

A 1964 article by Alan Dundes, with the encompassing title of 'Texture, text and context', brought philosophical and anthropological insights into the discursive nature of language use in a literary mode to bear in a direct practical way in the case of folklore texts of oral literary provenance.[14] Under the heading 'texture' here comes the raw material of language out of which the story or poem is made by its narrator. The choice of specific items of vocabulary; the aesthetic, poetic devices used, such as rhyming or alliteration; the shifts of register involving irony, humour etc.; the regional variants of articulation and grammatical expression used – factors such as these are a fundamental part of the linguistic and literary reality of the text. Under the heading 'text' comes the *message*, the plot, the content, consisting of genre and motifs and patterns of development that amount to a version of a tale-type, or ballad, or lament, or legend, etc. that is known in alternative formats, perhaps in other languages, but that constitutes a unique instance of literary creation in itself. Under the heading 'context' account is taken of both historical and social factors that have combined to bring into existence this specific 'text' with its specific 'textural' qualities. The narrator has acquired the story, poem, song, etc. from a prior source without, of course, reproducing the exact textural and textual elements of any previous version, and the formative influence of both geographical factors and historical circumstance will be evident in the latest narration. Also evident will be some of the effects of the social circumstances of this latest narration. Where did the performance take place and who was present? What was the nature of the social and communal situation in which the narration took place? What was the narrator's own response to these issues, both historical and social, including any commentary by the narrator on his or her own performance?

Such an approach to a literary or oral work as is envisaged by Dundes clearly perceives the 'text' as the outcome of systems of action within a universe of discourse whereby meaning is conveyed and communicated through the operation of a set of protocols shared by narrator and audience. As such, 'literature' arises out of such acts, events and situations that are components of a specifically 'literary' universe of discourse, though what constitutes the literariness of any particular universe and the acts or events or particular 'texts' within it is a matter of historical, cultural and social convention. 'Literature' proceeds from a process of linguistic action involving narration and reception of speech forms within a shared universe of discursive protocols involving the stylistics in which the speech forms are, so to speak, clothed and the genres into which 'literary' speech acts of this type may be categorised. When the products of such speech acts are the subject of notation as well as aural reception, then we have a written text which can stand apart from and survive beyond the social situation in which the speech events of the narration/performance took place. Such written texts are both a record of literary speech acts in the past and have the potential to communicate again as literature to readers acquainted with the universe of discourse out of which they rose.

Irish oral literature is comprised, to a very considerable degree, of texts reflecting and representing a history of 'literary' performance whose origin lies in the notation in written form of speech acts of a kind that were engaged in within a universe of discourse whose shared protocols of excellence (in regard to performance) and meaningfulness (in regard to content) were developed continuously over a very long period of time. The examples of Irish manuscript literature to be discussed below are mostly of comparatively recent provenance and have a vernacular character that contrasts with the literary products of the learned elites. It is the case, however, that all literary texts, courtly or popular, can be approached with an emphasis on eliciting their nature and significance as phenomena of discourse.

The commentary offered here on one particular item of Irish oral literature is simply intended to suggest the possibilities of analysis and interpretation that could be expected to derive from a fuller engagement with that literature undertaken from a perspective based on a fuller appreciation of the requirements of a discursive analysis. Briefly stated, the present perspective involves a concern with the texture, text and context of the oral/literary item envisaged as existing within a universe of discourse within which it has arisen and within which it continues to communicate meaning by means of acts of utterance, notation and reception (aural and visual) – each of which incorporates a greater or lesser degree of creative imagination in the performance of the story and in its knowing reception by its audience and later readership – individual and/or group listeners and readers. The item of manuscript literature chosen for discussion here, a piece of oral narrative tradition, may lend itself more easily to a discourse-oriented approach given its patently speech-act origin and nature.

An Préachán Dubh (*The Black Crow*)

The item of manuscript literature bearing the title *An Préachán Dubh* is a folktale of international provenance, versions of which are known far and wide in many Indo-European languages throughout the early modern and modern ears. There is even the disputed suggestion that a version of the tale occurs in the *Metamorphoses* of the second-century AD Latin author Apuleius Madaurensis. The early modern and modern versions of the tale are classified as Aa-Th 425 'The Search for the Lost Husband' in the scholarly catalogues of the folktale types that has been established for oral literary items of Indo-European tradition.[15] The tradition itself constitutes a universe of discourse within which tales such as *An Préachán Dubh* are circulated and transmitted both by word of mouth and by means of manuscript and even printed notation. The several hundred tale-types of this kind that have been identified and given scholarly classification are known collectively as *Märchen*, the German being the generally accepted international term for what is designated *seanscéal* in Irish tradition and *wondertale* in English.

The particular *seanscéal* with which we are concerned here, *An Préachán Dubh*, was taken down by hand from the narration of Seán Ó Conaill, a farmer-fisherman of Cill Rialaigh, Baile an Sceilg, Uíbh Ráthach in south Kerry in the month of August 1925. Ó Conaill, then aged seventy-two, narrated the tale, by his own hearth, apparently, during a collection visit to him by the young Séamus Ó Duilearga who was then twenty-six years of age. It appeared as number 17 in the '*Seanscéal*' section of the anthology of Ó Conaill-narrated material published by Ó Duilearga in 1948 as *Leabhar Sheáin Í Chonaill*.[16] There have been a number of reprints together with an English-language translation of the work (1981)[17] so that the 'original' Seán Ó Conaill 'performance' of *An Préachán Dubh* has continued, as discourse, to communicate its meanings – albeit in print – into the present, long after the demise of both its narrator and its recorder. And this 'posthumous' discursive process of narration, notation and publication has had as 'audience' and will continue to have as 'audience' the innumerable and largely unnameable readerships that the text of the item has had in its various printings and translation – in stark contrast to the few, if any, who were present on the occasion of the 'original' narration of the tale by Ó Conaill to Ó Duilearga in Cill Rialaigh in August 1925.

The texture of *An Préachán Dubh* consists of the actual speech sounds of that 'first' performance and their notation by Ó Duilearga in a written form that attempts to be faithful to the phonetic reality of the raw material as speech and to both the dialect particularities of Cill Rialaigh Irish in 1925 and the idiolect particularities of the individual narrator. 'I was only the storyteller's writing instrument,' says Ó Duilearga in his foreword to the 1948 book. 'I did not alter a syllable he spoke, and I wrote everything down as well as I could.' We might note in this respect what another scholar-collector, Kenneth Jackson, says in his 'Note on the Orthography' of the anthology of Peig Sayers-narrated material that he, Jackson, published in 1938 as *Scéalta ón mBlascaod*.[18] Having noted that the material had been taken down orally by him from the narrator in a modification of the international phonetic script, he explains that the original phonetic scripts 'are represented here in a simplified Irish orthography, based on the traditional spelling but adapted to the dialect' ... 'Absolute consistency and accuracy is not possible ... the aim is to give as closely as possible, within the limits of the orthography, exactly what the storyteller said, including all dialectisms, all individual peculiarities, and all instances of plain bad grammar.'

It would be possible to subject the Ó Duilearga text of the Ó Conaill tale to a line-by-line or even word-by-word analysis in order to make clear the phonetic, the lexical, the grammatical and the stylistic characteristics of the local dialect together with the narrative and rhetorical characteristics with which Ó Conaill endowed his performance of the tale. For instance, the third printed line of the published text goes as follows:

> *Bhíodh sae féin agus Máire ag imeacht na 'h aon lá a' máirseáil*

Further on we encounter the following sentence:

> *Có luath is do bhí sé sínte sa leabaig, do léim Máir' amach as a' leabaig, agus do bheir sí n'a láimh ar a' gcochaillín dubh, agus do ruith sí aníos chún na tine.*

The final sentence of the metanarrative with which the text ends goes:

> *Is amhla cailleav é, is dócha – bhí sé críona, mar níor ghuibh sé timpal ó shuin.*

In these passages we see the textural qualities of the story highlighted in the notation.

The literary qualities of any item of oral narrative will be intimately bound up with the degree of excellence which the 'native' audience and, later, the readerships of the text perceives in the texture (the raw material, as such) of the item, as much as in its text-as-content. In the case of *An Préachán Dubh* Seán Ó Conaill exhibits masterful control of description and dialogue, pace and mood, complexity of plot and its resolution through the flow of the tale as speech. This speech has a deceptively simple and limpid appearance, but it is a speech that, through its energy and fluency, tells a huge story in the small compass of six and a half pages of print. By comparison, another version of Aa-Th 425, this time called *Bull Bhalbhae*, again recorded from Seán Ó Conaill by Séamus Ó Duilearga – this time in April 1929 – comprises some twenty pages of printed text.[19] The textural qualities of the longer version, while still characteristic of the dialect and the idiolect in which it was narrated, appear to lack the rhetorical energy and urgency, the creative spark, of *An Préachán Dubh*, though its lexical and grammatical resources are no less. It could be argued that the shorter item more resembles the modern short story in its textural, rhetorical nature whereas the longer item, *Bull Bhalbhae*, has the textural excellence of another and older type of narrative. From a discourse point of view it could be said that each of the two items, in so far as they are different versions of the 'same' tale, inhabit separate universes of discourse, and aspects of the items' texts and contexts serve to support this contention.

Another example of this wondertale/modern short story binary is encountered in the story of *An Chailleach Bhéarrach agus Donnchadha Mór MacMánais* published by Dúbhghlás de hÍde.[20] Whereas in Aa-Th 425 the binary takes the form of two separate tellings of the story, in the de hÍde text the binary contrast exists in the narrative structure of the single telling. The frame-tale of the story has the qualities of a vernacular narrative drawing on the motifs and symbolism of medieval tradition. The inset to the frame-tale however has a very different character, one strikingly modern, and even contemporary, in some ways. The frame-tale tells how *Cailleach Bhéarach*, the hag/goddess, nowadays living in east County Galway as a kind of latter-day cruel landlord, is vanquished three times over by the local strong man and self-professed hero. Hitherto, we are told, a succession of males had succumbed to the rigours of such employment by the *cailleach* as farm labourers – an echo of the *cailleach*'s mythological status as sovereignty queen – akin to Queen Maeve who was said to have been never without one man in the shadow of another. *Cailleach Bhéarach*, like other sovereignty figures, is thus originally shown in this story as enduring through the generations of historical time as the eternal, otherworld partner of a line of mortal males. In this story however she is fated to relinquish her power, her status and her very existence in the triumph over her of this latest partner, Donnchadha Mór. Donnchadha Mór's victory is achieved through a combination of strength and cunning – the latter amounting to the abuse by him of the affections of the *cailleach*'s daughter with whom he pretends to fall in love so as to have her reveal to him the secret of how her mother might be overcome. When this happens, Donnchadha abandons the *cailleach*'s daughter and is indifferent to her perishing along with her mother in the general downfall of the feminine which his treacherous victory represents in mythological and perhaps psychological terms. Such vanquishing and displacement of the feminine is a very prominent theme in Irish written literature going back to early medieval times. We cannot be surprised to find it in oral literature too once a record of that oral narration starts to become available in modern times. What is noteworthy, however, in the case of this text is the way in which the 'message' of the story is delivered a second time and in a dramatically intimate and salient manner that, for me, comes near to the character and the effect of modern written literature.

The story of male victory here, achieved by means of the deception, abuse and abandonment of the female, is, as it were, prophesied in advance in the inset-tale told by the *cailleach* herself at the point in the frame-tale where she relinquishes her power and accepts that her reign is at an end. In this inset-tale the *cailleach* tells her life story and we hear how as a young girl (the structural equivalent of her own daughter in the frame-tale) she was abused and abandoned and of how, in her anger and shame, she took a terrible revenge that transformed her to the depths of her being.

Allowing for the qualities of surrealism – or even magic realism – in this story within a story, we can surely recognise a sense in which the hag/ goddess' account of her experiences is, after a fashion, a version of the stories of female degradation and its lifelong physical and psychological consequences with which we are obliged to be familiar in both the journalistic media and the narrative fiction of today. I am struck by a seeming powerful relevance of the *cailleach*'s – as it were – 'personal' story to today's world and by how it stands out, in rhetorical terms, from the frame-tale in which it is encrypted and of which it is a re-telling, or even a pre-telling in some mythic or archetypal sense. Again in this instance, as in the case of the two versions of 'The Search for the Lost Husband', a narrator employs sophisticated devices of narration to give an intensity of effect to one version that distinguishes it clearly from the other. Where

The Black Crow is a 'short story', as it were, by comparison with *Bull Bhalbae*, the inset-tale of the *cailleach* story can, perhaps, be taken to be an early, oral example of feminine writing – of *écriture feminine*, so to speak, as against the frame-tale legend.

Turning to the text of *An Préachán Dubh* we can ask how closely it corresponds to the outline of the plot of Aa-Th 425 as set down by Stith Thompson on the basis of acquaintance with the great number of versions occurring in various languages throughout the Indo-European cultural area. Thompson has thirteen plot elements that he identifies in this tale and only one of these is not found in *An Préachán Dubh* while the other twelve are present in the same sequence as that in which they occur in the Thompson outline. In the other Ó Conaill version of Aa-Th 425, however, the longer one recorded by Ó Duilearga some four years after *An Préachán Dubh*, the fundamental elements of the tale are, as it were, embedded in a more elaborate framework of motifs and actions that serve to produce a far longer text – derived of course from a greatly extended speech act on the occasion of the narration by Ó Conaill of the *Bull Bhalbhae* version. One could seek to compare also to both the Ó Conaill versions other versions of Aa-Th 425 that are known in Irish tradition. Over 200 other versions of the tale are noted by Ó Súilleabháin and Christiansen in *The Types of the Irish Folktale*,[21] with these having been recorded from all four provinces of Ireland. The most comprehensive study of Aa-Th 425 'The Search for the Lost husband' as it occurs in the Indo-European area as a whole is that of Jan-Ojvind Swahn, published in Sweden in 1955 as *The Tale of Cupid and Psyche*.[22] Swahn proposes some sixteen variations on what he regards as the basic theme of the tale and divides these variations into three groups that are associated with specific language areas. The two Ó Conaill versions – and, one can assume, the other Irish versions – conform to the variety of the tale that Swahn associates with German, English and Celtic-language narrative tradition. An analysis of representative texts of Aa-Th 425 from within these narrative traditions themselves could be expected to provide further evidence as to the development of versions of the tale over time and its shaping in relation to cultural contact and social circumstances.

'Surface' features of the text can embody these contacts and circumstances as a kind of ethnographic setting for the plot and action of the *seanscéal*. An example of this is the way in which the kitchen and the hearth of Seán Ó Conaill's own humble Cill Rialaigh house – of traditional type – is reflected in the description of the royal palace into whose domestic life the enchanted prince-hero – in the form of a crow – is introduced: *Do bhíodh a' préachán a' léimirig ar a hob is ar a' hiarta, agus do léimeadh sae anáirde ar na maidí snaidhm.*

In considering matters of context we can distinguish between the historical context in which a tale has arisen and been transmitted over time and across regions in its many and varied forms, and the social context in which any particular version has been performed as a speech act. Such speech act will have involved a specific narrator in the presence of a specific audience and will have occurred in a specific social setting. The extent of the historical context for *An Préachán Dubh* can, to some degree, be glimpsed in information we have concerning other versions of Aa-Th 425 as these are known to exist in Ireland and elsewhere, prior to Seán Ó Conaill's recounting of this version in 1925. Ó Conaill himself affords us further information regarding the immediate history, from his own perspective, of the version in question. Prompted, it is likely, by the collector recording the tale, he follows its narration with an account of his acquisition of it:

> The man I heard telling that was a traveller who used to spend a night or two with us. The name we had for him was Diarmuid a' Ghaidhrín (Diarmuid of the little dog). Diarmuid Ó Sé was his name and he said he was from County Cork ... It is not more than seven or eight years since I heard him telling it ... He must be dead, I think – he was old, and he has not come around since.

What the circumstances of the acquisition were we do not know in any detail, though we do know that it was common for travelling men, such as Ó Sé (an itinerant weaver) to 'earn their keep' as it were on their regular visits to a district by narrating stories for local fireside audiences and bringing the news from the outside world to the relatively closed and static local community. In return for such speech acts, the visiting stranger would get lodging and sustenance during the few days of his stay in the district and such hospitality was frequently available at the home of the local storyteller – as was, apparently, the case in the present instance. Such visitation and performance by travelling men, beggars, tinkers, weavers and other itinerants was a feature of the *airneán*, the night-time, house-visiting gathering of neighbours which was the *locus classicus* of narrative and other speech-act performances in Irish rural tradition.

Known by a variety of other names – *scoraíocht*, *bothántaíocht*, *cuairt*, *céilí* – these gatherings could also feature singing, the playing of musical

instruments, dancing and card-playing, with different households in
a parish being 'home' to different such activities on a regular basis.
Storytelling *airneáin* were predominantly male while female *airneáin* with
narrative genres such as legend, memorate, prayer were the accompaniment
of activities such as childminding, cloth-production, well-water drawing
and other domestic work. Where traditions of verse-composition existed,
house-gathering of local poets took place in which performance was
accompanied by peer-critique of both a technical and personalised nature.
Such fireside academies of poetry are the focus of Daniel Corkery's
powerful evocation of the 'Hidden Ireland' of the eighteenth century and
of its manuscript literature.[23]

A vivid portrayal of the operation of this fireside transmission of
literary tradition is contained in the account of how the longer *Bull
Bhalbhae* version of Aa-Th 425 was acquired by Seán Ó Conaill. He
himself tells of the circumstances in which he heard the story for the first
– and only – time prior to narrating it for Séamus Ó Duilearga.

> Dónal Sercí Ó Conaill I heard tell it in Diarmuid Ó Sé's house in
> Ceannúig a' Phriarire, and it was late in a dark, black night when I
> left him and I fell into the river and was well soaked …
>
> Dónal Sercí was a poor man who had nothing in the world but
> a small-holding. He would spend nights in relatives' houses telling
> tales and anecdotes. The whole townland would be listening to him
> if they heard he was there. It is my belief that he was eighty when I
> heard him tell this tale and that was the only time I heard the story.
> It is fifty-seven or fifty-eight years since I heard him tell it.[24]

This account, with its startling implication for the powers of recall of
the narrator, emphasises the continuity of discourse within which oral
literary tradition operated in the rural Ireland of the relatively recent past.
Ó Conaill, himself now an elderly man of seventy-six years, is narrating a
tale that he in turn heard narrated nearly sixty years previously by someone
who was born when Brian Merriman still lived in Feakle and Eoghan
Rua Ó Súilleabháin was only three years in his grave. The speech acts
involved in such oral narrative and poetic traditions as gave rise to *Cúirt
an Mheán Oíche*,[25] *Amhráin Eoghain Ruaidh Uí Shúilleabháin*[26] and *Leabhar
Sheáin Í Chonaill*[27] become, in different ways and in different times, part
of Irish manuscript literature through the process of notation in writing
and dissemination in first manuscript and later printed formats. Such a

progression from speech act through notation to publication underlies all texts of Irish literature that have survived – from the earliest Old Irish Poetry and tales that survive in medieval vellum to the stories and songs of early-twentieth-century folklore in the paper manuscript archive of the Irish Folklore Commission.

Every text of this literature can be regarded as existing in and participating in a universe of discourse within which it attained literary status by virtue of its textural qualities as speech act, its textual relations in terms of subject matter to other treatments and its imaginative and creative function in the contexts of audiences and readerships who recognise and acknowledge its achievement of excellence vis-à-vis the protocols of literary convention as these apply. Every text and every anthology of such texts can be approached with a view to situating them within a kind of calculus of discourse analysis that frames each text with an appreciation of the issues of intertextuality, of underlying textural quality and of contextual significance in historical and socio-cultural terms.

In many respects scholarship on Irish manuscript literature has always attempted to elucidate such issues as discourse analysis draws attention to in the tripartite frame of texture, text and context. To suggest that the universe of discourse approach is both a valid and a productive one is, perhaps, to do no more than to emphasise the possibility and the potential of a holistic approach that encompasses the linguistic narrows of grammar and etymology together with the poetic expanses of symbolism and creative imagination. Such an approach can encourage the filling out, as it were, of our appreciation of the literary worth of the texts and the underlying speech acts of such corners of the overall universe of discourse of Irish literary tradition as are represented by such publications as *Silva Gadelica*,[28] *Dioghluim Dána*,[29] *Éigse Chairbre*[30] and *Scéalaíocht Amhlaoibh Í Luínse*.[31] Such works capture in different ways speech acts that were considered noteworthy in the literal sense of deserving notation by virtue of their perceived excellence and importance. Originating in social contexts as different as the elite and aristocratic milieu of the royal palace and the bardic academy, on the one hand, and the humbler milieu of the kitchen hearth and the rural tavern, on the other, each of the items is a contribution to an ongoing Irish literary tradition. In its constituent components, this literary tradition is constantly re-creating, reinforcing and representing versions of Irish social and cultural identity which various sectors and groupings of Irish people have recognised as their own. Both regionally and over time there is, of course, constant change and transformation at work in this 'literary' expression and representation of identity – in conjunction with shifting social and historical circumstances and indeed with changes in the Irish language itself, its fortunes and the conventions of its literary use. Again here the notion of a universe of discourse within which Irish people have engaged in varieties of narrative and poetic conversation – a conversation, oral and written, that overall represents them to themselves as well as giving expression to their creativity – can be an appropriate one.

In conclusion, it is equally appropriate, perhaps, to mention ways in which the literary discourse of Irish manuscript/oral literature can register, outside of any consciously Irish literary identity, as a contribution to a more universal cultural discourse that encompasses both the individual psyche and a transcendent symbolism of creative imagination. Accounts of human interactions with the native otherworld, *an saol sí*, feature widely in Irish manuscript literature ranging from the mythological tales of early medieval times to the *sí-scéalta* and the *bean feasa* legends of the last century. In regard to the latter, oral narrative material of this kind, it is possible to envisage how such accounts amount to a type of communal psychotherapeutic resource for the speech communities among whom they circulate in performance and transmission. Stylised, literary narration of incidents involving otherworld agencies and realities can, it has been suggested, provide a kind of coping mechanism that enables individuals and the community to retain a sense of shared meaning in the face of life's afflictions and misfortunes. The stories are, in this light, both a record of the insecurities and the ambiguities of human existence and a device whereby the emotional traumas of living can be imaginatively alleviated. The efficacy of *sí-scéalta* in this regard is discussed in the work of Angela Bourke[32] while the present writer has addressed the functions of stories of the *bean feasa* in this light.[33]

Broadening the canvas from a focus on the individual psyche to the widest comparative literary contexts, we can mention the way in which Brian Merriman's *Cúirt an Mheán Oíche* has been read by Seamus Heaney in the light of Greek myth.[34] In this perspective Merriman's poem at its conclusion relates to the version of the Orpheus myth attributed to Ovid. In the classical myth Orpheus rejects feminine love and femininity in general as a consequence of what befell him in the attempt to win back his wife Eurydice from the UnderWorld. He now prizes his music and poetry more than woman's love. In punishment for this, the Maenads, the female devotees of Dionysius, tear him limb from limb. A similar fate is threatened to the *alter ego* hero of Brian Merriman's poem because of an apparently similar rejection and neglect of the feminine – the very charge concerning which the court assembles at *Craig Liath*.

To Heaney's insight into the more universal connotations of the conclusion of the *Cúirt* we can add the observation that the rejection or suppression of the feminine – on the parts both of Merriman and his poetic *alter ego* – is present in the poem from its beginning. At the opening of the poem we find the poet happily situated – by his own account – in a lifestyle and a mentality marked by a self-sufficient and self-satisfied masculinity that disregards and diminishes the feminine.

In native tradition such unbalanced and unbridled masculinity is a constant source of mysterious illness and possession (*fuadach*) by the *sí* and we may read such imbalance into *Cúirt an Mheán Oíche* from the poem's outset. If rejection and neglect of the feminine is the concern of the *aisling* court to which the poet's sleeping *alter ego* is summoned, the opening of the poem can be read as a self-accusation by the poet himself in respect of those masculine failings and excesses which bring all the trouble onto the head of his *aisling alter ego* at the poem's end. The first forty lines of *Cúirt an Mheán Oíche* show the poet inhabiting a landscape that is presented to the listener/reader as an early modern, Big House pastoral hinterland yielding up the male pleasures of hunting, shooting, fishing with their attendant subservient and exploited feminine background presence – if we take reference to such as '*an bháinseach úr 's an drúcht go trom*' in their traditional metaphorical senses.

The use by the poet of the term 'Reynard' for the object of a hunt by a throng pursuing with *géimreach adharc* (the blowing of horns) and *tréanrith gadhar* (the hard running of hounds) confirms this squire-like, male, Big House orientation. By the poem's end, of course, with the articulation and release into consciousness of the power of the feminine in the presence and the pronouncements of Aoibheall, the scene is transformed radically to one in which the poet himself, qua his *alter ego*, has become 'Reynard', the object of pursuit and the proposed subject of female wrath and violence.

These quasi-psychological and quasi-mythological readings of items of Irish manuscript literary tradition are, I would submit, capable of finding justification in that sense being discussed here of all literature coming into being always within universes of human discourse. Grounded in the articulatory and acoustic phonetics of the speech act, such universes of discourse contain 'literary' domains wherein those speech acts – and their consequent texts – that are conventionally adjudged to possess narrative and poetic excellence of a special and specially prized order are transmitted in performance and notation so that they constitute literary tradition. Irish manuscript literature, like all literary tradition, serves to represent people to themselves and to symbolise and sustain their creativity of imagination as makers and communicators of meaning in the face of transience and mortality.

CHAPTER 7

Irish Storytelling in Heritage Context

[Published in Neil Buttimer, Colin Rynne and Helen Guerin (eds),
The Heritage of Ireland (Cork: The Collins Press, 2000), pp. 171–7]

This chapter discusses the cultural nature of heritage and the reality that all representations of heritage are culturally selective. Following on from a somewhat theoretical exploration of these matters, the traditions of Irish storytelling are examined to illustrate the issue in a concrete way and to highlight central aspects and central difficulties of immediate relevance to the management of heritage presentation. Questions such as how best to 'stage' what was, essentially, a spontaneous performance; how to locate authentic material that is still of appeal to the modern audience; how to compensate for the male bias in storytelling tradition in an equality-conscious era, are touched on. Certain principles for, or, at least, approaches to, the successful representation of Irish cultural heritage managers. These apply equally to storytelling and to most other aspects of Irish tradition, artistic or material, religious or social, and have an application to cultural heritages other than Irish. They comprise the contribution of the discipline 'ethnology' to the study of how to interpret and represent all cultural tradition.

Present-day ethnology is especially concerned with understanding the cultural processes whereby local, regional and national identities are constructed, contested, transmitted and transformed in a continual process of representation and reinterpretation. Formerly it was concerned in more general and more descriptive ways with the comparative and historical study of peoples. Today's ethnologists combine field study of culture with the historical and comparative approach. They are concerned that an acquaintance with first-hand details of the actual functioning reality of cultural tradition should inform all attempts at interpretation and representation. The acquisition, through fieldwork, of such first-hand, detailed knowledge-on-the-ground is the aim of ethnography (literally 'the writing of culture'). Ethnography provides a platform of cultural knowledge on which the ethnologist builds up interpretation and analysis. Some ethnologists are their own ethnographers and some rely on the field collections of other and perhaps earlier workers and students of tradition. It is suggested here that heritage managers, in whatever corners of the heritage field, would do well to be aware of ethnology's implications for cultural representation.

TWO BASIC CONCEPTS

The application of an ethnological approach, which this chapter espouses, to any topic within the field of heritage management requires that two related ideas regarding the field itself be emphasised. These are:

i. that heritage of any description is always to be regarded, first and foremost, as culture;

ii. that heritage itself is invariably the product of a selecting out and a highlighting of aspects of culture in accordance with specific perspectives and specific interests. Some basic discussion of these ideas may be useful in the context of looking at one topic of Irish cultural heritage from the ethnological point of view as an example of the kind of approach to heritage and its management which is appropriate in an ethnological frame.

Firstly, let us look at the view that heritage of any description is always to be regarded, first and foremost, as culture. The term 'culture' has a long and varied history, not by any means confined to the humanities and social sciences. Indeed, its earliest associations are in the fields of husbandry (the culture of crops) and laboratory science (the culture of bacteria). Borrowed into the humanities and social sciences, culture has developed as a term with two separate ranges of connotation. The narrower of these has to do with what is sometimes thought of as 'high culture' or 'elite culture' – such things as the 'fine' arts, 'classical' music and ballet and 'high-brow' or 'heavy' literature within the European tradition, together with similar 'high' or 'elite' examples in other non-western civilisations. The other, broader connotation has developed from an appreciation of and a concern to understand the general human capacity and competence to adapt to environment, to reflect on life and find it meaningful and to represent and communicate this adaptation and meaningfulness in both material and symbolic work.

Attempts to define in any exact or exhaustive manner this broader, albeit more technical, meaning of the human and social sense of culture have been dogged by the realisation that since culture in this sense is as broad as human life in all its multifariousness, since in fact, in a sense, culture is the multifariousness of human life, then we can never hope to complete a list of its constituent elements. In place of such rag-bag definitions as have been attempted – seeking to enumerate all the aspects of human life involved (ideas, beliefs, art, morals, law, custom and so forth) – a definitional understanding of culture has been developing that regards it as comprised basically of knowledge: the kind of knowledge that an individual necessarily acquires in the course of growing up and being socialised into the adult human worlds of technology, social behaviour and meaning. Such 'knowledge' is not to be thought of as being simple or settled in its nature. Rather it is a shifting, dynamic, operational domain wherein each of us is continually making sense out of experience and adjusting our understanding, our behaviour and our communication in the light of prevailing circumstances and desired ends. Culture and cultural knowledge are thus properly understood as process: ongoing process over time in which we all participate as cultural actors. Also it should be emphasised that cultural knowledge is not confined to the verbal or cognitive forms of knowing that we traditionally consider as being located in our 'heads', the alleged seat of intellect and reason. This knowledge also comprises what we know 'in our hearts', the supposed seat of emotions and the traditional location of the values that inform our aesthetics and ethics. Likewise cultural knowledge includes the knowledge of 'how to do things', located by tradition in our fingers, in our feet, in our range of skills as put to work in technology, in art, in recreation.

Obviously no schematic model of culture, even culture-in-process, such as hinted at above, will comprehend the richness, the flow, the manifold and manifest wholeness and holistic nature of human cultural tradition as it is lived, yet some such model is conceptually valuable to those whose business it is to reflect on the nature of culture and cultural heritage. The model underlying the approach to heritage that this 'ethnological chapter' represents encompasses the aforementioned considerations of culture as knowledge-in-process. Furthermore, it takes the position that every individual, every group, every cultural community, whether on the local, the regional, the national or the global level, is continually engaged in giving external form (verbal, behavioural, symbolic) to shifting, dynamic transformations of those provisional formulations and realisations of knowledge – in all its 'locations' – that constitute the worldview and lifestyle of the individual, the group, the community at a given time and place. Kevin Danaher caught the sense of all this in his characterisation of folklore as 'the sayings and the doings' of ordinary people, as long as we can understand that what people say and do is said and done within a never-ending process of adjustment and transformation in the exercise of choice informed by the shifting meaningfulness of daily experience. Some forms of culture, some sayings and doings, in this process, come to be regarded as heritage.

The second idea to be emphasised here is that heritage is invariably the product of a selecting out and a highlighting of aspects of culture and culture process for specific purposes. This implies that the construction and promotion of heritage involve a kind and degree of conscious cultural choice that is additional to those group and community choosings and valuings that underlie the self-esteem and cultural pride stemming from that normal, spontaneous consciousness of cultural identity that is always part of the worldview and lifestyle of human groups. Such deliberate selection and deliberate highlighting as underlie the construction and promotion of heritage are themselves, of course, cultural in nature – though sometimes thought of as a kind of second-order cultural activity. They are to be understood as also subject to the dynamic play of adjustment and transformation that are at the heart of cultural knowledge. So just as culture is never a fixed or a finished quantum of knowledge or list of objects or prescription for behaviour or belief, so too heritage is to be understood as a field of cultural representation that is constantly responding to the adjustments and transformations and re-creations of social and cultural life and of social and cultural identity. That which is selected as heritage to represent the cultural traditions and the cultural identity of former ties cannot comprise a fixed or finished entity. It offers, rather, the opportunity for an imaginative engagement with phases of a culture process that was dynamic in its nature and that yielded certain externalisations or realisations of the then worldview and lifestyle that are capable of representing to our time the cultural world of a former era in which they had their 'first life'.

Just as culture changes over time, so too does heritage, and there can be a history of heritage just as there is culture history. A full representation of cultural tradition as heritage will try to address this issue and show the changing nature of heritage in respect of the cultural tradition in question, just as it will show the changes that have occurred in the tradition itself. Heritage management must thus be alert to what have been called 'the two lives' of cultural tradition. The first life is that of a relatively unreflective externalisation of worldview and realisation of lifestyle in artefact and repertoire, in custom and ritual and institution. The second life occurs when consciousness of the heritage status and potential of such externalisations and realisations is raised either by threat from outside or by reason of the attentions and activities of scholars and others as part of some intellectual and/or political movement, for instance romantic nationalism in the case of so many 'small nations' in Europe – including Ireland.

In more recent times a third kind of life has been visited on cultural tradition under the pressures of the modern tourist industry, where the need to entertain has frequently taken precedence over considerations of authenticity or scholarship.[1] At its extreme this can lead to distorted visions of cultural tradition and heritage being constructed and exploited chiefly as a commercial resource whose value is seen exclusively in terms of contemporary consumer products and services. We can try to discern how each of these lives or phases or levels of cultural knowledge and activity pertains to the consideration of any heritage topic. By way of example, let us consider in some detail the case of Irish popular narrative tradition, that is 'stories and storytelling', as part of Irish cultural tradition and Irish cultural heritage. Given the emphasis in the ethnological perspective on processes of construction, representation and transformation, our initial concern will be to explore narrative heritage as a heritage of storytelling 'events' in the first instance, and then to consider also the contents or repertoires that were performed in the course of these events.

IRISH STORYTELLING TRADITION

The perceived heritage of Irish stories and storytelling, taken together, is regarded as having the status of a 'grand tradition'. Irish people and Irish culture are supposed to have a special talent, a special capacity, a special appreciation for storytelling and verbal art in general. The *Táin*, the epic account of the cattle raid of Cooley and the central saga of the so-called Ulster cycle of early Irish literature, has a pre-eminent primary position in a canon of narrative excellence that stretches through the centuries to the prominent contemporary Irish novelists and short-story writers of the late twentieth century. As an element within this traditional heritage the figure of the traditional storyteller, the *seanchaí*, is taken as a representative personality who has become something of a model for latter-day interpreters and performers of Irish storytelling tradition within the heritage field. The image of the *seanchaí* – as promoted say in the stage and television performances of Éamon Kelly – has established itself as something of a stereotype, fixing or freezing actual process in traditional narrative expression into a characterisation that appears timeless and universal. Behind such a stereotyped characterisation there is, of course, a rich ethnography of the incidence of actual storytelling in the popular culture of the Irish countryside in the last hundred years. It is to this ethnographic richness beyond the stereotype that here, as in all other cases of heritage, we must go for enlightenment. Actual Irish storytelling has been studied and described most famously by the scholars of the Irish Folklore Commission, whose director, Professor Séamus Ó Duilearga, has published the seminal monograph entitled 'The Gaelic Storyteller' and the seminal anthology of stories and lore from a single, talented, tradition-bearer entitled *Leabhar Sheáin Í Chonaill/Seán Ó Conaill's Book*. The impression of Irish storytelling tradition that these works convey is that of a kind of rural academy of verbal art where the well-known, gifted performers had a privileged, star-quality status in the eyes of the community and the eyes of the visiting, recording collector-scholars. Subsequent studies by such as Henry Glassie, Clodagh Brennan Harvey and Máirtín Verling have shown how this rural academy/star-performer version of Irish storytelling tradition deviates from the cultural reality of storytelling in the Irish countryside of the early twentieth century where the forces of modernisation – including the displacement of Irish by English – operated increasingly to transform the patterns of social and cultural life away from the somewhat idealised picture presented by earlier scholars of Irish storytelling.

That somewhat idealised picture draws fairly directly on one strand within the earlier history of Irish storytelling, the strand deriving from the medieval institutionalisation of the *scélaige*, the professional storyteller as part of the entourage of king and chieftain. Such professional narrators operated in the context of the banqueting hall (entertainment) and the sleeping chamber (relaxation) among other customary locations, though in all such locations storytelling would frequently have had a quasi-political function also, in terms of praising the chief or king through recounting the glorious deeds of ancestors or famous antecedents and in propagandistic promotion of one faction over others. In fact the storytelling setting of nineteenth- and early twentieth-century rural Ireland was far more spontaneous and proletarian than the total academy characterisation – drawing on the medieval model – suggests. As such, however, storytelling continued into the last century as a central and valued expression of culture and heritage. Its importance is reflected in the ubiquity and variety of names for the commonest setting in which storytelling manifested itself. Some of these names are well known from media use of them in the context of presenting aspects of Irish tradition to a mass audience. *Airneán, scoraíocht, céilí* house, rambling house are terms that have become generally familiar from the extensive list of local terms for the cultural phenomenon within Irish life whereby narrative performance within an assembly of people took on the quasi-artistic, quasi-religious, quasi-psychological functions capable of intensifying life experience for individual and group and giving externalisation as verbal art to shared meaningfulness in terms of identity, memory and aspiration.

Another notable example of this kind of cultural phenomenon/ heritage in popular Irish tradition in recent centuries is the funerary ritual of the 'merry wake'. This was the gathering of relations and neighbours at the house of a deceased to wake or watch the corpse throughout the night hours. While the merry wake obviously cannot be regarded as constituting a storytelling event primarily, a combination of Christian prayers and ancestral verse-keening or lamentation formed an essential narrative accompaniment at the wake ritual. Both prayer and lament played their joint roles in the important social and sacred work that the traditional wake accomplished – namely the translation of the spirit of the deceased to the afterlife (conceived in both Christian and ancestral/fairy terms) and the cathartic release of the fear, sorrow and anger that is felt by individuals and community on the occasion of death. It should however be noted that 'storytelling' in the broader sense was also a feature of the merry wake, taking its place with other forms of recreation and activity, serving to realise and reinforce the intense, central preoccupations of the ritual over its two- or three-day course.

Other assemblies in which storytelling had a prominent, culturally intensifying role did not, by contrast with the wake assembly, depend on any dramatic occurrence, such as a death, to bring them into being. They were regularly formed and emerged in the course of ordinary daily life wherever people had the occasion or the opportunity to assemble – for a variety of purposes, some festive, some mundane. Examples of mundane occasions would be the occupational events and locations associated with potato and turf harvesting, night-fishing, bothy-herding or transhumance, childminding, knitting and quilting parties. Other similar groups of storytelling would include pattern days at a holy well or other sacred site, *Lughnasa* or harvest outings, bonfire days or nights, for instance May eve, midsummer and life-cycle festivities such as baptism or wedding parties as well as the wake ritual mentioned above. On each and all of these occasions in Irish tradition it was customary and normal for storytelling to 'break out', as it were, in a spontaneous expression of creativity and entertainment that was at once 'diversion', celebration and cathartic intensification of life experience. The performers of narrative on all such occasions were not at all necessarily star performers but could be anyone with an ability to perform who was moved to or was prevailed upon to contribute to the narrative occasion. Of course there were degrees of competence and excellence recognised and shared by members of the assembly/audience. This evaluation encompassed factors of repertoire, of rhetoric, of performance – histrionic and aesthetic. Certainly there were occasional star performers who were more popular and more in demand, so to speak, but one must emphasise again the relatively informal and spontaneous nature of these storytelling events.

THE TYPICAL STORYTELLING EVENT

Apart from the above locations of storytelling in Irish tradition there remains to be considered the *locus classicus*, as it were, of the winter hearth in the farmhouse kitchen where friends and neighbours gathered to pass the long hours of darkness and inclement weather. This is the setting of the *airneán* presented so vividly in the writings of Séamus Ó Duilearga and Henry Glassie, the former treating of the community of the cliff-top village of Irish-speaking Cill Rialaigh during the 1920s in south Kerry, the latter of the inland, English-speaking, border village community of Ballymenone, County Fermanagh during the 1970s. Each presentation is a reconstruction by an outsider of the structure and flow of the 'typical' storytelling event of local popular culture; each offers a rich tapestry of heritage to our later eyes. For Ó Duilearga the heritage issues most involved are those of illuminating and capturing a fragile remnant of the middle ages and bearing testimony to the noble and exemplary character of the bearers of that national heritage and of their way of life – lived in the teeth of modern misunderstanding, indifference and hostility. For Glassie the heritage issues involved relate in a more universal framework to a continual renewal and re-creation of human understanding and imagination by means of the intensification of the life experience out of the course of the daily round and the annual life-cycles of mundane community living, in bog and field and factory, in house and church and chapel, in utterance, in memory and in imagination. Glassie's account of the gradual intensification of communication in the course of the evening kitchen assembly, resulting eventually not only in story but also in music and song and food (for body and soul), is essential reading for all students of Irish storytelling and the heritage of Irish popular culture. Foremost among its virtues is the realisation it brings that, even in the *scoraíocht* or the rambling house (to use two other well-known appellations for the classic cultural site of the storytelling event), the telling of stories is not the unique, primary or professed reason for the coming together in assembly. Certainly there is an expectation that storytelling will occur, that stories will be told, that storytellers will perform – but only as a major and valuable incidental, so to speak, of the ostensible purposes of the assembly. These have more to do with desire for and delight in companionship (versus loneliness), the expression of neighbourly solidarity and group identity, a curiosity about local gossip and current affairs of an economic and political nature on the local and on wider fronts. Gossip and current affairs can lead to reminiscence or to make-believe; this in turn can prompt the recounting of a recognised item of the storytelling repertoire. The patterned process of proceeding with the storytelling event can be a protracted affair and may, on occasion, be unsuccessful or unproductive of any good storytelling performances. What is certain is that it contrasts very greatly with the starting-from-cold stage performances of storytelling slotted into the concert or cabaret settings of contemporary entertainment events that purport to represent the heritage of Irish storytelling. While there are talented stage exponents who tell stories today, one must distinguish between them and the storytellers of actual cultural tradition.

SOME DIFFICULTIES IN REPRESENTATION

The challenge of how to represent Irish storytelling heritage in terms of contemporary cultural settings and contemporary media evokes a variety of responses that all, in various ways, attempt to capture the perceived essential character and flavour of Irish storytelling in its 'first-life' mode. The above discussion of certain limited aspects of that first life will, hopefully, enable the reader to draw conclusions regarding the viability – on historical and ethnographic grounds – of representing Irish storytelling tradition in the mode of Éamon Kelly or the interpretative centre, of Kevin McAleer or the scholarly documentary. Apart from the characterisation of the storytelling event itself, however, attention must also be paid to questions arising from the content or texts of storytelling and the gender bias that their traditional performance exhibited.

As regards the texts and genres that constitute the repertoire of Irish storytelling tradition, ample information and reasonably adequate anthologies are available for the chief categories as a result of the work of scholars over the last hundred years and especially the work of scholars associated with the Irish Folklore Commission. This scholarship has linked the Irish popular storytelling repertoire to international storytelling scholarship. While a great deal remains to be accomplished – not least because of developments in the scholarly understanding of the role of storytelling within culture process that have given rise to new questions – there exists for heritage professionals a considerable amount of material that can ensure that excellent appropriate texts or items of repertoire can be utilised in any representation of popular narrative tradition – as a part of Irish heritage. A difficulty arises in repertoire terms from the fact that, historically, the type of story most highly valued and even most sought after, in the *airneán* of the rambling house, was the hero-tale of the 'Adventures of Fionn Mac Cumhaill' type with its stylised rhetorical features and its swashbuckling action. Neither this genre nor the other valued genre of the more international wonder-tale ('The Dragon-Slayer', 'The Quest for the Lost Husband', 'Cinderella' – known as *Móirín* or even 'Hairy Rucky' in Irish versions) are at all likely to appeal to modern general audiences. On the other hand, the humorous anecdotes and tall tales that prove popular in contemporary storytelling settings must be regarded as somewhat minor items of the narrative heritage. A real challenge exists here in regard to the adequate representation of the actual heritage of story within Irish popular cultural tradition.

As regards gender, the image conjured up by the term *seanchaí* is inevitably male, and often, as in the Éamon Kelly version, is replete with stereotypical *cáibín* and *dúidín*, the peaked beret and the clay pipe, and a penchant for spitting into the fire. The patriarchal, macho overtones of this image are best confined, in the light of ethnographic reality, to the domain of the native hero-tale or *Fiannaíocht* – named from the chief culture hero of popular Gaelic cultural tradition in Ireland and Scotland – though not all the hero-tales in the native repertoire concern the adventures of Fionn Mac Cumhaill and his warrior-band. The performance of hero-tales of this type, and, to a somewhat lesser degree, the performance of the international Märchen-type wonder-tale in its very plentiful Irish versions, was restricted to the male storyteller (*scéalaí* or *scéaltóir*). Indeed a taboo of sorts existed in relation to the performance of this type of material – especially the Fenian hero-tale – by females, in that it was held to be unlucky and even unnatural for a woman to narrate a story of this kind to an assembly – as unnatural, as the saying has it, as a hen crowing. The *seanchaí* of Irish popular culture in early modern and modern times has, by contrast, been male and female, the bearer and reciter of traditional lore rather than stories, lore comprising local genealogy, legends and history as well as prayers, verse, pithy sayings and the like. A certain female preponderance suggests itself in the ranks of known bearers and performers of certain kinds of *seanchas*/lore, for instance prayers, lament verse, mythological legend. The degree to which these gender distinctions can or should be reproduced in heritage representations of storytelling tradition is a question to be taken into account in the light of issues deriving from the feminist perspective which has recently and very properly been added to the hitherto largely male scholarly gaze and scholarly voice in matters of cultural tradition and heritage. The stereotyped figure of the heritage *seanchaí* needs radical alteration.

We now realise that our accounts of cultural tradition derive over-whelmingly from male sources and that attention in the study of these traditions has focused more centrally and sustainedly on matters male. Large areas of traditional cultural knowledge and cultural life – those centred on female consciousness and realised in female lifestyle and life-forms – are all but invisible in the cultural record, that is, in our account, from scholarship and otherwise, of the first-life mode of popular culture in Ireland. Thus the second-life heritage representations of that popular culture are all too easily left equally biased against the equitable portrayal of the human reality of the former era in question and its culture process and patterns. This consideration applies to the world of storytelling in cultural tradition and in heritage as much as to any other part of the field. The site of storytelling tradition regarded as the *locus classicus* – the winter fireside with friends and neighbours assembled – turns out, on inspection, to be an almost exclusively male affair. We now realise that there are other *loci* to which women gravitated at different times and in different circumstances, and that at these female assemblies repertoire of traditional narrative other than the male assembly ones were performed and transmitted. In this regard especially, the responsibility of the student of heritage to engage in research as an integral prelude to an ongoing integral part of representing cultural tradition adequately is paramount.

Finally, we can consider briefly the question as to what happened to the Irish storytelling tradition as represented by 'The Gaelic Storyteller'. Did it die? Did it stop? Did it change out of all recognition? Where is it, or its transformation, to be found today? These questions remind us of two fundamental facts. One, that storytelling is a universal human capacity and competence, a part of the human culture process in all conditions of society and history. Two, that in Irish cultural tradition a hundred years ago and more, storytelling was a kind of epiphenomenon arising from the social assemblies that occurred as a feature of the technical, economic, social, political and ritual symbolic sides of daily life. As society and social institutions change, we can be certain that cultural phenomena change also in their outward aspects, in their structure, in their function, in their meaningfulness. In the case of Irish storytelling tradition as we know it from descriptions of its operation in the late nineteenth and early twentieth centuries, the historical and ethnographic reality is that technical and socio-economic developments were altering in radical ways the forms of companionship, entertainment and communication from those circumstances that had hitherto been a vehicle for the occurrence and performance of tradition narrative, whether story or lore. The storytelling assemblies or the assemblies that led to storytelling as a part of their proceedings were displaced by newer kinds of social arrangements in the workplace, in the home, in the local world in general. The newspaper, the motor car and electricity all had a profound effect on the lifestyle of local communities; these are only three items from the many different aspects of the impingement of elements of modernity on Irish traditional life which those who would represent that tradition need to take into account. Harvey's discussion of the implications of just such factors of modernity for storytellers and their performances is an essential part of our understanding of all Irish traditional narration, medieval and modern.

It throws much light on the process of culture and of culture change in relation to verbal art.

CONCLUSION

In the post-modern era in which, by the reckoning of some, we now find ourselves, our attempts at representing cultural heritage, including storytelling traditions, can benefit greatly from understanding as clearly as possible the cultural nature of stories and their performance in different eras of history and in different life modes as, over time, a consciousness of tradition as heritage develops. It is to be hoped that the points of view that the present ethnological chapter presents for consideration will prove of interest to those whose task it is to engage in the important cultural work of representing and re-creating cultural tradition as heritage for the present day and, of course, for the future. In respect of storytelling itself, a recent report on the storytelling revival by Pat Ryan will be of particular interest. In respect of other areas of heritage – material, social and symbolic – the same general considerations apply.

Overall, the need is for heritage managers to be constantly alert to the necessity for further ethnographic research and further interpretation and analysis. In this, heritage management is yet another manifestation of that process which characterises all phenomena of a cultural nature. Like all culture, heritage too is endlessly diverse and adaptive, continually remoulded to reflect the ongoing dynamic of creativity in human life and its record.

CHAPTER 8

Orality and Modern Irish Culture

[Published as 'A Thousand and One Nights' (Prologue), in Nessa Cronin, Seán Crosson and John Eastlake (eds), *Anáil an Bhéil Bheo: Orality and modern Irish culture* (Newcastle upon Tyne: Cambridge Scholars Publishing, 2009), pp. 15–26]

A PERSONAL STRAND OF THE WEAVE

This chapter will attempt to illustrate aspects of orality of modern Irish culture by addressing three instances of orality in the personal and professional experience of the author. The first of these is the orality of the family and community culture into which I was born and in which I acquired literacy in Cork city during the 1940s. The second comprises the efforts my colleagues and myself made forty years later to engage ethnographically with the oral culture of community life in areas of Cork city that were perceived as having an enduring cultural vitality in the face of rapid social and cultural change. The third instance involves the methodological stance adopted by me in relation to the reading and decipherment of texts derived from oral narrative tradition in the Irish language. I am conscious of the difficulties and pitfalls of attempting to communicate adequately the oral nature of experience in a written medium and of how my own talent for communication – such as it is – has always, I believe, had an oral bent that has struggled at times to conform to literate convention and that has, on occasion also, been found to be rhetorically seductive without achieving uncontested, clear-cut status as academic discourse.

For the first twelve years of my life my parents and I lived in a small house, number eleven in a terrace of small houses that led down from the inner end of the Glasheen Road to the north-eastern side of the lake known as The Lough on the south-western outskirts of Cork city. The city/county boundary was known to bisect number eleven so that – since we occupied the opposing-end rooms upstairs and down – I slept in the county and ate my meals in the city. The elderly woman of the house, unmarried and without relatives, was a highly respected and independent-minded woman whose family home this had been and who supplemented her rental income from my parents with small earnings from the seamstress and knitting services she provided for her neighbours. Keeping a Victorian-style hat and coat in her wardrobe for very formal occasions, she wore a black shawl for her daily excursions to shops and her frequent, nightly visits to church and to her best friend, known as Penny-House, who had spent a period of her life in the United States of America and was now living together with a grandson in a tiny one-storey dwelling for which she allegedly paid a peppercorn rent. Electricity did not become available in the neighbourhood until after the Second World War and lighting was by town gas and paraffin-oil lamp. My mother cooked and boiled water on a gas stove while Nell – our landlady and my dear surrogate grandmother to whom I was far closer than to either of my actual grandmothers – cooked on an open fire and had only oil lamps for lighting, even after electricity was eventually installed. The house contained only one book on a permanent basis – even though my mother was a regular borrower of books from both city and county libraries, to both of which our boundary straddling gave her access, while my father read the evening newspaper every day and *The Catholic Standard* on Sundays. He worked for a life assurance company collecting tiny weekly amounts of premium money all over the city and entering up his account book and his weekly returns sheets very assiduously in a well-formed hand. Neither he nor my mother had gone beyond national school and their literacy competencies were of an interesting differential nature. As well as having a fine writing hand my father was a very good speller of words and was very quick at figures. He read very little, however, but remembered stretches of school poetry and a stock of Irish-language phrases that he picked up from the radio when we eventually acquired a 'wireless' with the advent of an electricity supply. On the other hand, my mother, though an avid reader of romantic novels – my father and I eventually got to buying her one in hardback edition every year as a Christmas present – was a very hesitant writer and never had much to do with matters numerate outside of the weekly household finances.

Incidentally, that one 'real' book I remember as being ours was an illustrated dictionary, lacking a cover, that was kept in the gas stove and put onto the window sill when any major cooking was taking place. It appears to me to have been normally let inside the stove when only the top gas rings were in everyday use. I can recall that the first illustrated word in it was 'adze'.

Nell was definitely a non-reader. I cannot recall her ever reading a single word and, as far as any writing went, there was quite a ceremony every Friday morning when she signed her name in the pension book. This was laid open on the centre of her otherwise bare table and she bent over it for several minutes in the course of inscribing her name, 'Ellen Donovan', in an open, ornamental script beginning and ending with flourishes of the straight pen she kept together with an inkpot on her sideboard for this weekly task, which I take to be the only surviving element of the literacy skills imparted to her in whatever course of schooling she had around about 1870.

Degrees of literacy have existed in Irish communities ever since the knowledge and practice of the technology of writing entered Irish culture in the early middle ages. The term 'primary oral culture' has not been applicable to any Irish community for 1500 years notwithstanding that the majority of the Irish population could not until relatively recently (about 200 years ago) read or write in any language. While being a 'literate culture' for such a long time, it is nevertheless the case that such literacy as has existed in Irish social life – ecclesiastical, politico/legal, commercial, educational, literary – has always been embedded, so to speak, as a set or archipelago of interconnecting and interrelated islands in a surrounding sea of orality. This state of affairs is the regular, normal condition of human verbal communication even in the case of the most highly literate societies and socio-linguistic contexts. Literacy, as such, exists and comes into play in a differential manner within any community or any group in line with various types of verbal activity, sacred, profane or artistic, and this is true also in the case of every individual language user in a community. An individual endowed to some greater or lesser degree with the various skills of literacy will utilise these – along with the skills of orality – as befits the communication requirements and opportunities that present themselves in any given socio-linguistic context. Some contexts may appear to be entirely literate, such as writing a letter or reading a novel in private; others may appear to be entirely oral, such as engaging in face-to-face conversation or reciting poetry. They can never be entirely separated from each other, however, in the sense that the speakers and writers and readers in a society which is not a 'primary oral culture' cannot escape the joint presence of orality and literacy in the make-up of their linguistic competence, no matter how clear their preference or commitment is to one or the other modality in any given context.

In that house in Croaghtamore and in the community of neighbours there, both orality and literacy thrived. I myself listened to Nell's endless invocations of her earlier life and the lives of her now-long-gone family, friends and neighbours in fireside sessions with my mother in the evenings and with neighbours who called during the day to sit and chat with her as she plied her sewing machine or her knitting needles while I played on her floor – sometimes re-enacting the activities of the coalman, the postman, the milkman, sometimes re-enacting what I took to be the behaviours of the soldiers fighting in the war whose course was reported to us by word of mouth, whether in gossip or on the 'wireless'. I was always delighted when one particular caller, a man who lived next door and seemed never to have work to go to, acted out in comic parody some of the exploits from Nell's repertoire of incidents pertaining to earlier days – 'long ago' and often involving 'Connie Kelly and that other man', a phrase that sticks in my memory of Paddy's antics. Another frequent caller was Mrs McMullen who – as well as regularly spending an hour or two in Nell's kitchen talking to her about old times and the gossip of the day – shared with my mother an appreciation of the pleasures of reading and took an interest in my progress in reading at school. I still have the copy of the Oxford University Press 1946 edition of *Tales from the Arabian Nights* with its introduction by E.O. Lorimer and its gorgeous illustrations by Gordon Nicoll that she gave me at Christmas 1948[1] – probably still only the second book in the house at the time. I think of it now as a highly appropriate (if demanding) gift for a child growing up in a situation where my mother's and my own reading – I remember sobbing myself to sleep upstairs having read an account of the death of Robin Hood where he asks to be buried at the spot where his last faltering arrow falls – was accompanied downstairs on a thousand and one nights by a constant call to service in the cause of oral narration. My father spent very many evenings at a local youth club, where he acted as committee secretary, and my mother would have happily read while I did my homework and maybe read along with her afterwards. Too often, alas, for literate ambition, Nell could be heard, when she had no other companion, observing to her fire-lit kitchen, 'Ah, sure, anyone that reads is no company.' Repeated a second time this would bring my mother to put a jacket of my father's around her shoulders and join Nell at her fireside for a session of memorate and anecdote in which she would, in fact, more than hold her own and from which she obviously got considerable verbal satisfaction and entertainment once she had overcome her resentment at having been obliged to forsake her library book.

When I began school I quickly mastered reading skills and became, for a time, the 'best reader' in the class. I moved on, outside the classroom, from the *Playbox* comic which my father brought me on the carrier of his bicycle every Thursday, to get books from the libraries my mother frequented, often now bringing me along to choose my own book from the children's section. On journeys to the branch of the county library we would walk across the UCC campus and she would regularly remark, as we passed the mouth of the stone corridor under the main arch with its double line of ogham stone inscriptions, 'Ah! If only those stones could talk.' She meant this, I am sure, in relation to the generation of students who had passed through the corridor and the college, but I have since seen an ironic further layer of meaning in it – a meaning not without relevance to the issue of orality and literacy both in a general sense of the ogham stones being the earliest form of Irish writing and in the particular sense of her call for the stones to talk in the context of her own (and my) quest for reading material.

Two other brief mentions of aspects of the oral-literate mix of life in Croaghtamore will bring this section to an end. An elderly neighbour, Danny Leahy, had a reputation as a poet and I remember hearing one of his compositions being read out for us by my father from the lined pages of a school copybook and hearing that one of the priests of the parish, Fr Cahalane, who had the reputation himself of being 'very well read' – he had an MA in history from the NUI – had great respect for Danny and his literary talent.

Every year as November approached on the calendar, 'dead lists' had to be got ready and deposited in a black tin box that sat on the altar rail of the Lough church. This involved writing out the names of deceased family and friends to be remembered and prayed for in the church services of All Souls' Day. Whatever of the list of our own family dead, I have a clear memory of the annual process of producing one for Nell. It was my father, the non-reading writer, rather than my mother, the non-writing reader, who wrote out the lists – though I was sometimes to be entrusted with part of the job. Nell's names, however, would be conveyed to my father via my mother, who would be requested/ordered by Nell herself to see to it that the list was prepared. I could, at this point, as I write this, apply myself to make out, from 'first principles' as it were, the names that must have been on our own list, year by year, but I have never forgotten the chief names on Nell's list and I remember here with reverence and with emotion the bearers of the names of Will and John and Kate Donovan who, along with Nell herself to an infinitely greater degree, are inscribed beyond erasure in my own oral-literate history.

BALLYMACTHOMAS

Fifty years after listening to fireside *seanchas* and reading stories of Robin Hood and the Arabian Nights in Croaghtamore I find myself in 1996 attempting, with my academic colleagues, to establish the Northside Folklore Project as a research enterprise of the emergent Department of Béaloideas/Folklore and Ethnology at University College Cork of the National University of Ireland. In the meantime my own life course has seen me take a primary degree in Irish and English at UCC and become a graduate student in an embryonic Department of Folklore at the University of Pennsylvania in Philadelphia under the guidance of Professor MacEdward Leach, a ballad scholar who was collecting oral traditions in the Avalon Valley in Nova Scotia. It was my very good fortune to be at Penn at the same time (1963/4) that Kenneth Goldstein was teaching folklore there along with MacEdward Leach and while another senior graduate student there was the Caribbean musicologist Jacob Elder. I had originally registered in the Penn graduate school English department intending to write a thesis concerned with the presence/influence of Irish-language vocabulary, phonetics and grammar in the nineteenth-century Anglo-Irish novel. MacEdward Leach encouraged me to take coursework in linguistics and anthropology and in this way captured me for folklore by bringing about the realisation on my part that a folklore informed by the perspectives and methodologies of these disciplines offered exciting and important potential for the study of Irish tradition. Propp, Chomsky and Dell Hymes, Anthony Wallace and Ward Goodenough together with Kenny Goldstein's *Guide for Fieldworkers in Folklore*[2] were on one floor of my formation just as – some years later when I pursued further postgraduate study in London at the Department of Anthropology at LSE – Raymond Firth, James Woodburn, Mary Douglas, Maurice Bloch, Edmund Leach and Ruth Finnegan were on another. My research interests as a consequence have covered a wide and perhaps somewhat eclectic range – the discursive analysis and interpretation of traditional narrative, the structural analysis of life-cycle ritual, a 'textual' approach to the study of traditional technology (the 'eloquence of tools') and a concern to bring an ethnographic quality to bear on the study of vernacular tradition in Ireland and on the history of that study.

My own fieldwork experience had consisted of two summers spent on solo community studies as part of the Irish anthropology field-training programmes of the University of Pittsburgh – one in *Corca Dhuibhne*, the other on the Beara peninsula. Now I was involved in a project of applied urban ethnography within Cork city aimed not only at identifying, representing, recording and interpreting the process and products of vernacular culture but of facilitating and guiding these activities to the greatest degree possible on the part of native, insider members of the local northside community among whom the work was being undertaken. We had settled on Ballymacthomas as a research site for a mixture of reasons, academic, logistical and fortuitous. As a placename, Ballymacthomas has something of a rural ring to it, but as a location it had seen several hundred years of town life during which its population, its housing stock, its economic history, its popular culture had been continuously transformed and reconstituted within a wider Cork northside context. As a site of vernacular cultural process it seemed to exist on some oral/literate cusp of the indigenous self-knowledge of Cork people – and even of some northsiders themselves. When asked where was Ballymacthomas some would say they had never heard of it while others would claim it as the place where they were born and reared.

We had a year of seminars in which we focused our research aims and eventually had some natives and children of natives of Ballymacthomas as co-participants to help us orient the initial fieldwork approaches. Walking the streets of the northside was one thing, engaging in cooperative collaboration with community groups and establishing rapport with 'gatekeepers' and likely informants and performers was another. We quickly discovered that there was a suspicion and even hostility on the part of many community leaders towards any study of the northside by academics from UCC. This, it transpired, was a consequence of many previous experiences by northside communities of having been 'studied' by students on various research projects. Considerable anger was expressed to us at a meeting we convened with representatives of all local groups we were able to contact, and we were conscious of how wary people were of this folklore project despite the collaborative and hopefully empowering terms in which it was presented. What dissolved this hostility and enabled us to move inside the arm's length at which we were initially held was our engagement in the discourse of Cork oral vernacular culture – partly that of the northside, following on our seminars with Ballymacthomas participants – and partly that of other streams of city cultural tradition of which some of us were native. Thus the bona fides of our academic and highly literate project was dependent on our ability to ground it in an oral realm and translate its expression into the language of vernacular speech.

As the project got going we developed a variety of training procedures aimed at introducing northside people into the mysteries of ethnographic fieldwork in their own community, and by far the most productive sessions I took part in involved using stories to illustrate whatever points of theory or methodology were at issue. In particular, 'confessional tales' of disaster and near-disaster in previous fieldwork on the part of the 'trainer', i.e. myself, were very effective at getting the point across and at eliciting spontaneous disclosure of similar experiences – and the fear of them – on the part of those undergoing induction. Such consciously 'oral narrative' externalisation of the various 'readings' assigned as part of the training sessions was an indispensable element, I believe, in the success achieved in equipping local people to undertake the work of ethnographic interviewing, something which was – and remains – a key objective of the Northside Folklore Project. While I do not for a minute suggest that any of us has a unique grasp of or insight into the orality/literacy dynamic of contemporary popular culture, I am nevertheless conscious of how aware I was of the rich oral soil out of which my own literacy grew as I engaged with the rich and creative orality of the northsiders who joined us in establishing the foundation for what is by now a going concern as a community research and archival resource recognised by the Heritage Council as a model for similar enterprises countrywide.

MODERN IRISH CULTURE

In one sense the importance of orality in modern Irish culture is beyond question given that all cultural process everywhere is the work of individuals who are speakers before they are writers, listeners before they are readers, and that in the case of even the most sophisticatedly literate of cultural productions and contexts, speech, i.e. oral language, is the origin and originating medium from which all text derives. As Walter Ong puts it so succinctly:

> In all the wonderful worlds that writing opens, the spoken word still resides and lives. Written texts all have to be related, somehow, directly or indirectly, to the world of sounds, the natural habitat of language, to yield their meanings ... Writing can never dispense with orality.[3]

If, today, it is seen as appropriate to treat all cultural process – qua discourse – as the construction and communication of 'text', then the primal presence of orality in Ong's sense can be seen to extend to all facets of Irish – and every other – culture. A methodology aiming at interpreting and analysing cultural texts, whether written or otherwise, that bases itself on an approach that has been successful in respect of oral, vernacular culture, can at least be said, I hope, to be starting from an appropriate place and to be setting out in the right direction.

My reading of the texts of mythological legends written down from the narration of oral performance has proceeded on the basis that the putative 'original' audience for such stories brought to the reception of the narrated version, on any one occasion, an acquaintance with multiple other versions and a body of indigenous knowledge regarding the characters, plots, motifs, symbols and stylistics of the performance, on the basis of which a judgement could be made as to the relative excellence of the particular narration in terms of its effectiveness as cultural communication. The effectiveness of any performance of an item of the mythological legend repertoire would, we can surmise, involve on the part of its listeners a mixture of entertainment, instruction and identity reinforcement at what we might regard as the public level of social community together with a potential for creative transformation and application at a private level of individual reflection. While the latter function – akin to the private reflection on a novel or a poem of the silent and separate reader of literature – is not easily accessed, the more public merits of oral narrative performance can be ascertained on the basis of an acquaintance with an adequately representative sample of other versions of the material in question and – thereby – an adequate acquaintance with the body of indigenous knowledge which the native audience brings to bear on the story and its performance.

In approaching texts in this fashion, one seeks to distinguish between three 'levels', as it were, on which the narrative operates – with such operation proceeding at different speeds, so to speak, in line with a Braudel-like perception of how history is to be envisaged as proceeding differentially on different planes. The tale of *Ana Ní Áine*, for instance, collected by Kenneth Jackson from the narration of Peig Sayers on the Great Blasket Island in 1936,[4] comprises a 'surface' layer of late-nineteenth-century, early-twentieth-century ethnographic reality reflective of the everyday world which any contemporary audience of such tales inhabited. Beyond, behind, beneath, within this 'surface' however there exist linages and symbols of an earlier, older, medieval ethnographic order whose significance as a set of cultural 'depth-charges' is never lost on the indigenous audience who perceive them as representations and markers of an enduring historical cultural dispensation to which they are themselves heirs and which they recognise as encompassing a core of identity – historical and cultural. The nineteenth-century merchant in Kenmare who is also the hereditary MacCarthy chieftain and the modern Catholic curate who is also the medieval *Seán Bráthair* monk are examples of such symbolic imagery in the Sayers tale. Beyond, outside, above both the ethnographic 'present' and the historic/symbolic 'past' of the story another layer of meaningfulness can be taken to be operating. This is a level that we may locate not 'farther back' in time but 'deeper down' in psychic space, in the individual consciousness and the unconscious of each listener to the tale and, indeed, each reader of any subsequent text that carries the tale into the domain of literacy. In the case of *Ana Ní Áine*, the figures of *Cailleach Bhéarra* and the Christus are, in my own reading of the story,[5] the unnamed, archetypal manifestations of this deepest, timeless layer of the story's significance. Overall, the narrative sophistication and cultural richness of a verbal performance such as Peig Sayers provided to Professor Jackson is the product of a combination of talent and personality on the part of the oral narrator and the familiarity and expectation of the native audience in regard to both the matter and the style of the oral presentation.

I can now recognise that my own approach to the study and interpretation of mythological legend has always proceeded from a perception of the necessity of a lively appreciation of the authority and authenticity of orality in any analysis of the textual notation of the story. It occurs to me that the foundation of this orientation was laid down long ago in the context of my reading of Robin Hood and the Arabian

Nights in the midst of the rich oral culture of Croaghtamore. Such an orientation is, I believe, to be found also in my attempts to elucidate the ethnographic, medieval (Christian/Celtic) and archetypal aspects of the life-cycle ritual of the merry wake in Irish tradition and the cultural 'eloquence' – instrumental and expressive – of the artefacts of traditional technology such as *ramhainn* (the long-handled, single-sided spade of Munster), *losaid* (the circular rimmed kneading-trough) and other features of vernacular material in the lifestyle of the *Ernhaus*. Given the scholarly understanding today of the ineluctably oral nature of all cultural text, I can only plead that the vernacular nature of my own interests and study has not been entirely misplaced.

Otherworld Harmonies and Heroic Utterance: The fruits of the literary act amongst us

[Talk given – in Irish – at the Merriman Winter School, Lisdoonvarna, County Clare on 1 February 1992. Published in *Comhar*, vol. 51, no. 5, May/*Bealtaine* 1992, pp. 94–9. The oral performance nature of the talk is readily evident in the style and structure of this unvarnished translation.]

If we are, this morning,[1] obliged to face into heavy-duty literary stuff at an early hour, let us realise that we do so on the morning of St Bridget's Day, that same Bridget who is the fecund matrix of craftsmanship in poetry and the arts; who is, for all time, both goddess and saintly patron of all Irish-language writers.

What I have to say is a contribution to your commemoration of the half-century of Irish-language writing that is to be found in the pages of the magazine *Comhar* since its foundation in 1942. That half-century, in terms of Irish writing in general, as the outside world understands it, stretches from the death of Joyce to the death of Beckett. We can also, of course, think of the names of Irish-language writers that can stand guard at the period's limits. I do not wish, however, to deal with individual authors, one by one, but to discuss culture and literature – especially Irish-language literature – in a more general way that pertains alike to both literary and oral narrative traditions.

In 1942, at the beginning of the period in question, there were many for whom Irish-language *writing* and Irish *language* literature were the same thing and such an identification is suggested on the face of the pamphlet

promoting the school itself, in so far as Seán Ó Tuama's *Nuabhéarsaíocht*[1]
and Tomás de Bhaldraithe's *Nuascéalaíocht*[2] are represented there as
standing for Irish-language writing. There was also the relatively common
notion that it was possible to opt consciously and deliberately for the
Irish language as the medium in which one would compose one's literary
output and that what was really needed so that worthwhile literature
would be produced in Irish was that sufficient verse and story narrative be
composed and published in Irish. This would guarantee, it was held, the
health of Irish-language literary production.

But there were others, even then, who understood that things were not
as straightforward as that, that no such certain trackways gave purchase
on and passage across the shakier expanses of artistic and intellectual life.
Among these others were, of course, the *Comhchaidreamh* intellectuals
who have the magazine *Comhar* and what has been published in it on
these matters as a lasting monument to themselves and to both their
courage and their high-mindedness during the dark days of world war.

Nor has there been any subsequent resolution, on either side, of the
difficulties of understanding and portraying the relationship of literature
and writing. My own approach to the issue begins from the simple,
perhaps childish, reality that is of fundamental importance nevertheless.
This is the reality that writing consists of physical signs, marks, *artefacts*,
made by hand, '*manufactured*' on clay tablet, on hide, on cloth, on paper.
Such marking, we must realise, has its origin in the trader's necessity to
keep accounts in the market place, to reckon bills and credit and debt,
and also in the earliest attempts by devotees of natural science to record
and keep track of the number and frequency of occurrence of celestial
movements, extremes of weather, landscape disasters and so forth. So that,
in a sense, writing, as physical marking for words, is a kind of secondary
development, posterior to early science and commerce. In so far as writing
is produced from letters, physical markings on paper, it might appear that
all writing is literature, or *letterature*, that is, made of letters. But the term
literature must be seen as having a considerably narrower scope for the
purpose of this school and this paper. Made of letters, yes, but not built on
the foundation of commerce or science but on the foundation of a creative
symbolism that renders physical marking eloquent of the imaginative
reaches of human life.

There is, of course, something of a paradox at the heart of this question
concerning the relationship to each other of writing and literature. If it
is the case that this thing called 'literature' amounts to less than the total

of everything written, nevertheless it amounts to more than just written forms of speech since we accept the existence of something called 'oral literature'. The term 'oral literature' in itself brings us up squarely against the paradox in question. Oral literature is speech, something that is not writing, but still it is literature, something that is ostensibly made of letters? Surely not! Rather is it the case that oral literature, while being speech, is perceived to possess a certain quality that we more frequently find associated with the domain of writing. In that domain itself, however, this literary quality is relatively rare in respect of the great oceans of writing, of all sorts, that surround us in our daily lives. Conversely, of course, we recognise that not everything spoken and heard is oral literature, in the same way that not everything in writing constitutes literature. Certain pieces of writing and certain pieces of speaking are, however, in all cultures, liable to be perceived as 'literature', as possessing that seemingly ineffable quality that the culture in question recognises and privileges in some way. The great question here is, of course, what that quality, that excellence, that special characteristic is, that causes peoples to attribute 'literary' status to certain pieces – be they writing or speech – rather than others. What is this *literaturnost*, this something that makes literature of writing and speaking or that has to be present in writing and in speech when we deal with 'literature'? This question has exercised the minds and taxed the brains of students of literature from Aristotle to Stanley Fish.

We can agree that it is certainly not its subject matter that renders a passage of writing or speech literature. Neither is it a question of style of writing or speaking, notwithstanding notions of *sublimitas* that have, traditionally, in the eyes (ears?) of some, been attached to the form as well as to the subject matter of literature. Despite powerful and acute efforts at analysis, modern linguistics has also failed to demonstrate that literary quality – as rendered in writing or speech – at the level of formal linguistic structure, phonetic, syntactic or other. No solution to the problem of saying what literary quality is, is ultimately available by means of any kind of inspection of the text itself or of the texture of the stretch of speech in question.

On another front, some contemporary literary theorists and some proponents of critical theory applied to politics try and maintain that the special recognition and privileging of 'literature' is always inadmissible on intellectual grounds – given the imperialist, the bourgeois and the monadic, individualist/capitalist ideology with which it is always freighted. In this view the question of the relationship of literature to writing is approached from a social rather than a textual perspective and its proponents arrive ultimately at the conclusion that the question itself is meaningless since what exists in reality is a succession of discourses giving expression to the competing scientific and economic and political forces in society that struggle for dominance, with no basis in any group or individual consciousness for proclaiming any one discourse to be 'literature'.

So, it appears that approaches to the question of what constitutes literature fail from both sides. The proponents of textual and textural analysis fail to resolve the issue as do, likewise, proponents of a social and political contextual analysis. Little wonder then that there is a sense today that the bottom has been knocked out of all traditions of literary canon and canon-making. Little wonder that there is endemic dispute and disagreement regarding the recognition of the boundaries of any field of literature or the identification of what should go in or what should stay out of any regional or national anthology of 'literature', as in the case, for example, of the three-volume *Field Day Anthology of Irish Writing*, and subsequent volumes of Irish women's writing.[4]

Also, at the practical level of writing and publishing, there has, for some time now, been a dissolving of traditional genres, so that one is no longer able to be sure, on theoretical grounds, that there are any real boundaries between, say, the novel and the short story or even between what constitutes prose and what constitutes poetry. In this event, one has to settle for speaking of 'passages of writing or speech' whatever formal structure or qualities or whatever genre-characteristics one may imagine them to possess.

And finally there are the poststructuralists – followers of Derrida – who deny that any passage of speech or writing can directly image any dimension or reality, any world or universe outside of itself as a quantum of language. Their position is based on the recognition that the linguistic sign, as signifier, has merely a conventional relationship to the meaning, the significance, it is taken to convey, so that we are all blind prisoners of language itself, inescapably enmeshed in its illusionary powers.

One could be led to believe, today, that writing is a dishonest, a worthless, even an insane pursuit; and especially that kind of creative writing that aims at reaching the level of 'literature'. As we celebrate a half-century of Irish-language writing in the pages of *Comhar* we are brought to ask, 'Is there any point to it at all?' From where can help be sought for those who – as writers and readers – are aware of the dilemma for literature and writing posed by much of the critical and scholarly thinking of the age?

For my part, I like to think that such help is available to us – as readers and writers – in the oral tradition of literature and literary performance; in the common comprehension, for example, of spoken linguistic and 'literary' excellence in the best passages of oral narrative that were once highly prized in Ireland's popular ancestral culture. It used to be a kind of shibboleth that modern, creative writing in Irish lay under some great compliment to Irish storytelling tradition and that those attempting to produce literature in the Irish language and the Ireland of today should draw freely from the well of traditional storytelling, its subject matter and outlook. While no one would be likely to take that stance today, I believe myself that the achievement of linguistic and literary excellence in traditional Irish storytelling should be seen in context, as a model for how individuals and communities of which these individuals are members can 'know' how to attain to that which they themselves regard as the plane of literature – by means of the operation of a system of spoken language signs within the overall communication patterns of their culture and their society.

The totality of culture is today best regarded as being comprised – within the paradigm of communication – of 'know-how' or *knowledge* shared: differentially among individuals and groups who make up a social entity; family, locality, region, country. We distinguish, colloquially, between different orders of such 'know-how', recognising: verbal (cognitive) knowledge – in our 'heads'; evaluative (affective) knowledge – in our 'hearts', and knowledge-in-action (operant) knowledge – in our behaviours, in our 'hands', our 'artefacts' and our 'manufactures'. Folklore – that is, unofficial, oral, cultural tradition – remains a fundamental and important element of such cultural totality of know-how, and, within folklore, oral narrative and its performance, whether as story or as song, continues as an important channel for the provision and recognition of oral literature by means of the use of words, of speech, of that excellence of articulation which is often marked out as possessing the quality of the literary.

Scholarly understanding of this heritage of oral tradition has undergone profound change since the middle years of the twentieth century. Over the last generation a new paradigm of understanding has established itself, involving a fundamental shift in the way in which scholars of tradition perceive their materials and objectives of study. The primary emphasis is no longer put on the glorious heritage of past cultural treasure, fixed in the keeping of the elders, but on the participatory processes whereby everyone plays a role in the social communication and creativity that characterises every group and sub-culture within society as a whole. Needless to say it is still possible to deal with a story or a song as a text on the page, but there is a deeper consciousness of the primary rhetorical nature of narration as a cultural phenomenon; of its linguistic nature as speech act. All text is, therefore, to be regarded as a record, a fragmentary record, of the words, the speech, the oral linguistic performance that underlies it, and all text is necessarily wanting as a representation of the linguistic behaviour-in-context that gives rise to oral literature in the views, the valuation and the ears of the local indigenous audience.

There is general awareness of the traditional 'sites' within Irish popular culture where storytelling 'happened', arose naturally, by itself, as an integral aspect of people's daily social intercourse. At such 'sites' – the winter hearth, the summer bog, the knitting bee, the wedding feast, the wake house, and so on – there was the regular expectation that the talk and the chatter of the assembled company would somehow develop towards an artistic or rhetorical discourse within which storytelling and singing of a standard judged excellent would occur in due course. The 'literary' plane would, step by step, be attained out of the midst of ordinary talk. During the pig fair in Dingle someone remarked to Tomás Ó Criomhthainn in the crowded public house as an elderly island woman opened up in song, '*Tá an ceol sí ar siúl*' ('The fairy music has begun').[5] A very interesting and plausible account of such growth of social communication towards the literary is given by Henry Glassie in the case of the ordinary life of one west Fermanagh community in the book *Passing the Time in Ballymenone*.[6] This account makes it clear, in terms of the community's own speech behaviour, how 'literature' can be understood as being essentially a form of linguistic communication. What underlies it is people's spoken interaction and it is this same spoken interaction that creates the literariness and the creative excellence and the inspiration that is adjudged to characterise certain speech. Close study of this account of Ballymenone speech and story is to be recommended, as is study of the preface Glassie has written to his anthology *Irish Folktales*.[7] We may note that this anthology – as is the case with every anthology of authentic oral literature – is untroubled by any of the editorial issues regarding canon and canon-making that were referred to earlier.

Glassie's analysis illustrates how, in Ballymenone's cultural communication system, *silence* and *speech* constitute a basic opposition. Anyone who fails to or chooses not to participate in common speech and speech patterns in the Ballymenone community runs the risk of being regarded as someone refusing participation in community life and in society itself. Such a person's capacity for human living seems called into question. Speech, in this case, is perceived as the sociable threshold of life itself. Across that threshold, within society, within the world of language use, there are different levels of social participation. An important cultural distinction operates in Ballymenone between the person who is likely to give only the short answer, the gruff response, 'Yes!' or 'No!' or 'Might!' or 'Maybe!' and the person who will engage in 'conversation', in response to a remark, to a question, to an opinion expressed and whose conversation will be marked by utterances that are measured, reflective and richly referential. In the storytelling assembly, the *airneán* or *céilí* or 'cooring' of Ballymenone, such 'conversation' is quickly established as the general communicative base from which the assembly advances linguistically to another, more intensive form of communication. This form, which flourishes in the initial stages of the storytelling assembly's activities, is known as 'crack' in the local parlance. 'Crack' in this usage has the nature of humour and wit and flyting or verbal 'besting' and when it has been in full swing for a while the people themselves report a further shift in the nature of the proceedings that raises it to a more intensive level again of communication. This shift is called the 'turn' and results in the production of what they call the 'bid', an original utterance that caps a phase of the speech, the crack, the conversation, and that is perceived as having a note of both elegance and authority going with it. The 'bid' remains in the mind of people present at the *airneán* and will be recalled on the next day and on the next occasion that an *airneán* assembles. ('Wasn't it well said by X last night', or 'Didn't X put it nicely when she said …'). The 'bid' is not a proverb or any other kind of ready-made speech formula. It is the creative, artistic response in speech to the vitality and intensity of communication of which it is itself an ornament and a temporary closure. Once 'bids' are coming into the *airneán* assembly in Ballymenone there is enough intensity and lift in the proceedings to allow, or indeed to require, a tale or yarn or song that clearly is and operates as 'literature' and that has the specially prized qualities of excellence and inspired delightfulness that are acknowledged as the qualities of literary linguistic performance. Spoken communication has, by now, achieved the plane of verbal art and, as such, verbal art always requires that sufficient uplift and intensity of speech be generated out of the company's social communication so as to stimulate the individual present who has sufficient ability and repertoire to produce the kind of linguistic performance that is recognisable to the outside observer as 'oral literature'.

The Ballymenone case is, I believe, highly instructive as to the nature of *literaturnost* for all who ponder the literary question, and who pursue its understanding in scholarship. I have spoken of intensity and upliftedness of speech as being required in the conversational basis from which literature is produced – Glassie's description makes clear what is involved here – but such intensity and upliftedness must not be equated with qualities of unevenness or roughness or wildness in the linguistic usage in question. This can be as smooth, even, simple and elegant or as rough, stressful and unbalanced as its 'author' wishes it to be for the purposes of the specific narrative which is intended, and, of course, in any one passage it may well be the case that alteration of style and effect is resorted to frequently. Whatever speech style is being used, however, that quality of intensification and upliftedness will be present if the passage is to be successful in achieving the literary plane in the minds and practice of the author/speaker and the reader/listener alike.

As far as *airneán* or traditional story assembly goes, we know now – thanks to the likes of Glassie – how the hard criteria of verbal art are satisfied. In the case of written literature, however, it is not at all as easily shown how it happens that this intensification of communication exists when the author and reader of the written passage are not necessarily located together in any kind of communicative assembly. And still I maintain that the question of literature will not arise in the case of any written passage unless there exists in the minds and in the linguistic performances of author and readers this kind of intensification and uplift.

Since author and reader are distant from each other – not only in terms of location but also in terms of time – it is, necessarily, in a way that is independent of each other that each engages in intensified communication and in the verbal art to which this may give rise. Consider the case of the creative writer at work. She attains to the level of art almost unknownst to herself, one may suppose, in the course of creating a text with no listening audience present to participate in the linguistic event, to respond to her, to encourage her, to sustain her. And yet she has to carry on composing words and hoping that they will be effective on the built-up or uplifted artistic level of linguistic communication in whose achievement the readers play a role that is equally important to that of the writer herself. In the reader's case, he, for his part, attains to this artistic quality of communication in some fashion that includes giving total attention to a text in expectation of having his consciousness shifted from the ordinary plane of daily life to some plane where more lasting kinds of truth and delight appear to be available.

This is not a clearly understood business, is even a slightly mysterious one, but it works for creative writing as surely as it does for verbal art in oral literature – something that we can understand, in terms of Glassie's account, as having the nature of a social as well as a cultural process. And at the heart of that nature and that process, in the cases of creative writing and oral narrative alike, is the reality that 'literature' is always artistic speech, artistic linguistic articulations and recording and reception; artistic verbal communication – whether seen or heard. This point bears emphasising.

Literature is *spoken language* whether it is fashioned from the raw materials of speech phonetics or the artefactual hieroglyphic materials of writing. The fundamental characteristics of 'literature' are thus rhetorical and poetical and these characteristics are what is recognised as belonging to the text or the narrative that is adjudged artistic, whether it is as 'prose' or as 'verse' that such a text is categorised in traditional terms. The 'speech act' is always at the heart of the production of literature, even though it is not always literature, spoken discourse which has the qualities of literature, that results from every speech act. And, for certain, it is not the *subject matter* of the speaker or writer that determines whether or not literature is in question. Every subject matter under the sun is available to literary discourse. It so happens that it is not the text or the spoken discourse itself, *per ipse*, that is the location of *literaturnost*, of literary quality. Rather is it located, on one hand, in the context of the audience and the readership who receive and register the result of the speech act and, on another, in the context of the excellence of performance, in rhetorical terms, of the speaking on the part of the writer or narrator. In this fashion we can acknowledge that literature is not a stable, permanent fixture but rather an occasional phenomenon potentially present during the listening of an audience in the case of oral literature and during the reading activity of individuals in the case of written literature.

We can observe how it is not necessarily the case that 'literature' is *there* – or 'happens' – for every listener/reader at the same time, since it is always, when/where it happens, the result of a dynamic, subjective, personal inter-relation between a stimulus of symbolic enactment and a response of individual consciousness. Such inter-relation and that to which it gives rise can never be mechanical or predictable. Instead, it inevitably has the nature of being a gift, a grace, for whose capacity to delight, to enthral, to inspire, to intensify, to transcend, we must simply be grateful. That intensification and that gratitude together constitute the fruits of the literary act amongst us.

With such emphasis on the living, discursive, artistic nature of literature, it follows that it is not in the 'text' itself, nor in the book on the shelf, that literature exists – any more than it exists in the manuscripts of the folklore archive or in *Leabhar Sheáin Í Chonaill*.[8] As physical signs these are pointers to and images of artistic linguistic communication; of literary discourse itself. If we wish to pass judgement on the corpus of Irish-language writing published since 1942, the fundamental question to ask is, 'Did it work? Did it give rise to the intensification, the inspiration, the delight that we call the literary?' The answer is, 'Yes, it did, portions of it, at different times and for different people; individual pieces of writing, whether long or short, whether oral or written.'

I imagine the creative writer undertaking her or his task, the task/risk of performing in the hope of striking it right, of getting on that writerly, storyteller, literary wavelength because of an urge to communicate in ways that go beyond talk or conversation or even wit. How the creative writer manages to do this successfully in the absence of an immediate audience to provide stimulation and encouragement must – to those of us non-writers – remain something of a mystery and a source of envy. But I'd like to think that there is the matter of mystery too in the performance of every *reader* and in the result that the reader achieves. I say this because I think that even at a distance from the writer the reader is able to respond with an equal intensity and creativity to the storyteller's performance just as the fireside audience responded to the traditional *raconteur* of the *Märchen* or the hero-tale.

Even if we are unclear as to how this happens, I am sure that we can all vouch for its reality – the reality of the pleasure and the power of the literary experience. The crucial thing I am claiming for this phenomenon is that it is essentially linguistic in nature and that literature is essentially a 'spoken art' whether it is constructed from the phonetic units and the syllables of speech or from the marks on paper that fill the pages of the book. The quality of *literatornost*, of 'literariness', of that which makes 'literature' of a piece of talk or a piece of writing, is a rhetorical or a poetic (formally and imaginatively intense) quality that is present in the communication between teller and told of which the story is the vehicle.

The communicative speech event is what always underlies the production of literature whatever the subject matter of the communication. If the linguistic fibres of that communication have those qualities of intensity, of creativity, of imaginative power, the 'literature' *happens*.

Portions of that writing in Irish since 1942 therefore 'speak' as literature to various people at various times and not necessarily to the same people in the same situations more than once. Similarly, portions of Irish-language writing from other eras 'speak' as literature in a similarly occasional and individual fashion according as individual readers occasionally engage with it as writing in ways that allow its capacity as artistic communication to be activated. Irish-language literary discourse – Irish-language 'literature' – is just such a process of artistic communication whereby authors and readers speak with each other on the field of consciousness, even if widely separated in time and space. Such literary discourse has existed in Irish for as long as the language has been cultivated as a storytelling medium and, as such, it is being borne forward today as a distinctive universe of discourse through the activities – literary speech activities – of the Irish-language writers of today *and* the activities of the readers who respond to them – in fragment and on occasion – at that level of communicative intensity at which we recognise that 'literature' occurs.

From the earliest times right down to today, there have been two notes, two voices, two modalities to be discerned in Irish-language literary discourse: otherworld harmonies, *an ceol sí*, and heroic utterance, *friotal na laoch*. Of course, no literary discourse in the world is so isolated in itself as not to be related to, or not to be a local version of, a more generalised human discourse and the claim is not made here that it is in Irish-language literary discourse only that these two modalities of otherworld harmonies and heroic utterance are to be found. What is most likely is that they are Irish versions of universal human modalities – just as we recognise the *sean-scéal*, wonder tale, and the *scéal gaisce*, hero tale, of Irish oral narrative tradition as local reflexes of the European and indeed the global repertoire of narrative. Nevertheless, I believe it is a proper, even a necessary, thing for writers in Irish today – who live in a world dominated to a very high degree by English-language writing and English discourse – to pay attention to the ancestral or elder modalities of Ireland.

One thinks of three reasons for saying this. First, as modalities, they involved the literary cultivation of the field to which in some sense the Irish-language writers themselves belong. It is the case that it has been in these modalities that 'literature' has been first and most easily achieved historically in Ireland. They offer the initial orientation towards verbal fulfilment and delight within native culture however much the individual writer intends to diverge, ultimately, from native or ancestral visions or values or practice. Second, the cultivation of these modalities offers the writer the opportunity of sustaining a sense of literary and cultural identity – should any one of them care to do so. Third, these modalities are fundamental in themselves. In Irish cultural tradition the psychic and symbolic potentials of the archetypal otherworld female and the archetypal hero remain of considerable significance to the interpretation of the everyday life experience of all audience and all readers.

However, if we *can* discern with some clarity these two notes, two modalities, in traditional literary discourse, the same cannot be assumed to be true in relation to contemporary creative writing/literature. One thing is clear enough – that it is not only men who write in the modality of the heroic utterance and not only women who write in the modality of the otherworld harmonies. Literary modality operates at a higher level of imagination and representation than the categorical principles of sex and gender, and contemporary creative writers in general try to escape from the gender biases that mark the history of both oral and written literature.

Hero tales – for instance the stories of the Fianna cycle – are what best exemplify heroic utterance in tradition. But of course there are female heroes known to tradition also, especially if we understand that the kind of heroism that is in question in this modality is ultimately the heroism that delivers to the individual ego the victory of winning through on the stage of social life. This is the category of story, of narrative, of literary discourse in which we can all, women and men, engage, in terms of speech or writing: 'My personal journey to identity and self-realisation' or 'How I grew up and took my place in the world' – whatever kind of place the latter proved to be. In the age in which we live, people are frequently counselled and encouraged to tell and to write this story about themselves as a form of therapy wherein they may be victorious over, or at least engage productively with, psychological and mythological monsters from within the life of their affections. Another kind of consequence, of course, can result from such self-narration: a consequence of delight and literary inspiration, when the narrator – speaker or writer – is a narrator of excellence, a craftsman or woman of speech who goes creatively about the business of telling the story. With this creative excellence may go a tendency for the tale to become a work of the purest fiction, but yet one that can capture the heart and soul of the reader as a 'true' account of a heroic adventure with which we can all identify.

As essential elements of the account of the hero's victory, we frequently find humour and irony and playfulness. These are not the first qualities to come to mind in any attempt to characterise examples and expressions of the second modality in question here – the modality of the otherworld harmonies. Here again, it is possible to say, in a fairly straightforward way, what was involved under this heading in traditional literary discourse: supernatural legend, the performance of the keening woman, the feminine, prophetic nature of poetic composition. There is a journeying here too but it involves going outside ourselves, outside human society to a dimension where mysterious cosmic powers hold sway over human lives and radically impinge on human society. It is not human victory or control or winning through that is revealed in this modality but a yielding to, an acknowledgement and a reinforcement of, the sense of the mysteriousness of life in its rhythmic dynamic, its mythic range, its majestic awfulness – a sense of mysteriousness that we are able to taste in those moments of ritual intensity when these second kinds of verbal art transmute for us into 'literature'.

In my reckoning, both of these modalities, heroic utterance and otherworld harmonies, are intertwined in each other throughout the course of that ancestral culture out of which Irish-language narrative and Irish-language writing speak. Even outside of its literary discourse, they are to be found together, side by side, in popular cultural tradition – in the 'wake', for instance – where the play-acting of the heroes, the 'hardy boys', is mingled with the otherworld harmonies of the keen, *caoineadh*. Within that discourse they are to be found mingled together in the works of the conscious, literary canon, as in the works of the oral storytellers. This is true as regards *Táin Bó Cuailnge* and as regards *Cré na Cille*. It is probably also true, I believe, in respect of the works of James Joyce and Samuel Beckett. It is certainly appropriate to recognise this characteristic blend of modalities in the written literary offerings in *Comhar* for the past half-century. In so far as we are able to do this, then we are ourselves, readers and writers of the Irish language, still on the Irish literary rails. Let us wish for a long, heroic and harmonious journey.

CHAPTER 10

An Bhean Mhíreáireach: An ethnopoetic analysis of a folklore text

[Published in *Béaloideas*, vol. 85, 2017, pp. 18–61]

In *Linguistics and Literature*, Nigel Fabb presents a narrative analysis of 'Ashey Pelt', a version of the Cinderella folktale told by 'a native of Ulster aged about sixty' and first published in 1895.[1] It is included by Katherine Briggs in her *Dictionary of British Folktales in the English Language*.[2] What follows below is an exercise in applying a similar narrative analysis to another folktale – one told in Irish by a native of Munster aged about seventy. It was first published in 1948 in *Leabhar Sheáin Í Chonaill*, the anthology of stories and traditions from Iveragh collected between 1923 and 1931 by Séamus Ó Duilearga, who was then in his twenties.[3] It is a version of the folktale known as ATU 901 'The Taming of the Shrew' told to Ó Duilearga by Seán Ó Conaill on 28 August 1927.

The kind of narrative analysis attempted here derives from ethnopoetics, a concern with the formal character of the performances of verbal art. Originating in the formalism of Propp[4] and Jakobson[5] in the 1920s, ethnopoetics has been developed in the work of scholars such as Tedlock[6] and Hymes[7] into a methodology that aims to represent and analyse traditional narrative performance in a fashion that does justice to the rhetorical and organisational skills of the storyteller who 'acts' a story for an audience who co-participate with the performer in realising the poetic effect of the performance.

Henry Glassie, in the Notes to *Ballymenone: Folklore and history of an Ulster community*, outlines briefly the development of the ethnopoetic perspective that informs his own research on English-language narratives and narration in County Fermanagh.[8] Ray Cashman also brings the ethnopoetic perspective to bear, tellingly, on the County Tyrone English-language narratives he studies in his *Storytelling on the Northern Irish Border*, and in his recently published second book, *Packy Jim: Folklore and worldview on the Irish border*, he also draws on ethnopoetics to deal with the narrative construction of worldview in the stories and storytelling of an individual Donegal English speaker from whom he has collected extensively.[9]

Such an ethnopoetic perspective on verbal performance can be encountered in recent criticism and commentary on the works of writers of prose literature. Jonathan Galassi, a translator of Primo Levi's poetry, speaks of John Updike's prose as being 'often hypnotically propulsive'.[10] It drives the reader forward, he says,

> with a vigour enriched by sonic patterns, layered, elaborately balanced metaphoric structures and a ceaseless flowing-ebbing-flowing rhythmic force. William Maxwell, Updike's adoring NEW YORKER editor, felt that his 1958 story 'The Alligators' 'read like one long poem'.[11]

John McGahern has recently been described by van der Ziel as 'a poet who worked in prose'. Van der Ziel also refers to articles on McGahern's work that draw attention to his use of such poetic devices as repetition and the chiasmic construction 'favoured by many classical poets'. Van der Ziel further asserts:

> McGahern had always been interested in the idea of 'rhythm'. That concept extended, in his usage, beyond that of the sounds of individual words or syllables within a sentence or a paragraph to include the repetition of images, words and phrases (even sometimes of whole conversations …), a concept which he compared to refrains in verse.[12]

A basic tenet of the ethnopoetic perspective on traditional narrative is to challenge a long-held assumption that such narrative consists – in written reproduction – of prose paragraphs. Instead, ethnopoetics holds the view that traditional narrative consists of lines or longer units of speech that proceed, like a musical composition, according to patterns and repetitions of verbal articulations that both underlie and give expression to the surface content of the story. Such units of the story and such patterns and repetitions of its narrative performance are marked by phonetic and grammatical features that can be missed in the written or printed representation of the story as paragraphs of prose. The text presented here from the narration of Seán Ó Conaill is set down in terms of a macro-structure of six episodes: 'Abstraction', 'Orientation', 'Complication', 'Evaluation', 'Resolution' and 'Coda'.[13] These episodes contain some fifty-two sections (or stanza-like units) of narrative speech, reproduced here in the orthography and spelling that Ó Duilearga chose to represent the narrator's verbal performance and that – in the absence of any phonographic recording – constitute the nearest we can approach to capturing the features of that performance.

Many other versions of this tale exist in the record of traditional Irish narrative including a version recorded from the celebrated west Cork storyteller Amhlaoibh Ó Luínse in 1943/4 by Seán Ó Cróinín[14] and a version recorded from Peig Sayers in the Great Blasket Island by Kenneth Jackson in the mid-1930s.[15] Such versions differ as to many of the details of the marriage arrangements, the exemplary killing of various creatures, the arranging of the testing of the wives and the final framing device which brings the narration of the story to a close. The narrative and rhetorical qualities of the various versions differ too, needless to say, in accordance with the specific performances delivered on the occasion of their narration, while the narrative context of every version is, of course, different also. The Ó Conaill text is treated here without reference to other versions as the unique product of the unique narrative performance recorded by Ó Duilearga in a particular social context on a particular occasion.

Following the text, a commentary is offered on the way the story proceeds – by means of linguistic markers of various kinds – to transition across section and episode boundaries from an initial framing device to a final one. Reference is made to only the most salient markers of transition that feature in this written representation of the narrator's performance. These markers are, for the most part, grammatical and no attempt is made to identify or deal with the equally essential markers of an articulatory and phonetic nature – such as intonation, tempo, volume – on which the written representation of the narrative performance is necessarily silent.

The commentary also offers, in places, a partial exegesis or interpretation of aspects of the story as it proceeds through the sections of the macro-structure. Such interpretative reading is given, where it is, as justification of the rhetorical features noted and pertains only to a subjective understanding by the present author of the semantic and cultural reception likely to have been afforded various sections of the narration by its actual – and potential – audience in Seán Ó Conaill's kitchen in Cill Rialaigh in August 1927.

Following the commentary, an attempt is made to outline some of the patterning and repetitions, the poetic parallelism by means of which the story proceeds through its sections. It must be borne in mind that the text here derives from the virtual dictation of the story by Ó Conaill to Ó Duilearga, who sat with pen and paper at the table in Ó Conaill's kitchen – a situation that would seem likely to have impeded and inhibited any narrator's verbal performance. That this difficulty was overcome to the degree that the attempt at performance analysis below suggests is a tribute to the very considerable narrative competence and sophistication of the storyteller and the scholarly diligence of the collector. If storytelling tradition was no longer such a vibrant or prominent feature of Iveragh community life when Ó Duilearga began his work there and if the speaking of Irish as the community language was declining, nevertheless Seán Ó Conaill had the reputation and status of being an exceptional storyteller in his own district in addition to being an extremely fluent Irish speaker. He appeared to Ó Duilearga to be anxious to have his repertoire of traditional narrative preserved in written form and to cooperate fully in the work of transcribing the stories.

In a 'Translator's Note' to her English-language version of the stories and traditions from Iveragh that Séamus Ó Duilearga published in 1948 as *Leabhar Sheáin Í Chonaill*, Máire Ní Néill quotes Ó Duilearga's opinion of Ó Conaill as a fine, incisive speaker of Irish, capable of wielding language as he wished.[16] She herself adds that Ó Conaill's command of his native dialect

> ... was enhanced by his devotion to the storytelling tradition of a former generation and also by his interest in the old printed books and contemporary Irish journals which he loved to have read to him and the contents of which, thanks to his superb memory, he adopted at will into his own repertoire. His narrative craft, however, was very much his own, and shows his personality in its vigour and idiomatic speech, couched sometimes in staccato sentences, sometimes in more fluent rhythms.[17]

Ó Duilearga, in his foreword, had stated that, with the exception of one short anecdote, all the items in the book were written down by hand and that Ó Conaill used to speak 'gently, slowly and evenly when he was telling a story' and that 'it was easy to write what he said, for, as he was reciting … he used to watch the pen in my hand and give me plenty of time'[18] (Ní Néill trans.). We also know from Ó Duilearga that such collecting sessions in the kitchen of Ó Conaill's house would frequently have an audience present of some half-dozen or more of Ó Conaill's neighbours who appreciated his narrative talent. Accepting such displays of narrative talent in such situations as traditional verbal art performance, we can approach representations of them – the text of an Ó Conaill story, for example – with a view to identifying the ethnopoetic qualities such a text displays. This is what is attempted here in respect of the story with the title 'An Bhean Mhíreáireach' told by Ó Conaill on 28 August 1927 and printed by Ó Duilearga.

The story is laid out below ignoring the paragraph divisions of the printed text. It is, instead, set down as a series of numbered sections that proceed from an initial framing device that presents an abstract of the setting and the agencies from which the story unfolds, through a succession of episodes that end in a coda that constitutes a final framing device. As in the case of a musical composition, the episodes of the story are not merely linear in occurrence but are woven together into a layered narrative performance that combines different levels of verbal articulation – phonetic, grammatical and semantic – into an artistic whole.

Sections are the fundamental narrative units of the storyteller's performance and are identified in terms of linguistic/rhetorical features that can be regarded as marking section boundaries in the variety of ways that are treated of in the commentary that follows.

The macrostructure of the text consists of a combination of the sections into a number of episodes:

<u>Abstract Episode</u> Section that contains a beginning framing device and that isolates and represents to the audience the initial settings and agencies on which the story turns.

Section 1
<u>Orientation Episode</u> Sections threaded through the storyline that characterise and enlarge on elements of the storyline without adding to its action or changing overall direction. Since these sections of *orientation*

are in non-contiguous distribution within the *complication* and *resolution* episodes they cannot themselves constitute a discrete 'episode' in the usual sense of the term. They are, nevertheless, best regarded as constituting an independent element of the episodic macrostructure of the text.

Complication Episode Sections that carry forward the storyline towards its crux and its resolution.

Evaluation Episode Section that represents narrator's perception of the crux of the storyline and the calling of the audience's attention to this by means of a shift or disruption in narrative technique – for example, use of shift to historic present tense in the case of the story Fabb analyses, or the distortion of syntactic pattern in the Ó Conaill story here.

Section 28
Resolution Episode Sections carrying forward the sequence of events from the crux of the storyline.

Coda Episode Section that rounds off the story and constitutes the end framing device.

Section 52
The Text

Abstract
1 *Bhí feirimeoir gustalach ann fadó go raibh triúr iníon aige.*
   (Long ago there was a wealthy farmer who had three daughters.)

Orientation
2 *Bhíodar ina gcailíní matha, suais le n-a chéile, ag obair is a' gnó dóip fhéin is dá n-athair. Bhí an té ba shin' acu – bhí sí an-mhíreáireach, agus ní bh fhéidir aon cheart a bhuint di.*
   (They were fine girls working together for themselves and for their father. The eldest of them was very shrewish, and it was impossible to get the better of her.)

Complication
3 *Nuair a bhíodar éirithe suas ina gcailíní óga, bhí an t-athair a' déanamh cleamhnais don cheann críona, ach ní tógfí bhuaig í ó chuaig an ainm mhíreáireach so amach uirthi.*
   (When they had grown up to be young women, the father tried to make a match for the eldest one, but she would not be taken from him because of the shrewish name that had gone out about her.)

4 *Seadh, dhin sé cleamhnas ansan don tarna ceann, agus do phós sé í, agus do thug sé sprae mhaith dhi.*

(Well, then he made a match for the second one, and gave her in marriage with a good dowry.)

5 *Tamall ina dhiaidh sin ansan, do phós sé an ceann óg, agus chuir sé in áit mhaith í, agus thug sé sprae mhaith dhi.*

(A while after that he gave the youngest one in marriage into a good place and gave her a good dowry.)

Orientation

6 *D'fhan a' ceann críon' aige sa tigh i gconai; agus do bhí sprae mhuar mhaith le fail aici dá bhfaghfaí éinne a thógfadh í. Do chuala buachaill éigint í bheith ann agus go raibh mórán airgid le fail aici agus do bhí fhios aige í bheith míreáireach chomh maith le héinne eile.*

(The eldest one stayed at home, and she was to get a good big dowry if anyone would take her. A certain young man heard of her and of the money she was to get and, like everyone else, he knew she was a shrew.)

Complication

7 *Tháini' sé fé n-a déin, lá agus duairt sé lé n-a hathair gu'b' shin é thug é a' déanamh cleamhnais leis a gcailín sin a bhí aige.*

(He came for her one day, and said to her father that what had brought him there was to make a match with this girl of his.)

8 *'Tá sí sin ann,' aduairt a' t-athair leis, 'má thógann tú í, agus rud maith le fáil aici,' aduairt sé, 'agus ní bheadh suí ann romhat in ao'chor dá bhfaghfí éinn'eile dhi, mar tá sí míreáireach, agus tá sí 'n-a gnóthadóir mhath, chomh math le héinne, ach i dtaobh a míreáirí ní thógfadh éinne í. Din-se do rogha rud anois,' aduairt sé, 'tá sí le fail agat, más math leat í thógaint. Sin iad na lochtaí anois innst' agat. Tóg í, nú fág it 'iaig í.*

('She is there for you if you'll take her,' said the father to him, 'and she is to have plenty,' said he, 'and she would not be here for you at all if anyone else could be found for her, but she is shrewish; she is a good worker, as good as anyone could be, but because of her shrewishness no one would take her. Do what you wish,' said he, 'you may have her if you like. I have told you the faults. Take her or leave her!')

9 *Duairt a' buachaill go dtógfadh, nárbh aon locht leis é sin inti on uair go raibh sí go math chun ga'h ní eil' a dhéanamh. Duarthas leis go raibh. Fuair sé sparán airgid léi ansan agus pósach iad. Bhí capall maith ag an ógánach agus iallait, agus d'imíodar leo ansan a' teacht abhaile.*

(The young man said he would take her, that he thought that no fault in her since she was so good at everything else. He was assured she was. He got a purse of money with her then, and they were married. The young man had a good horse and saddle, and they set off on their way home.)

10 *Phreab sé ar a chapall, agus í seo ar a chúlaibh.*

(He leaped on the horse, and she rode pillion behind him.)

Orientation

11 *Duairt sé leis a' mnaoi, agus iad ag cur díobh, ná raibh aon ainmhí ba mheasa leis ná an capall, agus cú a bhí aige, agus cráin mhuice – gu'b iad na trí nithe ba mheasa leis a bhí aige.*

(On the way he said to the wife that the animals he valued most were this horse, and a hound he had, and a sow – these were the three things he valued most of all that he had.)

Complication

12 *A' teacht abhaile, ní hé an bóthar ceart a ghuibh sé, ach seana-bhóthar, agus do bhí geat' iarainn árd roimis ar a' mbóthar san. Thug sé aghaig a chapuill ar a' ngeata chun do léimfeadh sí é.*

(He did not go home by the right road but by the old road, and there was a high iron gate across that road. He set the horse towards the gate to jump over it.)

13 *Ach d'úmpaig sí ar leataoibh bhuaig mar ná féadfadh suí é léim[e]; bhí sé ro-árd di. Nuair nár léim sí an geata, do tháinig sé anuais di, tharraig a phiostal as a phóca, agus do lá'ch í, bhain di an srian is an iallait, agus d'fhág ansan í.*

(But she turned aside from it because she could not jump it; it was too high for her. Since she did not jump over the gate he dismounted, pulled a pistol out of his pocket, and shot her, took off the reins and the saddle and left her there.)

14 *'Sin mar a dhinim-se le haon ní ná dineann rud oram!'*

('That is how I treat anything that does not obey me!')

15 *Chuir sé an iallait is a' srian ar a dhrom, agus ghluaisíodar rompa, agus chuadar go dtí an tig.*
(He put the saddle and reins on his back, and they continued on their way and went to his house.)

16 *Bhíothas go fáiltheach rómpa nuair a thánadar – a athair is a mháthair.*
(There was a welcome for them when they arrived from his father and mother.)

Orientation

17 *Amáireach ansan, bhí an bhean so go maith chun a gnótha dhéanamh, comh maith le héinne.*
(Next day this woman did her work well, as well as anyone could.)

Complication

18 *Ach lá eile 'n-a dhia san ghuibh sé féin is a bhean amach a' máirseáil sa bhfeirm, agus a' chú so acu. Ch'nuic sé bó a' teacht isteach thar claí insa talamh agus duairt sé leis a' gcú imeacht agus a' bhó san a chuir amach. Ach ní' dhein a' chú rud air, mar ná raibh aon taithí aici ar aon ní dá shaghas nuair ná ficfeadh suí giorria ná mada rua.*
(But another day after that, he and his wife went out to walk the farm, and this hound was with them. He saw a cow coming in across a wall onto his land, and he told the hound to go and put the cow out; but the hound did not obey him, as she had no experience of such a thing unless she saw a hare or a fox.)

19 *Ní dhin sé ach a phiostal a tharrac amach agus a' chú a lá'cha.*
(What did he do but pull out his pistol and shoot the hound.)

20 *Sin é mar a dhinimse les ga' h aon ní ná déanfadh rud orm.*
('That is how I treat anything that would not obey me!')

Orientation

21 *Tháinig dhá shúil don mhnaoi agus eagal' a dóthain uirthi, a' capall a mharú roimis sin, agus a' chú a mharú anois.*
(The wife's eyes dilated with fear at his killing the hound now, having already killed the horse.)

Complication

22 *Ghluaisíodar leó ansan, agus do thángadar abhaile.*
(They continued on their way and came home.)

Orientation

23 *Ní duairt a' bhean aon fhocal ach teacht abhaile; agus ní misde a rá ná*
    go raibh sí 'na seirivíseach mhath, ábalta ar ga'h aon ní a dhéanamh go
    gcuirfeadh suí a lámh ann.
    (His wife did not speak a word on the way: and it may be said that she
    was a good servant, able to do anything to which she put her hand.)

Complication

24 *Tamall eile 'n-a dhiaidh sin ansan, bhí cráin mhuice 'ge, agus do chua sí*
    isteach sa gharaí, agus duairt sé léi gabháil amach as san, agus ní ghuibh.
    (He had a sow which went into his garden some time after that, and
    he said to her to get out of that, and she did not go.)

25 *Níor dhein sé aon ní ach a lámh a chur i n-a phóca agus a phiostal a*
    tharrac amach, agus í lá'cha;
    (What did he do but put his hand in his pocket and pull out his
    pistol and shoot her,)

Orientation

26 *agus do bhí an bhean a' féachaint air.*
    (while his wife was watching him.)

Complication

27 *'Sin é mar a dhinim-se,' ar seisean, 'leis ga'h aon ní ná déanfadh rud orm'.*
    ('That is how I treat anything that would not obey me!')

Evaluation

28 *Ní duairt a bhean focal ach teacht abhaile agus aire thúirt dá gnó. Bhí sí*
    'n-a cailín grástúil, comh macánta agus do chua sí isteach go tig riamh.
    (The wife said nothing, but came home and attended to her work.
    She was a gracious girl, as gentle as ever went into a house.)

Resolution

29 *Tamall i'n-a dhia san, cheap athair a chéile dínnéar a bheith aige féinig*
    agus ag an dtriúr cleamhnaithe a bhí aige, agus do chuir sé scéala chúha
    teacht a' trial air an lá san áirithe.
    (Some time afterwards his wife's father thought of having a dinner
    for himself and his three sons-in-law, and he sent word to them to
    come on a certain day.)

30 *Do thánadar, agus do bhí dínnéar math aca, bia 'guis deoch a ndóthain aca; agus a' caint is ag eachtraí dá chéile.*

(They came, and they had a good dinner, plenty to eat and drink; and they were talking and yarning together.)

31 *Chuaig a' triúr driféar ansan go seómara leo féin, agus gan éinn' eile eatortha, agus do luíodar ar bheith ag imirt chártaí.*

(Then the three sisters went into a room by themselves and began to play cards.)

Orientation

32 *Bhí an triúr cleamhnaithí sa chistin agus fear a' tí, agus iad a' caint is a' comhrá, ag innsint scéaltha dá chéile.*

(The three sons-in-law were in the kitchen with the man of the house, talking and conversing and telling stories to each other.)

33 *Ach do bhí úna mhuar ar a' gcuid eil' aca í seo mar bhean, agus an ainm a bhí uirthi roimis sin, í bheith chomh maith, chomh mánla agus do bhí sí.*

(And the others were so surprised at this woman being so good and gentle, considering the name she had before.)

34 *As sain do tháinig sé anuas eatartha ceoc' aca aba cheanúla agus b'ómúsaí go raibh a bhean air.*

(From that it led on to which of them had the most affectionate and respectful wife.)

Resolution

35 *Duairt a' cliain déanach leo go gcuirfeadh sae féin céad punt gill leo go raibh a bhean féin níos ómúsaí air féin ná bhí mná na beirt' eile. Chuireadar féin síos ansan céad an duine ar an mbord.*

(The latest son-in-law said he would bet a hundred pounds that his wife was more respectful than the wives of the other two. Each of them put a hundred pounds on the table.)

36 *'Conus a bhe' fhios againn anois é?' aduairt a' chéad duine. 'Be' fhios againn é,' aduairt a' cliain déanach.*

('How shall we know it now?' said the first man. 'We shall know it,' said the latest son-in-law.)

37 *'Anois,' ar seisean, 'nuair a bheig na cártaí gearrth' amach aca, agus na cúig chárta i láimh na'h éinn' aca agus ceann aca imearth' aca leis, glaodhadh a' chéad fhear ar a mhnaoi.'*

('Now,' said he, 'when they have the cards dealt out, and each of them
has her five cards in her hand, and has played the first card, let the
first man call his wife.')

Orientation

38 *Do bhíodar a' fair' orthu ansa go dí go raibh na cártaí aca 'n-a láimh agus
    iad á n-imirt.*
    (They watched them until they had the cards in their hands, and
    were playing them.)

Resolution

39 *Ghlaodhaig a' chéad duine ansan ar a bhean. D'fhreagair sí é agus duairt
    sí go mbeadh suí chuig' anois á mbeadh na cártaí seo imearth' aici. Nuair a
    bhíodar imearth' aici, phreab sí 'n-a suí agus tháini' sí aníos a' trial air.*
    (Then the first man called his wife. She answered him, and said she
    would be with him when she had played these cards. When she had
    played them, she jumped up and came to him.)

40 *'Cad dob áil leat díom?' aduairt sí. 'Téighre síos mar a rabhais!' ar seisean
    léi.*
    ('What do you want of me?' said she. 'Go back where you were!' said
    he to her.)

41 *Seadh, nuair a suathach na cártaí arís, agus nuair a gearrach amach ar a'
    mbord iad, bheir ga'h éinn' aca ar a cuid féin;*
    (Well, when the cards had been shuffled again and dealt out on the
    table, each of them took up her hand,)

Orientation

42 *agus do bhí na fir a' faire orthu i gcónaí.*
    (and the men were watching them all the time.)

Resolution

43 *Bhí ceann aca imearth' ansan aca nuair a ghlaodhaig a' tarna fear ar a
    bhean.*
    (One card had been played when the second man called his wife.)

44 *'Bead chút anois nuair a bheig na cártaí seo imearth' agam!' ar sise. Seadh,
    nuair a bhí, d'éiri' sí 'n-a suí agus chua' sí ag triall air.*
    ('I will be with you now when I have played these cards!' said she.
    Well, when she had played them, she stood up and went to him.)

45 *'Cad dob áil leat díom?' aduairt sí. 'Imig ort arís mar a rabhais!'*
aduairt sé.
('What do you want of me?' said she. 'Go off back to where you were!'
said he.)

46 *Seadh, shuathadar na cártai aris a' triú huair. Bheir ga'h éinne ar a cuid*
féinig, agus d'imiríodar ceann aca. Ghlaodhaig a' triú fear ansan ar a
bhean, agus níor dhein sí aon ní ach béal na gcártaí a bhí 'n-a láimh a
úmpáil fútha ar a' mbord a' preaba 'n-a suí.
(Well, they shuffled the cards again the third time. Each of them
took up her hand and played a card. The third man called his wife,
and what did she do but lay her cards face down on the table and
jump to her feet.)

Orientation

47 *Bhí an bheirt eile á cimeád chún go n-imiríodh suí na cártaí a bhí 'n-a*
láimh, ach níor dhein sí rud ortha.

(The other two wanted to keep her to play the cards she had in her
hand, but she would not do it for them.)

Resolution

48 *D'imi sí, agus do chua sí a'triall ar a fear.*
(She left and went to her husband.)

49 *'Cad dob áil leat díom?' aduairt sí.*
('What do you want of me?' said she.)

Orientation

50 *Bhí an t-airgead ar an mbórd.*
(The money was on the table.)

Resolution

51 *'Bailig chút é sin ar an mbórd agus cuir id' phóc' é!'*
('Gather up for yourself what is on the table and put it in your pocket!')

Coda

52 *'Smachtaíonn ga'h éinne an bhean mhíreáireach ach an té go mbíonn sí*
aige.'
('Everyone manages the shrew but he who has her.')

COMMENTARY

The collector of the story, Séamus Ó Duilearga, printed it with the title 'An Bhean Mhíreáireach'. That this was a name by which its narrator, Seán Ó Conaill, knew it can be surmised from his use of the term *míreáireach* four times in relation to the female subject of the story. The term is a variant of the word *míréireach* (*mí* - negative prefix + *réir* = 'bidding/command') meaning 'unbiddable/insubordinate'. The narrator's last use of it, in his closing personal commentary/coda, is printed by Ó Duilearga as a quotation from 'S.Ó.C' in a footnote to the printed text. Ó Conaill's comment has the distinct feel of a proverbial saying with ironic and humorous overtones and serves as a definite and distinctive final framing device. As such it should be allowed to stand as an integral part of the narrator's 'text'. There is, also, the possibility that Seán Ó Conaill's comment was made to the collector in conversation about the story prior or subsequent to its narration, in which case its recording in a footnote would have more justification. In either case it confirms the likelihood of the story's printed title as deriving from the narrator and – taken here as the narrator's final meta-linguistic pronouncement – constitutes a stylish close to the story's performance.

Abstract
Section 1
No overt framing device occurs at the start of the story other than the use of the word *fadó* which, with its sense of 'once upon a time', functions here to indicate the 'traditional narrative' status of what follows. A primal familial situation of father and daughters is presented without mention of any mother/spouse figure. They live in a past distant from the narrative's 'present' time and operate as a harmonious self-enclosed unit.

Orientation
Section 2
The daughters are described as *cailíní matha, suais le n-a chéile* – ('good girls, genial and kindly with each other') – taking the word *suais* here as an abbreviated form of *suaiseach/suaibhseach* rather than as an idiolectical variation of the adverb *suais*, since the phrase *suas le na chéile* could be said to have overtones of competition (i.e. the sisters 'up against each other') which would not be appropriate in this context. The monadic nature of the situation is emphasised by the metric quality of the binary-construction

phrases *ag obair is a' gnó dóip fhéin is dá n-athair* ('working and profiting for themselves and their father'). Here the rhythm of the two stressed 'o' vowels of the verbal noun pair *ag obair/a' gnó* is echoed in the more elongated rhythm of the stress pattern of *dóip fhéin is dá n-athair*, giving a sense of cyclical recurrence that is strengthened by how the pronominal forms *dó(ip)* and *dá* themselves alliterate and chime with the open vowels of the preceding verbal nouns. By contrast with this monadism, a departure from the static benign presentation of the three sisters in the primal situation of their dependence on/submission to the father is signalled by the periphrastic repetition of the verb 'to be', *bhí an té ... bhí sí* ('the person who was ... she was'), to declare the eldest daughter to be uniquely unbiddable.

Complication
Section 3
The verb-phrase *Nuair a bhíodar éirithe suas* ('When they had grown up') marks a time shift to a later 'present' in which the father is engaging in the process of making a marriage settlement for the eldest. The occurrence of the terms *ba shin* ('that was') (Section 2) and *críona* ('old') in relation to her differentiates the eldest from her sisters within the cultural category of *cailíní óga* ('young women') and separates such 'young women' category from the blander and patronising category of *cailíní matha* ('good (little) girls') invoked in Section 1.

A further differentiation from the monadic situation of Section 1 is indicated here in the assertion that the unruly nature of the eldest daughter has gone out beyond the boundaries of the household so that no-one (i.e. no other household with a likely male spouse) will accept her as a marriage partner. Where the father is said (using the third-singular past tense of the verb 'to be') to have been *a' déanamh cleamhnais* ('attempting to make a match'), with the sense of doing so repeatedly/over time, the failure of his efforts is reported in terms of the impersonal form of the conditional mood of the verb: *ní tógfí bhuaig í* ('she would not be taken from him') – an indication of the intrusion into the primal monad of the judgemental attention of the surrounding community.

Section 4
The punctuative sense of *Seadh ... ansan* ('Well ... then') marks the crossing to a new section from the stalled state of affairs of the previous one. Here decisive action is possible, and occurs in the brief telling of the

marrying off of the second sister – the middle one of the three. The series of three single-syllable verbs in which the rapid action is recounted – *dhin sé … phós sé … thug sé* ('he made … he married … he gave') – hint at the frustration of the father with his efforts in respect of the eldest daughter and the zest with which he accomplishes the disposal of the next one. The trio of verbs spell out the trio of actions that he would have expected to apply to each of his trio of daughters in the normal course.

Section 5

This section continues the progressive sense of the previous one. *Tamall … ansan* ('For a while … then') effects the section transition and also signals a going forward within a family-settlement sequence that has had a defective beginning and that now proceeds, *ina dhiaidh sin* ('in the aftermath'), in respect only of the second and third daughters. The sense of the correctness of the marrying off of the second and third girls is endorsed by the statement in both cases of their endowment with *sprae mhaith* ('a good dowry') and even the sense of an increasing success in the settlement process in that the youngest daughter is said to have been, in addition, settled *in áit mhaith* ('into a good situation'), i.e. a good farm-holding.

<u>Orientation</u>
Section 6

Transition back to the stalled condition of marriage expectation in regard to the eldest daughter is effected by the statement that she remains, apparently permanently, at home with her father: *d'fhan … aige sa tigh i gcónaí* ('she remained in the house with him'). This is in spite of the here repeated assertion that a large dowry remains available for anyone who might be found to take her in marriage. There is, however, an unmarried young man who hears of her and the extent of her 'fortune' and who knows, as all do, that she is unbiddable.

<u>Complication</u>
Section 7

Transition to a statement of the young man's in indirect speech. A shift from a previous seemingly permanent state of inaction is signalled in the phrase *Tháini' sé fé n-a déin, lá* ('He came in search of her one day') where not only is one specific day – *lá* ('one day') – highlighted (for action) but the action of the young man's coming to meet the eldest girl then is pointedly said to have been undertaken in order, actively, to fetch and acquire her – *fé n-a déin* ('in search of her'). Here it is not her father who is any longer the chief agent of the effort to arrange her marriage but the young man who announces to him that this is itself the reason he has come – to effect a marriage settlement with that daughter, the eldest, who is now the only *cailín* ('unmarried female') that he has of his family of daughters.

Section 8

Section boundary crossing is marked here by transition from oblique narrative to a sustained passage of direct speech whose dramatic tone is emphasised by the opening binary contrast of *Tá sí ann/Ní bheadh suí ann* ('She is here, alright/She wouldn't be here for you at all'), and the even more curt closing contrast of *Tóg í, nú fág it 'iaig í* ('Take her or leave her behind you'). Direct speech here delivers directly the circumstances of the shrewish nature of the eldest daughter and her continual unmarried state despite the 'fortune' going with her and her excellent capacity for work. Direct choice in full knowledge of this is urged by the father on the suitor.

Section 9

Boundary transition is marked by reversion to indirect speech in which the suitor's acceptance of the eldest daughter is reported. Her unbiddable nature notwithstanding, he is happy to take her as wife since she is so good at all household business. The reassurance he receives in regard to this latter – presumably again from her father – is indicated using the impersonal form of the verb 'to say': *Duarthas leis* ('It was said to him'), which has the narrative effect of detaching the action from the immediate father/suitor negotiation focus and hurrying the story on to the accomplishment of the marrying off at last of the eldest daughter – something that is also told using a perfunctory-sounding, impersonal verb form – *pósach iad* ('they were married'). One notes the shift of narrative perspective in the relating of the bestowal of dowry in this third marriage settlement. Whereas in the case of the two earlier marriages we are told that the father 'gave' (*thug sé*) the *sprae mhaith* ('substantial dowry'), in the case of this third marriage what we are told is that 'he [the suitor] received (*fuair sé*) a bag of money'. Once married, the couple went off on the young man's horse and again here the narrative perspective shifts significantly from the original location to another household – that of the young man. Even though an eventful journey will be recounted before their arrival there, the transition of the eldest daughter from her former home to her new one is communicated succinctly here already in that we are told that the couple 'went off' in order to 'come home' – literally 'to be coming home' (*a' teacht abhaile*).

Section 10

The action verbs at the end of the previous section indicating the journey the young couple undertake are re-emphasised and redoubled in effect in this single-line section containing only a single verb form *Phreab sé* ('He sprang'). In telling of this sudden, iconic, springing into the saddle, with his new wife riding pillion, the narrator gives us a hint of the forceful personality of the suitor-become-husband and the authoritarian nature of the relationship to which his new wife is to be subject.

Orientation
Section 11

The iconic instantaneousness of the previous section transitions to indirect speech recounting by the husband, in the course of their journey, *agus iad ag cur díobh* ('as they were going along'), of the possessions he holds dearest – an alliterating trio of *capall, cú agus cráin mhuice* ('his horse, a hound of his and a sow'). The significance of these possessions can be understood in terms of the usage of traditional narrative where the iconic attributes of the knight, the noble hero, are his sword, his steed and his hound – as related, for instance, in another narrative, '*An Ridire Rua gan Ghruaig gan Gháire*' ('The Russet Knight without Hair or Laughter'), also written down from Seán Ó Conaill by Séamus Ó Duilearga.[19] The possessions list mentioned by the new husband here subverts any claim for the identity or status of his character, in the narrative, as a nobleman or otherwise honourable gentleman-farmer. The shining sword of royal honour and identity that occupies first place in the traditional reckoning of the icons of nobility is absent here and is replaced – and relegated to third place, as it were – by the lowly sow, *cráin mhuice*. In the absence of the royal sword and its connotations, the list of his most valued possessions – and their fate in his hands – shows the new husband as a cruel tyrant whose marriage is focused primarily on the acquisition of wealth and the ruthless imposition of his authority.

Complication
Section 12

A resumption of the action of the journey whereby the newly married eldest daughter is going to her new abode whereas the new husband is said here to be *A' teacht abhaile* ('Coming home'). Again we can note this shift in narrative perspective, effected in the choice of verb, in order to place the new husband's homeplace at the centre of the world into which he is bringing his new wife. The difficulty of attaining to that centre for the new wife (his new possession) is presaged in the incident of the husband's setting of his horse at an impossibly high iron gate. Crucially here the horse is indicated to be a mare – as are, crucially, all three of the prized animals indicated to be female – in the use of a female pronoun in the phrase *chun do léimfeadh sí é* ('so that she might jump over it') and in the phrases (Section 13) *d'umpaig sí* ('she turned aside'), *ná féadfadh suí* ('she was unable'), *ró-árd di* ('too high for her').

Section 13
The interruptive conjunction *Ach* ('But, however') marks transition to a section demonstrating the dire consequence for the female creature of deviating from her master's will and failing to carry out her master's wishes. The latter's cruelty is emphasised in the curt phrase *agus d'fhág ansan í* ('and left her [abandoned her] there'), that marks the moving forward of the couple to the next demonstration of the husband's tyranny.

Section 14
Transition to a brief direct-speech expression of the lesson the husband wishes to inculcate: 'Obey me, or else …'

Section 15
Now without horse, *ghluaisíodar rompa* ('they continued moving onwards') transitions back into the resumption of the journey which brings them to the new husband's house. The rhythm of the trisyllabic verb with its two-syllable pronominal adverb gives a sense of a determined forging ahead that carries them, now on foot, 'all the way', so to speak, to the house. We note the verb *chuadar* ('they went'), for their going to the house, and the way this contrasts with the action verb of the next section.

Section 16
The use of *thánadar* ('they arrived') here marks a shift of narrative perspective from the journeying of the young couple to their being now situated at the house of the husband's parents. The welcome the young couple receive from the husband's father and mother is expressed by the use, on the narrator's part, of an impersonal verb form which gives something of a qualified and perfunctory tone to the welcome – as if

the parents are to be regarded as at a somewhat cautious remove from the wilful doings of their strongminded son. Equally to be noted here is the belated – as it were – appositional nomination of the father and mother as the subjects of the verbal phrase of welcome whose impersonal – more 'distant' – form has been used. *Bhíothas go fáiltheach … a athair is a mháthair* ('Welcoming was made … [by] … his father and mother').

Orientation
Section 17
Transition is signalled in the words *Amáireach ansan* ('Tomorrow then') which bring the narrative to a point where the eldest daughter and new wife is seen to be, in the aftermath of her eventful translation to her new household, a dutiful housewife *chomh maith le héinne* ('as good as any'), in the very words her father used of her when her husband had come to seek her in marriage. No suggestion is given of any insubordination or holding back from housework on her part.

Section 18
Ach lá eile ('But on another day') moves the story on to a further expression of cruel dominance to be shown to her by her new husband in the case of a second of the trio of the possessions he holds dearest – his hound. The hound accompanies them on a *máirseáil* ('perambulation') about the farm. The verb here conveys something of a regimentation of movement that suggests order and control which originates in the person and authority of the husband. It is he alone who is said to perceive intrusion onto the land of the farm by a cow who crosses a boundary line. The hound is spoken to and instructed to go and expel the cow straight away. Nothing of the narrative style here suggests or presages danger or violence.

Section 19
The husband's response to the inaction of the hound appears initially to also lack action – the minimising *níor dhein sé …* ('he did not do …'). However the word *Ach* ('But'), following and qualifying the 'not doing', marks transition to a section that recounts – in simple, matter-of-fact fashion – a violation not only of domestic life but of the natural order too. The task being required of the hound lies outside the natural range of her talents as hunter of quarries such as hare and fox. Despite this and despite her stated status as one of the husband's three prize possessions, she is peremptorily shot by him in cold blood before the eyes of his wife.

Section 20

Transition marked by shift to direct speech in which the husband tersely confirms and emphasises the ruthlessness of his demand for instant obedience on the part of all who lie in his power. The implication that his wife is potentially included within the *ga' h aon ní ná déanfadh rud orm* ('every last thing that would disobey me') is a further expression of the inhuman quality of his marital behaviour.

Orientation
Section 21

Transition out of direct speech to an account of the wife's growing terror in the face of her husband's sequential death-dealing actions: *Tháinig dhá shúil don mhnaoi* ('Her eyes dilated [with fear]'); *eagal' a dóthain uirthi* ('she was filled with fear').

Complication
Section 22

Transition from wife's fearful contemplation – the spot, to which one might say she is rooted in terror – to a moving on in the couple's progress around the farm and to their coming home.

Orientation
Section 23

Having come home in silence – transition could be regarded as being marked by the negative muteness of *Ní duairt a' bhean* ('The wife did not say [anything])' – the wife enacts the role of a servant, competent in all that she turns her hand to, day after day.

Complication
Section 24

Transition to another occasion, sometime later, *Tamall ina dhiaidh sin ansan* (a while after that then) when yet another (a third and final) demonstration is provided to the wife of the husband's seemingly mindless cruelty and tyranny. This time it is in respect of the remaining one of his three prize possessions – his sow – that in its turn too fails to obey him.

Section 25

Another use of a verbal construction initially indicating inaction, *Níor dhein sé aon ní* ('He did nothing'), but followed by deadly action recounted, or drawn out, as it were, in slow motion – slower than that of Section 19 – with his hand reaching into his pocket, pulling out his pistol and shooting dead his prize sow.

Orientation
Section 26

The quiet assertion of the narration that this further violence takes place within the wife's gaze – *agus do bhí an bhean a' féachaint air* ('and the wife was watching him') – follows on in unbroken utterance from the articulation of the third act of killing on the husband's part. One may surmise a rhetorical marking by the narrator of the wife's silent witness, in terms perhaps of a slower and maybe quieter delivery of the words of this very short section.

Complication
Section 27

The section transitions to an almost identical, direct-speech repetition of the deadly pronouncements of sections 14 and 20. The wife's dire plight is given its ultimate expression in this second reiteration of the husband's threats.

Evaluation
Section 28

Re-assertion, in another case of the negativing of direct speech narrative, of the situation of the wife's condition of mute compliant submission in the circumstances of her husband's household. The narrative here, nevertheless, also refers to her as a *cailín grástúil* ('a gracious young bride') and declares her to be as gentle and as docile a young bride as ever entered a household. This evaluation of the eldest daughter – in the context of the cruel circumstances of her marriage – contrasts both structurally and semantically with the portrayal of her at the beginning of the narrative. Its relevance will, it can be argued, continue to operate for both the narrator and his audience – throughout the remainder of the narrative as a redeeming counterweight image to that of the apparently cowed and fearful personality immediately obedient to the summons of her master at the story's later *dénouement*. A slight stumble, as it were, in the narrator's grammar while effecting this evaluation marks it out even more as a place in the narrative where the point of view and the values of the narrator (and, through him, of the audience also) bear on the performance – and surface, as it were, on the face of the narration. The verbal form in the phrase *comh*

macánta agus do chua [sí] ('as docile as ever entered') contains the third
person singular feminine pronoun *sí* which is superfluous here. It may
be surmised that the narrative complexity of maintaining the seemingly
opposing representations of the eldest daughter/young bride as at once
insubordinate and compliant (in terror) at different levels and time frames
of narrative performance distort the grammar of the narrator's rhetoric in
what might be regarded as sympathetic variation. Here the narrative can
be said to be drawing the listener's/reader's attention to its poetic function
by means of a disruption of syntactic and metrical pattern.[20]

Resolution
Section 29
The sense in which we could identify the previous section as evaluation
is further pointed up here by the reference to the wife's father as *athair a*
chéile ('his father-in-law') in the course of a narrative transition – marked
by the phrase *Tamall ina dhiaidh sin* ('After a while') – to the resolution
episode. The masculine possessive adjective *a* in *athair a chéile* can only
refer to the male speaker in Section 27 so that we can consider that the
narrative here appears to jump across Section 28 in an 'elision' from the
narrative sequence of a passage (Section 28) that is rhetorically lifted out,
so to speak, and rhetorically marked, in order to allow the narrator to
acknowledge the crux of the story and draw his audience's attention to it.
The emphasis now appears to be placed again on a male world – that of
the father-in-law and his three sons-in-law whom he invites to a meal –
without any direct mention of the three daughters.

Section 30
The account of the assembling in the father-in-law's house of the
three husbands, of the fine meal he affords them and of the ensuing
conversation and table-talk is marked both by the absence of any reference
to the daughters and by another peculiarity of the narrator's syntax in the
omission of the plural pronoun to which the verbs of the phrase *a' caint*
is ag eachtraí dá chéile ('talking and conversing with each other') refer. We
can recognise this as further evidence of the structural tension in the
narration noted in the evaluation episode at Section 28.

Section 31
Ansan / 'After that' gives transition to the situation where the three
daughters – unmentioned in the meal-assembly until now – are shown

withdrawing to a room on their own where they fall to playing cards. This card-playing to which the daughters resort in a separate room while their father and husbands continue to entertain themselves in the kitchen with conversation and the exchange of news and gossip strikes one as somewhat of a reversal of the traditional order in the community culture from which this narrative was recorded. It is perhaps best regarded as a schematic device required by the story in question, as is the silence and non-participation of the father in the remainder of the narrative action. One could also speculate as to whether such reversal might serve, in the deeper structure of the narrative, for both narrator and audience, as something of a distancing of the storyline from community values that are rejecting of the marital cruelty and tyranny that the story recounts.

Orientation
Section 32
The continuation of the all-male conversation and storytelling in the kitchen of the father-in-law's house.

Section 33
The normality of the gender division (already compromised by the reversal noted in Section 31) is, as it were, interrupted, *Ach* ('But'), by the curiosity and wonderment – perhaps scepticism – of the other males at the gentle affable mien of the eldest daughter.

Section 34
Out of their amazement at this state of affairs the question suggested itself to them – *tháinig sé anuas eatartha* ('it came up for discussion between them') – as to which of their wives could be said to be fondest (*ceanúil*) and most respectful (*ómúsach*) of her husband.

Resolution
Section 35
Transition to indirect speech through which the latest son-in-law ends all speculation by wagering a hundred pounds that it is his wife who is more respectful of him than are the other two wives of their husbands. We can note that the terms of the wager – as laid down by the cruel husband – do not cover spousal affection (*ceanúlacht*) ('fondness, affection'), as was included in the preceding discussion. The other husbands agree to the wager – laid now regarding respectfulness only – without reference to affection.

Section 36

Transition marked by switch to direct speech exchange whereby the first son-in-law queries how the wager is to be resolved and the third immediately assures him that indeed it will be resolved.

Section 37

'Anois,' ar seisean ("'Now then," said he') gives emphatic direct speech transition to the determination by the latest son-in-law of the nature of the ploy by which the wives will, in turn, be required to leave their card-playing and come to their husbands' call at crucial junctures of the play.

Orientation
Section 38

Description of the unusual circumstance of the intense watching-from-the-sidelines, so to speak, by the males of their wives' card school to the point where the first hand is just about to be played.

Resolution
Section 39

The first of the callings-out – for his wife by the first son-in-law to have been married – is expressed by the use of the verbal form *Ghlaodhaig* which carries the meaning of shout or shouted command. This renders all the more pointed the delayed and casual fashion in which this wife – the middle daughter – responds to/obeys her husband's 'command'. Indirect speech declares her intention to finish playing her hand of cards before responding to the call, which she does promptly once her cards are played.

Section 40

Transition to a rhetorically balanced direct-speech exchange wherein the wife queries why she was called and is told to return to the card room and to carry on as before. The import of the wife's simple query as to her being called away from the game – *Cad dob áil leat díom?* ('What is it you want me for?'), a query that each of the wives will make in turn – is weighted far beyond the apparently relaxed and casual enquiry here, for both narrator and audience, as it surely is also – inside the narration – for the eldest daughter, whose question, when it comes to be asked, could be considered as involving huge personal risk in the circumstances of her husband's previous behaviour.

Section 41
Seadh ('Well then'), the connective use of the copula plus neuter pronoun, effects transition to a description of the resumption of the card game by the wives.

Orientation
Section 42
A resumption of the male gaze recounted in Section 38.

Resolution
Section 43
Another male interruption of the wives' card game as the second husband calls out his wife – the youngest of the daughters.

Section 44
Transition to direct-speech report of how this daughter answers her husband's 'command' – asking him to wait until she played her hand of cards and only then coming to him.

Section 45
Another direct-speech exchange, mirroring that of Section 40, wherein this husband's response to his wife's direct querying of her being called out is to tell her to return to where she has been with her sisters at the card game.

Section 46
Again, as in Section 41, the connective use of the copula plus neuter pronoun *Seadh* ('Well then') transitions to an account of the resumption of the wives' card game and the calling out/commanding of the eldest daughter by her cruel and violent spouse. With no break in speech, the narrator's account of this command proceeds to tell how his wife instantly put down her hand of cards and sprang to her feet. One can note the use by the narrator here of a verbal construction *níor dhein sí aon ní ach …* ('she did nothing except'), a construction initially suggesting inaction and lack of urgency as was also initially the case in the accounts of the killing by the husband of his hound and his sow. In all cases the effect of this construction is to heighten the dramatic effect of the ensuing action.

Orientation
Section 47

The dramatic action at the end of the previous section is paused, as it were, in transition, while the other wives watch their sister and wait for her to play her hand of cards. *Ach níor dhein sí rud ortha* ('But she didn't oblige them') is how the narrator expresses – with a degree of delicacy – her failure to fulfil their expectation on the brink of her immediate fulfilment of her husband's command to come into his presence. Her refusal of their expectation is here rhetorically played off against the dire consequences of previous refusals (for horse, hound and sow) of his commands. Here, in her father's house and in the company of her sisters and their spouses she is held (in narration) suspended for a moment between a normal unhurried response to her husband's summons – as she and we have witnessed in the case of the summoning of the other two daughters – and a headlong terror-stricken response prompted by her experience of previous outcomes to his commands.

Resolution
Section 48

D'imi sí ('She left') is how the narrator expresses the eldest daughter's vacating her place of emotional and existential suspension and he follows it with another verb of motion *agus do chua sí* ('and she went') plus the gerund form *a'triall* ('a-journeying') to convey the extent and the import of this transition. It is a transition not only in the form of the narrative performance, but also in the meaning of her move into the presence of *a fear* ('her man') – a designation which I think we can here distinguish from the term *a fear céile* ('her husband'). At the beginning of the story the males who marry the daughters are referred to as *buachaill* ('unmarried (young) male') or *cliain* ('son-in-law'). In the course of the card game test, the other two husbands are each referred to as the *fear* ('husband') of their spouses but the marriage partner of the eldest daughter is not referred to by this term until she, as it were, chooses – against all the odds – to opt for him as her true husband, despite everything, and in the presence of all her family in her original family surroundings. In a fundamental sense it is she who finally renders him a husband through her choice of him out of the midst of her family, and the narrator's choice and use of terms for the suitors/spouses throughout the narrative gives appropriate rhetorical expression to this.

Section 49
Transition to a report of direct speaking on the part of the eldest daughter for the first time in the narrative. She asks the same question of her husband as her sisters asked of theirs – thereby aligning herself with the normal in marital relations that such questions in such circumstances imply. Hitherto, in the story, she has been silent, indeed increasingly mute as her terror of her spouse is revealed – to her and to the narrator's audience – in the course of the episodes of violence. Here she confronts him in a way previously unthinkable and, in doing so, faces him down, as it were, in the presence of and with the resources of her family of origin (the combined feminine of her sisters and herself, each of them married women, substituting in part at this point for the lack of a mother figure in the story).

Orientation
Section 50
The plainness of the statement *Bhí an t-airgead ar an mbórd* ('The money lay on the table') transitions the temperature of the narration back from the breathless dramatic heat of the previous section and quietly focuses attention on the money wagered. That money is, in a sense, the wealth the eldest daughter brought to her marriage in the form of the *sparán airgid* ('purse of money') that constituted her dowry from her father – together with the wealth of her sisters' dowries.

Resolution
Section 51
Transition to direct speech invitation by her husband to the eldest-daughter-come-into-her-own-as-his-wife to make her own of their joint wealth and possessions as represented by the money of the wager. Constituted of the wealth of all three couples, the wager taken to herself by the eldest daughter can stand for their common well-being and her own victory, by way of fortitude, patience and courage, over the deficiencies and distortions of the initial relationship with her spouse. His *Bailig chút é sin ar an mbórd* ('Gather up for yourself what's on the table') has a tone of affection in it and his telling his wife to put the money into her pocket is of marked significance in the context of the previous references to pockets in the story where on every occasion a weapon is taken out to end a life. The words themselves that constitute his reply to her question stand in contrast to the dismissive responses of the other two spouses to

that same question. His words can be construed as displaying a disarming – if unexpected – tone of warmth, intimacy and generosity. They can be taken as restoring to the eldest daughter/wife her personal agency and autonomy in the eyes and ears of the story's audience despite the seeming unrelenting harshness of the patriarchal premise – and outcome – that the story appears to suggest.

Coda
Section 52

As referred to above at the start of the commentary, this direct speech statement is taken here as the narrator's final framing device to his narrative performance. It consists of the narrator's own meta-commentary on the story and on his performance of it in his narration. It brings to a close for his listeners the performance status of his narrative and differentiates for them between the make-believe world of storytelling – in which the way to subdue an insubordinate female is known to all, as is witnessed in this traditional tale of the communal repertoire – and the real social world where marital relations are mediated in an internal world of deeper, more complex emotional and psychological terms than are featured in the case of the characters of any traditional tale. Such differentiation had already been communicated in the rhetorical complexities of the evaluation episode. It is repeated and reinforced here in a framing device whose tone is that of playfulness in the aftermath of a sophisticated narrative performance.

Performance patterning

Attention is drawn here to features of the narrative performance represented by the Ó Duilearga text such as repetition (duplication, triplication of linguistic elements), parallelism, contrast and substitution together with other aspects of rhythmic structure and syntactic dynamics.

  Section 2 *ina gcailíní matha* ('fine girls')
  Section 3 *ina gcailíní óga* ('young women')

Patterning here is across a section boundary and constitutes both repetition and contrast. The contrast lies in the opposition of the *cailíní matha* ('fine girls') of Section 1 with the *cailíní óga* ('young women') of Section 2. A shift in both semantics and intra-narrative time is here contained within the repetitive grammar pattern of preposition + possessive adjective + noun + qualifying adjective.

Section 3 *don cheann críona* ('to the eldest one')
Section 4 *don tarna ceann* ('to the second one')

Here, a repetitive grammar pattern conveys contrast in the age order of the daughters and we can note how the contrast is accentuated in a differentiation in the rhythmic structure of the phrases in that the phrase in Section 2 has a noun + adjective sequence whereas in Section 3 there is inversion to an adjective + noun sequence with – presumably – accompanying stress-pattern and intonation variation.

Section 4 *(do) thug sé sprae mhaith dhi* ('he gave her a good dowry')
Section 5 *thug sé sprae mhaith dhi* ('he gave her a good dowry')

Linguistic repetition here expresses the repetition of action in the storyline. In Section 3 the inclusion of the verbal particle *do* in the verb form *do thug sé* ('he gave') gives a deliberative sense to the action expressed, whereas its omission in Section 4 indicates the more automatic sense of the bestowal of the second dowry and its expression in the context of the two short sections in which the marrying off of the two younger daughters is narrated.

Section 5 *an ceann óg* ('the youngest one')
Section 6 *a' ceann críon'* ('the eldest one')

As with the repetitive pattern in sections 2/3, a contrast in the age order of two of the daughters is conveyed. One can note a symmetry between the contrast patterns of the pairs of sections in that reference to the oldest (*críona*) daughter is initial in Section 2 and final in Section 5 while reference to the younger daughter in each case is the other way around. The difference in the representation of the article *an* ('the') may be taken in this case to be an instance of orthographic variation in the recording of the speech of the narrator.

Section 8 *Tá sí sin ann* ('She is there')
    Ní bheadh suí ann ('She would not be here')

In this comparatively lengthy section the father of the girls is speaking plainly to the suitor for the eldest daughter's hand of the situation whereby she is available to him only because no one else can be found for her – because of her shrewish nature: 'She is there for you' versus 'She wouldn't be there for you at all'.

    Tóg í ('Take her')
    Fág it 'iaig í ('Leave her')

The father brings the suitor's decision down to the starkly expressed contrast of 'Take her' versus 'Leave her after you' – with the addition of the adverbial phrase *it 'iaig* ('behind you') giving the ultimatum a finality of both sense and rhythm beyond what a bare 'take her/leave her' could achieve.

> *aduairt a' t-athair leis* ('said the father to him')
> *aduairt sé* ('said he')
> *aduairt sé* ('said he')

The rhythmic structure of the father's reported speech in the section ties together the first two instances here of the verb *aduairt* ('said') into a complementary pair giving emphasis to the narrator's perception of the fraught nature of the possible marriage arrangement for the eldest daughter. The third instance – *aduairt sé* – is a slight drawing back by the narrator from his own animated insertion, as it were, into the drama of the presentation to the suitor of the terms of the possible marriage. The narrator acts the part of his story character in this section in spite of the triple occurrence of the markers of reported speech.

Section 9   *Duairt a' buachaill go dtógfadh* ('The young man said he would take [her]')

The three occurrences of the verb *(a)deirim* ('I say') in the narration of the speech of the father in Section 8 that leads to the binary 'Take her/ Leave her' are invoked and bound together in the opening word of the narrator in Section 9: *Duairt* ('He said'). What he is reported as saying is *go dtógfadh* ('(he) would take') the eldest daughter, so that here *duairt* and *tógfadh* parallel and echo the expressive use of these linguistic forms in the previous section. The verb *(a)deirim* ('I say') occurs again in Section 9, this time in the impersonal past tense form *Duarthas* ('Was said') which, as it were, lacks the urgency of its earlier use and implication in this and the previous sections.

> *Fuair sé sparán airgid léi* ('He got a purse of money with her')
> *D'imíodar leo ansan a' teacht abhaile* ('They set off on their way home')

In respect of the marriages of the two other daughters, the narrator tells in sections 4 and 5 how the father, in each case, 'gave a good dowry' to each girl. In the case here of the marriage of the eldest daughter the narrator tells how it is the suitor who is given the dowry. This shift from the verb *thug* ('he [the father] gave') to the verb *fuair* ('he [the suitor] received') has the effect of shifting the focus of the storyline and the 'gaze' of the hearers from the setting of the father and his home to the world of the suitor and new husband. Such a shift is further emphasised in the use of the verb *ag teacht* ('on their way') to describe the direction of the journey on horseback of the newly married pair. It is not a 'going' to her new home on the part of the eldest daughter but a 'coming' to that home on the part of the couple.

Sect. 10   *Phreab sé ar a chapall, agus í seo ar a chúlaibh* ('He leaped onto his horse with her as pillion behind him')

This brief section captures in its starkness the situation in which the eldest daughter now finds herself. Nothing has been told previously of her willingness or otherwise to enter into this marriage despite her acknowledged reputation for being unbiddable. Once the suitor was assured of the girl's domestic competence – despite her temperament – and once the dowry was paid, *pósach iad* ('they were married') (Section 9). The impetuous, vigorous, motion of his bouncing onto the back of his horse on which his new wife has already been deposited is conveyed by the use of the verb *phreab* ('leaped') with its connotations of startling suddenness and decisiveness. Coming in the narration after the telling in Section 9 of how 'they set off on their way home', it points up and reinforces a sense that two powerful opposing personalities are here irrevocably joined together in some fateful fashion.

Sect. 11   *an capall, agus cú a bhí aige, agus cráin mhuice* ('this horse, and a hound he had and a sow')

In speaking of his three prize possessions, the new husband takes on here, in the ears of an audience familiar with traditional narrative, something of the aura of the hero, the nobleman, the knight-at-arms whose emblematic possessions are also three in number. Two of these can be matched with the husband's allegedly treasured possessions: the noble knight's royal steed with his horse, the noble knight's royal hunting dog with his hound. The mismatch remaining between the noble knight's royal sword and the husband's sow gives the lie to any true identification of him as a noble or gentleman in the ears of the audience – something which bears centrally on the course of the story.

We can note how the names of the husband's possessions alliterate – *capall, cú, cráin* ('horse, hound, sow') – and how, as is clear from the usages of sections 13 and 18, the horse and the hound are, like the sow, female. Their identification in the story with the new wife and her plight becomes obvious as the narration proceeds and as they succumb, one by one, to the cruel, implacable will of their master.

Sect. 13   *Ach d'úmpaig sí ar leataoibh* ('But she turned aside')
            tharraig a phiostal as a phóca ('pulled a pistol out of his pocket')
            agus do lách í ('and shot her')
Sect. 18   *Ach ní dhein a'chú rud air* ('But the hound did not obey him')
Sect. 19   *a phiostal a tharrac amach* ('pull out his pistol')
            agus a' chú a lácha ('and shoot the hound')
Sect. 24   *agus ní ghuibh* ('and she did not go')
Sect. 25   *a phiostal a tharrac amach* ('pull out his pistol')
            agus í lácha ('and shoot her')

These non-contiguous sections are linked in a parallelism of duplication and triplication of action, absence of action and consequence of action. These repetitions are threaded through the sections in a fashion that increasingly reinforces the meaning through the use of linguistic forms of diminishing length.

Sect. 14   *Sin é mar a dhinimse le haon ní ná dineann rud orm*
            ('That is how I treat anything that does not obey me')
Sect. 20   *Sin é mar a dhinimse les ga' haon ní ná déanfadh rud orm*
            ('That is how I treat anything that would not obey me')
Sect. 27   *Sin é mar a dhinimse [ar seisean] leis ga' haon ní ná déanfadh rud
            orm* ('That is how I treat [he says/said] anything that would
            not obey me')

Another linking of non-contiguous sections in an expanding parallelism that spells out the dire fate of those subject to the husband's tyranny. The switch from the indicative mood *ná dineann* ('who does not do') in 14 to the subjunctive mood *ná déanfadh* ('who would not do') in 20 and 27 has the effect of emphasising the sense in which the new wife is being shown how all have to choose to obey, as does the switch from the term *le haon ní* ('anything') in 14 to *les ga' haon ní / leis ga' haon ní* ('anything') in 20 and 27.

We can note how the narrator as it were allows himself to be co-opted into the expanding parallelism of these three sections to the extent that in the final threatening declaration of the husband, the husband's direct speech is interrupted by the meta-comment *ar seisean* ('he says') that has the effect of breaking the declaration into two parts and thereby doubling its import. This marks a kind of crescendo in the narrative, wherein the cruelty and menace of the husband is represented to his wife and to the tale's listeners in the fullest degree following the storyline's gradual 'bringing home' of the newly married pair in the verbs of motion occurring since Section 9: *d'imíodar* ('they set off'), *ag cur díobh* ('going along'), *ag teacht abhaile* ('on their way home'), *ghluaisíodar rompa* ('they travelled on their way'), *do thánadar abhaile* ('they came home').

Section 28   *Ní duairt a bhean focal ach teacht abhaile agus aire thúirt dá gnó*
                ('His wife said nothing but came home and attended to her work')

The new wife's response to this is to remain silent and in silence to apply herself to her domestic duty. We have noted in the commentary above how the narrative here (Section 28) – in the absence of even a single word of direct speech by the wife in response to the ultimate revelation of her oppression and the seeming immersion of her in the business of her new 'home' – takes on an evaluatory aspect which is both organisationally significant in the macrostructure of the text and rhetorically significant in that it foregrounds and permits the acknowledgment of a value system which the narrator – and through him the traditional audience of his performance – would wish to bring to bear on the events of the story.

Section 29   *triúr cleamhnaith* ('three sons-in-law')
Section 31   *triúr driféar* ('three sisters')
Section 32   *triúr cleamhnaith* ('three sons-in-law')

Following the intense and unique focus on the individual figure and individual plight of the eldest daughter/new wife in Section 28, the narrative continues here in a more prosaic tone that returns the eldest daughter to the common situation of her sisters in their triple marital alliance with the three sons-in-law of their father whose summons to his house they obey.

Sect. 36   *'Conus a bhe' fhios againn anois é'* ('How shall we know it now')
         'Be' fhios againn é' ('We shall know it')
Sect. 37   *'Anois,' ar seisean* ('"Now," said he')

The patterned repetitions of the four words – *beidh* ('will be'), *fhios* ('knowing'), *againn* ('our'), *anois* ('now') – verb, noun, pronoun, adverb – over three phrases of reported speech of diminishing length briskly leads the storyline from the uncertainty and curiosity of the other sons-in-law regarding the marriage of the eldest girl to the definitive *Anois* ('Now then') of her husband, whose command of the situation is total and who displaces the father completely in the remainder of the narrative.

Section 38   *Do bhíodar a' fair' orthu ansan* ('They watched them')
Section 39   *Ghlaodhaig a' chéad duine ansan ar a bhean* ('Then the first man called his wife')
Section 42   *do bhí na fir a' faire orthu i gcónaí* ('the men were watching them all the time')
Section 43   *nuair a ghlaodhaig a' tarna fear ar a bhean* ('when the second man called his wife')
Section 46   *Ghlaodhaig a' triú fear ansan ar a bhean* ('The third man called his wife')

In the first two of these three set pieces, the calling out from the card game of the wives by their husbands, the command is preceded by the telling of how the husbands looked on from the other room – from afar, as it were – at the wives as they played. The absence of the phrase *ag fair' orthu* ('watching them') preceding the third 'calling out' quickens the action and immediately carries both the narration and those listening to it directly to the heart of the dramatic denouement and resolution of the story.

Section 39   *D'fhreagair sí é agus duairt sí* ('She answered him and said she')
             Phreab sí 'n-a suí agus tháini' sí aníos a' trial air ('She jumped up and came to him')
Section 44   *'Bead chút anois nuair'* ('"I will be with you now when"')
             d'éiri' sí 'n-a suí agus chua' sí ag triall air ('she stood up and went to him')
Sect. 46   [ ]
Sect. 48   *D'imi sí, agus do chua sí a'triall ar a fear* ('She left and went to her husband')

Similarly here, the heightened sense of the approach to a climax is effected by the absence of any spoken reply by the eldest daughter to the command of her husband to come from the card game – when her two sisters have, in turn, given delaying answers to their husbands' commands and stayed to play out their 'hand'. She, instead, instantly turns down her cards on the table and goes to her husband.

Section 40   *'Cad ab áil leat díom?'* ('"What do you want me for?"')[21]
Section 45   *'Cad ab áil leat díom?'* ('"What do you want me for?"')
Section 49   *'Cad ab áil leat díom?'* ('"What do you want me for?"')

This query – 'What do you want me for?' – serially put to their husbands by the three sisters is given identical expression in each instance. It tolls bell-like through the sections, gaining a deeper tone on each occurrence as it brings the story, its characters and its listeners to the place where the narrative is able to portray a final return to the values of equality and generosity in the domain of marriage.

Sect. 40   *'Téighre síos mar a rabhais'* ('"Go back where you were"')
Sect. 45   *'Imig ort arís mar a rabhais'* ('"Go off back to where you were"')

A parallel dispensing of the younger wives not only back to the card-playing room but to the continuance of their married lives in the company of husbands who care for them and with whom they are free to be themselves. The repetition here of *mar a rabhais* ('where (as) you were'), preceded in the second instance by *arís* ('again') works to intensify an expectation that the eldest wife too will be returned to a situation which, in her case, is one of both fear and oppression as well as being one of card-playing.

Section 51   *'Bailig chút é sin ar an mbórd agus cuir id' phóc' é'* ('Gather up for
                yourself what is on the table and put it in your pocket')

For the first time the words of the eldest daughter's husband treat of her in her own individual right. She is told in relation to the money on the table – belonging to her sisters' husbands and to her own husband too – *'Bailig chút é sin'* ('Gather that up for yourself')[22] and she is told *'cuir id' phóc é'* ('put it in your pocket'). The two phrases, in their brevity and in the balance between them, represent and express in emphatic form the new dispensation being envisaged in the relationship between the pair.

We can note the phonetic patterning of two forms: the pair of two short syllables *'bailig'*, *'cuir id'* (containing only short 'front' vowels) followed in each case by a single stressed syllable *'chút'*, *'phóc'* containing a long 'back' vowel. They stand alone, as direct speech, unattributed by the narrator, but in the rhetorical complexity of the narrative performance they function to give emphatic utterance to a restorative and compensatory judgement on the issues treated of in the story. This judgement can be seen to be that of the narrator and of the audience for whom his performance was traditionally enacted, in addition to being an expression by the cruel husband of his recognition that he has achieved his aim of controlling and taming his wife.

Section 52

This meta-utterance acts as the narrator's final framing device that brings his performance to a close. He places the term *bean mhíreáireach* ('insubordinate wife') at the centre of a pair of contrasting phrases. The first, *Smachtaíonn ga'h éinne* ('Everyone controls' (i.e. knows how to control)), purports to state a general truth in an unambiguous fashion and does so in terms of the substantial and somewhat compacted phonetics of its constituent elements. The second phrase, at the 'other side' of the term *bean mhíreáireach*, a term constituting the title of the story, consists of a succession of single-syllable words that – following the conjunction *ach* ('but') – express an exception to the general, and a contrary particular truth, whose simple phonetic representation punches home, as it were, the unrhetorical and imprescriptible quality of specific social relations, in their diverse reality, as can apply to any particular instance of the dynamics of a marriage.

Irony and humour here combine to indicate the didactic significance that is embedded in this traditional narrative performance within a community setting where the initial absence, in the tale's abstract, of a wife/mother will have carried for its audience a cautionary import regarding the well-being of the daughters and, especially, the well-being of the eldest girl.

CHAPTER II

Language Teaching, Sociolinguistics and the Irish Folklore Text

[Published in *Teangeolas*, no. 15, winter 1982 (Linguistics Institute of Ireland), pp. 20–7]

An issue of interest to both language teachers and practitioners of sociolinguistics is the social and educational context in which any particular language is taught. This context, in its entirety, plays a very large role in determining the choice of language-teaching material used in schools, the philosophy and style of the teaching itself and the motivation of both pupils and teachers in the language-learning/teaching enterprise. The degree to which it is possible to know this context fully, even in the case of a single language, is limited. In the case of Irish in the Irish state education system, the feeling exists very strongly that a good deal of context research is urgently required in order to enable all those involved with the teaching of Irish to perceive clearly the goals that can reasonably be set in regard to conferring competence in the language on the general school-going population; in regard to identifying the methods and materials by means of which this can be most efficiently undertaken; and also in regard to the best ways of evaluating, at various stages, the progress that the pupils and indeed the education system itself is making on the road to achieving its aims. A good deal of the research that has been, and is, at present, undertaken by Institiúd Teangeolaíochta Éireann (ITÉ) was and is designed to provide data that will allow answers to be formulated to the questions mentioned. The findings of the Committee on Language Attitudes Research, published almost a decade ago, were another important source of information of this kind. There is a recognised need to try and bring all such research up to date since historical factors affecting social and political circumstances, as well as personal attitudes, have all – doubtless in inter-linked ways – been changing in the years since the original data was collected.

One very serious aspect of the contemporary social and educational context of the teaching of Irish here would appear to be – on anecdotal evidence at least – that in large areas of what is regarded as true Gaeltacht, young children are coming to the state school system with English as their first language despite the fact that, in many instances, these children come from homes where Irish is the first language of both parents. We need urgently to know the extent to which this phenomenon actually exists and how the parents, the teachers and indeed the pupils affected see their role in it. At present, it is impossible to say if such a phenomenon should be regarded as the completion of the process of the historic language shift that reached a peak in the second half of the nineteenth century or whether what is going on here is a fresh language shift that poses an entirely new obstacle to the successful maintenance of Irish as a vernacular. It must be emphasised that, until some actual data come to light as a result of careful investigation, our understanding of what is involved must remain very poor. Fortunately, ITÉ itself has recently undertaken a small-scale project focusing on Gaeltacht areas, and the findings will be eagerly awaited.

So much for the local and national context of the teaching of Irish. There is also an international context to be taken into account. While the prevailing circumstances and the external history of every language are unique, nevertheless a sufficient degree of comparison is possible, worldwide, to enable global statements regarding languages and education to be made in a way that is still relevant to the circumstances of the individual education system. One formulation of such global statements is incorporated into a basic anthropology textbook by Peter B. Hammond. In discussing the question of the relative adaptive value of particular languages, without prejudice, as he puts it, to 'the firmly established principle that, as groups, people in every society are intellectually equally endowed', he sets down the following:

> It has been suggested that the Japanese may be the last of modern peoples to evolve their own language of science. Hereafter, most aspiring Urdu-speaking astrophysicists, like their counterparts who speak Amharic, Albanian, or any Austronesian tongue, may have to

study in a European language for their advanced degrees. Thus, in the evolutionary perspective in which all peoples must sooner or later come to some kind of terms with industrially based technology and the changed patterns of living it makes necessary, some languages can be regarded as being, at least for the present, evolutionarily more 'advanced' than others.

It a true, of course, that the languages of all peoples, like most of the other aspects of their traditional ways of life, could make the changes necessary to adapt. But many may not, simply for the reason already stated: it is less wasteful in energy and time to adopt the language of another people that has already undergone the modifications necessary to the efficient communication of new information in a rapidly changing world. Such an assertion implies nothing about the intrinsic worth of other languages under traditional cultural circumstances. Nor does it necessarily follow that those languages that may be considered as less evolved in the strictly scientific or technical sense will, as a result, die out. As long as they are well adapted to dealing with major aspects of their speakers' experience they are likely to persist. Indeed, in providing an efficient means of communicating about most traditional aspects of their users' way of life, they may be perceived as more 'advanced' than the new foreign language adopted for communication about science. The old ways of talking may persist as long as the old ways of life go on – or as long as those who remember the native language survive. But, barring external preventive intervention, an old language may certainly become extinct, sooner or later.[1]

The crucial sentence here, in the context of the teaching of Irish, is, I feel, the one where a language's capacity to deal with major aspects of its speakers' experience is suggested as the vital factor in determining that language's chance of survival. One is acutely aware that only very small numbers of the Irish population have, to any significant degree, Irish as the medium of any kind of life experience outside of the classroom itself. If in the Gaeltacht now a growing number of households have also turned from Irish as the vernacular of the nuclear family, then it is time to reappraise the situation regarding the teaching of Irish and time to see if there may not be some fresh ways in which it can be ensured that some major aspect of his or her life experience is encountered through Irish by the learner of the language in the Gaeltacht or outside it. This, of course, it may be argued, is not a matter solely, or perhaps at all, for the schools, and the sociolinguistic endeavours of *Bord na Gaeilge* and other bodies, both voluntary and official, are to be welcomed in removing from the backs of those involved with Irish in the education system a burden in regard to the promotion at large of that language that was undoubtedly too exclusively placed. Nevertheless, some serious thought will always be required regarding the question of whether the kind of Irish and the kind of Irish teaching to which the general school-going population is exposed is likely to be – as it should be – an enhancement of their humanity in the first instance, an enrichment of their life experience that is a valuable and a pleasurable element of their cultural formation and socialisation into the adult Irish world.

It is granted that these are very serious demands to make on the teaching and the teachers of Irish but I would argue that unless it can be regarded as being at least on a par with the other humanities-type subjects, the teaching of Irish will always suffer from being open to the charge of being an unnecessary imposition on the Irish school-going population. At a time when many voices call for a reduction in the amount of time and resources devoted to the humanities subjects, at second and third levels at least, all who are involved with teaching Irish must see to it that their materials and their methods are those most likely to perform a genuine service to the proper education of students. In what follows I am suggesting one small and, I hope, practical way in which the value of Irish in the education of the learner can be raised. This increase in value can be achieved through an increase in the intrinsic richness of the language material utilised and studied. What I propose should not in any way increase the difficulty or lessen the functional potential of the teaching material in question.

For language teachers as a whole the effect of the accelerated technological changes of recent decades on the various languages that are being taught in Irish schools has been of significant import. Developments in regard to syllabus design and choice of language materials have reflected these changes. In general, there has been a shift away from the vocabulary and the language registers of the more verbally artistic domains towards the functional and the utilitarian. The apparent increase in the relevance of the materials to the contemporary world as experienced by the students themselves is matched by the apparent dilution of the 'strength' of the language sample constituting the materials, with its accompanying apparent loss of idiomatic richness, semantic range and creativity (in the exploitation of humour, irony, rhetorical effect, and so on). It has been unfortunate that, in the case of Irish, genuine efforts to overcome difficulties associated with dialectical variety have seemed to further the process that distances much of the kind of language materials learners of Irish encounter today from the kind of Irish to be encountered among any of the historically Irish-speaking communities. This is not a question of vocabulary only, nor of the prescription of standardised morphology and orthography. It has also to do with a shift in the quality of the language taught, a shift at some level or levels of usage from the sentence up.

Such developments cannot, of course, be attributed exclusively to teachers, or language programme designers and writers, or – least of all – to the learners themselves, nor can they be attributed solely to any or all elements of the education system for the simple reason that some such development in language usage is generally acknowledged to have been taking place in urbanised/industrialised society in general in the course of the last few decades. The reasons – or even the explanations – for such change are doubtless very complicated and far beyond the scope of this article. At their extreme, however, they present in Ireland the appearance of relative inarticulateness to the reflective older speakers of either Irish of Hiberno-English, who find in the speech of the younger generation a fall in the standards of language usage. Henry Glassie reports interesting instances of such an evaluation on our part of the older inhabitants of Ballymenone, County Fermanagh. One informant there ended his description of modern labour with the, to him, pathetic image of men on the job sitting through their brief lunch break in silence. Glassie paraphrases the communal judgement of Ballymenone on the question as follows:

> Silence is the key idea. It betokens at once stupidity and cowardice. Unchallenged by adversity, having it too easy, modern people have let their minds wither, and they have lost the courage it takes, and the generosity it takes, to reach out through conversation to help their fellows and establish through words a community founded on mutual aid. I have heard old men say it is a shame they do not speak their 'own native tongue', but it is not the loss of Irish, three generations past, that most concerns them, it is the loss of rich articulate English. Modern people stumble around in the language, repeating over and over the same dirty words – 'effin this and effin that' – without clearly expressing themselves ... but whatever its source, it is a fact, and they

see it as symptomatic of laziness, stupidity, and selfishness. Modern people do not 'take the time' to speak efficiently. Words are the force of community. What has been lost is the spirit of neighbourliness that depended on cooperation, and chat, daily in the bog, nightly at the hearth.[2]

It is not in any way contended that this trend in language usage is universal or automatic in every speech community of modern industrialised society. The effects of mass communication and the standardising influences of centralised bureaucracy are altered in every community's case by factors of history, culture, social organisation and individual personality. Nevertheless, a 'decline' in the standards of language usage is widely reported today at all levels of education and also in society outside the school. Allowing that in every community there may well be class and group and individual exceptions to it, such a trend has serious implications for language teaching and one can wish for careful research to be undertaken to determine the nature of the 'decline'. It is likely to be shown in Ireland, I think, that there is certainly a striking change in the speech patterns and in the 'ethnography of speaking' – as well as in the vocabulary – of urbanised, industrialised Irish communities by comparison with the language usage of earlier periods. This is but one aspect of the general cultural transformation of Ireland from the traditional to the industrial world that has been going on for several centuries but whose full effect has only recently been brought to play in the most forceful way on large sections of Irish society.

One of the effects of this transformation has been to peripheralise traditional knowledge and to weaken its cultural transmission in the form of the stories and other lore that constituted, until comparatively recently, the repertoire of traditional communal wisdom in many Irish communities. It cannot be without significance for language teaching in Ireland, and specifically for the teaching of Irish, that the institutionalised performance of this repertoire played such a central role in traditional Irish society in regard to the socialisation of the young, the reinforcement of the cultural identity of the community in general, and the promotion of the value of verbal art. Certainly, today, changes in social and economic organisation have swept away nearly all of the traditional contexts of the institutionalised performance of this repertoire and, in disuse, the repertoire itself has largely faded from the memory of the Irish people. In general it has been replaced by knowledge acquired from the formal channels of cultural transmission that predominate in contemporary society, channels of which formal schooling is one of the most universal in effect.

Some attempt has been made to utilise traditional oral narrative and other items of the 'folk' repertoire of traditional Irish society as school texts for use by students of Irish at the upper stages of second-level education. A constant difficulty however has been that this kind of material, by its nature primarily oral and the product of a social context of which the student has no experience, has little apparent attraction for the great majority of students, who are prone to regard it as antiquated, lifeless and without any meaning for their own lives. The contemporary relevance, the creative vitality, the meaningfulness of such traditional material must of necessity remain hidden from the urbanised students of today whose attention is directed to it at the level of story or content. It is not as story, however, but rather as the record of masterful linguistic performance that demonstrates language skills of the very highest order that such texts are presented by Donnchadh Ó Cróinín in the case of one, well-known, Munster seanchaí – namely Amhlaoibh Ó Luínse. In his preface to the anthology of Ó Luínse texts that he edited, Ó Cróinín has written:

> ... *tá scéalaithe agus scéalaithe ann – nó do bhíodh – ach d'fhéadfá a rá go bhfuil an deighilt seo le déanamh orthu: scéalaithe a thugann uatha díreach ar an gcuma go dtáinig chúthu, ar feadh a gcumais, agus an saghas eile a dheineann a gcuid féin den rud a ráinig i raon a gcluas, agus a mhúnlaíonn le toil agus le tuiscint é ... [agus] ná féadann gan bua na samhlaíochta atá acu féin a imirt ar an ngnáth-rud, sa chás gur rud nua airís agat é, geall leis. Tá a bhua féin ag gabháil le gach aon taobh acu, ach ós searbh gach gnáth níl barr le baint d'fhear na samhlaíochta: sa deire thiar, is é a choiníonn an saol ar siúl.*
>
> *Leis an dara saghas a bhain Amhlaoibh Ó Luínse, agus ní hamháin go raibh bua insinte agus bua samhlaíochta aige, ach tá ceard agus eagar agus críochnúlacht le braith ar gach aon scéal dar inis sé, idir fada agus gairid dóibh.*[3]

[Storytellers vary but one can say that they may be divided as follows: there are those who narrate just as the material came to themselves – as well as they are able. Then there are others who make their own of what their ears had heard and who fashion it willingly and knowingly ... so that their imagination gives rise to something new, as it were. Both types have their own virtues. However, since the ordinary can grow stale, pride of place goes to the one with imagination. When all is said and done it is he who keeps life going.

Amhlaoibh Ó Luínse belonged to the second type and not only was he narratively and imaginatively gifted, but every story he told, long or short, was marked by craftsmanship of composition and by polish of delivery.]

O Cróinín contrasts the clear, direct elegance of the Ó Luínse texts with what he refers to as the *culaithirt Ghaeilge ar chnábalach iasachta* ('Irish clothing on a foreign frame'), something that is so frequently to be found, in print, masquerading as the modern Irish language. In recommending the Ó Luínse texts as good material for language learners, he characterises their linguistic virtue as follows:

> *Is é bua is mó a chítear domhsa bheith ag baint leis an leabhar so ná bua na cainte atá tríd síos ann: caint chruinn, ghonta, shnasta, mheáite, agus gach aon abairt ar bhráid a chéile chomh greanta le clocha na trá.*[4]

[The chief virtue I see this book as having is the virtue of the kind of speech it comprises throughout; speech that is exact, pithy, balanced and accomplished – each sentence nestling in with its companions as trimly as stones on a beach.]

The aspect of such folklore materials that I would myself wish to emphasise here is that they are the products of speech that have generally been produced in conditions of heightened creativity so that they exemplify a side of the Irish language that is infrequently taken into consideration, I believe, in either the preparation of language materials for beginners or the selection or construction of study texts for more advanced learners. I have in mind here those characteristics of language and of language use that we may call the rhetoric (or even the eloquence) of Irish, a term that represents those features of traditional language use that function to such communicative effect in Irish oral narrative but that are not to be found in the lexicons or the grammars that are among the working tools of both the language teacher and the creator of language-teaching materials. It is probably true that everyone with any aptitude for, or interest in, language has some degree of personal 'feel' for rhetoric or eloquence in the sense in which I am using these terms here. It would be especially desirable in the case of Irish, however, to have some research findings as to the nature, distribution and frequency of occurrence of these rhetorical characteristics in a substantial and representative corpus of the language. The texts of traditional Irish oral narrative that survive, either in print or in the archive established by Coimisiún Béaloideasa Éireann (and now part of the Department of Irish Folklore at UCD), could readily constitute the makings of such a corpus. Such information as I envisage would be a valuable addition to the resources available to teachers and to those who prepare language-teaching materials in Irish and, it is to be hoped, would be some contribution to an attempt, seen by many as desirable, to enrich the language samples to which students and other learners of Irish are exposed. This is not an argument for the reintroduction of dialect forms or proverbs nor for any comparable change at the levels of vocabulary and grammatical structure. Rather is it an assertion that, from the beginning, the learning of Irish should bring students into contact with specimens of the language that are imbued with at least some of the aesthetic and rhetorical characteristics of the spoken language at its most vital. This should not, necessarily, in any way interfere with considerations regarding the basic vocabulary and the basic grammatical structures to be first tackled or with the general functional or communicative orientations of the syllabus materials introduced. It would nevertheless be a significant advance in terms of the quality of language teaching available to students of Irish at every level.

Some thought needs also to be given to the question of using some folklore texts as teaching materials for the more advanced post-primary student and certainly for the adult learner of Irish. It may be that modified versions should be provided of anecdotes, jokes, funny stories, riddles and other 'minor forms' of oral narration that, while being confined to basic vocabulary and structure, would nevertheless reinforce for the student's ear and eye an authentic style of Irish expression. I would not exclude proverbs and proverbial phrases from the list of forms to be considered for use in this fashion. Excessive and unthinking use may have been made of them by earlier generations of language teachers. Nevertheless, they represent a considerable element of any corpus of the living speech of a community. In a work on the general theory of cliché, a Soviet scholar has recently written:

> The lexical stock of any spoken language includes a fair number of so-called complex clichés, i.e. set word-combinations which are reproduced in a form fixed once and for all. These include various idiomatic phrases, e.g. at one's finger-tips, complex terms, e.g. atomic

weight, all kinds of proverbs, proverbial phrases, winged words, quotations and folk aphorisms, newspaper and literary clichés and the like. Unfortunately, the relevant statistics are lacking as to their proportion in the national language and in human language in general. However, an analysis of any more or less sizeable text suggests that they comprise a high proportion of the lexical stock.[5]

Supra-syntactic analysis of the minor forms of oral narrative would probably have implications beyond the identification of those rhetorical characteristics which I see as very important, since, as Jeffrey L. Kallen remarks, 'Language theories may also profit by examining the total range of verbal behaviour including artistic or contextually-structured genres.'[6] Thus in a general way, the kind of analysis I am interested in seeing done for the purpose of enriching Irish language-teaching materials would be likely to bear fruit in terms of linguistic theory also and it seems appropriate that, in a country laying claim to such an impressive national heritage of oral narrative, such analysis should be undertaken. And it is not only in structural linguistics that the results of such research would be valuable. Writing as long ago as 1971, Dell Hymes stated:

> The folklorist is accustomed (inured might be the word) to having some other discipline, such as linguistics, pointed out to him as important to folklore. I should like to point out the importance of folklore for work in linguistics. Certain lines of folkloristic research, I maintain, are essential to the progress of the trend in linguistic research called 'sociolinguistic'.[7]

Seeing the 'ethnography of speaking' – the description and explanation of the use of language – as fundamental to all sociolinguistic research, Hymes argues that it is with respect to the concepts of *performance* and *genre* that folklore primarily contributes to the achievement of the sociolinguistic goal. Study of the *use* of folklore, as of language, is, he claims, what leads to an adequate theory of the place of both in social life. With the increased understanding today of the possibility of treating folklore as the product of complex processes of cultural performance and communication, it is possible to analyse folklore texts in ways that yield important data on that creative aspect of language use which Hymes claims has been the focal point of Chomsky's theoretical impact in linguistics. The goal of accounting for the occurrence of novel sentences cannot, in Hymes' view, be achieved by linguistics alone since linguistics has no method for establishing criteria that can account for the appropriateness of the novel sentences. It is also his view that folklore research is in a prime position to contribute to a general theory of just such creative aspects of language use and he sees the analysis of verbal performance in terms of expressivity as offering, in its potential for the discovery of new kinds of units and organisation in language, an opportunity for a major advance in sociolinguistic knowledge as well as in folklore.

Thus, it would appear that the investigation of Irish oral narrative texts, advocated in this paper for the purpose of improving the quality of Irish-language teaching materials, can if required find additional justification through the contribution it would make across the broadest fields of language study.

PART 3

The Otherworld Feminine

Introduction

Representations of a supernatural female agency occur in the art, the mythology and the religious ideology of a great number of cultural traditions all over the world. Archaeology presents us with artefacts from archaic times that portray the female form in various guises that appear to portray fertility and maternity. Psychology portrays the mother figure as of primeval significance in human consciousness and development. It is not, of course, the case that there is any single universal mother-goddess tradition. Lotte Motz offers 'a balanced and informed view of these issues that does justice both to historical cultural diversity and to psychodynamic reality in the matter of goddess traditions'.[1]

The evidence of pre-history and of mythology shows us that in the old European, neolithic era, before the spread across the European world of Indo-European speaking cultures, the cult of the mother-goddess prevailed throughout. Ireland, too, was inhabited for thousands of years before the coming of the Celts, our first Indo-European immigrants, by peoples whose ideology encompassed religious and cosmological sensibility towards a divine female agency who was the origin of the physical universe itself and of the life forms contained in its landscapes. On this last, western outpost of the old European world, the incoming patriarchal Indo-European cosmology of the Celtic-speaking cultures, established here by the technological and political hegemony of relatively small numbers of Celtic-speaking settlers, took on a significant characterisation from the previously dominant matriarchal ideology. Such accommodation is a universal feature of acculturation when, by conquest or peaceful settlement, ancestral culture is transformed by contact with new cultural forms that replace older expressions of worldview. In the Irish case, the cosmology of the incoming Indo-European, i.e. Celtic, ideology had already acquired an element of that identification of the cosmic forces of fertility and reproduction with a divine, sovereign, female landscape figure that finds its fullest expression in the early medieval literature of

Wales and Ireland. Cultural accommodation by Celtic ideology, in Gaul and Britain, to the pre-Celtic supreme-mother-goddess tradition of neolithic old Europe was intensified in Ireland, where an abiding sense of a supreme, sovereign, female cosmic agency operated on the incoming culture to a degree that resulted in a continuing, powerful sensibility to the presence in landscape of a divine, female agency – a sensibility that remains at the heart of Irish ancestral cosmology and legend.

At the learned level of Irish medieval literary tradition the figure of the mother-goddess is transformed into that of a territorial sovereignty queen whose autonomy and independent authority is diminished and exploited in the politico-literary propaganda of patrilineal dynasties competing for political hegemony. At the popular 'folk' level, however, the figure of the divine female agency, the mother-goddess of landscape, retains her autonomy and majestic authority in the local lore of place and thereby constitutes a traditional cultural resource contributing richly to the creativity of the popular imagination. All over the Gaelic world in Ireland and Scotland, down to the present age, traditions of the *cailleach*, the supernatural female elder, are to be found attached to natural features of the physical landscape – mountains, lakes, rivers, tumuli, caves whose shape she has moulded and whose location she has fixed – and feature also in the abundant stories of supernatural encounter between humans and the native otherworld within that sacred feminine landscape.

Accepting that the concept of a mother-goddess figure is prominent in Irish culture from the earliest times, the essays in this section discuss ways in which some aspects of the figure of the otherworld feminine continues to feature in the oral and vernacular expressions of that culture.

Following an initial presentation in the round, so to speak, of the character and ubiquity of the 'eternal female', the question of the personification of the sovereignty of such a figure in both the natural world of landscape and in traditional literature is explored – in particular the personification bearing the name *Cailleach Bhéarra* in both medieval literary tradition and in later vernacular oral culture. The continuity and adaptation of legends of *Cailleach Bhéarra* is then presented in terms of the analysis of and commentary on the texts of a number of tales collected for the Irish Folklore Commission in the earlier twentieth century. This material is evidence of a continuing presence in popular Irish cultural tradition of the perception of a female agency – connected to a supernatural realm.

Such continuing presence constitutes an instance of an issue treated within a number of recent publications dealing with new approaches to Celtic religion and mythology. This is the question of the accommodation of the new Christian religion in Ireland and Britain to the old indigenous religion of the Celtic-speaking peoples of the two islands. John Carey has discussed the process whereby the 'old gods' were, in many cases, subject to absorption into a Christian dispensation of cosmology.[2] The literature of the period of early Irish is now understood to exhibit a multi-layered, multi-faceted nature in respect of its expression and representation of the imaginative world of mythology and religious culture. The orthodoxy of Christian learning and letters is threaded with figures and concepts from an enduring native world of ritual and belief. Joseph Nagy would claim that important elements of that native worldview lived on up to modern times not only in the narrative transmission of legends of otherworld encounter but also in the dynamic of the verbal performance of such legends and its potential effect.[3]

The goddess figures of medieval Irish literature and of later oral vernacular tradition draw on the amalgamation of that earlier cosmology with Christian culture. In particular, the figures and the stories of the sovereignty goddesses have a central and significant place in the early literature. Máire Herbert recounts that significance of the goddess figure in the mythic narrative representation of society in early and middle Irish literary tales.[4]

While these medieval tales of the sovereignty goddess are seen to function in a political discourse of male hegemony concerned to establish the legitimacy of particular claimants to ruling authority, the non-sovereignty female figures of later pre-modern tradition are represented both as personifications of the life forces of landscape and territory and as the imaginative inspiration and narrative legitimation of the operations of a set of actual females who play important roles in life rituals of birth and death of the pre-modern rural communities.

The country midwife – the 'handy woman' or *bean chabhartha* – along with 'keener' or *bean chaointe* of funerary ritual, have close connection to a native otherworld which is understood as the realm of the goddess. Another figure of vernacular narrative legend tradition drawing on the otherworld feminine is the *bean feasa* ('wise woman') figure resorted to, in legend, by individuals who are victims of misfortune and who are portrayed as being helped – through her agency – in finding ways of coping with their plight. The functioning of vernacular legend narration/ performance in these instances can – along the lines suggested by Nagy – bear some comparison with the coping mechanisms acknowledged by modern therapy in regard to the alleviation of distress.

The otherworld feminine features in the thinking and writings of major figures of both the Irish literary revival and the Gaelic League movement. W.B. Yeats and Douglas Hyde each drew on the literary and oral vernacular traditions of the sovereignty queen and the legends that demonstrated the continuing allegiance of tradition to the concept of a native, indigenous otherworld realm. In this way each can be seen as having brought Irish oral narrative traditions of the otherworld feminine to bear on the literary imagination and the cultural identity of modern Ireland.

Cailleach agus Céile: The Gaelic personification of sovereignty in nature and culture

A nature/culture or wilderness/society dichotomy characterises much of the symbolism of traditional culture and pre-modern civilisation and finds expression in the collective representations of popular tradition as well as in the symbolic productions of the learned and the literate. In the Gaelic culture of medieval Ireland the dichotomy in question is centrally reflected – in vivid and generative fashion – in terms of a series of female sovereignty figures. These figures personify the territory, and the social order prevailing upon it, of the human realm, and also the territory and the non-human life orders of the surrounding wilderness, whether that wilderness is the wilderness of air or earth or water. The female sovereignty personification of the human realm is the figure of a divine spouse, consort of the royal and rightful male ruler. Wilderness sovereignty, on the other hand, is personified in the figure of a terrible, threatening, divine hag who animates the wild world and guards its life forms. These two figures – hag and spouse – constitute binary opposition whose classificatory potential in Gaelic culture and in medieval Gaelic literature has been somewhat obscured by a concentration of emphasis on the divine spouse and sovereignty queen term of the polarity, largely due, no doubt, to the greater prominence accorded this latter in the written record of learned tradition.

The terms *cailleach* and *céile* suggest themselves today as apt Irish-language versions of the elements of the binary opposition I am highlighting. However, despite their alliteration, their euphony and their modern Irish and Scottish Gaelic dictionary meanings, it must be pointed out that there are difficulties inherent in their use in this way in the context of their semantic ranges in the earlier Irish language of medieval times.

I take it that *cailleach* is formed from *caille*, borrowed from Latin *pallium*, and that its earliest associations as a personal term are with the supernatural realm of the Christian order.[1] It has the primary meaning of 'nun' or 'woman in religion', viz. the phrase *cléirigh agus cailleacha* and the term *ceall cailleach* for abbess. It develops the secondary secular meanings of 'elderly woman/housekeeper' and these are the senses in which it is employed pejoratively in the sagas to mean 'secular and (wholly human) crone'. In the sagas however it also comes to have connotations of the native, ancestral supernatural as when we get a reference to the Morrigan *i ndelb na sentainne caillige*.[2] This latter association of *cailleach* with the native rather than the Christian supernatural realm is the one most directly attested at the non-learned level in the various *cailleacha* of oral tradition, such as *Cailleach an Daingin*, *Cailleach Neifinn*, *Cailleach na nGabhar*, *Cailleach na Beinne Bric*, *Cailleach an tSruth Ruaighe* and so on in the corpus of Irish and Scottish folk narrative.

Likewise with the term *céile*, its adaptation to secular, profane usage would appear to be a secondary development from an original usage chiefly in ecclesiastical terms: *céile* as in *Céile Dé*, *Céile Mac Maire* alters in sense to the legal *céile* ('the recipient of a fief') and eventually acquires the generalised sense of 'other fellow/opposite number' and the narrower sense of 'spouse', 'husband' or – less frequently – 'wife'.

Whatever the historical etymological soundness of the *cailleach/céile* version, however, I am intending to propose a hag/spouse opposition as a structural feature of medieval Gaelic culture, certainly in relation to the symbolic classification encountered in the narrative traditions of that culture at both the learned/literate and, in so far as we know it, at the popular and oral level of tradition. In this fundamental binary structuring of its symbolism the Gaelic medieval world is no different to the worlds of other cultural traditions. Running through most schemes of primitive and traditional classification is the principle of duality – an ordering of phenomena, of experience, and of the symbolic representations of experience through simple classificatory oppositions.

In its most developed forms this principle gives rise to the dual organisation of society as a whole with a corresponding organisation of the perception of the cosmos, the physical environment and the attributes of the world in general and all things in it. In such circumstances all reality consists of two halves, as for instance in the yin-yang conformations of much Chinese tradition. Another example, from nearer the micro end of the scale of social complexity, is the culture of the *Avatip*, a Papua New Guinea Sepik River lowland community studied by Simon Harrison of the University of Ulster. *Avatip* society is divided into two moiety-like descent groups, each with specialised magical and ritual powers. Harrison reports that this magical division of labour actually defines the community's political unity and its identity against outsiders.[3]

With full-blown dual organisation, while we can speak of individual dualities, it is of the essence that the sets of various and manifold dualities are themselves structured into a single, all-embracing classification. That this particular alignment of binary oppositions is a characteristically western construct and does not constitute a cultural universal is amply demonstrated in relation to a succession of non-western societies in Carol MacCormac and Marilyn Strathern, *Nature, Culture and Gender* (London: Cambridge University Press, 1980). While I am not claiming such a universal degree of symmetry for the expressions of the *cailleach/céile* conformation in medieval Gaelic tradition, the hag/spouse duality in question is a very powerful one and provides a linkage principle between a series of separate dualities that are used in Gaelic tradition to symbolise each other in conceptual and indeed in affective terms.

The underlying fundamental dichotomies which find expression in this fashion are those involving, on the one hand, the contrast of the social world and the tame territory in which it is located and operates with the world of wild nature which surrounds it, and on the other hand, the contrast of the natural world of which human society is a central feature with an otherworld located in the supernatural realm. Figure 12.1 shows these dichotomies first singly and then in conjoint alignment.

Figure 12.1 Fundamental dichotomies

Social World	Wilderness
Natural World	Otherworld
Here	Elsewhere
Humans	Supernaturals

I need not emphasise, in regard to Figure 12.1, how, in Irish tradition as in those other cases where a major world religion is superimposed on native, ancestral faiths, there is ambiguity as to the nature and location and agencies of the supernatural world of the otherlife elsewhere. In learned as in oral tradition, Irish medieval and folk narratives reflect a creative tension between native conceptions of a contingent otherworld, a *saol sí*, in parallel, as it were, with human life, and the Christian conception of a transcendent otherworld that eye has not seen nor ear heard. *Cailleacha* feature in their turn in the creative exploitation of this ambiguity, whether at the learned/medieval level as in the ninth century 'Lament of the Old Woman of Beare' or at the later/popular level of early-twentieth-century folk narrative.[4] In a legend from the repertoire of Amhlaoibh Ó Luínse we hear, for instance, of the offer a *cailleach* figure makes to the young girl Peig Ní Dheasúna to provide her with a vision of an ambiguous next life, part Christian, part fairy: *'Beidh radharc mór agat le feiscint'* ('You will be able to see a great wonder'). On this occasion, as in the many others in Gaelic popular narrative tradition when this motif occurs, the young girl declines the offer.[5]

In partially aligning the perception and symbolic classification of life forms (animal and vegetable) and environmental forces (geological and atmospheric) with the conception and the manifestations of the supernatural in human affairs, Gaelic medieval culture is doing something which is a standard feature of occidental traditional culture, and what I am attempting to draw attention to is the way in which images of a female supernatural-cum-wilderness personage are a central specific device by which in Gaelic culture this alignment is accomplished. There are, of course, other devices that operate in the culture to manifest the same alignment. The portrayal and development of Fionn Mac Cumhaill in narrative tradition, as it has been presented recently by Joseph Nagy, can be seen to be evidence of the operation of this wilderness/otherworld alignment also in terms of a male hero figure.[6] Finn is perceived paradoxically as being both central to and yet outside civil society in his association with mantic poetry and divination on the one hand and with the natural environment and the wild creatures native to it on the other. This file/fénní polarity which Finn expresses is a manifestation of the structuring principle that lies behind the narrative discourse of Irish tradition at both the learned and the popular levels of transmission. It is my contention that the manifestation of this principle in the form of a female figure – intermittently representing social and natural sovereignty in alternatively intimate and alien, fecund and destructive, attractive and repulsive guise – is both very ancient and very widespread in Gaelic tradition. John Carey has argued for seeing such a duality of aspect in the Irish war goddesses.[7]

I am suggesting that indeed the same duality permeates the presence of the supernatural female on all sides and at all levels of Irish narrative tradition. In particular I want to suggest that at the non-learned level of the later folk narrative tradition we can still see operating this structuring principle of literate medieval Gaelic culture. In the later folk tradition the principle is predominantly manifested again and again in the person of a female ancient, a *cailleach* who has localised associations with the south-west of Ireland but who is known to Gaelic tradition throughout this country, throughout much of Scotland and in the Isle of Man. This senior mythological figure is widely known as *Cailleach Bhéarrach* or something approximating to *Cailleach Bhéarrach* such as *Cailleach Bheurr* or *Cailleach Bheathrach*. The name is often taken to mean Hag of Beare or Beara, the historic territory of the *Corcu Loigde*, an Érainn tribe of west Munster, the chief residence of whose over-king was at Dunboy near the present-day Castletown Berehaven. Certainly the learned ninth-century lament establishes the name *Caillech Bérri Buí* in its association with the place Beara.

At the popular level of oral tradition, however, the *cailleacha* with names whose second element appears to be a version of the placename Bérri/Bearra should, I believe, be understood to be named not from this toponym but rather in relation to the collective perception of a hostile, peaked wilderness which they personify. We can note immediately that in the oral tradition of the Beara peninsula itself the supernatural female in question is termed *an Chailleach Bhéarrach* ('leis an gCailligh Bhéarraigh'), making it clear, I believe, that we should distinguish between this *cailleach* of later oral tradition and the *cailleach* of the ninth-century lament, who was authoritatively assigned the toponymic Béarra association in learned medieval materials. At the level of popular oral tradition it would appear that a degree of folk etymology has come into operation here, in both Ireland and Scotland. This folk etymology draws on conceptions of a female wilderness/otherworld spirit that perhaps owed something to the influence of Norse mythology but that certainly perceives the supernatural female not primarily in terms of the tribal/territorial sovereignty queen image but as a sovereign spirit of the wilderness. Such a supernatural female personification of the external, peripheral wilderness is named in oral tradition from her chief characteristic of being *biorach* (sharp, inimical, peaked). The form Berach was a relatively common personal name in early Ireland and I believe that it is from the conception of such a peaked wilderness goddess, rather than from the place Beara, that the representative *cailleacha* of Gaelic oral tradition are named.

Iron Age Celtic materials on the continent are known, of course, to include images of a peaked or horned god from as early as the fourth century BC. This figure, named *Cernunnos*, 'the Horned or Peaked One', has associated with him images of the serpent, the bull and the stag. These are understood to emphasise his symbolic significance as a chthonic or earth figure with a strong fertility association. The Ulster hero *Conall Cearnach*, the Bumpy One, and the Welsh *Owain*, Keeper of the Forest, are regarded as later insular and partly humanised reflexes of this great male supernatural figure. Here, of course, in medieval Gaelic culture as well as elsewhere in the Christianising world, we find the animal and fertility association of the horned god eventually transferred to an image of Satan with horns and hooves and an accompanying goatish ruttishness. Against this, Professor Mac Cana has surmised that with the establishment of Christianity in early medieval Gaelic culture, it is at the level of the lowest order of society that the cult and memory of *Cernunnos* would have survived longest.[8] The evidence I have looked at in the Gaelic oral narrative tradition, that in Ireland and Scotland carries a medieval repertoire to the brink of the modern world, suggests that it is rather *Cailleach Bhéarrach* who functions in popular oral tradition to express (in terms of a female divine figure) that conflation of association of chthonic powers, the vitality of the wilderness and of animal life, and fecundity in people and nature that we find operating in earlier portrayals of the horned god. Non-learned, oral tradition is here, I believe, carrying forward archaic conceptions of the nature of the earth, of animal life and of human order – conceptions that found ancient and perhaps earliest expression in terms of the female personification of various aspects of the cosmos.

I have mentioned the way in which I believe our understanding of the nature and fullest potential of the *cailleach/céile* polarity has been obscured by an over-emphasis on the sovereignty queen aspect of the supernatural females of learned Gaelic tradition. Perhaps it would be truer to say that there has been in relation to the learned tradition a mistaken emphasis on either the divine spouse aspect or the war goddess aspect, to the detriment of our understanding of the intermittent presence of both statuses together in the figures and the imagery of the personification of female sovereignty in nature and in culture. John Carey's treatment of the war goddess and Máire Bhreathnach's querying of the sovereignty goddess as also a goddess of death[9] begin to suggest the continual co-existence in the supernatural female of those ranges of association that I suggest are encompassed in the underlying nature/culture, wilderness/society dichotomy. I think it is possible to show that just as these war goddesses and sovereignty figures of the learned tradition exhibit the characteristics of their antitheses, so too the *cailleacha* of later oral tradition and specifically *Cailleach Bhéarrach* – who is perhaps the most representative figure among them – exhibit characteristics across the range of the *cailleach/céile* polarity and are not confined solely to the role of wilderness hags, devoid of all quality save that of being blightingly inimical to human life. In Figure 12.2, I show the basic set of opposing characteristics within which the other binary qualities, i.e. 'fertile/barren', 'intimate/alien', 'attractive/repulsive', etc., are developed.

Figure 12.2 Cailleach antitheses

Cultural	Supernatural
CAILLEACH/CÉILE	
Natural	Wild

The ranges of these qualities and their underlying primal opposition of the natural to the cultural-cum-supernatural are associated with and exploited in all the representations of the supernatural female in Gaelic tradition at both learned and popular levels, whether the immediate dramatic and narrative characterisation is that of sovereignty queen, war goddess, spirit of the flocks or crops, wilderness hag, etc. There are of course differing emphases in differing areas of Gaelic tradition. For instance in oral tradition, Scottish *cailleacha* narratives seem chiefly to emphasise sovereignty in flocks and herds while Irish *cailleacha* narratives seem chiefly to emphasise sovereignty in crops. This may of course be an outcome of narrative as much as of social or cultural history and I am not attempting here to account for such variation.

By way of discussion I wish to refer to two texts from late Irish oral tradition, both published by Douglas Hyde in *An Sgéulaidhe Gaedhealach*.[10] These texts derive from the narrative repertoires of the storytelling traditions of counties Roscommon and Galway, respectively, and were written down before the end of the nineteenth century. The first of them is entitled *Cailleach Ghleann na mBiorach agus an Tarbh Dubh* and involves the overthrow of the reign of a supernatural hag who appears to represent the untamed sovereignty of horned animals. The overthrow is accomplished by a human male figure assisted by a bull who is the progenitor of all domestic cattle and the sworn enemy of the *cailleach* in question. On the bull's advice, the hero equips himself for the physical confrontation with a flail as a weapon so that it is possible to regard the human hero as here ultimately confronting the supernatural guardian of wildlife with the aid of the energy and technology of plant and animal domestication.

The following is a resumé of the text:

- A *cailleach* lived underground since time immemorial on the side of *Gleann na mBiorach* in County Kerry, never leaving the mouth of her cavern.
- People feared her greatly and no-one would venture by night into the gleann, from where tremendous animal noises were regularly to be heard during the hours of darkness.
- One morning, before sunrise, *Murchadh Ruadh Ó Conchubhair* carries a sheaf of oats through the *gleann* to the black bull that he grazes there.
- At the mouth of the *cailleach*'s cavern, *Murchadh* witnesses a heron dropping to the ground an eel which is then taken inside the cavern by an eight-legged dog, as food for the *cailleach*.
- Later, the black bull speaks to *Murchadh* and tells him that the *cailleach* was the source of the great plague that destroyed the domestic cattle herds in ancient times and that all present-day cattle are the progeny of himself and the single heifer who survived the plague along with him.
- The bull explains that the heron is the *cailleach*'s mother and that *Madra na nOcht gCos* ('The Dog with the Eight Legs') is her son.
- The bull instructs *Murchadh* to light a fire of his – the bull's – dried *bualtrach* (bull's droppings) at the mouth of the *cailleach*'s cavern and to wield a flail against herself, her mother and her son.
- The bull offers that he will himself confront and vanquish the *cailleach*.
- *Murchadh*, a non-arablist, gets his wife to borrow a flail from a neighbour and he gathers and dries a great mound of the bull's droppings.
- Smoke from the fired *bualtrach* draws the *cailleach* and her kin out of the cavern and they do battle against *Murchadh* and the black bull whom the *cailleach* identifies as *Domblas Mór*, her great and ancient adversary.
- The black bull and *Murchadh* finally overcome and kill the *cailleach*, her mother and son; *Murchadh* breaking his borrowed flail in the course of the battle.

- The bull leads *Murchadh* into the cavern to fill a bag with gold and silver from the *cailleach*'s hoard. As *Murchadh* exits, the cavern is engulfed in an earthquake and the black bull entombed.
- Back at home, *Murchadh* explains the broken flail and his new wealth in terms of his having beaten the troublesome bull and sold it to a prince from Connaught.

Some points of commentary immediately suggest themselves:

1. The *cailleach* here, from the beginning, combines attributes of otherworld and wilderness in the remote Kerry fastness. She lives in a classic otherworld location and is nurtured in her chthonic permanence by magic creatures.

2. The human hero, with his oat-sheaf and his grazing bull, is in clear and domesticated contrast to the wild and supernatural *cailleach*.

3. The black bull, through a horned animal, is here part of the man's world even to the extent of sharing human speech. This feature is, however, ambiguous in its function. It serves to de-emphasise the creature's animality or alignment with the wilderness realm of the *cailleach*, while at the same time it lifts the bull–man relationship out of the realm of the ordinary and human and gives emphasis to magical, otherworld elements that are the supernatural counterpart of the wild, the non-human, aspects of life.

4. What is at issue in the story and in the *cailleach/Murchadh* juxtaposition is sovereignty. The *cailleach* is as much a sovereignty figure here as she is a wilderness hag even though her sovereignty is envisaged in terms of animal life in the natural realm rather than social life in the human world. At the outset of the story, both *cailleach* and human hero have a partial sovereignty in their respective realms. The overthrow of the reign of the *cailleach* in *Gleann na mBiorach* by *Murchadh* here re-enacts the gaining and establishment of human pre-eminence in terms that oppose the combined forces of maleness and culture to the essence of femaleness and nature. It is with the aid of artefact and technology that *Murchadh* is victorious – fire fuelled by the droppings of a domesticated animal and the flail as a piece of agricultural technology available to the hero through social relationship (his wife borrows it from a neighbour).

5. *Murchadh*'s reward for victory over the *cailleach* is his consolidated pre-eminence in the human realm of this, natural life. This much is signalled in the story in two ways. First, he loses his speaking

bull whose engulfment in the *gleann* correlates with *Murchadh*'s own emergence more fully into the human world of human, and especially male, technical and social supremacy. Secondly, he acquires great material wealth and physical comfort for the remainder of his life. In the motif of his carrying off the *cailleach*'s gold we see, as it were, transferred to the human hero the wealth previously attaching to the sovereignty of the flocks and the crops. One is reminded here of the tears of gold shed by the Norse goddess of fertility and sensuality Freyja, whose two daughters are named 'Jewel'.

The second text to which I wish to refer is from County Galway and presents the *cailleach* – this time actually named *Cailleach Bhéarach* – as a goddess of the harvest and especially the corn crop. It is analogous to a corpus of oral narrative texts in the Folklore Commission archive which continue the theme of the male conquest of the supernatural female and the acquisition, thereby, of knowledge and wealth. Since I have discussed this County Galway text at length elsewhere I give here only a schema (Fig. 12.3) and a summary version of the plot.[11]

Figure 12.3 Triple victory of hero

Contest	Implement	Advantage
digging	spade	hound's milk
mowing	scythe	steel spikes
reaping	sickle	destruction of <u>Dardaol</u>/Beetle

The following is a summary of the narrative structure of the story:

Summary
Frame-Tale
    a. *Cailleach Bhéarach* and her daughter set up, farming, in *Gleann na Madadh*.
    b. A succession of labourers expire in her service in vain attempts to match her prowess.
    c. The warrior-like *Donnchadh Mór* boasts that he will overcome her and takes service with her for unusually high stakes. He is to be fed on a cereal diet along with one pig-meat dish on Easter Day.

d. *Donnchadh* wins affection of *Cailleach Bhéarach*'s daughter but is left prostrate at the end of a day's spade-work.

e. Daughter renders superhuman strength to *Donnchadh* by dipping his bread in the milk of her mother's hound. *Donnchadh* vanquishes *Cailleach Bhéarach* and is rescued from her wrath by the daughter. Similarly with the daughter's help, Donnchadh vanquishes the *cailleach* at mowing – blunting her scythe.

f. Before reaping of oats, daughter alerts *Donnchadh* to existence of magic beetle in handle of *Cailleach Bhéarach*'s sickle. *Donnchadh* destroys the beetle and inflicts ultimate defeat on *Cailleach Bhéarach*.

g. At his request, she reveals her great age and she relates to him the story of her life and binds him to secrecy regarding it while she lives.

h. At the end of his term of service, *Donnchadh* extracts the fullest reward for his contract.

i. Shortly after, *Cailleach Bhéarach* sickens and dies during a great storm, together with her daughter and hound.

Inset-Tale (the story of her life)

i. When the *Cailleach Bhéarach* was a young girl she was betrayed in love by a neighbour's son.

ii. In revenge, she acquired magic gifts from the smith and used them to kill her former lover.

iii. She gives birth to a daughter at the smith's house and, in disguise as a man, becomes his helper at the forge.

iv. As punishment for accidentally injuring the smith, she is transformed into a sow for a period of 100 years.

v. Subsequently, she is restored to her daughter and given riches with which she buys her farm at *Gleann na Madadh*.

We may note that the character *Donnchadh Mór* is presented in the tale as a stereotype of the male hero and a fitting adversary for the supernatural hag. In the course of the story, he is seen to be in relationship with (a) his own mother, (b) the *cailleach*/hag, his adversary, (c) the hag's daughter who is a kind of lover to him. With these three females we see represented in this one text the three aspects of the supernatural female that are prominent in Gaelic tradition overall: *magna mater*, divine hag of war and death, sovereignty queen/spouse. The point of the whole tale is, of course, to recount the eventual overthrow of the hostile, repulsive, deadly persona of the goddess by a male hero who is aided and enabled in this by the personification of the goddess' maternal and spouse-like aspects.

In the folk legend versions of such an encounter and such a victory for a semi-human, semi-divine male hero over a supernatural female figure, we appear to have an echo of a very ancient formulation of the female personification of the cosmos and the articulation of this conception in terms of a myth. This myth concerns a female divine who symbolises the fecundity of the natural world and the ultimate order of the supernatural realm whence the sovereignty of the male ruler in this life is legitimated by means of an encounter between him and the goddess. If many of the folk legend versions of such an encounter are cast in the form of a contest and a vanquishing, at the learned and literary level the encounter typically resolves itself in terms of the consummation of a union between the male sovereign of the human, social world here and the divine female personification of the sovereignty of both the wild, natural world and the supernatural otherworld elsewhere.

And it is not in Ireland only that the Gaelic notion of such mystical marriage of king and landscape survives into early modern times. James VI and I addressed his first English parliament in 1604 in terms that have been convincingly analysed by Michael Enright to reveal the influence of Gaelic tradition on the monarch. In presenting and pressing his campaign for Anglo-Scottish unification, James represented himself as the spouse of a bride who personified both his kingdoms: 'I am the husband and all the whole isle is my lawful wife.'[12] Enright attempts to show that there is a direct link between James' utterances and the common Gaelic heritage of Scotland and Ireland in the matter of a foretold mystical union between a supernatural female personification of the sovereignty of a territory and the rightful ruler of that territory. Enright holds that at his accession to the throne, James, like many of his Scots subjects, must have felt that a prophecy had been fulfilled. Such prophecy, and especially the marriage metaphor, was, Enright holds, probably known also to Scottish lowlanders in the later sixteenth century. He quotes verses from Alexander Montgomerie and others to this effect and shows how this symbolic theme could hardly have escaped the attention of James, especially the version of it deriving from Thomas of Erceldown's alleged thirteenth-century divination that 'one day a man in the ninth degree of Bruce's blood would rule "all Bretaine to the sey"'.

Whatever of such intrusion by the sovereignty queen into the 'matter of history', I think that a case exists for trying to build up as rounded a picture as possible of the nature and significance of figures such as the *Cailleach Bhéarra* as we have encountered her in the two texts discussed above. The model which I think we can begin to develop to account for the forms and significations of the supernatural female in her hag/spouse polarity of representations needs obviously to be relevant to both literary and legendary figures other than *Cailleach Bhéarrach* if it is to be of much use. The kind of framework of significations which I am suggesting (see Fig. 12.2 again) as the background from which some such model can emerge is relevant also, I suggest, to at least three other types of literary figure. In the first place, I think it can allow us to look again at the apparently straightforward 'sovereignty queen' figures with a heightened sensitivity – such as Dr Máire Bhreathnach articulates – to ways in which they may be simultaneously perceived as carrying other cultural significations. Secondly, I think that such a model will account efficiently enough for the complex significations of the various martial and/or druidic foster mothers of heroes – such as Cú Chulainn's *Scáthach* and Finn's *Bodbmall* – whose spheres of influence encompass liminal stages of the hero's development wherein intermittence and alternating polarity is appropriate.[13] Thirdly, there is the case of the supernatural females of the voyage tales. These tales may themselves be regarded as serving an initiatory or transitionary function in having the hero translated out of the human realm into a liminality that is part wilderness, part otherworld. Dr Christa Löffler has shown, in a detailed study of the voyage to the otherworld island, that the female personification of that liminal island is a figure who can justly be regarded as part *céile*, part *cailleach* in my sense of this polarity.[14]

Additionally, I would suggest that the *cailleach/céile* polarity, operating as something intrinsic to the representation in Gaelic tradition of the supernatural females, can throw further light on the origin and sociocultural significance of such legendary proletarian figures from later oral tradition as the Scottish *glaistigh* and *nigheag* and the Irish *leannán sí* and *bean sí* who are to be regarded, in this fashion, as highly specific kinds of hag/spouses in their own right. A re-examination of the material relating to these and probably further types of supernatural female in Gaelic tradition undertaken with a *cailleach/céile* polarity in mind should prove instructive.

CHAPTER 13

The Inner-Outer Otherworld of Hyde and Yeats: Translation and worldview in the Irish literary revival

[Published in *Éire/Ireland*, vol. 35, nos. 1 & 2, 2000, pp. 26–42]

Describing W.B. Yeats at the end of 1898 as 'a Loner and a Nationalist and a Drug-user on a high', Roy Foster holds that Yeats spent the late 1890s waiting for the millennium – political, aesthetic and erotic – to arrive. When, however, the millennium not only failed to arrive but transformed itself into a personal apocalyptic anti-climax centring on Maud Gonne's revelation of her secret love life and her marriage to Major MacBride, Yeats had, Foster says, a kind of breakdown.[1] Certainly Yeats is seen as having 'set to' reconstructing his life, exploiting, in Anthony Cronin's phrase, 'his wonderful capacity to become a new person'.

This reconstruction and renewal is seen as constituting 'a farewell to Celtic mists', as Foster puts it, an abandonment of the regions of youthful and romantic enchantment for the sterner, more adult concerns of political and daylight reality. In a review of an anthology of Celtic literature compiled by George Russell, Yeats wrote dismissively in 1904 of a '... region of shadows ... full of false images of the spirit and of the body', images to which his own personal response was, he claimed, one of 'frenzied hatred'. This claim was only a year or so removed from Yeats' review of Lady Gregory's *Cuchulain of Muirthemne*, in which the poet speaks of stories serving as 'a chief part of Ireland's gift to the imagination of the world' and defends this claim by declaring that the one thing in Ireland that stirred him to his roots was 'a conception of the heroic life come down from the dawn of the world and not even yet utterly extinguished'.[2] Some critics see a conflict between this delight in the heroic and the granting of free reign to the individual imagination to pursue that 'experimental digging' in 'the deep pit' of the self, which, Yeats now said, can alone produce great literature and to which he would henceforth commit himself. The 'heroic' is, in this light, seen to be incompatible with the 'self'.

I want to suggest that the counterpoint between so-called 'Celtic realms' and 'self-excavation' is more harmonious than has perhaps been allowed, and to explore the native, ancestral, alternative otherworld dimension. This sphere – debased in the terms 'Celtic twilight' and 'Fairyland' – is still available, even today, as a mythological and archetypal resource for individual and for community nurturance. The basic human quest, common to national and to individual psyches, is a quest for unity – not so much of territory, or politics or peoples, but a unity of soul within itself and with cosmic soul. Seamus Heaney has recently spoken in terms of Yeats' efforts to do something towards which Douglas Hyde and the early Gaelic League were striving in a different way – the restoration of spiritual values and a magical worldview, which Ireland and the Irish had lost in the colonisation of not only the Irish landscape but of the Irish imagination as well. The calculus of this imaginative loss is expressed largely in the progress of language shift and in this shift's significance as imaginative impoverishment, reaching to the deepest depths of self, in the case of individual artist and of anonymous generation alike.

Seamus Heaney today paraphrases Yeats' words about the place that does not exist, the place that is but a dream, in his own contemporary struggle to articulate a sense of Irishness which is beyond the refutations of politics – and even of history. The traditional native, ancestral, alternative, otherworld realm, a recognition of which and a sensitivity to which was basic in the popular cultural heritage Hyde promoted – and on which Yeats drew – was capable of providing a framework for the resolution of fundamental problems of an ontological and a cosmological order, the large issues of the relationships among self, history and eternity.

A fundamental element of this ancestral Irish otherworld orientation was the recognition that daily life is lived on the brink of another order of being, which is neither closed off nor far away. Normality in this regard consists of the possibility, indeed even the prospect, of transition between the two orders, on the part of individual consciousness. This kind of awareness of an imminent otherworld and this propensity for regular otherworld experience is commonly regarded as the territory of religion or psychology rather than of literature, especially if we chiefly mean by this latter term, texts of the western canon of modern writing. Reading such texts of modern literature is not viewed as participation in group ritual. On the other hand, cultivating an ancestral oral heritage through participating in the performance of legends and songs that transmit sacred group knowledge or group wisdom – for which the native term is *coimcne* – had itself a sacred aspect. This aspect is palpable in the reverence shown for landscape, for features of landscape, and for the forces, personified or un-personified, believed to shape both landscape and cosmos – and, ultimately, to control human affairs. Such reverential awareness of a potential otherworld in the world-all-'round is a manifestation of a degree of union or harmony between the individual psyche and the larger totality of psychic or imaginative life, which appealed to both Hyde and Yeats as a kind of redemptive resource for the Irish and for humanity in the face of dehumanising contemporary forces working against the interests of imagination and of soul.

For a period spanning the turn of the century, both men held the cause of art and the cause of the Irish Gaelic cultural heritage to be the same; each sought to nourish and to liberate an inborn creativity and spirituality threatened and thwarted on all sides. In Hyde's case, the vision and the energy of the man became the vision and the energy of a hugely successful social movement, the Gaelic League, which in its first twenty years radically infused the lives of Irish men and women of all classes, creeds and backgrounds with an imaginative charge.

The imaginative repossession of themselves and of the past transformed those lives, giving them a gaiety, a self-esteem, a confidence. In the case of Yeats, his individual repossession of the fused heroic and aristocratic heritages to which his imagination laid claim was to lead him deep on a journey into his own particular consciousness and on into a universal consciousness of the human condition that is paradigmatic not just for Irish people but for all people.

Important aspects of that poetic journey invoke features of landscape and cosmos and the permeable boundary between these and centres of human consciousness that seem to echo aspects of Irish ancestral cosmology. It may be useful to describe some of the latter in the context of a basic framework: an ambivalent concurrent allegiance within Irish tradition both to Christianity and to the pre-Christian (pagan, Celtic, or simply native Irish) religious proclivity that endures in Irish life, as in Irish literature, as a defining characteristic of Irish worldviews and Irish styles of life.

This ambivalence in Irish popular religious tradition issues as a deep-seated syncretism in conviction, in ritual practice, and in the oral narrative materials that reflect traditional experience and traditional imagery of otherworld and afterlife. Little violence is done to the popular religious and oral narrative tradition by categorising it into a polarity captured in an essential way in the pair of terms *athair-mhac/ máthair-chailleach*. These are not, however, easily or simply translated into equivalent English terms.

Athair-mhac, with the literal meaning 'father-son', represents official Christian orthodoxy. Eoghan Rua Ó Súilleabháin, the eighteenth-century poet, used it famously on one occasion to cast a barb at ecclesiastical authority:

> *Má tá an tAthair Mhac mar an Eaglais*
> *Níl brí 'nár ngnó*
> *Is ní fearra dhúinn an tAifreann*
> *Ná suí ar an móin*[3]

'If the Father-Son resembles the church on earth, then we're all done for' is the sense of it. Séamas Caomhánach held that the term *athair-mhac* derived from the usage of early Greek Christian tradition. At any rate it demonstrates the masculine and patriarchal nature of Irish Christianity in the modern period. That at least is what I *intend* it to do.[4]

On the other hand, I suggest that the term *máthair-chailleach* signifies a loyalty and an allegiance to another, ancient, pre-Christian and pre-Celtic understanding of the basis and operation of life – a loyalty and an allegiance that endures in Irish popular cultural tradition. *Máthair-chailleach* has the literal meaning 'sacred elder mother', and I intend it to indicate the acknowledgement of and reverence for an ultimately female, cosmic principle at the heart of reality, to which Irish popular religion continues to give syncretic witness. This personified figure of the divine female was, in the earliest years of the twentieth century, generally accepted as a literary device, often representing Ireland itself. The *Cailleach Bhéarra*, Queen Maeve of Connaught, *Caitlin Ni Uallacháin*, Deirdre, Gráinne all have, in the writing of the time, the status of literary image. But in the legends of popular narrative tradition, which Hyde's followers in the

Gaelic League were collecting and publishing, the status of the divine female was much more than that of literary icon. Even though no cult of *máthair-chailleach* existed outside such syncretic Christian devotions as those to Saint Gobnait, Saint Bridget and so forth, with their holy well patterns, nevertheless legends about *Cailleach Bhéarra*, about Áine, about Clíona, about Aoibheall, and about other women of the *sí* should be understood as religious texts pertaining to sacred figures within popular consciousness. These figures were intimately connected with the essential aspects of life: health, fertility, well-being, goodness, death, otherworld and afterlife.

Hyde's vision and the vitality of the early Gaelic League were engaged with just such an ancestral sense of the Irish landscape and the Irish cosmos. For Yeats, too, there was an enduring engagement with the wisdom and the energy that underlay and flowed through place-names and place-lore. (*Dinnseanchas* is the native term: the traditional repertoire of sacred knowledge about an essentially sacred landscape.)

What I wish to do here is to draw attention to contrasting central features of the two alternative orthodoxies that coexist in Irish tradition, the Christian and the ancestral, so as to throw more light on the latter as a specific Yeatsian context. The basic situation is more complex than this, of course, since there are at least four different historical eras of Irish religious orthodoxy known to us – each with its own syncretic configuration. First we recognise a meso-neolithic old European era – which we should perhaps be regarding as a succession of separate, particular eras if only we had the evidence. Second we have an Indo-European, i.e. a Celtic, era. The Christian/medieval era follows, and gives way to an era of scientific enlightenment and atheism, which coexist with faith in the modern age.

The first of these, the old European era, can be thought of as an age that, if not matriarchal per se, is certainly not patriarchal here in Ireland or elsewhere in Europe. This is the era before the arrival in Ireland of Celtic speakers with their male, Indo-European gods and their Indo-European patriarchal social organisation. Later comes Christianity, another patriarchal ideology, spreading from the Middle East on the heels the Mediterranean *imperium*, which had absorbed it in its later stage. The *imperium* never reached Ireland at all, in terms of military occupation; but Christianity continued the westward movement beyond Roman Britain and took root, flowered, and went native here in a distinctive imaginatively productive and culturally glorious fashion. Yet the memory of the goddess and of a sphere charged with sacred vitality has endured; so cosmological ambivalence has remained – especially in popular cultural tradition – as a distinctive characteristic feature of Irish life and Irish literature. Officially and avowedly Christian, the Irish people give allegiance to the goddess too – and to her alternative otherworld realm – not out of nostalgia, not out of ignorance, not out of superstition, but out of a sense that *her* legends represent an archetypal wisdom regarding human life, a knowledge valuable beyond theological fashion and productive of human well-being in both individual and communal terms.

The central elements of the two alternative Irish cosmologies may be summed up in two contrasting pairs of features. For Christianity we have:

(a) God the Father reigning in heavenly glory through all eternity, with a hallelujah chorus of endless praise from choirs of angelic spirits. It was this Father who at the beginning of time created the entire universe from nothing.

(b) Jesus, the Son of the Father; coming on earth among us humans to teach us about our Eternal Father and to bring us to say 'Thy will be done on Earth as it is in heaven'. In His own case, of course, it was His Father's will that He should die for all of us on the cross, saving us from the eternal punishment and death that we merit.

These tenets were enthusiastically embraced by Irish people and by Irish culture and are the inspiration for marvellous verbal art such as Old Irish lyrics, the poems of *Bláthmhac*, the later poetry and song of *athrí* or repentance, and *Caoineadh na dTrí Mhuire*, the celebrated passion lament. There can be no doubting how deeply the gospel entered the Irish psyche. A stark and moving assertion of this is contained in the apocryphal legend of an Irish slave in Iceland questioned one night by his Viking master as to what names his people gave to the supernatural beings in which they believed. One name the slave said his people believed in was *Íosa, Mac Dé*, Jesus, the Son of God, and he said that his own hope also lay with this *Íosa*. Here indeed was a steadfast Christian! But if the voice of that slave is a true voice of Irish religious tradition, it may be claimed that another true Irish religious voice exists, speaking of a different supernatural reality. The pair of features at the centre of this alternative reality – by contrast with a pair at the centre of the Christian reality – follows:

(a) The eternity of a physical universe as the corollary of an eternal ancestral otherworld. The matter of this physical universe always was and always will be there. There was no first instant when it was created *ab initio* – but its shape has been formed by the operation of a female agency, whose handiwork is the setting alike for human lives and for the life of *an slua sí*, the denizens of the ancestral otherworld. Over all lies the female agency rules.

(b) The temporal landscape as the domain of the *seantuinne*, the *cailleach*, the divine female elder. Her corporeal presence is manifest alike in various natural features of landscape – for example *Dá Chích Anann* (Anú's Two Breasts), a mountain range in Kerry – and also in constructed features of lands such as in the mounds of the Boyne passage graves, and especially Cnogba (Knowth), the hill or mound of the goddess Boí, understood in the medieval record to be the telluric womb of the supernatural female who reigns as sovereign.[5]

The Irish, ancestral, supernatural female agency moves and operates throughout her terrestrial jurisdiction, flowing as the rivers named for her flow. Examples here are the great river names of Shannon and Boyne, and Bandon, the widespread river-name Bride, down to the little Owenabee River, *Abhainn* or River of Boí (the same goddess appellation as Knowth) that flows into Cork Harbour.

Under the names *Buí Bhéarra* or *Cailleach Bhéarra* she is widely known in landscape and topography throughout the whole Gaelic world of Ireland and Scotland for more than a thousand years, and in this persona she carries into the Christian middle ages and on into the early modern and modern worlds until today, the affection for – and Irish allegiance to – an alternative female ultimate authority discerned still at the imaginative heart of life long after the successive cultural transformations of Indo-European patriarchy and Christianity in Ireland. This affection coexisted with the hegemonic masculinity upheld by official Christian dominance in matters of mythology and ritual.

Apart from this contrast in the personification of cosmic or supernatural agency, Christianity and Irish ancestral faith contrast also in terms of where and when that agency relates to human life, in terms of space and time as applied to conceptions of otherworld and afterlife. We can say something briefly about each.

Taking space and spatial relationships first of all, we may ask, Where is the otherworld? Where is, in the Christian case, heaven – or hell? Who can tell? Of one thing we are certain: the Christian heaven is not here, all about us (*pace* Wordsworth, the growing boy). Since the early middle ages, the Christian heaven has been envisaged as a location outside our own realm, somehow up beyond the sky in its infinity of depth. And, of course, Christ 'ascended into heaven': *Ár nAthair atá sna flaithis go hard* / 'Our Father who art in heaven on high' as the poetic Gaelic version of the Lord's Prayer has it. A heaven from which the Father sends his son down to earth – *Vom Himmel hoch* in the phrase of Luther's great hymn to the Nativity.

In ancestral tradition, on the other hand, the otherworld, styled *an saol sí*, the life and land of *sí* since Celtic predominance, has been understood as being located to hand: to be 'round about'. Indeed it is not thought of as anywhere else but our own sphere and the *sí* otherworld 'throughout' each other, as the Hiberno-English phrase has it. This 'throughoutness' contact is not in ancestral tradition manifest, however, except at certain occasions in the calendar or in the life cycle, and even then perhaps to only certain kinds of individuals or categories of people: wise women, midwives, children, those males endowed with special artistic or athletic skill, and so forth. Such might experience, even visit, the *sí* otherworld to no ill effect – often indeed to good effect, with their existing special endowment further enhanced as a result. *An saol sí* was perceived, basically, as existing in the same dimension of the universe as human life. If it was the domain of the goddess/*cailleach*, palpable in the landscape, then it was also palpably located under the same sky as ourselves.

As for temporal relationship, that is, *When* is the otherworld?, we again see fundamental contrast between the Christian and the ancestral answers. In this life, according to Christian teaching, we are on the edge of eternity at all times, but we do not actually enter eternity until our life on earth comes to an end. After bodily death the soul departs for a spiritual existence conceptually constructed from a dualist, rationalist division of matter and spirit, body and soul – a philosophy, no doubt, incorporating elements of both Aristotelian and Cartesian thought.

In ancestral cosmological tradition it is, on the other hand, during our own lifetimes here on earth that we can experience, and even enter into, the native otherworld of the *sí*.

Admission into that otherworld may be accompanied by a loss of synchronisation in aging, since the *sí* otherworld tends to be the 'Land of

Eternal Youth', from whence visitors like Oisín return to a human world that has aged in their absence. Whatever of lack of synchronisation, the basic belief is that it is possible to be equally in otherworld eternity or timelessness and in our own lifetimes on those occasions when otherworld contact is manifest. Also we can see that when such otherworld visitation takes place, the human person enters into and returns from the *saol sí* in body and soul, as it were, though what should be emphasised here is the non-dualistic nature of the human person in ancestral thought, which, in this view, is without the Aristotelian or Cartesian or Christian division into matter and spirit. Such a non-dualist sense of person is hinted at in the common Irish language usage of the term for 'soul' (*anam*) as in phrases like 'She has great life in her' (*Tá an-anam inti*), or 'They devoted/ sacrificed their lives to a cause' (*Thugadar a n-anam ar son cúise*). Here the sense of *anam* is something more than that of the Christian ghost, which ascends into heaven after the death of the body. It is more the vitality or the life principle of the body in the intensities of living here on earth. Now the greatest, most marvellous and most mysterious intensification of living in ancestral tradition is to encounter and, perhaps on occasion, to enter into the *sí* otherworld as so many heroic and representative figures, male and female, are portrayed in tradition as having done. Examples range from Cú Chulainn to locally renowned hurlers and pipers and from Biddy Early, the north Munster wise woman, to locally renowned midwives and wise women and keeners at the wake.

All human life does come to its individual end, of course, no matter how perceived within philosophy or religion or literature. Ancestral Irish tradition has the deceased ancestors joining the ranks of the anonymous *slua sí*, the 'other ranks', as it were, of the native otherworld, destined to be an eternal retinue of the sovereign goddess and her regional transforms, the *sí* queens like Áine and Clíona and Aoibheall, who vivify the local landscape with their presence in geotectonic form and in oral narrative performance.

This specific ancestral Irish view of otherworld and afterlife has been subject to academic investigation recently, by scholars including John Carey of University College Cork and Patrick Sims-Williams of the University of Wales. In 'Time, Space and the Otherworld', Carey argues that the ancient sacred óenach, or ritual assembly, constitutes a pattern for narrative accounts of otherworld contact; Carey sees such patterning as a distinctive feature of Celtic Irish culture:

> ... for the ancient Irish the otherworld lay not only beyond the limits of [human] existence but also at the very heart of society. It was the source from which values and authority derived.[6]

Certainly it is true that in the later rural folklore and popular culture to which both Hyde and Yeats looked for inspiration, legends of contact with otherworld forces, themselves personified as sacred, supernatural female figures, were a source of personal legitimisation and social empowerment for individuals in a variety of social roles. Prominent among these were the women who occupied a set of female personae who rendered crucial service to the community in times of personal crises like those of childbirth, illness, misfortune and death, when the sensibilities of an ancestral cosmology – alternative to those of the official religious orthodoxy – were, perforce, joined to a Christian sensibility, to 'the will of the Father', in the task of finding meaningful the vicissitudes of human experience. In such times of heightened intensity of living, Irish popular culture and ancestral tradition call on deep imaginative roots. In 'Some Celtic Otherworld Terms', Sims-Williams comes to the conclusion that the two basic conceptions in ancestral cosmology as to the location of the otherworld are pre-Celtic in origin.[7] These conceptions are, first, that the *sí* otherworld is located underground, literally in the landscape, whether in the 'natural' hillside cave or rock outcrop, in the 'natural' spring well, or in the 'artefactual' or constructed ring fort (the *lios* and the *dún* of native tradition); and, second, that the *sí* otherworld is located overseas – perhaps on a sea island or perhaps in a mysterious underwater region to which access can be had only by going under the waves.

Both of these conceptions are, in Sims-Williams' view, a legacy from a pre-Celtic, pre-Indo-European world that gave its primary cosmological and religious allegiance to a female personification of divinity. So that, in a sense, the *sí* otherworld in Irish tradition has been indeed the Land of Women – *Tír na mBan* (or even of Woman) – from archaic times down to the late-nineteenth-century Roscommon and Sligo landscapes in which Hyde and Yeats became acquainted with the legends and so-called superstitions of the *cailleacha* – the hags and the wise women and the fairy queens. This landscape, all over Ireland and Gaelic Scotland, was, to the native sensibility, redolent with signifiers of the presence, authority and power of the feminine supernatural and its/her realisation in a physical universe – which is also vitally sacred. Joan Radnor has summarised the relation of landscape to femininity both in the pagan Celtic and the medieval Christian tradition in Ireland:

> ... this Otherworld is symbolically a female realm. Its geography is suggestively female: access is through a passage-way into a mound, or down a well or under or across water.[8]

The names associated with the female personifications of a feminine otherworld and a feminine cosmic power are a study in themselves. Two stand out in particular because of their continuity and their comparative ubiquity: the names Anu – with its Christianised Áine, or Anne, form – and Boí, with its association in the medieval literature with the south-western Beara peninsula as well as with the Boyne burial chamber. As Áine, as Boí, or as any other of the many local *cailleach* versions of the personified female cosmic force, the mother goddess has survived in popular oral narrative and in the religious sensibility of popular Irish cultural tradition in a way that escapes the kind of syncretism that has at the learned level given rise to the legends and cult of Brigit/Bríde/Bridget – at once pagan goddess and Christian saint.

I emphasise that it is at the level of popular cultural tradition that this memory of and this allegiance to the *máthair-chailleach*, the hag-goddess-mother, prevailed, surviving into modern times. At the learned, literary level of tradition from the early middle ages the figure of the *máthair-chailleach* was subverted to the cause of dynastic, patriarchal politics and turned into a sovereignty queen figure. The image recalls the general Indo-European ideology of the *hieros gamos*, the mystical marriage between the king and his divine consort who represents his territory and – in his unequal possession of her – represents also the projection of his patriarchal sovereignty.[9] This sovereignty queen myth has been central to a good deal of Irish literary and Irish political tradition from the use of Boí as sovereignty consort to Lug in the dynastic charter legend of the Uí Néill, through the *spéirmhná* of the *aisling* and the *seanbhean bhocht*, to the Mother Ireland images of modern times – including, most pointedly in this context – those that Yeats invokes and to whom he gives poetic and dramatic life in the decade between 'The Countess Cathleen' and 'Cathleen Ní Houlihan'.[10] As a kept woman, or a woman for the keeping by the victorious of the competing warring royals, the sovereignty queen figure serves always, in her myth, to empower and legitimate male authority and a patriarchal order. Thus is the *máthair-chailleach* shorn of her cosmic autonomy and of her pre-eminence as a matrix of vitality, fertility and identity in both local landscape and the cultural life of people.

This is at the official, learned, aristocratic level of Irish literary and all cultural tradition. Underneath the learning and the nobility, however, from the late ninth century to the late nineteenth, a wider, more generous and definitely more autonomous sense of the *máthair-chailleach*, the super-natural female, endures in the legends and the unofficial religious sensibilities of the plain people. Here she is no kept woman, however noble or tragic, but the universal, ever-present personification of the deepest level of cosmic reality as it presents itself to human consciousness. The ancestral otherworld, the *saol sí* of Irish tradition, is above or perhaps beneath all else, the major projection and imaginative elaboration of the perceived encounter between consciousness and reality on this island.

The story of this encounter, with its deepening of consciousness and gradual elaboration of symbolic expression, is what is recounted in the *Dinnseanchas*, the ancient place-lore, in terms of a sacred landscape; in the *Lebor Gabála*, the Book of Invasions, in terms of a mythic social and political history; in *Cath Maige Tured*, the Battle of Moytura, in its description of the paradigmatic event of Irish mythology and cosmology. In that battle (fought in County Sligo) the forces of destruction and chaos inimical to human society are finally vanquished by Tuatha Dé Danann, the Peoples of the Goddess, thereby establishing for all time the hegemony of the feminine supernatural in Ireland. This hegemony is subsequently shared with *Clanna Mil*, the Milesians, the later invaders who represent the human population of the island, in an agreement whereby Tuatha Dé Danann withdraw from the superficial world into *sí* otherworld locations. The contract emphasises both the proper sovereignty of the feminine supernatural in human affairs and the living, shaping, sustaining presence of that feminine supernatural in a landscape not merely physical, as it pulsates with the, as it were, atomic energy of the senior cosmic power.

I believe that it is to this traditional or ancestral sense of a sacred landscape yielding epiphanies concerning relations among the individual person, and external nature, that both Hyde and Yeats were initially drawn; each then tried in different ways to teach others to encounter this sacred landscape as a resource for renewing the national and individual psyche in pre-independence Ireland. Readers of Matthew Fox and Philip Sherrard today or of Simone Weil and Teilhard de Chardin a generation ago may find this call familiar.

There is, of course, another discipline again that has, since the turn of the twentieth century, grappled afresh with the notion of an alternative order of reality – a concept known apparently to all conditions of humankind in all cultures. This discipline is psychology and, in the West at least, the twentieth century has seen the revelation of knowledge concerning the otherworld realm understood by Freud and by Jung as the world of the unconscious – though Freud and Jung individually understood it in different ways. The basic concept of the unconscious itself allows us, however, to understand traditions and writings about all otherworlds – ancestral or Christian or New Age – as a kind of code for the life of the unconscious in all of us. This necessarily means that it is in ourselves, in our minds and imaginations, that heaven or the *saol sí* truly exists for us. In terms of this psychological point of view, and especially in terms of the subspeciality of psychodynamic studies, certain creative, sacred, almost divine, potentials of the human person can come into play in our lives as we gain insight into the operation of those aspects of ourselves that are usually hidden away from daylight, deep within the individual and collective unconscious. Such insight is understood as releasing into everyday conscious behaviour something of a primordial power that resides within every individual.

One recalls again Yeats' expressed wish to forsake the mists and shadows, which carried false images of the spirit and body, and to undertake an experimental digging into the self. Any such digging, whether for poetic or therapeutic ends, breaks into that realm of deep imaginative energy that may in Irish usage properly be called *anam* ('soul') in the native sense in which no distinction is implied between soul and body or between this life and some spiritually non-corporeal realm. The non-dualist, physical-cum-sacred universe, cosmic and psychic, is the place where the poet and the therapist work; it is in this place too that Irish ancestral tradition has always located the profoundly important work of 'soul-making'. The phrase *ag déanamh a anama*, which lexicographer Dinneen glosses as 'is making his peace with God', signifies as well in the ancestral religious discourse, and can, I maintain, be glossed there as 'is renewing his or her primal vigour'. This process involves making contact with sources of cosmic and psychic power in the repertoire of legend and placelore and the ritual visitation of landscape features, which were a shared heritage of the Irish-speaking countryside. Such imaginative visiting and revisiting of the persons and places of renewal bring us to an otherworld, to *Tír na nÓg* / the Land of Eternal Youth; to *Tír na mBan* /

the Land of Women, the realm of the goddess, the *máthair-chailleach*; to *Tír na nAircitíopaí* / the Land of Archetypes; to *An Domhain Toir* / the Eastern World; to Byzantium.

The legends and the folk wisdom that Hyde and Yeats alike recognised in the Irish countryside as cultural and spiritual treasure had, and can perhaps still have, immense value as creative materials of imaginative and psychic renewal. In some ways Yeats might be seen as never having really left behind him the Celtic realm (which is not, of course, a Celtic realm but an Irish realm) in the course of his digging of self. His excavations and articulations of the deeper and wider and higher gyres of life and consciousness and soul can be seen as remaining grounded in his initial, youthful encounter with the archetypal energy he sensed in the legends and lore of the landscapes of Sligo and Connaught and Ireland. These landscapes are the scenes of the triumph of Tuatha Dé Danann at Moytura, of Medb's reign at Cruachan, of the hegemony of the *máthair-chailleach* throughout Ériu – itself both the name of the land and of the 'lady' – as R.A. Breatnach has styled the divine consort aspect of the sacred female in his seminal clarification of the sovereignty queen myth in native *literary* tradition. Here again we are up against the Irish ancestral cosmological conviction that the landscape is the living realisation of a feminine sacred order and that the human lives consciously lived within such a landscape are capable of – and even liable to – regular imaginative enrichment through knowledge of and contact with the sacred cosmic powers.

Yeats, in fact, chose to continue to seek such imaginative enrichment and such creative sources of renewal not in the formulations of any ancestral tradition, but rather in his own formulations of psychic theories and of concepts such as the antithetical self within the wider, geographic and historical cosmos. Perhaps we should allow that, as an individual modern artist, Yeats had no alternative – since his own poetic impulse could not possibly be uniquely channelled within any one tradition. The effect, however, of the relative loss to the poet of such earlier contact with sources of creative renewal, which imaginative intimacy with the Irish landscape had brought with it, needs also to be considered. Francis Stuart has spoken of always sensing a gap in the mature Yeats between what Stuart terms 'the life' and 'the art'; and perhaps this observation of Stuart's could, in some way, be related – if only chronologically – to Yeats' emergence from and disengagement from the sacred landscape of ancestral Irish tradition.[11] Does the truth of his early masterfully confident assertion that 'whatever we build in the imagination will accomplish itself in our lives' begin to flag in the life of its author himself?

Of course, imagination – especially traditional imagination – and the creative accomplishment of its work in psychic life then, as now, was under general pressure on the wider social front. In the worldview of Irish, religious, educational and literary circles in the 1890s, sacred ancestral tradition and its expression as legend and ritual custom were generally regarded as merely 'folklore' and 'superstition' – with all of the overtones of the picturesque, the regressive and the ignorant which these terms imply. Both Hyde and Yeats were radical in their perceptions of the serious, adult import of ancestral cosmology within the oral narrative tradition and within popular culture, in an Ireland where the Victorian *pater familias* reigned supreme in the official, public order. This was a social world in which the values of rationality, technical ingenuity and efficiency, civic order, moderation and respectability were privileged. Even within the Christian churches there seemed to be an absence of those qualities of imagination or soul that were associated with traditional Irish spirituality. Certainly in both Victorian Catholicism and Victorian Anglicanism there would seem to have been a rejection, a shutting-out, on the part of the official mind, of any knowledge of the ancestral Irish perception of the physical universe as charged with the energy and presence of a divine order, and of any knowledge of the ways of regular, renewing contact with this presence, through legends and customs.

On the wider Victorian front we can understand many of the artistic and cultural movements of the late nineteenth century as resistance to this shutting-off of the sources of spiritual, creative and imaginative renewal by the prevailing intellectual establishment. The widespread turn-of-the-century interest – literary, academic *and* popular – in spiritualism and the occult should be seen in a similar light.

I believe that we should see Hyde and *Conradh na Gaeilge*, the league, founded in 1893, as a further resistance to and a rejection of the prevailing orthodoxy of spiritual suffocation. The great and immediate organisational success of the league may have been derived from the way in which the early league's vision and activities held out the prospect that renewing imaginative energy and repossessing cultural identity would give access to ancestral sources of such renewal.

It was widely recognised from the beginning that the Gaelic League was more than a mere language organisation. Later the league became inextricably enmeshed in the politics of cultural and militaristic nationalism. In its early phase, however, its vision, Hyde's vision beyond language instruction, was one of spiritual, of sacred otherworld, import. When Hyde lectured on de-Anglicising Ireland, he had more in mind than the speaking of the Irish language. What he was talking about was really the state of Irish people's metaphysics, their discourse with their native supernatural, their psychic and spiritual well-being. The kind of revival he envisioned as the goal of the early Gaelic League was not only a revival of the grammar and vocabulary of a specific linguistic code, but also a revival of human soul in an Ireland seen as languishing and suffocating in the arid desert of Victorian imperial culture. *Athbheochain na Gaeilge*, the aim of the Gaelic revival, certainly entailed promoting the speaking of the Irish language but, in a deeper and more important sense, it entailed setting loose *anam* – that is, creative energy, gaiety, celebration, and self-knowledge within Irish tradition, setting it loose from the hegemonies of the day.

There is something of an Irish-Protestant-led counter-counter-reformation in the nature of both the Gaelic League and the Anglo-Irish literary revival. Hyde and Yeats were both seeking scope – cultural, artistic, imaginative and creative – for the Irish soul and for the human soul. Their visions met separate fates in history. On the one hand, there was a hardening and a reduction by nationalism of the generous, initial vision of the Gaelic League, which had attracted a diverse multitude of supporters to its promise of imaginative renewal. On the other hand, Yeats is seen to leave behind the boundary of Ireland and Irish tradition in his lonely exploration of the widening gyres of individual artistic consciousness in its relation to the unconscious and the eternal within universal culture.

Whatever success or failure we may judge attended the efforts of Hyde and Yeats to realise their visions and succeed in their literary and cultural missions, we should remind ourselves that a century later the Irish landscape, then an imaginative runway for their visions, remains to be discovered and encountered anew by those with access – ancestral or academic – to the repertoire of sacred legend and oral tradition by means of which it renders itself comprehensible to its inhabitants. To listen to what it says about life does not oblige us to take up any cult, whether of arms or of a mother goddess. Rather does it sustain and enrich us in our attempts to do justice to the full range of human imaginative and psychic resources, feminine and masculine, that exist within each one of us and that we see and hear mirrored and echoing in our universe on all sides – if we really look and really listen.

CHAPTER 14

The *Bean Sí* in the Flesh: A rethink about goddess mythology and Irish tradition

[Paper read at *Litríocht agus Cultúr na Gaeilge* conference, National University of Ireland, Galway, 19–20 October 1990]

The currently fashionable interest in goddess mythology is obviously associated with the development of feminist perspectives, in literary and sociological analysis, as part of the women's movement. One of the concerns at the heart of this development has to do with the cultural and no doubt the social liberation of women from the stereotyping imposed on them as an outcome of the patriarchal nature of both the universe of discourse and the underlying, or concomitant, social orders that result from a combination of Indo-European and Judeo-Christian traditions within western civilisation.

Within this vast and profound enterprise, the study of individual linguistic and literary traditions can help to elucidate the ways – positive and negative – in which men and women, and masculinity and femininity, in a general sense, have been represented in the symbolic logic of specific cultures. My own interest in the study of representations of the female in Irish tradition was first expressed in relation to what I saw as a vision of liberation, and especially female liberation, in Brian Merriman's *Cúirt an Mheán Oíche*, where, as I have argued, the autonomy and the energy of the early Irish sovereignty queen is, in the author's poetic imagination, brought to bear, out of the realm of the mythological, on to the civil and sociological circumstances of the men and women of Merriman's contemporary world.[1] The liberated women – and men – of the poet's vision draw on an ancestral archetype of the sovereign female, so as to provide joy, significance and legitimation for their own lives. The poem's power and popularity within Irish popular as well as literary tradition is evidence of the enduring relevance of the quest for just such a relationship as the poem engenders – a relationship not only between literature and life, but between the mythic and symbolic realm and the everyday social and political reality of individual people's particular existence.

In that individual reality, access to the liberating energy and the joyful autonomy of mythic and archetypal figures is less straightforward for flesh and blood men and women than it is for the poet's characters. But it is possible to trace some patterns, at least, of the kind of access to the power of myth which Irish people have had available to them within their ancestral cultural tradition. In what follows I deal with evidence that suggests that in that tradition certain human female roles in society were constituted and reinforced in significant ways from the mythic and symbolic realm. More specifically, I want to claim that this reinforcement involved an ancestral, *bean sí* archetype other than that of the celebrated sovereignty queen, whose myth is, after all, a device of masculine hegemony. Encountering, embracing, wedding the loathly hag cum radiant goddess confirms the male hero in his reign as earthly sovereign with political power and social prestige.[2] His female partner remains otherworldly and may well be transformed back into a wild death-dealing hag once more. The feminist quest for models for female autonomy are ill-served, I think, by trying to present the likes of Macha and Maedb or Aoibheall and Áine as appropriate archetypal figures. Despite the power of poetic creation in Merriman's poem, the fact is that, outside poetry, in historic and ethnographic reality it is the male hero in his warrior and ruler roles that the sovereignty queen myth legitimates and energises. The formidably masculine qualities of a Gráinne Ní Mháille and a Margaret Thatcher are, of course, evidence that it is possible for individual women to compete, and even triumph, in the so-called man's world. It shows us also how carefully we must distinguish gender and gender construction from physiological sex and reminds us too that life can always overwhelm categories and systems with which we try to classify and interpret it.

In general, however, the symbolic logic of Irish and other western cultural traditions keeps the female at a distance from the centres of social and political power. Specifically, in the case of the symbolic logic of Irish tradition, female power and autonomy is assigned to either an otherworld realm, where, as sovereignty queen, a divine spouse is supernatural consort of the royal male ruler of human society, or else to the outer wilderness beyond the social realm, where, as personification of landscape and the wildlife of flora and fauna, a divine hag constitutes an abiding, if peripheral and marginal, threat to the well-being of humans and human affairs. This hag-spouse, binary opposition, the opposition of supernatural *cailleach* to supernatural *céile*, runs deep in Irish tradition. On the one hand, it appears to find its most intense and characteristic expression in the well-known medieval literary narratives of the encountering by a male hero and future royal ruler of a loathly hag, who is transformed to a radiant young beauty through physical intimacy with him and who, revealing herself as supernatural sovereignty, prophecies and delivers political dynastic sovereignty to her human partner. On the other hand, it finds expression also in the accounts from oral tradition of a variety of *cailleacha* who reign in remote valleys, in mountain passes, on islands and sea rocks and are tellural guardians of the natural world, of the cereal harvest, of animal herds. These *cailleacha* constitute adversaries to human endeavour and have to be vanquished in the tales by a variety of male heroes who draw on supernatural sources to gain the victory.[3] Thus, in both instances, at both literary and oral levels of tradition, the apparent inevitability of male social hegemony is advanced.

In an article in *Béaloideas*, I claimed that the figure of one *cailleach* – *Cailleach Bhéarra* – subsumes both sides of this dichotomy in the representation of female power as something marginalised or excluded from centres of authority in human society.[4] The sense of *Cailleach Bhéarra* as sovereignty queen has since been reinforced by the findings of Tomás Ó Cathasaigh in a study in *Éigse*, where he emphatically endorses T.F. O'Rahilly's earlier identification of *Cailleach Bhéarra* with the sovereignty personification called Buí or Bua, the alleged wife of Lug, after whom both the burial mound of Knowth/Cnogba at Brú na Bóinne and the Island of Dursey, together with other sea rocks at the end of the Béara peninsula, are called.[5] The sense, on the other hand, of *Cailleach Bhéarra* as wilderness figure and personification of crops and flocks is, in oral tradition, very widespread and very well known. In the folklore of Ireland and Scotland, *Cailleach Bhéarra* shares this function with a variety of other well-known hag figures, under a variety of other names.

Both of these senses of *Cailleach Bhéarra*, however, tie her in to the sovereignty myth, which, in Gaelic patriarchal discourse, ultimately serves to elevate, ennoble and glorify a male warrior-cum-hero. It is most significant for my purposes here, in attempting to focus on archetypal sources for female autonomy in the human social sphere, that *Cailleach Bhéarra* material also contains a third sense beyond the sense of her as spouse-like sovereignty queen, or terrible, wilderness adversary. This is the sense of *Cailleach Bhéarra* as eternal, enabling, nurturative, female agency – whether as creative earth mother, as wise tutor/counsellor, or as magical and artistic performer.

Elsewhere, I present evidence from the archives of the Irish Folklore Commission for this side of *Cailleach Bhéarra*.[6] It is extensive both in range and in quantity and establishes her as a figure of autonomous power, stability and wisdom. Here, I want to urge that it is this wise, benign, nurturative, enabling and above all creative supernatural figure, whether in the person of *Cailleach Bhéarra* or of the numerous other named and anonymous *cailleacha*, known to ancestral Gaelic tradition, who offers to Irish and to all women, and indeed men too, a native, archetypal model that can serve them in their efforts to ground their conviction of the dignity, the autonomy, the creative vitality of every individual human life in Irish mythology. Certainly, it appears to me that this version of the *cailleach* formerly animated and energised a series of female personae in Irish cultural tradition that historically offered individual women the opportunity to perform crucial social and cultural roles that in return brought them significant status and authority as women in their own right. I am thinking of such as *An Bhean Feasa, An Bhean Ghlúine, An Bhean Bhán, An Bhean Chaointe*; perhaps even also of such less specific personae as those of a *Bríd na nAmhrán* or a lullabying mother, given the magic power that Breandán Ó Madagáin infers in lullaby performance.[7]

Each of these personae is connected with, and able to draw on, the energy of a native mythological resource in different ways. Together, they share privileged access to, and protection from, the risks of contact with, the ancestral otherworld realm *an saol sí*. Look for instance at the legends that explain the acquisition of her power by the *Bean Feasa*. As in the case of the best known of the Munster *Mná Feasa*, Biddy Early, it is, inevitably, a 'fairy' gift.[8] Look at the legends that explain the practical wisdom and the skill of the *Bean Ghlúine*, whose legendary ministrations to a female of the *slua sí* are reinforcement for the local community in its placing of such great trust and confidence literally in her hands.[9] Look at the strictness of the taboo on the handling of a just-deceased corpse, by even its closest relatives. Only the *bean bhán* is, as it were, licensed and proof against such intimate, physical contact with such a liminal potentially contaminating phenomenon as a fresh corpse. Only when she has performed her practical, and especially her ritual, services is the symbolic potential of the corpse to pollute and injure the family and the community contained in the prophylactic prescriptions of the laying-out.[10] And the prophylaxis works both ways – for the deceased as well as for the bereaved. As an important element of the wake ceremonial in general, the laying out of the corpse is a proper and necessary part of the deceased's successful and safe transition to the otherworld realm, in both its Christian and ancestral perceptions.[11] Failure to achieve such transition leaves the deceased's spirit 'troubled' and liable to return.

It is heightened concern that her dead love be safe from such troubling harm in the awful circumstances of the absence of his lost corpse that causes Liam Ó Raghallaigh's young widow to claim, in her lamenting of his death, that if things were as she would have them, then it is not one but three women who would lay him out:

> *Bheadh triúr de na mná bána ann*
> *le haghaidh mo ghrá 'chur ar a leabaidh.*[12]

The case of the *bean chaointe* can be dealt with at more length here. First, let me say that the *saol sí*, with which these female personae have privileged contacts in Irish tradition, is not only the 'fairy' world of the anonymous *slua sí, bunadh na gcnoc, uaisle beaga, daoine maithe*, etc., of later folklore,[13] but the more fully realised realm of the goddess, the world of the Tuatha Dé Danann, and the other ancestral divine figures whose recusant existence has, in vernacular imagination, survived fifteen centuries of Christianity. Within this ancestral supernatural realm we can surely agree that the figure of the goddess looms very large and encompasses a significance far wider than is contained and articulated in the sovereignty myth. It is, of course, the non-sovereignty queen reaches of that wider significance which, in my reading, informs those female personae whose own significance and authority in Irish popular cultural tradition operated independent of patriarchal origin or patriarchal legitimation.

If, as what I am arguing implies, the flesh and blood women who fill the social roles associated with these personae act, as it were, in the place of, or in the person of, the goddess, when they perform their important functions in the community, then it is in the place of the benign, wise, creative, nurturative person of the goddess that they operate. And this is true even in the case of the *bean chaointe* who should not be regarded as somehow congruent with the reverse side of the sovereignty queen figure, which relates to death – a relationship that Máire Bhreathnach has made explicit in her *Zeitschrift* article.[14] Rather is the *bean chaointe* to be associated with the creative, enabling, protective aspect of the goddess in that her artistic *caoineadh* performance at the wake is what in large part effects the safe transition of the deceased to the peaceful otherworld realm. Then again, the continued performance of her services during the journey from the wake house to the graveyard is welcomed in the tradition as an added protective measure, proper to both the well-being of the deceased in the otherworld and that of the bereaved family and community in this. The latter remain, throughout the period of the wake and the funeral, liable to contamination and injury from supernatural forces operating in the context of the intimate contact between human society and the otherworld, which the corpse symbolises, and as such they remain in need of the services of the *bean chaointe*. Thus, the *bean chaointe* and her charmed cries are regarded in tradition as a lucky thing, bringing magical benefit to all.

However, neither the sovereignty goddess nor her grim reverse transform, the goddess of death, are absent from the symbolism of the traditional funerary ritual, since the 'banshee', the supernatural death messenger, can surely be identified as their dual reflex. The complex of symbolism and nomenclature associated with this supernatural death messenger has been discussed extensively, in all its regional variety, by Patricia Lysaght, who suggests that certain aspects of the Irish death messenger, as met in later folk tradition, has developed from a more general family or guardian spirit – the Norse *fylgja* type – which is found also in other parts of Europe.[15] She concludes, however, that the complex of symbolism of the death messenger tradition in Ireland 'is to be understood in terms of the fundamental nexus of sovereignty', as outlined in succinct summary by Proinsias Mac Cana.[16] Indeed, Lysaght suggests that Aoibheall, the territorial goddess of the land of Thomond, in coming to Brian Boru before the Battle of Clontarf to prophesy his death, as recorded in the twelfth- and thirteenth-century sources *Cogadh Gael le Gaillibh* and *Annala Locha Cé*, is a kind of precursor of the death messenger tradition in later Irish folklore.

From all this it can be said to follow – for those who allow that mythological tradition can constitute a template for the interpretation of cultural reality – that the goddess is present at the wake in at least two respects. First, she is present as the supernatural persona of the death messenger. And, secondly, she is present in the human personae of the *bean bhán* and the *bean chaointe*. For the moment, I take the *bean chaointe* to be the more prominent of these human personae for reasons that are, I hope, apparent. We can, I believe, now proceed to see this female pairing – 'banshee' and *bean chaointe*; the one supernatural, the other flesh and blood; the one prophetically crying death into the human community, the other poetically crying death out of the human community – as symbolising also how she intervenes dramatically in human affairs at that very time which is, conventionally, in Irish tradition, the time of closest contact between the human world and the native ancestral otherworld of the *sí*; a time when profound transition and transformation takes place, both in the life of the deceased and in that of the deceased's family and community.

If the *bean chaointe* can indeed be said, in this fashion, within the logic of Irish traditional funerary symbolism, to represent the goddess, the ultimate *bean sí*, in her creative and protective and enabling aspect, then we can readily appreciate how the *bean chaointe* is a rival, as it were, to the *sagart paróiste*, the officer or agent of the official Irish religious ideology whose concern it also is to facilitate the transition of the soul of the deceased to, in this case, the Christian afterlife. A kind of contest in this regard is reported in oral tradition as having frequently taken place in the course of the funeral procession and at the graveyard. This is a contest resulting from the active enmity towards the *bean chaointe* of the majority of parish clergymen. It appears that a priest of the parish in which the burial was to take place would often arrange to meet the funeral procession en route to the graveyard, or, in some cases, would join in the procession in its later stage. The clergyman would take up the leading position in the procession, riding or walking in front of the coffin which was borne on the shoulders of four men, in relays, or else – for longer funeral journeys – was in a horse cart. Whether shouldered or drawn, the coffin would be attended throughout by one or more *mná caointe* and, in the case of a coffin borne in a horse-drawn cart, the chief *bean chaointe* would ride in the cart, sitting on the coffin and leading the entire party of female mourners in the *olagón*.

The priest, meeting such a funeral, was likely on occasion to confront the keening women and to attempt to disperse them and drive them out of the funeral. A verbal duel frequently took place on such occasions between the clergyman and the *mná caointe*, with insults and mockery and curses being exchanged. During the nineteenth century there were instances when, in such situations, physical violence was resorted to by the priest. Seán Ó Súilleabháin reports that his own father witnessed this happening at a funeral that took place about 1880 – the priest using a horsewhip, on that occasion, to repel his female opponents.[17]

At first glance, this contest is about the imposition of male clerical authority on areas of the social life of that sector of the Irish rural community hitherto beyond the domain of church control. Such extension of clerical social control is certainly at issue here but we can see a deeper significance also in the confrontation if we remember that the *bean chaointe* is, in terms of the ancestral cosmology of the Gaelic world, a representative of the mother goddess and her cultural transforms. In the confrontation of priest and *bean chaointe* we can see, opposed to each other, office-holders and, as it were, official representatives of the two alternative cosmologies that underlie the value and belief systems of Irish popular tradition down to modern times.

This kind of idealised schema of opposition and opposing actors is, of course, by its very nature, an abstraction. Hopefully, however, it has its use in illuminating the significance in cultural terms of the actual behaviour of actual historical people. In that actual history and ethnography, of course, no such clear-cut distinction between the practices of popular Christianity and ancestral folk religion is evident. We hear, for instance, in the oral tradition of south Cork recorded from Seán Ó hAo/Hamit by Seán Ó Cróinín, that there is remembered there a priest who used himself begin the *olagón* outside the wake house as the corpse was carried out for burial – the *mná caointe* then taking up and continuing the *caoineadh* to the graveside.[18] And we know of widespread accounts of how it was Mary – *Muire Mháthair* – at the foot of her son's cross on Calvary, who made the first *caoineadh* and of other accounts of how, in her grief, *Muire* smoked a clay pipe to give her ease at Christ's wake. Thus is Mary, the mother of Christ, drawn into the symbolism of ancestral mortuary ritual, being associated with the origin of two of the central features of the wake.[19] This, of course, complements the *bean chaointe* image of Mary, the Virgin Mother, in Gaelic song tradition, an image that Angela Bourke has established so convincingly.[20]

Another blending of the Christian and the ancestral is evident in the tradition of Brigid/Naomh Bríd, who has the soubriquet 'Muire na nGael'. Her significance as both goddess reflex and as legendary Christian saint has to do with fertility, craft and poetic creativity which is prophylactic and enabling – the very qualities suggested in the non-sovereignty queen tradition of the goddess which informs the *bean chaointe* and other female personae that afford expression in Irish tradition to the person and personality of the autonomous woman. This confirms further, for me at any rate, the correctness of the assertion made by Liam de Paor, among others, that Bríd is a fitting patron for Irish feminists – however involved the working out must be of ways in which the creative energy of a Bríd archetype can be caught in contemporary social life.

The creative energy of the goddess is brought into the heart of mortuary ritual in the Irish wake tradition and we can see in the widest cultural context here that the wake is, in a sense, a location for the re-enactment of one of the central myths of Irish culture. This is the myth telling of the establishment and the confirmation of the reign of the goddess, and of the people of the goddess, in the face of the forces of destruction, of anti-structure, of chaos that are perceived to surround and threaten life and to underlie the occurrence of death. On the social level the rupture of relationships that death entails is mirrored and resolved in the *communitas* – the liminal relaxation of the rules and structures and calculations of ordinary daily life – that characterises the wake period. This *communitas* dissolves, as it were, the social world and reconstitutes it anew, with necessarily new alignments and social relationships, in the aftermath of the demise itself and of an institutionalised process of grieving for the individual deceased. On this social level, throughout the early modern period, the wake in Ireland was, as we know, in many areas, the occasion for games and play-acting and physical boisterousness that gave graphic expression to such social dissolution and liminality. These unrestrained behaviours are, however, almost entirely absent in the record of the mortuary traditions of the south-west of Ireland – the region perhaps especially associated in medieval tradition with cults and legends of the hag goddess of the landscape. It is likely that the regional distribution of the occurrence of mimes and imitative games at wakes is attributable to varying degrees of dissemination in Ireland of the popular culture of early modern Europe with its emphasis on the institutionalised expression of the carnivalesque.

Everywhere throughout Ireland, however, the wake, whether unrestrainedly merry or not, is the occasion for another kind of creative and artistic performance at the centre of which we can situate the *bean chaointe* and her important magical work of poetically crying the deceased into a non-patriarchal otherworld which is, in very immediate ways, symbolically to hand. The creative playfulness of verbal art is thus what both protects the human community and effects the transfer to the otherworld of the deceased. While the emphasis in the *caoineadh* tradition seems to be on a kind of recitative of stock phrases and stretches of repetitive onomatopoeic utterances largely without literal meaning, we know that individual family members with a poetic gift were liable to compose extempore verse (later perhaps consciously reworked) as a unique artistic contribution to the intensity of the *caoineadh*. I suggest that the fact that our most celebrated examples of this are either by women, or put in the mouths of women, appropriately reflects the greater prominence of the female voice and person in the business of the *caoineadh* and the wake as passage ritual.[21]

Other kinds of verbal artistry also find significant expression within Irish tradition on the occasion of the wake. These centre on storytelling, with the wake assembly being entertained throughout the night hours by the recital of such as hero tales, wonder tales, historical legends, memorates, genealogies, verse, proverbs, riddles and other items of the major and minor genres of Irish oral narrative tradition. The wake house is in fact one of the major locations for the creative and re-creative performance of this type of material so that in this respect the wake house resembles the 'rambling-house' or the *teachairneáin*. In the wake house, as in the *teachairneáin*, verbal artistry is accompanied by a certain amount of singing, music-making and even dancing – and also by card-playing. During the dark hours of the nights over which the wake lasts, the assembly resorts, in this fashion, to that repertoire of verbal and other artistic and re-creative performance that was regularly indulged in, in due season, as a community activity of the rambling house, commencing the coming of *Samhain* and the onset of the winter half of the year. The period of six months from 1 November to 1 May was traditionally the season when a) the medieval bards taught their oral learning and poetic craft in the bardic academies and b) when the common people also gathered, night after night, to listen to and witness and partake in the creativity of the rambling house. *Samhain*, the great Celtic feast day of the otherworld and of the dead ancestors, marks the beginning and initial high point of the season for this kind of creative communal performance in the round of the traditional calendar. At the feast of *Samhain*, the old Celtic year waned and the new year began, so that *Samhain*-time has a liminal, interlunary-like significance. It is a time when, in Irish tradition, the gateway between this life and the ancestral otherworld of the *sí* is wide open and household visitation from the *slua sí* ('fairy host') and from dead ancestor is expected to occur. Ordinary time and space are disordered at *Samhain*.

The Reeses have emphasised this aspect of the *Samhain* festival:

> A period of disorder in between the old year and the new is a
> common feature of New Year rituals in many lands but it is soon
> followed by the re-creation of an orderly world which lasts for
> another year. At Hallowe'en the elimination of boundaries – between
> the dead and the living, between the sexes, between one man's
> property and another's and, in divinations, between the present and
> the future – all symbolise the return of chaos. It is noteworthy that
> the 'day with a night' which the Mac Óc (a god-hero) equated with
> the whole of time were those of *Samhain*. This day partakes of the
> nature of eternity. What Hallowe'en inaugurates is winter, and much
> of the uncanniness of night, when man seems powerless in the hands
> of fate, will prevail until the dawn of another summer.[22]

Samhain certainly is the pivotal point of mythological time in Irish
tradition. Great mythic events occur, or perhaps eternally recur, at
Samhain-time. While the first Gaelic Irish are said to have arrived on the
island of Ireland at *Bealtaine* (May Day), the beginning of summer, the
Tuatha Dé Danann ('the tribes or people of the goddess') who constitute
the Celtic pantheon of otherworld divines and semi-divines in Irish
mythological tradition, had finally wrested the physical island of Ireland,
and with it the hegemony of social existence, from the *Fomoraigh*, the
dark forces of chaos and disorder, at *Samhain*-time in the celebrated *Cath
Maige Tuired*. This battle is seen as the ultimate paradigmatic contest in
Irish mythological tradition and Irish cosmology.

I would like to refer specially to a comment on the story of the battle
by Elizabeth Gray who has discussed the cosmological significance and
mythological status of the texts of the tale of *Cath Maige Tuired* which
have survived. My speculation regarding a possible symbolic alignment
between the myth of the Battle of Moytura and the ritual of the wake
I judge to be supported by what Gray asserts regarding the continuing
representative nature of ancient Irish mythic material for the native
Irish culture of later times. Referring to the transformation by the
secular learned class, together with monastic scholars, of Irish myth into
Christian pre-history, she emphasises what she calls the significance of
such material for the future as well as for the past.

> Even as a branch of native history, stories about the gods, the Tuatha
> Dé Dannan ('The Tribes of the Goddess Dana') remained paradigms

for human action and models for the interpretation of human experience ... More specifically, such tales still served to establish legal precedent, to explain customary ritual, to justify political authority, to illustrate medical practice and to define social order.[23]

Such stories can point us in the direction of deciphering the symbolic significance of prominent features of post-medieval Irish tradition in a way that takes due account of the cultural antecedents of such features. In Irish cultural tradition the Battle of Moytura is held to recount how there came to be established the reign of the ultimately non-patriarchal otherworld powers with whom the human Irish population was thereafter to regard itself as co-existent and who, in the course of time, became the anonymous *slua sí* ('the fairy host') of the imminent, contingent otherworld of ancestral cosmology. There is, surely, a sense in which the same forces that opposed each other in the Battle of Moytura – the sovereign power of the representatives of the goddess, on the one hand, and the disruptive and destructive force of death and disorder on the other – are again brought into conjunction in the assembly of the wake. It is as if the pivotal, paradigmatic contest of mythological tradition is re-enacted in the passage ritual that marks the closest and gravest connections which the human realm has with the otherworld in ancestral cultural tradition in Ireland. In the traditional calendar such closeness of worlds is symbolised and protected against in the festival of *Samhain* and the prophylactic performances which it calls forth and to which it gives rise. The wake assembly is like a kind of movable *Samhain*, similarly oriented to the conjunction of human and otherworld realms, and utilising similar performances of communal and especially female creativity to protect the human community from the dangers of contact with the immortal forces of the otherworld on whose threshold the community is liminally poised within the ever-renewing cosmic contest between death and life.

The status of the *bean chaointe* in Irish popular cultural tradition and the respect accorded individual *caoineadh* performers derives from some such common understanding of the importance of the service she renders to the community. Very often this is expressed analogically, in oral tradition itself, as the perception of an identification of the *bean chaointe* with the male *file* whose own poetic gift is, of course, widely understood in tradition as being also of supernatural origin. In *Seanchas ó Chairbre*, Seán Ó h-Ao ('Hamit') says, '*Do bhíodh sean-mhná i dtigh an tórraimh and ba chuma nó filí iad ... do thosnídís ar bheith a'caoine agus do chuiridís a mbíodh i dtig a' chuirp a'gol lena gcaoine, do dhinidís a' caoine chó breá san'* ('There used to be keening women in the wake house and they were for all the world like poets … they would begin keening and they would put all in the corpse house crying with their keening, they used to keen so well').[24] And in 1938, in the parish of Enniskeane in Cinéal mBéice, in County Cork, a seventy-eight-year-old male informant reflected on the old women 'keeners' that used to be at every wake: 'Tis no harm that there's no "keening" at wakes and funerals now; it was too lonesome – when the old "keeners" opened up in the middle of the night after the Rosary … and they'd had a dropeen … You'd rather be underground.'[25] One can also note here the points of view that emphasise the female aspect of poetic composition and the essentially female nature of the poetic craft itself in Irish cultural tradition. Descriptions of the bardic school as a kind of lying-in institution for those giving birth to verse and interpretations of the poet as bardic mistress to his lord and patron alert us once more to the intricacies both of gender construction and of the symbolic relationship of the sexes in cultural representation. What is patent, however, is the continued perception within Irish cultural symbolism of powerful female conduits for supernatural wisdom and power.

With the transformation, in historical process, of the sociocultural world in which the *bean feasa*, the *bean ghlúine*, the *bean chaointe* held sway, the grip of a patriarchal universe of discourse within Irish culture on Irish society in general was consolidated. To what degree other personae and roles were developed or are now being developed in order to provide goddess mythology with outlets on human affairs, within or without popular Christianity, is beyond the scope of this chapter.

CHAPTER 15

Continuity and Adaptation in Legends of *Cailleach Bhéarra*

[Published in *Béaloideas*, vol. 56, 1988, pp. 153–78]

Reference to *Cailleach Bhéarra* in both medieval materials and in modern scholarly surveys of the medieval Gaelic world is pervasive. She appears as an unstable and yet a pre-eminent presence whose status is attested equally in Irish and Scottish Gaelic tradition and in the modern scholarship of these traditions. Professor Mac Cana's reference to her in his survey of Celtic mythology is typical both in its emphasis and in its qualification.[1] He speaks of *Cailleach Bhéarra* as being 'as famous in modern Irish folklore as she evidently was in the early literary tradition'. The textual basis of her earlier fame is clearly of an implicit nature only, yet Mac Cana just as clearly accepts the ascription to her by early tradition of a cluster of roles: a geotechtonic role in landscape formation; a status as divine ancestress with numerous progeny of tribes and people; the characteristic of being an epitome of longevity in passing repeatedly through the cycle of youth and age; and a role as sovereignty symbol in, for example, her representation in the medieval materials, under the name Buí, as the wife of Lugh, elsewhere himself the model representation of kingship. The Scottish scholar J.G. Mackay has referred to her as 'the most tremendous figure in Gaelic myth today',[2] while Professor Wagner, in a recent article – thinking, surely, not only of the famous ninth-century poem – calls her 'the most famous old lady in Irish literature'.[3] Ann Ross, too, has accorded her considerable prominence, not only in her book *Pagan Celtic Britain* but also in her specific publication on 'The Divine Hag of the Pagan Celts'.[4]

Attempts to identify the nature and the significance *Cailleach Bhéarra* carries within the Gaelic world quickly lead one to the realisation that we are dealing with an extremely complex figure. At different stages and at different levels of Gaelic tradition the figure of *Cailleach Bhéarra* has been used to represent different clusterings of cultural meaning so that we are faced with a multiplicity of forms and functions of *Cailleach Bhéarra* that prove very difficult to distinguish and whose historical and/or functional relationship to each other continues to be obscure to a great degree. In one viewing *Cailleach Bhéarra* would appear to represent a version of traditions of a mother goddess emanating from the worlds of Indo-European and even old European cosmology. In another she appears as a representative figure of the divine hag of the Celtic and early Irish worlds who has close connections with the sovereignty queen tradition. Yet again, *Cailleach Bhéarra* can be seen as a version of a supernatural female wilderness figure peripheral to and usually inimical to the human world. Indeed *Cailleach Bhéarra* in modern Gaelic folklore, in both Scotland and Ireland, is most frequently understood as one of a range of such wilderness figures and I am of the opinion that these owe their existence in Gaelic traditions, later and early, at least in part to the influence of Norse cosmology in its personification of the forces of wild nature. This is an aspect of *Cailleach Bhéarra* tradition that has not, I believe, hitherto been generally acknowledged.

An examination of Scottish material relating to the supernatural female bearing the names *Cailleach Bhéara/Bheurr* reveals a multitude of association between her and the forces of wild nature, especially the storms of winter, the storm clouds and the boiling winter sea. She is also, in the Scottish material, very much the spirit of the high ground, of mountain and moor and is seen frequently to personify wildlife, for instance the life and well-being and fertility of the deer herd.

Norse folklore is pervaded with creatures representing the forces of wild nature and in Scottish tradition *Cailleach Bheurr* is frequently said to have herself originated in Norway from where she allegedly carried rocks out of which she formed the coasts and mountains of the Scottish mainland and of the Western Isles. If many of the Scottish legends of *Cailleach Bheurr* contain such motifs of Nordic provenance, there is equal evidence of a Norse element in the make-up of other varieties of Scottish hags of the peripheral wilderness who also personify wild nature and are held to threaten human life. Such personages, and especially *Cailleach Bheurr*, are credited with the formation of various aspects of the physical landscape and are often said to reside in a cliff or a sea rock where they rule the waves of the sea. The *Cailleach Bhéarrach* of the Irish Beara peninsula is locally associated with a standing stone in the vicinity of Eyeries. Eyeries is a place-name that my former colleague Dr Roibeárd Ó hUrdail suggests may possibly be of Scandinavian origin in being derived from the Norse *eyrr,* which means 'a gravelly beach', and is found in well-known placenames of the Scottish coast, in the Isles and in Man. Oileán Buí itself, of course, named for *cailleach* or *sentainne,* one of whose earlier names was Buí, bears also the Norse-derived name 'Dursey' and there is little doubt but that the south-west Irish coast is, or was once, rich in Norse association. I mention An tOileán Tiar (Blasket) and Carraig Aonair (Fastnet) as two other major south-western locations having Norse-derived alternative names.

Cailleach Bhéarra's reputation as a figure of significance would, then, appear to span the worlds of Celtic mythology, Gaelic medieval literature and modern Irish and Scottish folklore with, in each case, a possible Norse connection. Eleanor Hull and Alexander Haggerty Krappe have both written valuable articles on aspects of *Cailleach Bhéarra* in later popular tradition – Hull in the English journal *Folklore*[5] and Krappe in volume 1 of *Études Celtiques.*[6] Eleanor Hull raises the question whether the myth of *Cailleach Bhéarra* might not be a comparatively late one since she is, says Hull, unknown outside the Gaelic world and, within that world, gets no mention in such mainstream medieval sources as *Sanas Chormaic,* the *Cóir Anmann,* the *Dinnseanchas* or *Acallamh na Senórach.* She is mentioned, we may note, in *Aislinge Mheic Conglinne* and also in the *Expulsion of the Déssi* – the later twelfth-century version – and under her earlier name, Buí/Boí, she appears in the *Metrical Dinnseanchas.* Despite this relative dearth of mention, Hull concedes that *Cailleach Bhéarra* tradition, especially in its geotechtonic aspect, might well have an earlier and more distant source than the boundaries of the Gaelic world. Krappe takes that earlier, distant source for granted and sees *Cailleach Bhéarra* tradition as a Gaelic reflex of a theme or themes whose provenance is wider and older than the entire Celtic world:

> *La Cailleach Bheara est une ancienne déesse agraire et chthonienne équivalent gaelique de la Déméter grecque, déesse de la fertilité mais aussi de la mort. S'est rattachée à elle une légende développée d'un ancien rite qui, en Phrygie, courait sur Lityerse.*[7]

Hull in fact quotes in translation from the text of a modern Irish narrative – published by Douglas Hyde in *An Sgéulaidhe Gaedhalach*[8] – that seems to echo the Phrygian tale of how, in a reaping contest, Hercules eventually overthrows Lityersés, son of Midas, who in those days reigned over the corn harvest on the banks of the Maeander.[9]

In such a context one must recall Professor Gerard Murphy's remark that 'many Irish folk-tale motifs are as old as the days of primitive Indo-European unity'[10] and the contention, on archaeological rather than on literary or linguistic grounds, by Professor Jan Filip of a significant degree of continuity into the Celtic world from late Stone Age times in the matter of the *magna mater*.[11] If early-twentieth-century storytellers in the west of Ireland have as an authentic part of their traditional repertoire from medieval and earlier times an account of how a local champion overcomes the female divinity of the corn harvest in a reaping contest, then it would appear that Gaelic oral narrative tradition, in Ireland at least, was still, into our age, carrying forward an extremely ancient formulation of that pattern of opposition between otherworld supreme divinity and semi-divine/semi-human hero whose outline in Irish mythology Professor O'Rahilly tried to establish. Not only that, but Hyde's text, if it is genuine, could well supply the affirmative answer to Tomás Ó Cathasaigh's question in *The Heroic Biography of Cormac Mac Airt*[12] as to the existence of an as yet unrecognised 'otherworld goddess vs hero' opposition as predicated in the syntagmatic and paradigmatic relations inherent in O'Rahilly's theory. Incidentally, a second source of such 'goddess vs male hero' opposition is alluded to by Máire MacNeill in *The Festival of Lughnasa*, when she speaks of the shadow of a female person – sometimes called Ana/Áine, sometimes *Cailleach Bhéarra* – looming behind the male divinity of *Crom Dubh* from whom, in the Lughnasa legends, Lugh ultimately wins the harvest.[13] Again here popular tradition would appear to be preserving the names and the older strands of meaning – as chthonic and fertility goddess – of a figure who, at the learned and aristocratic level of tradition, is long-since transformed in function to being a sovereignty queen.

At the learned, political, literary level of Irish tradition, the chief significance of the female divine in general develops away from the ancient chthonic and harvest associations and – through the figures of the goddesses of war and death – is ultimately invested in figures representing the sovereignty of the rightful ruler and the personification of the territories and even of the whole land of Ireland itself. The medieval conception of such sovereignty figures carries on down to the eighteenth-century *aisling* genre of modern Irish poetic tradition. The tired and clichéd nature of the eighteenth-century tradition was however – as I have argued elsewhere[14] – to be radically revitalised by Brian Merriman who, by invoking in *Cúirt an Mheán Oíche* the medieval form of the sovereignty myth, liberated into the modern Gaelic world the powerful, full-blooded personification of sovereignty in the guise of Aoibheall of Craig Léith.

One of the chief ways known to us in which *Cailleach Bhéarra* is established in medieval tradition in the ranks of the sovereignty queens is the use of her name to identify the subject of the celebrated Old Irish 'Lament of the Old Woman of Beare'.[15] In the second quatrain of this poem the line *Is me Caillech Bérrí Buí* occurs and it is a line rich in ideological import with its overtones of Christian religion, Celtic mythology and localised political topography. Buí was claimed as divine ancestress by the Corca Loigde – a leading tribe of the Érainn of west Munster – whose territory once included the whole of the Beara peninsula and the chief residence of whose over-king was at Dunboy (Dún Buíthe). Such political use of the significance of *Cailleach Bhéarra* in the realm of poetry is presumably paralleled by her similar utilisation in prose, as for instance the subject of the now lost tale *Serc Caillighe Bérri do Fothad Cannaine* where, we may assume, the desire to shape political reality produces a further claiming of her as ancestress and divine legitimatrix on behalf of aspirants to political authority.

The author of the ninth-century lament, it is agreed, proceeds to exploit ideological ambiguities in inventing the figure and name-form of the aged female who is at once the lingering representative of a profane, native eternity of earthly sovereignty and the Christian nun finally embracing the prospect of an eternity of the heavenly sovereignty of the male Christian God. In his 1953 edition of the lament Gerard Murphy wrote:

> Her name which is *Sentainne Bérri* … has already become *Caillech Bérri*. *Caillech Bérri* would once have meant 'The Nun of Beare' but had doubtless at the time the poem was written already, in ordinary speech, become the equivalent of an obsolescent *Sentainne Bérri* which could mean only 'The Old Woman of Beare': *sentainne* is obsolete in Irish today and *cailleach* for long has meant, not 'nun', but 'old woman'.[16]

Sentainne Bérri then is one ancient ascription of the divine female that gives her a localised mythological and quasi-political association with south-west Ireland and in particular with the Beara peninsula at whose tip lie both Tech Duinn and Dursey Island, otherwise Oileán Buí.

I find it very interesting indeed that Professor Wagner, in his recent *Zeitschrift* article,[17] should identify both these earliest names for *Cailleach Bhéarra*, viz. Sentainne (Bérri) and Boí/Buí with derivations from the Indo-European forms **Senona* and **Bovina* meaning, respectively, 'female elder' and 'cow-like-one' – the latter being, Wagner claims, a characteristic appellation of Indo-European manifestations of the *magna mater*. On Professor Wagner's terms, then, both the rivers Shannon and Boyne are named ultimately for the female divine who herself begins to become known as *Cailleach Bhéarra* around about the late eighth or early ninth centuries when the famous lament was composed. From my point of interest in considering prose narrative versions of *Cailleach Bhéarra* legends a further remark of Gerard Murphy's in his 1953 edition is here crucial:

> The change from *Sentainne Bérri* to *Caillech Bérri* doubtless first occurred colloquially among the illiterate. When it had firmly established itself, the learned may have invented the legend that the Old Woman of Beare became a nun and received the *caille* or nun's veil ... thus justifying the title *caillech*. In quatrains 11, 12 and 22 of the poem, the Old Woman of Beare is clearly looked upon as a nun.[18]

From other quatrains of the poem it is equally clear that the Old Woman of Beare has been the consort of kings and thus the embodiment of the sovereignty principle in much the same way as Gormfhlaith and Líadain embody it in the poems attributed to them. Using the traditional associations of the *Cailleach* or *Sentainne Bérri* as mother-goddess, as shaper and guardian of the land, and as sovereignty figure, the author of the lament is able to express, to quote Professor Mac Cana, 'the deep incompatibility between Christianity and the world of pagan belief', something that Mac Cana calls 'one of the great crucial themes of the Irish past'.[19] Most commentators on the lament see this contrast, or opposition, to be something pivotal in the poem and a major source of its imaginative tension. Such imaginative tension, generated between native and Christian ideology and motif, is a source of a good deal of Irish artistic output – visual as well as literary – in the medieval period. Whether this ambivalence of cosmology inherent in the lament itself and, for example, in poems such as 'Hail Brigit', attributed to Orthanach Ua Coíllámha in the early ninth century, found any similar expression then in prose tales featuring *Cailleach Bhéarra* in the colloquial repertoire of the bearers of popular Gaelic tradition, we can now never know in any direct way. We can, however, examine what has come down into modern times, amalgamated in complicated ways with later and with learned material, as the popular traditional repertoire of the last generations of *scéalaithe* and *seanchaithe* in the Gaelic world.

Cailleach Bhéarra is prominent in this repertoire, both in Ireland and in Scotland, and some attempt can be made to impose order on the multiplicity of significance which she seems to possess in this material. One may attempt to establish the developmental stages in the narrative and other history of the person and the legend of *Cailleach Bhéarra*. Or one may in synchronic or structural terms attempt to construct a model showing the relationships to each other of the various aspects of *Cailleach Bhéarra* tradition. Such a structural model has been proposed by Professor Paul Friedrich of Chicago to cater for the significance and development of Aphrodite through antiquity.[20] By means of his model Friedrich is able to resolve apparently opposing aspects of the Aphrodite tradition, for instance the sexuality and purity that are, in her texts, simultaneously affirmed. The apparent absence of any substantial early corpus of *Cailleach Bhéarra* myth or legend probably means that textually based work on her earlier significance, parallel to Friedrich's on the significance of Aphrodite, is less likely of accomplishment. Nevertheless, in the case of *Cailleach Bhéarra* and her surrogates, we should, I believe, regard them as possessing separate – and perhaps structurally opposing – clusterings of cultural meaning in the context of the Indo-European, the Celtic and the Gaelic worlds. The early Indo-European heritage in the *Cailleach Bhéarra* character can be seen in the more modern material primarily in the earth mother and fertility goddess aspects of her figure. Similarly in relation to a more specifically Celtic heritage of significance for the divine hag we should highlight the primacy of the hag of war and death aspect, an aspect, incidentally, that also has strong overtones of the notion of a powerful sexuality. Primacy of the symbolism of the sovereignty goddess, the divine consort of the rightful ruler, then remains as the aspect of the tradition developed latest and at the learned and literary level only. It is this aspect which has, however, made the term *Cailleach Bhéarra*, or a rendering of it, well known throughout the later Gaelic world as a name for the subject of a large corpus of legend regarding various manifestations of a supernatural female ancient.

The significance of *Cailleach Bhéarra* in modern Irish and Scottish folklore has thus to be understood, I think, in relation to the two separate

yet related levels of tradition: the literary, learned traditions of the early
middle ages in which the term *Cailleach Bhéarra* is established as the name
of a sovereignty queen in politics, in prose and in poetry, and the common,
popular, unlearned level of Gaelic tradition (concerning which there is
little direct evidence until modern times) which seems to have contained
a range of manifestations of an ancient female divine with the general
characteristics of the old European *magna mater*. Since the middle ages
and due partly to the fusing of the learned with the unlearned traditions
in the social upheavals of the early modern period, the name *Cailleach
Bhéarra*, or a version of it, has come into widespread use throughout the
Gaelic world, in Ireland and Scotland, as a name for these *magna mater*-
type female supernaturals in materials placing a marked emphasis on the
terrible mother, the wilderness-personifying and the threatening side of
their nature.

In Ireland the forms *Cailleach Bhéar(r)a* and *Cailleach Bhéar(r)ach* are
the usual ones found in oral tradition. In Scottish tradition the range of
oral variants includes *Cailleach Bhéara, Cailleach Bheur, Cailleach Bheurr,
Cailleach Bheurrach, Cailleach Beartha, Cailleach Bheathrach*, and it appears
that in Scotland, in regard to the transmission of the name at the non-
literary level, a degree of folk etymology has come into operation that
draws on conceptions of a female nature and wilderness spirit owing
something to the influence of Norse mythology. The second element of
the name in Scotland is often understood – alike by tradition-bearers and
by scholarly commentators – to mean 'keen', 'sharp', 'pointed' (< *beur*) or
else 'quick-witted', 'sharp-spoken', 'eloquent' (< *beurru*(ch)).

In Irish tradition too, the oral form *Cailleach Bhéarrach* and the allied
form *Cailleach Bhiorach* suggest the operation here also of an element
of folk etymology in regard to the transmission at the non-learned
level of the name *Cailleach Bhéarra* as a term for a female supernatural
who is perceived as much as wilderness spirit as sovereignty queen. A
detailed analysis of the full range of the forms of the name will prove
instructive. I suggest that it may well reveal that a majority of the hags
known to popular tradition over Ireland and Scotland who carry a name-
form suggestive of identification with the Béarra of the poem should
be understood to be named rather from a female personification of the
peripheral wilderness whose chief feature is that of being *biorach*, 'sharp',
'shrill', 'inimical'. The form *Berach/Beorach* was a relatively common
personal name in early Ireland and the forms *Cailleach Bheurr/Bheurrach*
are perhaps the most widely encountered form of the name of our *cailleach*

in the Scottish material. It is surely relevant that the forms *an Chailleach Bhéarrach, leis an gCailligh Bhéarraigh* are the oral forms that occur on the Beara peninsula itself to refer to the 'Old Woman of Beare beside Dursey' and I think it may be argued that, at the level of popular oral tradition, even in Beara itself the connotations of *Cailleach Bhéarrach/ Bheurrach* are primarily those of the generalised wilderness figure rather than those of the divine hag -cum- sovereignty queen of learned tradition. George Broderick's suggestion that the Manx traditional song about Berrey Dhone is possible evidence that Bérri was there the hag's original name and not merely a toponym is of the greatest interest and needs to be taken into account in the larger context I am suggesting.[21] Though there are relatively few instances known to us of the 'political' use of the figure of *Cailleach Bhéarra*, we are, I think, gaining a general understanding today of how the names and alleged exploits and associations of many eminent figures – lay and clerical, profane, sacred and divine – were put to use by the composers, compilers and transcribers of medieval Irish genealogies, origin legends, saints lives, praise poems, and so on. We should also, I believe, allow for the operation of a similar kind of judicious exploitation of traditional lore, and the traditional associations of aspects of that lore, in the creative performances of both medieval and modern storytellers at the popular or folk, as distinct from the learned, level of tradition. In particular, in relation to the figure of *Cailleach Bhéarra* and the associations attaching to her in Irish and Scottish Gaelic tradition, we have, I believe, evidence of skilful manipulation by the modern traditional storyteller operating in non-learned circles, that bears comparison, in its own way, with the manipulation of aspects of their common heritage by the learned practitioners of the medieval material. In either case we can perceive, along with the recounting of central motifs associated with traditional figures, the ordering of the material and – presumably – its delivery in the case of the taletellers, after a fashion that gives creative expression to current imaginative tensions and to the contemporary social and cultural status quo.

To begin to illustrate this I would first of all propose to examine the text of a story collected by Professor Jackson in the 1930s on the Great Blasket Island, from Peig Sayers, and published by him in the anthology *Scéalta ón mBlascaod*.[22] The story is titled, presumably by Professor Jackson, 'Ana Ní Áine' and there is no mention in it of the *Cailleach Bhéarra* as such. Nevertheless I think it is possible to associate this text with category 4 or perhaps with categories 1 and 4 of the seven categories of late Irish oral narrative material relating to *Cailleach Bhéarra* that I outline in Figure 15.1.

Figure 15.1 Classification of oral Irish narrative featuring *Cailleach Bhéarra*

	Tentative Classification of Oral Irish *Cailleach Bhéarra* Narrative
1	Three hag-goddesses of south-west Munster
2	Creator and shaper of physical landscape
3	*Cailleach Bhéarra* as source of proverbial wisdom
4	Great age of *Cailleach Bhearra* is explained and the greatest marvel she witnessed is recounted
5	Corn goddess: late winter sowing, threshing, reaping contest
6	*Cailleach Bhéarra* featuring in Fenian/Romantic tales, e.g. *Céadach*; *Ridire an Gháire Dhuibh*
7	*Cailleach Bhéarra* featuring in international tales, e.g. AT 425, *The Search for the Lost Husband*; AT 1525, *The Master Thief*

This classification derives largely from an examination of material in the archives of the Department of Irish Folklore in UCD (formerly the Irish Folklore Commission) and has a tentative status only in relation to the full range of late Gaelic oral narrative. While *Cailleach Bhéarra* herself is not named in the Sayers/Jackson tale, its structure and the main import of its plot suggest very strongly that the heroine Ana Ní Áine alias Áine Nic Chártha is, in fact, a representation of the divine earth mother who is known – under the name Anu – as mother of the gods and who also appears as Áine an Chnuic in later popular legend. Such representative figures frequently occur threefold in Gaelic tradition and indeed legends of south-west Munster present *Cailleach Bhéarra* as one sister of a mighty trio associated with the three great peninsulas of the south-western Irish coast. The other two sisters, in that case, are called *Cailleach Bhólais* and *Cailleach an Daingin*. I am not suggesting that the Ana Ní Áine of the Sayers/Jackson text is 'really', say, *Cailleach an Daingin* (in the story she is actually located at Kenmare which is in the groin – between two of the peninsulas in question) but I am saying that what happens in the story appears to be, at one level, a restatement of the central theme expressed a thousand years previously in the 'Lament of the Old Woman of Beare', and that there is some justification for seeing Ana Ní Áine in the twentieth-century text as a version of *Cailleach Bhéarra* or, more accurately, of the female divine so often given the name *Cailleach Bhéarra* throughout the Gaelic world.

At another level in the Blasket story social issues pertaining to the world of post-Famine nineteenth- and early-twentieth-century rural Ireland are handled and commented on by implication. The way in which the narrative structure of the text manages to cope with this duality of signification and brings the story, at both levels, to a highly unified and, culturally, highly meaningful conclusion strikes me as evidence of the continued sophistication, in terms of verbal art, of certain of the twentieth-century successors of the medieval *scelaige* who employed similar skills at both the learned and, we must presume, the popular levels of tradition.

For the purposes of discussion I present a summary version of the narrative structure of the Sayers/Jackson text and offer five points of commentary that will, hopefully, illustrate my approach to understanding the full cultural significance this text encompasses.

Frame-Tale Summary

1. Rich man's daughter marries, as mature woman, a young gentleman from Ulster.
2. A travelling man prophesies that she will live on always until a certain monk prepares her for death.
3. She lives on through the generations and is eventually in a cradle rocked by a distant female-line descendant.
4. A new curate of the parish comes to the house and an encounter takes place between him and the female ancient who reveals herself to him for what she is.
5. The curate then reveals that he is the cleric in the prophecy related to the old woman so long before; he questions her regarding the wonders she has seen during her long life.
6. She relates to him the greatest wonder she ever saw; he prepares her for death and she expires.
7. Her name, we are told, lives on as an epitome of longevity.

Inset-Tale Summary (The Greatest Wonder)

1. When the old woman was a young girl she went sailing to Skellig one day in the company of a priest and others.
2. In the dark and chill of a sudden storm they encounter a female spirit in a cloud.

3. The priest, having elicited that this is the spirit of a priest's paramour damned for the killing of an infant, reads from a prayer book until the woman vanishes in a flash.

4. The boat-party returns home without visiting the Skellig Rock.

Commentary

1. The tale is opened for us in a setting … *Is dócha gur fadó riamh anis* … ['It is probably a long time ago now'] which is presented as being considerably anterior to the 'present time' of the narration itself. The first character introduced is a man called MacCarthy who is of Kenmare. This man, we are given to understand, is rich and powerful. Peig's audience would have understood, perhaps, that MacCarthy was a strong farmer or even that he was a merchant in the quasi-urban setting of Kenmare town itself. There is in him also, however, an invocation, by association, of the hereditary chiefs, not only of the Kenmare district, but of much of south-west Munster in medieval times; that same MacCarthy that Aogán Ó Rathaille invokes so powerfully in his poetry, and locates in the same general place.

2. That MacCarthy's only daughter here remains unmarried until she is a mature woman (*críona cruaigh go math*) establishes the solidity and continuity of the world of the original setting. Into this world is introduced the daughter's husband, a young gentleman (*fear óg uasal*) from Ulster. He is no commoner and he arrives into the tale from a land having, in southern Irish narrative tradition, associations with magic and witchcraft and mysterious powers. His introduction, and the incident of the beggarman with second sight who makes the prophecy, shifts the tale into the realms of the supernatural but without any dramatic rupture of the surface of everyday, ethnographic reality familiar to an early-twentieth-century rural Irish Gaeltacht community.

3. The narrator herself had remarked at the tale's outset that while the heroine's name in 'real life' is Ana Nic Chártha, she is known in this story as Ana Ní Áine (… *gurb ainm di Ana mc Chártha, ach ní tugtar 'sa scéal ach Ana Ní Áine*). In fact the narrator goes on to refer to her in the course of the tale as Áine (*tháinig áthas ar Áine*) and as Áine Nic Chártha (*chuir sé an ola dhéanach ar* Áine nic Chártha). The name-form Ana Ní Áine certainly lends itself to notions that considerably deepen the reach of the tale

into the cultural past the narrator shares with her audience, and a further remark of Máire MacNeill's in *The Festival of Lughnasa* – regarding St Ann – is relevant here: 'Her name has attracted legends of Anu, the mother of the Irish gods, and of Áine, one-time goddess and long-living woman of the Sidhe.'[23] However, it is as a surname that Áine is used here in the Blasket text, which is itself unusual. And what are we to make of the first element ˙Ana? Is it a Gaelic form of Ann the mother of the Virgin Mary? The temptation is, for me, to regard it as in some way a version of the old goddess name Anu/Danu and to regard the full style of Ana Ní Áineas as the casting into 'modern' form of a reduplicated version of one of the major appellations of the *magna mater* in Irish tradition from very early times. We need in no way imply a conscious or co-ordinated knowledge by the Blasket narrator or her Blasket audience of the learned, historical provenance of such a name in order to allow that the name-form Ana Ní Áine could, in late popular tradition, invoke associations in the minds of a native audience for this narrative that touches on the senior female divine whose presence lurks behind the male gods of native tradition from the beginning. The unfolding of the narrative of the tale we are discussing certainly leaves me in no doubt but that we have here a manifestation of the same character about whom the transcriber of the 'Lament of the Old Woman of Beare' had written in an explanatory headnote:

> This is why she was called the Old Woman of Beare: she had fifty foster-children in Beare. She passed into seven periods of youth, so that every husband used to pass to death from her, of old age, so that her grandchildren and great-grandchildren were peoples and races. and for a hundred years she wore the veil, after Cuimíne had blessed it and placed it on her head. Then age and infirmity came to her …[24]

4. In the Blasket text it is not Cuimíne Fota, the seventh-century successor of Brendan in the abbacy of Clonfert, who acts the part of the Christian cleric placing on the ancient female the veil of Christian salvation. Instead, appropriately to a text and a narrative repertoire that derives largely from a post-medieval world, it is Seán Bráthair Ó Conchubhair, a monk well known

in Irish popular tradition as having been doubly confirmed in his
Christian priestly character by virtue of having himself, on one
occasion, lapsed temporarily into a renunciation of Christian
belief through yielding, in Rome, of all places, to the power and
meaning of pagan Irish superstition.[25] His appearance in this tale
as the medieval *alter ego* of the modern Catholic curate strengthens
again the sense of historical depth in the narrative. The female
representative of an ancient cosmology is here confronted by a
male clerical representative of medieval Christendom through the
ministry in 'modern' (or contemporary) times of a clergyman who,
in the text, bears the hallmarks of being a Catholic curate of the
early-twentieth-century Irish rural scene.

5. Just as the figure of Seán Bráthair Ó Conchubhair introduces
medieval folklore motifs into the tale, so too the actual encounter
and confrontation between the Catholic curate and Áine Nic
Chártha (which is also the encounter of Seán Bráthair with Ana
Ní Áine) is accomplished in terms of the use of the international
folklore motifs of a) the pursuit and redemption of the priest's
paramour, and b) the recounting of the greatest marvel witnessed
in a preternaturally long life. The former of these motifs is
included in the exempla given by Caesarius of Heisterbach in his
Dialogus Miraculorum, compiled about AD 1220.[26] In the Blasket
text the greatest marvel is recounted by Áine Nic Chártha in what
is an inset-tale. The woman in the cloud in this inset-tale is to
be seen as a kind of pre-figuration of Áine Nic Chártha herself
in her role as the personification of the goddess just as the priest
of the inset-tale is to be seen as a kind of prefiguration of the
Catholic curate who personifies Seán Bráthair Ó Conchubhair.
At the centre of both frame- and inset-tales there seems to be an
implicit violation of taboo in regard to culturally proper constraint
on the juxtaposition of female sexuality/fertility with male clerical
status. In the inset-tale the violation takes the form of infanticide
following on illicit relations between the woman in the cloud
and an unnamed cleric. In the frame-tale the potential of some
similar type violation is hinted at in the scene where the Catholic
curate innocently lays his hand to the cradle, in the kitchen corner,
to rock the supposed infant. In doing this the curate causes the
historical and mythological ground to open under his feet, so to
speak, and brings about the revelation of the protagonists' true

identities on the part of the protagonists. Following this he is able to lead Ana out of an eternity of existence in this world and into the eternity of the Christian afterlife in heaven, thus, after a fashion, affirming again the sovereign triumph of Christianity over Celtic religion. In Irish tradition legitimate sovereignty has always had its source in the otherworld and the conferring of this sovereignty has frequently involved an encounter in which marvels are witnessed. We need not then be surprised when the sovereignty of Christianity and its male deity as represented in the Blasket story by Seán Bráthair Ó Conchubhair continues to be asserted in the context of a recounting of the greatest marvel witnessed in the long life of the representative of the supreme female divinity of the Celtic world in Ireland.

In Figure 15.2, I show the triple opposition in terms of which the tale's central motif is rendered:

Figure 15.2 Triple gendered opposition in central motif

Female	Male
'Celtic' divinity	'Christian' divinity
Cailleach Bhéarra	Christus
Ana Ní Áine	Seán Bráthair Ó Conchubhair
Áine Nic Chártha	Catholic curate/*sagart óg*

The vitality of cultural continuity in this Blasket text is, I think, clear, and is not, in general terms, in dispute in relation to oral narrative tradition. What it is equally important for us to try and understand as clearly as we can is how this traditional material is – in performance and transmission – adapted and shaped in relation to contemporary social and cultural circumstances, so that the embodiment of its chief cultural meaning is brought about in an historically and socio-economically realistic fashion from the point of view of the contemporary audience for its narration. It is by means of some such constant adaptation that the functional relevance to society of traditional material is maintained and the means by which such adaptation is achieved has to be the creativity of narrative performance. This creativity can be thought of as a function of both the talent and the personality of the narrative performer responding to the expectations and pressures deriving from the social context of the particular narrative event;

an event whose reality as a form of social communication is always poorly represented by even the most meticulously transcribed text. In relation to *Cailleach Bhéarra* in Irish oral narrative tradition, however, texts are almost the only record of the spontaneous storytelling, featuring her, that we can study. Careful examination, classification and analysis of such texts can still be expected, I think, to yield certain clues as to the nature and operation of functional adaptation in the traditional creative performance of the material.

Creativity of performance seems to me to find expression on sociological and psychological levels as well as on that level of rhetoric and verbal artistry where the narrator's sophistication in the use of language and the exploitation of linguistic resources (including semantic ones) finds expression. Geoffrey Gantz has remarked, in relation to the linguistic and other sophistications of learned, medieval Irish tales, that they encompass, as he puts it, 'both impacted myth and corrupted history'.[27] I think a case can be made for adding to this list, in respect of the later folk narratives, both a kind a stylised sociology and also a dimension in which the personality of the narrator expresses itself on the particular occasion of performance in response to factors that even the fullest and most exhaustive ethnography of the tale-telling situation cannot hope to register. I should like to pursue a little the question of the addition of a stylised sociology since, in relation to the psychological dimension I am proposing, almost nothing can at present be said – at least by me – at a level other than the subjective and the anecdotal.

In Professor Jackson's Blasket text the age-old characters and the culturally profound significance of their encounter are presented to us in a setting that is, on the surface, that of post-Famine rural Ireland. The detail of the story, in both the frame and the inset-tales, has been meticulously chosen by the skilled narrator so as to be immediately comprehensible to a contemporary audience in terms of their own personal life experience. The profounder meanings of the narrative communicate themselves at several deeper levels. We cannot hope to understand or even illustrate this process of surface renewal from a single text or even from all known versions of a single tale or legend.

Ideally, what is needed is a complete ethnographic and textual record of the entire community's engagement in the creative performance of its oral narrative repertoire over as long a period as feasible. Such a record would enable one to attempt to identify and analyse the social substance in which traditional incidents and characters are clothed. Another approach might be to take all known versions of legends relating to a single traditional personage such as *Cailleach Bhéarra* and to attempt to analyse their sociological or ethnographic embodiment in terms of regional socio-economic and historical variation.

In an effort to begin to do this latter I have extracted from the archival material in the Department of Irish Folklore texts relating to *Cailleach Bhéarra* that I have tentatively assigned to the seven categories of oral narrative already outlined in Figure 15.1, and I would suggest that it is possible to see in this material evidence of at least some aspects of the sociological and ethnographic embodiment of traditional characters and incidents in late Gaelic oral narrative tradition.

We might take, for example, the material designated by category 5 or, rather, that section of it relating to the harvesting contest between *Cailleach Bhéarra* and a succession of human figures one of whom eventually vanquishes her. Category 5 material in general shows *Cailleach Bhéarra* as very definitely a corn goddess and consists of versions of three main incidents:

a) How people tricked her into revealing to them the secret of her early and abundant corn harvest; she lets it be known that she sows in late winter and harvests the still-green corn before the coming of autumn gales. *Coirce na bhFaoillí* is attested in both Irish and Scottish Gaelic tradition as a name for this late winter corn.[28]

b) How she taught people to thresh corn in an improved manner using a hazel and holly flail and threshing one sheaf at a time on a clean floor. The account typically ends with a *leath-rann* of which the following is an example: *Suaisteán cuilinn agus buailteán coll, Fasaire aon phunainn ar urlár lom.*

c) How she lorded it at harvest time over the reaping of corn and put to death a succession of male reapers whose legs she used to sweep from them in the cornfield when they failed to match her own prowess with sickle or scythe.

At least twenty-eight versions of c) exist – all from Connaught and one of them, the longest, is seemingly a retelling of the version Hyde published in 1901.[29] These twenty-eight versions vary considerably as to length and to the narrative skill of those who told them to the Folklore Commission field-workers. The question has to be considered as to what effect Hyde's publication of his text of this tale in 1901 had on the repertoire of the west of Ireland communities from which the Folklore Commission received more than two dozen versions a generation later. From a combination of both internal and contextual evidence it may be assumed that the Hyde text is not the sole source of all the later versions though it has, doubtless, influenced some of them. The specific nature and precise extent of this influence remains, for the present, as an interesting topic to be investigated. The versions also vary in the degree to which the traditional material is clothed in the early-twentieth-century rural reality which was the ethnographic context in which, as tales, they functioned.

The biggest single adaptation, found in a majority of the texts, is that it is a mowing contest, rather than a reaping contest, in which the hag is finally vanquished after her long reign of terror and destruction. I would tentatively interpret this as an adaptation arising from the far greater familiarity of the generality of the plain people of the west of Ireland communities from which the Irish Folklore Commission field workers collected, with the saving of hay rather than of corn on any large scale in recent times.[30] Whether the distribution of those versions where it is still a reaping contest could be correlated with areas of a greater familiarity with grain cropping than is generally to be found throughout the essentially spade-culture territory of much of the western Gaeltacht in the early twentieth century is difficult to ascertain. Clearly, however, running through all these versions is the notion of *Cailleach Bhéar(r)a/ Bhéar(r)ach*, thus named, as one of the gentry – or at least one of the strong farmer class – living in the local 'big house' on occasion, or, alternatively, on a substantial holding, hiring farm labourers, working them hard and feeding and sleeping them as would any nineteenth-century squire or minor landlord. She is portrayed as being concerned with rents and wages and land purchase, and the main events of the tale are always fleshed out with these concerns and with other realistic details from the humbler lives of the tales' audiences: turfcutting, buttermaking, knitting, walking to the market in Galway, even emigrating for a while to England. The setting here is, in some ways, reminiscent of Cois Fharraige in Máirtín Ó Cadhain's short stories. In other ways it reflects the sheep country of Clare/Galway and east Galway with its meadows and grazing lands behind straight stone walls, its comfortable farmhouses and relatively more developed economy and social organisation.

Against these backgrounds of contemporary ethnography the central confrontation takes place that pits the strength and cunning of the human hero against the prowess of a supernatural female who is vanquished at last by means of human deviousness assisted by an element of magic advantage that is provided as often as not by a blacksmith or his daughter. The version Hyde published has a triple confrontation in terms of, firstly, spade work, then the mowing of hay and, finally, the reaping of oats, as Figure 15.3 sets out.

Figure 15.3 Triple confrontation and defeat

Contest	Implement	Advantage from CB's Daughter
digging of stubble	spade	hound's milk
mowing of hay	scythe	steel spikes
reaping of oats	sickle	destruction of Dardaol

In this version it is *Cailleach Bhéarra*'s own daughter (fathered by a blacksmith?) who provides the advice and magical advantage to the human hero Donnchadh Mór Mac Mánais.

There follows a summary version of the narrative structure of the Hyde text.

Frame-Tale Summary

1. *Cailleach Bhéarach* and her daughter set up farming in *Gleann na Madadh*.
2. A succession of labourers expire in her service in vain attempts to match her prowess.
3. The warrior-like Donnchadh Mór boasts that he will overcome her and takes service with her for unusually high stakes. He is to be fed on a cereal diet along with one pig-meat dish on Easter Day.
4. Donnchadh wins affection of *Cailleach Bhéarach*'s daughter but is left prostrate at the end of a day's spade-work.
5. Daughter renders superhuman strength to Donnchadh by dipping his bread in milk of her mother's hound. Donnchadh vanquishes *Cailleach Bhéarach* and is rescued from her wrath by daughter.
6. Before haymaking, daughter supplies Donnchadh with steel spikes with which he can cause *Cailleach Bhéarach* to blunt her scythe, thus himself gaining victory a second time.
7. Before reaping of oats, daughter alerts Donnchadh to existence of magic beetle in handle of *Cailleach Bhéarach*'s sickle. Donnchadh destroys the beetle and inflicts ultimate defeat on *Cailleach Bhéarach*.

8. At his request she reveals her great age and she relates to him the story of her life and binds him to secrecy regarding it while she lives.

9. At the end of his term of service Donnchadh extracts the fullest reward for his contract.

10. Shortly after, *Cailleach Bhéarach* sickens and dies during a great storm together with her daughter and her hound.

Inset-Tale Summary (The story of the *cailleach*'s life)

1. When the *Cailleach Bhéarach* was a young girl she was betrayed in love by a neighbour's son.

2. In revenge she acquired magic gifts from the smith and used them to kill her former lover.

3. She gives birth to a daughter at the smith's house and, in disguise as a man, becomes his helper at the forge.

4. As punishment for accidentally injuring the smith she is transformed into a sow for a period of 100 years. Subsequently she is restored to her daughter and given riches with which she buys her farm at *Gleann na Madadh*.

Commentary

1. Donnchadh Mór is presented to us as a type of male hero: he is as strong as any stallion and as fleet of foot as any stag. There is no fair or assembly that he will not clear with his ash-plant when anger comes over him. He is set up as a fitting adversary for the *cailleach draoidheachta* ['magic hag'] as *Cailleach Bhéarach* is described in the text as if the supernatural elements of her persona were likely to be overlooked in the mundane ethnographic setting of her farming activities.

2. Donnchadh, the supreme type of the male, has relationship in the text with three females who can be aligned with those aspects of the female supernatural that I have suggested are prominent in the totality of *Cailleach Bhéarra* tradition:

   a) his own mother, elderly, venerable, wise from whom he has himself sprung and been nourished and who can fathom the wiles of *Cailleach Bhéarach*. She stands in the relationship to him of *magna mater*.

   b) *Cailleach Bhéarach*, who is primarily a nature and wilderness goddess here, inimical guardian of the fertility of the

vegetable world (as in so many other texts of the animal
kingdom too). She stands in the relationship to the hero of
the divine hag of war and death.

c) the daughter of *Cailleach Bhéarach* who accepts and returns
the hero's love and, in this role of pseudo-spouse, sustains
and equips and enlightens him in his confrontations with
his adversary (her mother). She stands in the relationship to
the hero of (semi) divine consort or sovereignty queen and
is possessed of at least some of the traditionally associated
motifs,[31] for example she is loathly – *Bhí gnúis uirthi chomh
gránna leis an mbás* ['Her countenance was as horrible as
death'] – she supplies a draught of magic liquid that confers
sovereignty/physical endurance, etc.

3. The sustaining, nourishing, enhancing relationship between
Donnchadh and the *Cailleach Bhéarach*'s daughter is reflected in
the endearment term *A chuisle mo chroí* which is used towards
Donnchadh by his mother and which he himself uses to pseudo-
spouse when she provides for him in his confrontation with her
mother. Correspondingly, terms exchanged between Donnchadh
and the *Cailleach Bhéarach* express the opposite of endearment:
*'Níor thug mé tosach d'aon fhear ariamh, agus níl tusa dul d'á fhaghail
uaim,' ar sise.* ['"I never gave precedence to any man and you are
not going to get it from me now," said she'.]

> *'Faobhar, a Dhonnchaidh, le faobhar gearrtar féar.'*
> *'Ni headh, a chailleach,' ar seisean, 'acht le fear maith agus le
> sean-speil gheár.'* ['"Edge, Donnchadh, hay is cut by edge."
> "Not so, hag," said he, but by a good man and a sharp old
> scythe.']
> *'Ha, Ha, a chailleach bhradach, tá tú gabhtha anois …'* ['"Ho,
> ho, you thieving hag, you are caught now."']

4. In the inset-tale we get an autobiographical account of the
earlier life of *Cailleach Bhéarach* which incorporates the motifs
of homicidal violence and illicit sexual relations in a manner that
appears to echo the violations detailed in the inset-tale of the
Sayers/Jackson text discussed earlier. In the latter, however, it is
the issue of the illicit relationship between woman and priest who
is murdered whereas in the Hyde text the killing has occurred
prior to what I take to be the fathering of the *cailleach*'s daughter
by the smith/magician.

5. Just as the Jackson text ends with an explanation – in terms of the story recounted – of a piece of local linguistic usage, i.e. *Tá sí comh críona le hAna Ní Áine* ['She is as old as Ana Ní Áine'], so the Hyde text ends with an explanation in terms of its own story of the placename *Gleann na Madadh* ['The Glen of the Dogs']: we are told that hundreds of dogs congregated in the district on the morning following the death of *Cailleach Bhéarach*, her daughter and hound. In this way, in the case of both texts, the narrator provides an innocent and superficial explanation for the existence of the legend in his/her repertoire. We can easily see, however, how a strong case can be made for understanding that the significance of such texts for their traditional audiences would have included mythological and religious considerations having an impressive continuity from earlier ages.

I would set this Hyde text along with that text collected from Peig Sayers by Professor Jackson which I have commented on earlier and see them both as impressive examples of what the later Gaelic taletellers at the popular levels of tradition in Ireland could make of the material they inherited from a long past. These two published texts, along with many others as yet in archival form in Ireland and Scotland, deserve in some ways to be regarded as works of literature, certainly as artistic products in their own right. Their creativity, however, and the artistic meanings they carry – and here I may be allowed to hazard a final assertion – are never to be regarded as primarily a matter of some literary aesthetic or some transcendent, inspirational vision. Rather is it the case – both for the tales' immediate audiences and for our later scholarship on them – that their creativity and significance as art must be estimated in terms of their sophisticated exploitation of the repertoire of association and nuance that belongs to a universe of discourse rooted in a communal social and cultural reality. An important part of this reality was communal knowledge of history and ancestral tradition, and *Cailleach Bhéarra* material in that popular ancestral tradition in Ireland and Scotland constitutes, I believe, one kind of evidence for my assertion.

Non-Sovereignty Queen Aspects of the Otherworld Female in Irish Hag Legends: The case of *Cailleach Bhéarra*

[Published in *Béaloideas*, vol. 62/3, 1994–5, pp. 147–62]

In relation to all types of narrative material dealing with divine hags, sovereignty queens, war goddesses, earth mothers, and so on, it seems to me that there are at least two fundamental principles underlying our traditions – and our partial knowledge of these – in so far as they derive, to a degree, from pre-Christian and medieval worlds.

The first principle is that of the perception, or the conviction, of the existence of a female cosmic agency; the second principle is that of the necessary existence of human relationships with such an agency. Evidence regarding the operation of these principles in our traditions is variously perceived as being itself religious, cosmological, mythological, ritual, legendary and so forth, and we are obliged to build up our knowledge of such principles in piecemeal fashion and in the light of the displacement by Christianity of the central transmission of such knowledge within both religious and literary tradition.

From what I know of legendary and other material in both Nordic and Celtic tradition, I think the existence in them of the two principles stated is beyond dispute and I believe that the two traditions share some further characteristics that can be alluded to.

There appears to be, on both sides, a basic duality in the perceived nature of a female cosmic agency. In Nordic tradition the divine female is perceived both as relentless battle goddess and as spirit helper/counsellor of the hero. In Celtic, or at least Gaelic, tradition she is portrayed as both a fierce goddess of war and death, and a radiant sovereign of fertility. All this is at what we might call the learned or literary level of tradition.

At the popular, or oral, level I have been struck by some further correspondences in the matter of Gaelic hags (*cailleacha*) and Nordic giantesses. These have to do with the associations of both hags and giantesses in our traditions with winter, with the wilderness and its life forms, and in particular with the raven as an avian manifestation of the destructive versions of the female agency.[1] At this popular level of tradition also, I think an ambivalence is evident as to the nature of the 'hag' or 'giantess'. She can be both hostile and destructive to, or helpful and supportive of, human life, and I think we should recognise this ambivalent or dual nature of the divine hag in popular tradition just as it has been explicitly recognised on the learned and literary level by (in the Gaelic case) such scholars as John Carey, Máire Bhreathnach, Marie Sjoestedt and others.[2]

Reidar Christiansen made two interesting remarks about the possibility of early contact between Nordic and Celtic peoples as playing a role – together no doubt with areal or even universal cultural principles – in producing at least some of the kinds of correspondences I have in mind. He writes that while such traces of contact are more likely to occur in the folktale proper, they are by no means absent from material of the historical type. He specifically refers to a poem called *Krákumál*, perhaps written in the Hebrides, which has an allusion to an Irish conception: the screaming goddess of war.[3]

He also mentions the hag, the mother of the giants, the ultimate opponent, as a still more complicated case – because it involves, as he puts it, more far-reaching problems, ones that I take to be cosmological and religious in origin.[4]

Within Gaelic tradition, specifically, there has been development whereby at the learned, literary, historical, political level of medieval tradition the figure of the female cosmic agency has been transformed from being a figure of religious ritual and cosmological myth/legend into being a figure of literary politics. This is the figure and the person of the sovereignty queen whose myth is so prominent in medieval Irish tradition and whose literary reflex has been such an enduring part of later Irish and, indeed, Anglo-Irish literature. As I have argued elsewhere, however, popular oral tradition in both Scotland and Ireland has retained the figure of the earth goddess with a wider range of connotations than are encompassed in the sovereignty queen myth and this chapter is devoted to exploring some of these non-sovereignty queen connotations.[5] I want to do this kind of exploration in relation to material concerning one particular goddess-figure who is very prominent in both the medieval, learned and the later, popular, oral traditions of both Ireland and Scotland and who, thus, features in tradition as a whole, both as sovereignty queen and giant hag, and whose persona in the preserved texts widely encompasses the ambivalent, and even multi-faceted, nature of the earth goddess as female cosmic agency and her relations with humans and with human life.

The goddess-figure in question is the Hag of Beare (*an Chailleach Bhéarra*) who at the learned, literary level has associations as sovereignty queen and eponymous ancestress with the burial mound at Knowth, on the Boyne; with the Corcu Duibne lineages of the Irish south-west; with prominent quasi-historical personages such as Cuimíne Fota and Fothad Cannaine and with the mythological Lug – the god-prototype of sacral kingship.[6] As sovereignty queen as such, the Hag of Beare is styled with the personal names Buí/Baí and Digdi. Later oral tradition (and perhaps also early medieval oral tradition) calls her simply *Cailleach Bhéarra*, the Hag of Beare, and her learned associations (of sovereignty and politics) with the Beara peninsula of the Irish south-west coast are absent from the general corpus of Irish and Scottish material – though present in material from Munster. Her name, also, undergoes folk-etymologisation in popular tradition outside Munster, and especially in Scotland. Nevertheless, she is to be identified widely in Gaelic legend generally as a popular reflex of that same earth mother who developed into a sovereignty queen in learned medieval tradition.

Since the repertoire of the later Gaelic storyteller contains an amalgam of material, some of which originated on the literary-learned medieval level, any attempt at clarifying the non-sovereignty aspect of *Cailleach Bhéarra* legendry needs to develop criteria for identifying legends deriving from the learned, medieval-literary sovereignty queen myth.[7] My own approach to this problem is based on the assumption that the sovereignty queen myth effectively legitimates male authority and male social supremacy, while non-sovereignty queen legendry tends to emphasise female autonomy and empowerment. In excluding from consideration legendry material deriving from the former, I have been mindful of the eight motifs of the sovereignty queen myth as identified by R.A. Breatnach[8] and the sovereignty queen nature of legendry material that presents the *Cailleach Bhéarra* as a personification of the corn harvest[9] or of animal flocks or herds.[10] On the basis of such discriminations we may proceed to examine the character of each of four general categories of non-sovereignty queen *Cailleach Bhéarra* legendry that I propose.

In the non-sovereignty queen legends about *Cailleach Bhéarra*, the Hag of Beare, that I have located and looked at, broad categories of classification suggest themselves as follows:

1. *Cailleach Bhéarra* as she who created and dominates landscape;
2. attributes of *Cailleach Bhéarra* regarding her physique, her nourishment and her hygiene;
3. the physical eternity of *Cailleach Bhéarra* – which is, in fact, finite;
4. *Cailleach Bhéarra* in conflict with and displaced by Christianity.

I have space to mention only some of the more prominent motifs associated with these categories of *Cailleach Bhéarra* non-sovereignty queen legendry. Some of these are of course shared with legends of other supernatural female figures in Ireland and Scotland. Some may well also be shared with Nordic legends or found in an even wider context.

I

In the first category, that dealing with *Cailleach Bhéarra* as creator of and presider over the landscape, the following motifs are prominent:

- the dropping of cairns of stones on mountain tops and of large rocks in waterways and in lakes is attributed to the activity of *Cailleach Bhéarra* as a geotechtonic power;
- the location of certain islands in the sea, and lakes in the mountains is attributed to her;
- her activity was responsible for certain rock formations on the sides of hills and mountains and also for dolmen-type natural structures on flat land;
- the track of her foot or hand may be seen to this day in certain rocks;
- thunder, storm winds, tides and wave power all attest the energy of her abiding presence in the physical realm.

Two interesting applications of this presiding domination theme occur in material from Mayo and Sligo. In that region legends attribute the building of certain round towers and church steeples to the prowess of

Cailleach Bhéarra as a stone-mason, so that she becomes the creator of the more massive and enduring aspects of the cultural landscape as well as of the physical.[11] In this we can detect a blending of traditions of *Cailleach Bhéarra* with those of the *Gobán Saor* – the journeyman master mason (a late popular reflex of the Celtic god of craftwork) who is widely credited in Gaelic tradition with the building of the round towers of Ireland.

Also in Mayo and Sligo we find a tradition, attested at half a dozen locations, in material from different folklore collectors, that it was *Cailleach Bhéarra* who deprived humans of their original ability to walk immediately after birth.[12] The human child, we are told, once had this ability, but *Cailleach Bhéarra* laid her hand to the small of its back (or pressed her two thumbs to its back) so as to impair it, and it henceforth took a year or more before the human infant was able to walk. Only for that, we are assured, the newborn child would be able to walk and jump at birth like the calf and the foal and the lamb. Indeed what *Cailleach Bhéarra* wished was to deprive humankind of its ability to walk upright at all, but she only succeeded in delaying the onset of this ability in every individual. We are told that the marks of her fingers can be seen on the thighs and waists of adolescents – as a permanent reminder, no doubt, of *Cailleach Bhéarra*'s primal encounter with humankind. The attribution in this way to the activities of *Cailleach Bhéarra*, the earth goddess, the personification of female, cosmic agency, of the growth/stretch marks that occur as a feature of the 'landscape' of the human body, matches in the individual corporeal sphere the attribution to her of the origin of features of the physical landscape such as huge scrape-like screes on the sides of mountains, for example *Scríob na Cailleach*.[13] In each case the features involved are manifestations of an evolutionary or developmental dynamic – the one biological, the other geological – whose energy or life the earth goddess, and, in this material, *Cailleach Bhéarra*, represents. Isomorphism between the human body and the physical universe is a feature of archaic cosmologies,[14] and we have here, in this Mayo and Sligo legendary material, the suggestion of the similar manipulation of both the physical landscape and the human body by a supernatural female figure from whose oppressive clutch humanity has, with difficulty, emerged. Whether this interesting echo of ancient worldview derives from early medieval or from more modern sources remains, at present, unclear.

There is here too something of the winter goddess of Nordic traditions who opposes the emergence of spring and its images of fertility, seeking to prolong the frozen grip of winter and its severe weather which she personifies. In the Mayo/Sligo material *Cailleach Bhéarra* is presented as a similarly sterile opponent of human autonomy and fertility, and we are told that, when any new season's animals or blossoms or fish are seen, people say *Marbhfháisc ar an gCailligh Bhéar(r)aigh*, i.e. 'May death take the *Cailleach Bhéarra*.'[15]

Lévi-Strauss held that, in mythology, 'it is a universal characteristic of men born from the Earth that at the moment they emerge from the depth, they either cannot walk or they walk clumsily', and that traditional narratives relating the origin and continuing existence of such ambulatory impairment bear witness to the persistence of the notion of the autochthonous origin of man.[16] Edmund Leach has severely faulted such general propositions of Lévi-Strauss on the grounds of ignoring what he terms 'the cultural limitations of time and space',[17] and any reading into this Sligo/Mayo *Cailleach Bhéarra* legendry of mythological and archaic religious significance invites similar censure – on the lines of censure that Tomás Ó Broin has recently made of the hasty and simple-minded identification by some scholars of the *Lia Fáil*, the Stone of Destiny or Coronation Stone at Tara, with the Delphic *omphalos* and the Indian *yupa*.[18]

Nevertheless, there is, in this material, food for thought – and indeed speculation – regarding the import of the legend of the *cailleach*'s involvement with the human frame and its functions. Common terms in Irish and Scottish Gaelic equivalent to 'spinal marrow' are *smior seantuinne* and *smior-cailleach* which literally translate as 'marrow of the elderly female' and 'marrow of the hag'.[19] The term *smiorcalach*, an adjective with the meaning 'friable; liable to crumble', is derived by Dinneen from *smior*, 'marrow', and *cailleach*, 'hag', and the perceived fragility of the human spine and especially the spine of the newborn infant may be invoked in this respect in relation to the Sligo/Mayo legends in question that suggest the origin of that fragility in a primal human encounter with the predominant 'hag' of Gaelic mythological tradition.

II

In the second category, i.e. information regarding the physique and nourishment of the *Cailleach Bhéarra* together with details of what we may call her hygiene and sleep patterns, the following features are prominent:

- From Beara itself we learn that her physique and energy were such that during a single tide-cycle she was able to gather her marine food (plants and fish) from over a huge stretch of named points in the south-west Munster region.
- From different locations and collection dates in both Connemara and Erris we learn that a neighbour to *Cailleach Bhéarra* who accompanies her in walking from her Mayo home to Galway to obtain wool-teasing equipment has the feet quite literally 'walked off' him. Her antidote to the damage she has done him is to advise soaking his feet overnight in vats of butter which are dry by morning, the butter having been absorbed by the mortified feet.
- Her diet is commonly given as marine based – though also as consisting of either exclusively cow's milk or exclusively cereal crops. The marine or sea-shore diet features most prominently in material from the south-west Irish coast and here, invariably, accounts of it take the form of a quatrain, such as:

> *An meadhbhán Fáide fíorghlaine*
> *An díolasg ó chuantaibh Chléire*
> *An burdán geal aduaidh ón Leamhain*
> *Agus an cineamh ó mhullach Bhéimís*

which can be roughly translated as:

> Clear, clean edible seaweed of early spring
> Another kind of edible seaweed from the
> harbours of Cape Clear
> The bright salmon of the Laune river to the north
> And the wild garlic from the top of Béimis mountain.

Perhaps the single most significant thing about this quatrain is that it contains the quotation of a half-quatrain from the twelfth-century *Agallamh na Seanórach*, a learned compilation of Fenian lore,[20] where this occurs in a description of the resources of the place from which Fionn Mac Cumhaill and his warrior band went to fight the famous Battle of Ventry – *Cath Fionn Trá* – against invaders from the otherworld that Gaelic tradition frequently locates *i gcríochaibh Lochlann* – in the Nordic lands. There is an implication here for the dating of *Cailleach Bhéarra* legendry to which further reference will be made below.

In this second category also we are told that *Cailleach Bhéarra*

- never ate or drank except when she was really hungry and thirsty;
- that her little finger or the palm of her hand had never known sunlight;
- that she never slept except when she was tired and sleepy;
- that she was always washing the mud from her bare feet and legs in the course of her constant travels so as never to carry the mud from one puddle as far as the next.

III

We may now turn our attention to the third category: the finite physical eternity of the reign of *Cailleach Bhéarra*.

Cailleach Bhéarra is, in most respects, the epitome of longevity. We can recall the proverbial wisdom regarding the three longest-lived creatures – the yew tree, the eagle and the *Cailleach Bhéarra* and how she remembers when lakes were little spring wells or barley grew around what is now a sea-rock.[21]

In Irish oral tradition the widespread motif of the innumerable ox bones in the loft of her house that defy counting demonstrates the apparent impossibility of reckoning in human terms the length of her days. A visitor – sometimes a Christian saint or priest – seeks to count the bones that *Cailleach Bhéarra* says have been deposited there for each year of her life and fails, despite great time and effort, to even begin to reckon their number.[22]

In the Irish legends I have looked at regarding her longevity, however, there is also a strong sense that the alleged eternity of physical existence of the *Cailleach Bhéarra* is, paradoxically, finite; that it had a beginning and has had, or has, an end; that it may be enumerated. A Carna, County Galway legend recounts how *Cailleach Bhéarra* learns of the birth the previous night of the daughter of her own great-granddaughter.[23] Another Galway account tells how, in answer to St Patrick's query as to her age, *Cailleach Bhéarra* says that she has buried (i.e. outlived) nine times nine generations nine times over in nine successive graves.[24] And there is the proverbial wisdom that the life of the *Cailleach Bhéarra* endures for only as long as it takes all traces of one carefully constructed potato ridge to vanish from the soil,[25] whereas a well-known estimate of the span of the physical world itself is that it endures as long as three successive ploughed ridges (or boundary furrows) will leave a trace in the earth: *Trí iomaire treabhtha* (or *críche*) *go deireadh an domhain*.

In a corpus of legends regarding the 'worst', i.e. the coldest or the wettest, night that 'ever came out of the heavens' – sometimes named *Luan Lae Bealtaine* (Mayday Monday) – we learn that other creatures – the eagle, the deer, the otter, the salmon – are, in fact, much older than *Cailleach Bhéarra*.[26] Her age and origin are prescribed here by the notion of a flood that once covered the land of Ireland and one is reminded of use of the Flood in *Lebor Gabála* (Book of Invasions) to locate in a time continuum the earliest human settlements of Ireland.[27] The *Lebor Gabála* text represents a great tenth- and eleventh-century literary and learned grafting on to a biblical stock of important aspects of native mythological and cosmological tradition. It should not, perhaps, surprise us to discover that oral tradition also reflects in similar fashion the adaptation and adjustment into a Christianised account of prehistory and human origins here, of the *Cailleach Bhéarra* – as major representative figure of the great chthonic mother and earth goddess of the Celtic and, indeed, old European religious systems.

In relation to a possible *Lebor Gabála* congruence, attention may be drawn to the borrowing into *Cailleach Bhéarra* legendry of the half-quatrain out of *Agallamh na Seanórach* mentioned earlier and I would like to suggest that we have here, in each case, some slight evidence of the possible age span of the *Cailleach Bhéarra* material in question – it being, conceivably, fashioned within a renewed literary creativity, learned and popular, of the eleventh and twelfth centuries. Thus, later Gaelic oral traditions of *Cailleach Bhéarra* are to be viewed as themselves the products of a Christian world and not as any direct survival from a remote pagan past. Within that Christian world, nevertheless, they bear witness to the continuing sensitivity of popular tradition to elements of an ancestral cosmology that survive in popular mythological narrative and that point to the person and the power of the supernatural female.

IV

We will now consider the displacement of *Cailleach Bhéarra* by Christianity. An informant from Mull reported in 1935 that *Cailleach Bhéarra* was a young girl when Adam and Eve lived in the Garden of Paradise[28] and, certainly, the sense of *Cailleach Bhéarra* as part of an alternative cosmology to the Christian one comes through in the legends. In some versions of the innumerable bones legend, the enquirer is St Patrick himself who, having, as it were, identified *Cailleach Bhéarra* as the supposedly ageless figure of the goddess, demolishes her in a flash.

A Mayo version has her making her way to Lough Derg – which, we are told, was the chief seat of pagan pilgrimage in pre-Christian Ireland – to work her powers against the recently arrived new religion. Patrick intercepts her and pursues her to the top of Croagh Patrick, his own holy mountain, where 'he ran her to earth'.

In Munster tradition encounters with local Christian saints cause the *Cailleach Bhéarra* to be petrified to a rock which still stands with its back to land on a spot named *Ard na Caillí* or *Tráigh na Caillí* (Hag Height, Hag Strand, etc.). *Cailleach* Point on the south-west Mull coast has a similar rock formation similarly explained.

We should notice that in the Irish south-west, where it is a local saint rather than Patrick himself who displaces *Cailleach Bhéarra*, the local saint is most often a female. This is further evidence of the strong association of the south-west with the cult of the goddess and its transformation in Christianity into traditions of local female Christian saints who – as in this case – oppose the chief non-Christian representatives of their own origin. *Gobnait* and *Caitiarann* are specifically mentioned in this regard.[29]

Another legend features what one might term a layman opposing *Cailleach Bhéarra* on behalf of the new faith. In a version from County Galway we hear that a servant boy of the *Cailleach Bhéarra*'s went out to turn hay on a day when she predicted rain. When she upbraids him he questions her certainty as to the weather.[30] She says that the lark and the deer have spoken to her of imminent rain. He then utters the memorable and significant quatrain:

> *Ná creid fuiseog is ná creid fia*
> *'s ná creid briathra mná*
> *Más moch mall eirgheas an ghrian*
> *Is mar is toil le dia a bhéas an lá.*

[Believe not the lark nor the deer
And believe not the word of woman [vs word of male divinity]
Whether sunrise is early or late
The day will be as God disposes.]

This quatrain is frequently found in oral tradition independently of *Cailleach Bhéarra* legendry. Here, however, it is used against her. The quatrain in question is an utterance which manages to combine opposition to *Cailleach Bhéarra* and her nature religion, on the part of Christianity, with a patriarchal sexism which, of course, Christianity, however wittingly or unwittingly, introduced in the context of the ancestral cosmology of the Celtic lands in which supernatural female powers are prominent.

A less harsh – if equally dismissive and patriarchal – judgement on female cosmic agency is, perhaps, vouched for by the young lad in a County Mayo legend which recounts the death of *Cailleach Bhéarra* as a result of her falling from a steeple she had built. She fell, in this account, because of her agitation at hearing the young lad shout up at her when passing:

> *Feicim do thóin, a Chailleach Bhéarra!*
>
> ('*Cailleach Bhéarra*, I spy your arse!')

I conclude with a comment about mythological legends, such as those of *Cailleach Bhéarra*, vis-à-vis later popular religion and popular culture. I believe that as an expression of the convictions of any traditional cults of the earth goddess, in her many forms, in Ireland, the legends of *Cailleach Bhéarra* are now empty of religious significance and exist only in print, in archive form or in the vestigial memories of passive carriers who have no personal conviction regarding such a female cosmic agency. Like so much else of ancestral and popular religion in eighteenth-, nineteenth- and perhaps even early-twentieth-century Ireland, any consciousness of an alternative cosmology to an increasingly orthodox Christian – and largely Roman Catholic – one has been obliterated. There is, undoubtedly, a sense in which Irish Catholic devotion to the cult of the Virgin Mother of God owes something of its intensity and its loyal endurance to its touching on sensibilities that earlier fed on notions of the mother of the gods, the female agency who reigned in physical life and whose assistance or hostility was said to account for many of the blessings or vicissitudes of human existence. Similarly, I would argue that the much wanted Irish openness to a sense of spiritual transcendence is not unconnected to ancestral cultural sensibilities regarding an otherworld realm that was imminently close at hand – the realm of the *sí* where so often it is a female divine who is perceived as reigning in peace and beauty. Indeed, the lively susceptibility to interpret life events in terms of contact with this ancestral otherworld realm that was found in popular culture in Ireland and Scotland until relatively recently, leads one to believe that even though personal conviction regarding the person and the authority of the goddess is now no more, it was very real – at least among some segments of the community – in early modern times.

Proinsias Mac Cana has declared that the authoritative self-assurance of the divine heroine is extended to her human counterpart in literature – meaning, largely, medieval literature, no doubt.[31] My question is whether such self-assurance also continued to have some influence on the status of flesh and blood women in society – especially in the lower ranks of society whose numbers in Ireland multiplied so rapidly from the end of the seventeenth until the middle of the nineteenth century.

A huge population of the plain people of Ireland was, in those times, effectively beyond the reach of strict pastoral control or orthodox teaching by any church, and that population's continued official and consciously deliberate overall allegiance to Catholicism impinged to only a limited degree on ancestral loyalties in regard to the forces of the native otherworld realm. These loyalties include, in a pre-eminent way, loyalties to the name and the legends and the authority of the goddess – and more specifically to her *cailleach*/hag persona – in its benign and nurturative as much as in its destructive and threatening forms.

I believe that it can be shown, in terms of the cultural logic operating in pre-Famine Ireland at least, that a range of social personae held, on due occasions (of birth, sickness, 'trouble', death), by flesh and blood females had, as an important part of their legitimation and autonomy, in the eyes of popular society and in popular culture, the archetype of the humble hag-goddess and her otherworld authority.[32] The country midwife (*bean ghlúine*); the wise woman (*bean feasa*); the corpse washer and 'layer out' (*bean bhán*) and the crying woman at wakes (*bean chaointe*) among others, all seem to me to derive their power and authority from close contact with an essentially female otherworld force or agency. This contact is itself the subject of many other legends,[33] and I can do no more here than draw attention to their potential too for analysis in this fashion.

PART 4

History and Politics

Introduction

This section begins with some consideration of the relationship between the 'history' of the academic historian and the historical content of vernacular tradition that is regarded as 'folk history'. Penetrating discussion of this topic has been provided in the writings of Guy Beiner who holds – and demonstrates – that local traditions are repeatedly reshaped through what he terms 'negotiations of memory'.[1] These consist of a continuous process that includes such modes of transmission as oral narration, print media and social commemoration. Beiner's discussion is in relation to the history and folk memory of an iconic historical event – the landing on the Mayo coast in 1798 of a French expeditionary force in support of a proposed uprising.

Other instances of such transmission are examined in this section in relation to the utilisation by Brian Merriman of the *aisling* tradition of the otherworld sovereignty queen to critique the social world of the late-eighteenth-century Irish countryside and in the case of the remembrance in oral history of the attempted French expedition landing in Bantry Bay in 1796.

The continued existence in the mentality, the poetry and the worldview of the Irish-speaking population in the eighteenth century of traditional concepts of sovereignty and otherworld female agency has been persuasively argued in a recent work by Vincent Morley.[2] The question of the continued existence of such traditional mythological themes in the culture and the politics of the modern world had been raised by Richard Kearney in relation to the necessity of distinguishing what he terms 'authentic', i.e. liberating ways of invoking myth, and 'inauthentic', i.e. perverse ways that are void of the creativity and imagination that contact with mythic energies can promote.[3]

Another and far more recent iconic historical event – the 1916 Rising – is discussed in the light of these matters, and the issue of its constituting a mythological potential for the conduct of social and political life is considered in the light of its commemoration. The degree to which a folk mentality informed, to some degree, the thinking and political ambition of a taoiseach who was heir to much of the mythology of 1916 is explored and a final article examines how such mentality and official political mindset militated to a not insignificant degree against the acceptance and the recording of the social and cultural realities of an increasingly urbanised and industrialising Ireland.

Along with developments in folklore at University College Dublin and in anthropology at NUI Maynooth and Queen's University Belfast, the Department of Folklore and Ethnology at University College Cork proceeded with such study and recording as is envisaged here in ways that have been discussed by Cliona O'Carroll[4] and Marie-Annick Desplanques[5] who bring out the co-participative and emancipatory nature of this form of folklore and ethnology. These were features that were aimed at from the beginning in the planning for the Cork Northside Folklore Project – a research undertaking and archival resource that finds its place in the wider field of Irish ethnology and its study – to which the present work is a contribution.[6]

CHAPTER 17

The Hidden Ireland: Myth and reality

[This text originated as a radio talk in a Thomas Davis Lecture series entitled 'Ireland after William']

The term 'the hidden Ireland' has had general currency in this country for nearly a century now, since Professor Daniel Corkery published under that name his celebrated study of eighteenth-century Munster Gaelic poets.[1] Corkery probably intended it to be a controversial title for a book that had as its avowed aim the redressing of the balance of ignorance and neglect which had been the lot, so he claimed with considerable justification, of the world of native Irish learning and those attempting to carry on its cultivation in Ireland after the age of King William. In a sense Corkery was proposing the 'hidden' Ireland as a 'real' Ireland in contrast with the official, parliamentary Ireland of Lecky's history of the ascendancy Irish world as reflected in the novels of the Anglo-Irish literary establishment. The full extent of a complete account of any such 'real' Ireland would of course go far beyond the confines of the literary aspects of the Irish eighteenth century to which Corkery mainly confined himself. He himself acknowledged this in his introductory remarks to the book:

> To fill out the vision of that land, so dark, so scorned, yet so secretly romantic to those who know it, one would need to have as well a full account of the Irish adventurers of that century, of such men as Morty Óg O'Sullivan and Art O'Leary – to take two of many figures so different, so very different both from 'Barry Lyndon' – the 'Irishman' of fiction and Barrington's 'Irishmen' of history.

One also needs an adequate account of the wandering priests and friars moving hither and thither between this country and the continent, suffering so deeply, striving so gallantly to keep the institutional side of the church from utterly fading away. Finally, with a comprehensive study of the folk-poetry – the most precious heritage of all produced by the Gaels in that century – as well as of the folk-music then composed, we should feel that we had fairly explored the riches of that starving people. Until those other avenues are also opened up one cannot have any deep idea of their hidden lives.[2]

Two questions immediately suggest themselves as fundamental to this issue. What exactly is meant by Ireland here? Is it a place, a people, a collection of peoples, a state of mind, a memory, a personal experience, a combination of all these? Or something else again? And from whom is 'Ireland', however we characterise the meaning of the term, hidden, and why? In *The Hidden Ireland* Corkery claimed to show that for the Irish-speaking poets and people of eighteenth-century Munster – and the implication of his title is surely that this is also true for other regions of the country – Ireland is a very real, if abstract, presence, a presence to be symbolised and personified in the imagery of allegorical *aisling* – or vision poetry. In such poems, Ireland, in the person of a beautiful woman, the helpless and pitiful victim of foreign oppressors, speaks to the poet of the liberation and regeneration that is to follow in the wake of a restoration of rightful rulers to the hegemony of the land of Ireland. Meanwhile the peasant poets and the plain people in general are seen to languish in undeserved misery, excluded from civil society and exploited by rapacious landlords and merchants.

In his well-known essay published in 1969,[3] Professor Louis Cullen has argued that Corkery's concept of a 'hidden Ireland' in the eighteenth century ignores the actual economic realities of the day and – ironically – in imposing an unhistorical stereotype on the poetic record of the times even manages to invest the people and situations he describes with the same kind of remoteness that Corkery himself objected to in the writings of such as Somerville and Ross. Cullen's own analysis of eighteenth-century Gaelic poetry purports to show how widespread was the involvement in a cash economy, the preoccupation with prices and with ways of getting on in life, with the realities of commerce, of small industry and of an emerging class structure. Professor Seán Ó Tuama has argued that Cullen's objections are invalid since he has misunderstood the nature of the hidden Ireland concept Corkery promoted and that Corkery is, in some ways, a better social historian than Cullen since the historical evidence is that, contra Cullen's view and notwithstanding real social differentiation, the Gaelic aristocracy and the eighteenth-century tenant population were united emotionally within a common Gaelic cultural system.[4]

The danger here is that we will fall into the trap of seeing Corkery's and Cullen's views of Irish society in the eighteenth century as mutually exclusive so that we are compelled to come down on the side of *either* ideology *or* economic analysis as the true and proper framework within which to comprehend the people, and their motivation in the events and situations of everyday eighteenth-century Irish life. Such false opposition between some warm and heady myth promulgated by Professor Corkery and some clear and cold reality promoted by Professor Cullen will simply, if it is allowed to take hold, serve to delay and make more difficult our achieving of any satisfactory understanding of this highly significant and challenging period of our history. The fact is, and its statement is surely a truism, that the past is irrecoverable, and that no scholar can hope to reproduce for us the lived reality of, for instance, eighteenth-century Irish life in any way that is other than an approximation to the hugely complex and ultimately subjective experience of the men and women whose lives constituted that reality and the record of whose activities and thoughts is necessarily so incomplete. In this sense Ireland in every period of its history is a hidden Ireland and it is the never-ending task of historical reformulation and restatement to provide us with the partial insights that are the best we can do in our concern to re-create, to know, and perhaps to learn from the past.

The starting point for any consideration of the condition of society and the history of culture in Ireland after William must surely be the transformed and transforming nature of Irish society and Irish culture in the more or less peaceful aftermath of the wars and expulsions, the destructions and plantations of the previous century. But just as the military struggle between King James and King William in Ireland must be seen in the context of the great European war then in progress, so the social and cultural transformation of Ireland in the eighteenth century has to be understood in relation to the contemporary transformation of European society from the Atlantic to the Urals and beyond, a transformation characterised by one of its recent historians as the end of the old order in rural Europe.⁵ Put at its simplest, this involved a shift in social organisation from the hierarchy of social orders – each defined in terms of hereditary power or lack of it – to a class hierarchy, where class is defined in terms of accumulated wealth. Thus the transformation of the Irish countryside from being a pre-capitalist and largely pastoral, political economy, a transformation that began to take significant effect at the end of the seventeenth century and that has been working its way ever since towards an economy that is urban-dominated and capitalist-industrial, is in no way a uniquely Irish phenomenon. The two great phases of it that are of most relevance to the notion of a hidden Ireland in the eighteenth century are, first, the emergence throughout most of Ireland since the mid-seventeenth century of a new social world consisting of two great orders of people – a new land-owning or land-holding ascendancy on the one hand and a vastly more numerous order of tenant farmers and cottiers on the other; and, secondly, the creation and gradual predomination of class distinctions within this new world as a result of population pressures and increasing economic competition in the course of the eighteenth century.

These developments, it must be stressed, take place against a general background of increased trading activity and the growing importance of towns and town-life whose influence at all levels was ever-increasing in the countryside. Georgian Ireland saw sustained economic growth, with the increase in trading bringing about a very considerable increase in wealth. This wealth, at first almost the exclusive property of the landed gentry, was to pass, in the course of the eighteenth century, to other classes of Irish people and from mid-century there is evidence that even the poorest classes were in the position of being able to shield themselves, economically, from the effects of a bad harvest.⁶ A transformation of this kind could not take effect smoothly, with equal rapidity or to the same extent throughout Irish society. Nevertheless all the evidence we can consult regarding the lives of the people of Ireland in the eighteenth century, whether that evidence be from parliamentary, statistical, economic, literary or folkloric sources, points to the fact that there was a universal and wide-ranging appreciation of and accommodation in various ways to the economic and social realities of life.

Such accommodation in the multitude of spheres that make up every individual's life can never be automatic or monolithic, yet patterns of accommodation are visible – at least to later observation – and these patterns help us to gain some understanding of the nature and complexity of the accommodation that is taking place. This is the ground on which disciples of Corkery and Cullen are allegedly divided into romantic and utilitarian camps. My own position is that I believe that just as the actual accommodation to real life of real people everywhere ranges over and encompasses the socio-economic and the ideological in a way that is not easily compartmentalised, so too our attempts to understand such accommodation in the case of eighteenth-century Ireland must be sensitive to as wide a spectrum of human and cultural realities as possible. Gerard Murphy among others (as Professor Cullen himself noted) has pointed to the continued existence of aspects of a medieval mentality underlying the popular culture of early modern Ireland.[7] These medieval aspects, as much as the early modern European parallels, need to be taken into account when the evidence of the behaviours and choices of the plain people of eighteenth-century Ireland is being examined – whatever the source and nature of the evidence is. The need to be sensitive to similar phenomena of overlap and dovetailing of the traditional and the modern in an earlier era is adverted to by Professor Brian Manning in relation to popular involvement in the Irish rising of 1641.[8] Drawing on ideas of John Bossy, he questions the usual argument that the strength of Catholicism in Ireland in 1641 was largely due to the success of the counter-reformation, accepting, instead, that

> the Catholicism which the Irish peasantry was defending was not the Catholicism of the Counter-Reformation but an older Catholicism deeply rooted in the ancient way of life of the country people and the traditional Gaelic world ... Many of the clergy and some of the religious orders, notably the Franciscans, were in close touch with popular beliefs and practices and defended them against the rigorous enforcement of the Tridentine legislation. It was not so much the strength of the Counter-Reformation as its weakness that was crucial. The Irish people who rose in revolt in 1641 were unsettled and disoriented by the break-up of the Gaelic system of landownership and the Gaelic social order. They rose in revolt in defence of their ancient culture, the old order, their traditional way of life, and they were able to identify this with Catholicism because amongst the Catholic clergy and religious orders they found leaders and defenders of their customs and traditions.[9]

Thus the reality of the people's participation in 'history' is shown to be far more complex than might at first appear.

The range of ways in which the eighteenth-century Gaelic poets adapted to the transformation of Irish society in their own time and the effect of these adaptations on their poetry give some indication of the complexity of the issues involved then also. Some poets stay, so to speak, at the rural, non-commercial, extra-urban end of the spectrum of transformation. Others cross into the world of the town and the class society. Geographical factors matter here of course and the passage of time obviously made it easier for the later-eighteenth-century writers to adapt to the newer forms of social organisation. Whatever they themselves felt about it, their world was becoming inexorably oriented to commerce and to town life. Where Aogán Ó Rathaille finds it almost unbearably painful to contemplate the changes he sees coming to pass, later poets are able to adapt to these to the extent that they can compete for popularity in the market place and in the tavern.

A great part of the poetic achievement of Brian Merriman at the end of our period is, it seems to me, his ability, within the traditions of Gaelic poetry, to inhabit not only consciously but in a masterful way the contemporary, emergent world in which he found himself and to propose the civil and psychological liberation of the individual in that world in terms, not of the restoration of an old order based on the Stuart or any other royal line, but rather in terms of personal maturity and independence. A crucial point about Merriman's great poem *Cúirt an Mheán Oíche* is that the vision of a regenerated land and people that it projects draws its power from Merriman's invocation and creative transformation of the ancient Gaelic sovereignty myth in a form that predates the allegorical *aisling* tradition by at least a thousand years.[10]

Here indeed we have evidence of continuity in mentality of the kind Gerard Murphy has noted, and it is, in this instance, a dynamic and revolutionary continuity that shows up the rhetorical and exhausted nature of the imagery of the conventional eighteenth-century *Aisling*. The practitioners of this conventional *aisling*, if we are to take at face value their dream of restoration for the old orders of society, have surely to be seen as themselves victims of mystification by the very tradition they seek to maintain – given that they are, in reality, members of an increasingly class-oriented society, taking advantage, in a variety of ways, of this possibility, however treacherous or shameful their behaviour might appear when seen from the perspective of the traditional literary elite. Corkery's *Hidden Ireland* is a work whose very foundation, in many ways, rests on that perspective, seeing in the recent experience of dispossession by a majority of the old aristocracy an explanation for all the misfortunes and insecurities of the eighteenth-century Irish. This is to overlook the pressures for social change deriving from deeper and very powerful forces that operated throughout the European world in the course of the eighteenth century.

The upheaval at home, dire and all as it was, has to be seen as part of a great transformation of the western world whose local effect is not wholly unwelcome to the hitherto less well-off. Louis Cullen has recently written an acute passage observing this:

> There is of course everywhere evidence of the impact of landed upheaval − resentment by the dispossessed, insecurity among the new proprietors. The former landowners resented change, a fact illustrated in the Munster poetry which mirrors their aspirations for a restoration of their lands and the dispossession of the upstarts, as they regarded the new owners who had replaced them. The land system which came into existence as a result of landed settlement in the seventeenth century has been represented as a degradation of the rural population, but this view cannot correctly be drawn from the Munster poetry which laments not oppression, but dispossession. Leases were deplored, but simply because, set, in their view by the wrongful owners, they were the legal expression of the new system. In poetry which is not aristocratic, far from the lease being regarded as oppressive, leasehold was viewed as a token of security. Tenants on the whole benefitted from the spread of leasehold in place of the arbitrary and more uncertain tenures hitherto common. Where they did not, it was generally a consequence of the collapse of prices, as in the dire first decade of the new century, when after prices fell abruptly, rents, reasonable at the time of leasing, overnight become oppressive in their incidence.[11]

If we turn now to consider some of the evidence we have for the continued existence in our period of an older part-Celtic, part medieval-European mentality − not in the ranks of the poets, but in the popular culture of ordinary people − we will see, I believe, further proof that there is more to comprehending the Ireland of the eighteenth century than simply plumping for either the romantic/poetic or the economic self-interest schools of thought on the subject.

Ireland in the eighteenth century is a country similar to many other colonial lands, then and since, where the encroachment of a more developed technology and of capitalist formations on a pre-urban, pre-industrial, pre-modern, traditional society gives rise to rapid and radical social transformation. The language-shift (now, alas, almost complete) which has been a fundamental element of transformation in all the Celtic countries since the seventeenth century[12] lends, of course, a tremendous finality, in cultural and in psychological terms, as well as in social, to the changes that are taking place in the Ireland of the eighteenth and indeed the nineteenth centuries – but again here one must beware of the temptation to see language-shift as a phenomenon unique to the Celtic experience. In studying overall this 'process of modernisation', as it is called, the historian seeks to understand, to make sense of, people's behaviour as they react to the transformation of their social world and their daily lives. The flow of events however is to be seen as filtered through both the universe of discourse of the forces and values of modernisation and at the same time through the universe of discourse that is the folk mind with its own traditional value systems and codes of symbolic articulation. In this situation the events of history, so called, are perceived differently and can communicate different meanings within the two universes. A knowledge of the forms and content of the traditional universe is essential for any attempt to round out the picture of what is really going on in people's lives as the people themselves experience them.

Some pioneering studies in the exploration of this relationship between what has been termed 'matters of history' and 'matters of tradition' have been published,[13] but we await major publications of this kind in regard to the modernisation of Irish society in the eighteenth century. I would suggest that collective forms of agrarian protest in Ireland from the mid-eighteenth century constitute one area where this kind of exploratory research would encounter rich material for analysis. It is likely, I believe, that the colour-symbolism, the disguises, the ritual behaviours of peasant protest in Ireland in the face of the forces of modernisation can be shown to be evidence of the coming together for a time of the worlds of politics and folklore so that it was possible for highly meaningful political statements to be made then in traditional forms that to us today are merely the work of irrationality or frenzied excess. Certainly for the south of France as late as the mid-nineteenth century popular traditional culture can still be regarded as providing a powerful collective framework for the expression of new ideas about politics and society. Unless the opposite is proved, I think we can take it as being the case in Ireland also that the transition from a traditional peasant society to a modern political one did not follow a simple line of progression from black to white, and that the traditional universe of discourse of the ordinary people is as much a part of the history of, say, Irish eighteenth-century agrarian outrage as any orders in council or parliamentary petitions.

Yet another area of the history of the eighteenth century in Ireland, the study of which can benefit from our paying attention to the continued survival in popular culture of aspects of native ancestral mentality, is that of messianism – in political affairs as much as in religious or ecclesiastical. Professor Breandán Ó Buachalla has published a lecture on the subject and its connections with the tradition of vision poetry which is of considerable relevance to the point I am attempting to establish.[14] Ó Buachalla holds that eighteenth-century *aisling* poetry is not only a literary convention but the clear manifestation of a popular pre-political mentality drawing on traditional sources of prophecy and wisdom to anticipate, not a revolution, but a return to the former state of affairs that allegedly existed previous to the catastrophe which gave rise to contemporary misery and oppression. As such it would be an important element in the continuing vital existence of the folk universe of discourse with which I am concerned. Now, messianism in Irish tradition is a subject of very considerable scope and in the space remaining to me I can only treat of one aspect of it that has a peculiarly direct link with our period.

The 'Barbarossa' legend – of the hero who waits under enchantment for the opportune time at which he can be restored to his people in order to free them from their bondage – is widely known throughout Europe and an analysis of the versions of it that have been encountered in Ireland has recently been published by Dr Dáithí Ó hÓgáin in the journal *Béaloideas*.[15] He suggests that the legend was brought to Ireland, as it was to Sicily, by the Normans, but of more concern to us here is the fact that several patriotic prophecies have become associated with the legend in this country, one of which concerns the allegedly final battle in Irish history after which Ireland will be finally rid of her foreign, i.e. English, oppressors. Readers of Thomas Flanagan's novel *The Year of the French* will recall what prominence he attributes to the nostrums of the prophecy men of Mayo in the last years of the eighteenth century. In Munster versions, the Barbarossa legend gets mixed up also with the stories of *Donn Fírinne* the ancient Celtic god of the dead who still appears as a character in twentieth-century traditional folk narrative.

It is the Donegal versions of the legend, however, that proffer, for our purposes, the best evidence of the vitality and assimilative powers of the folk universe of discourse not only in the eighteenth century but long after. The hero of the legend, the sleeping warrior, is known in various other parts of the country by a variety of names, some historical, some not. In all Donegal versions save one, he is either an O'Neill or an O'Donnell – often, most interestingly for us, one Ball Dearg O'Donnell who is thought to lie asleep under the great *grianán* or stone fort of Aileach awaiting the call to arms. In fact a real Ball Dearg O'Donnell existed and can be shown to have had the historical facts of his sojourn as a rebel leader in the north of Ireland assimilated to the versions of the Barbarossa legend current there.

This O'Donnell was, in reality, the Irish-born son of a Spanish officer of Irish ancestry, who arrived in Ireland from Spain, pretty much as a soldier of fortune, in 1690, four days after the Battle of the Boyne. Having led a rebel army in Ulster for some time – partly due, apparently, to his acceptance by the people as a saviour from over the water – he abruptly changed sides and joined the Williamites at Sligo. Later, he returned to Spain and died a major-general in 1704. That such a figure can have entered so quickly and so deeply into popular tradition is an indication of the power of the folk universe of discourse at the beginning of the century of our concern. That the Barbarossa legend was still being collected in counties Donegal and Galway as recently as the 1940s and 1950s is a further indication of how dangerous it can be to neglect the influence of tradition on history during the eighteenth century.

My aim, in this lecture, has not been to suggest, even if Corkery's notion of the 'hidden Ireland' of the eighteenth century does not receive universal acceptance today, that another and still *more* mysterious Ireland of that era exists – hidden in the largely forgotten byways of the folk mind. What I do want to urge however is that no source of evidence can be left untapped when we attempt to uncover the meaning of historical events, and that a good deal of evidence remains to be brought to light regarding how a great many eighteenth-century Irish people perceived their everyday existence and the transformations to which it was subject in the course of the near-century from the Battle of the Boyne to the Dungannon Convention that preceded the establishment of legislative freedom in Ireland.

Regarding entries in Anglo-Saxon chronicles of a much earlier period of history, John Earle has written: 'To posterity they present merely a name or two, as of a battlefield and a victor, but to the men of the day they suggested a thousand particulars, which they in their comrade-life were in the habit of recollecting and putting together. That which seems to us a lean and barren sentence, was to them the text for a winter evening's entertainment.'[16] The sentiment expressed in this quotation is one that applies equally – in my estimation – to the remains of Irish eighteenth-century traditional culture – except that I believe that more than an evening's entertainment is involved. The fullest possible attention to that culture on the lines I have suggested can be expected to yield a not inconsiderable enhancement of our understanding of the history of the era that is the subject of this series.

CHAPTER 18

History or Folklore: *Cé acu an cuntas cam?*

[Lecture given to the Irish Historical Society colloquium 'Popular Culture and the Writing of History' at the History Department, National University of Ireland, Galway on 17 November 1995]

This title seems to imply a simple opposition between the truth of history and the distortions of folklore or, conversely, the truth of folklore and the distortions of history. In fact, I want to discuss aspects of some recent developments in the study of culture and cultural materials that move us on beyond any such simple and, apparently, implacable opposition and to suggest that the distortions and the truths of both history and folklore coexist within a general cultural discourse that is the source of the raw materials that both disciplines recognise and engage with and that draw from the discourse of ethnography – historical and contemporary.

Seán Ó Conaill of *Cill Rialaigh*, a cliff village near Bolus Head and *Baile na Sceilg* at the western end of *Uíbh Ráthach* peninsula, described the structure of the traditional calendar for Professor Séamus Ó Duilearga in the 1920s when the latter was engaged in writing down from Ó Conaill's dictation as much of the local repertoire of folklore, in all its genres, as Ó Conaill, then a man in his seventies, could bring to mind.[1] Regarding the structure of the traditional calendar, Ó Conaill reports two sets of quarters and two sets of corresponding quarter-days or head festivals. One set of quarters and festival days are elements of an ecclesiastical calendar involving the celebration of Christmas and the feasts of various saints, namely St Michael, St Patrick and St John the Baptist. The other set are elements of a calendar owing its existence to prehistoric Irish farming communities, and the names of the quarter days in this instance are give in Celtic form: *Lá le Bríde* and *Lá Lúnasa*; *Oíche Bhealtaine* and *Oíche Shamhna*. Ó Conaill himself calls the ecclesiastical set *Ráithí Cama na Bliana* ('the Crooked Quarters of the Year'), while for him *Ráithí Fírinneacha na Bliana*, 'the True Quarters of the Year', are represented by the Celtic or agricultural set. It is obvious however in Seán Ó Conaill's folklore repertoire and in Irish folk tradition in general that the 'true' and the 'crooked' reckonings coexists within a sequence that flows in the physical seasons and in the human imagination without interruption or turbulence – and certainly without any sense of oppositional enmity. We might speculate that there is a model here for the coexistence of the differing versions of the past and of cultural truth produced by our two disciplines.

Needless to say, both disciplines have their own histories – and, no doubt, their own folklore too. The history of history is incomparably longer, in the western world at any rate, than the history of folklore, though the materials that each studies – expressions of cultural identity and experience and representations of that identity and experience in the past – in all kinds of material, social, behavioural and symbolic manifestations, have been in existence as long as humankind itself and for longer than any knowable starting point for history – in however venerable a guise. In another sense, of course, every society has always had its native historians-cum-folklorists whose business it was to preserve, to cultivate, to perform and to transmit historical and cultural lore, the kind of lore termed *senchus* in early medieval Ireland. Despite the considerable divergence between the historian as *fear léinn* and the tradition-bearer as *seanchaí* in its more modern sense, I think we can and should recognise ways in which scholars of history and of tradition – the historian and the folklorist – remain necessarily involved with each other in their professional concerns.

The loosest relationship between history and folklore is surely that both share a kind of antiquarian curiosity as one of the roots from which they have in their different ways flowered. It was to the historical record that the founding fathers of folklore looked in the eighteenth century to justify and legitimate their claims – however romantic – regarding the riches of the peasant repertories of popular culture that they strove to record and preserve. The original English term by which the field of folklore scholarship was known was 'popular antiquities', and until the middle of the last century a kind of antiquarian paradigm prevailed among folklore scholars. One might say that there was a general perception of the study of tradition and of tradition materials as being an engagement with the relics of past ages that were now threatened with extinction under the pressures of the modern era. To a largely understandable extent Professor Ó Duilearga, who personifies Irish folklore studies in so many ways, is representative of the emergent discipline of folklore throughout the nineteenth and earlier twentieth centuries in regarding himself as being engaged in something of a fire-brigade operation to save a national heritage of popular cultural tradition from complete oblivion by recording and archiving as much of it as possible. If Séamus Ó Duilearga saw the folklore heritage he was after as a national or even a nationalistic one, the earliest antiquarianism-inspired collectors in Ireland were not as overtly nationalist even if their inspiration can be traced to the romantic nationalism that stems in part from the ideas and writing of Wilhelm von Herder. In Herder's perspective the language and the folk literature of the ordinary people served as the taproot of national identity, and one notes that the slogan still shown on the cover of *Béaloideas*, the journal of the Folklore of Ireland Society, quotes high authority indeed for the mission work of collection: it reads, '*Colligite quae superaverunt fragmenta, ne pereant*'.[2]

A conference in 1950 at Indiana University which Seán Ó Súilleabháin, archivist of the Irish Folklore Commission, attended to represent the Irish profession, probably marks the end of the antiquarian phase in the discipline in general.[3] Increasingly, from then, the antiquarian paradigm is displaced by a shift of interest from folklore as product of the past to folklore as process of performance and communication – including of course communication of perception of the past. Structuralist and Marxist approaches to the analysis of folklore texts and performances with a great deal of attention paid to context and function also date from that time. I am assuming that historians are able to point to similar developments within history, though I take it that the story there has been much more complicated and, perhaps, contentious.

A more specialised and perhaps more recently cultivated relationship between history and folklore can be attributed to their common involvement with the study of the use of oral testimony to represent the past. 'Oral history', 'life history', the 'memorate', the 'personal experience account', the 'historical legend' are among the kinds of oral testimony that have been of interest to both historians and folklorists, and again the figure of the native historian can be invoked here. Studies of the practices and repertoires of 'native historians', whether in early medieval Ireland or in more recent African societies as studied by such as Jan Vansina[4] or David Henige[5] or Elizabeth Tonkin,[6] have uncovered principles underlying the construction of a group's or a society's understanding of its past that are highly instructive for both disciplines in regard both to the present and to former ages whose history and whose folk traditions may be the focus of our researches. Work on the ethnography of speaking and on the 'speech act' by folklorists and linguistic anthropologists following pioneer studies by Dell Hymes and John Gumperz have produced new insights into the social and cultural reality of how people actually use language in social context to represent their preferred understanding of their identity and their past.[7] The constructed and processual nature of all tradition, including historical tradition, has been emphasised with a corresponding implication for the general and larger-scale pronouncements of historians and folklorists alike regarding the meaning and the representation of the past.

Despite such advances in the understanding of both popular culture and the writing of history as essentially forms of dialogue in which both 'natives' and 'professionals' alike participate, there remains a potential gap of mistrust and misgiving between our disciplines in regard to each side's capacity – as perceived by the other – to get it right, to tell it straight, to escape from the distortion factor of the academy and the folk as the case may be. One example of this is the objections that historians might raise in relation to the book by Daithí Ó hÓgáin entitled *The Hero in Irish Folk History* – judging Ó hÓgáin's perspective to lack any sensitivity to context, to process, to construction, to the distortions of mythology and memory in relation to the historical representation of characters of the past.[8]

A second example of an even more sweeping kind of dismissal from the other side of the history/folklore question is to be found in an article contributed by Henry Glassie to a festschrift for G.B. Thompson of the Ulster Folk and Transport Museum published in 1988 and entitled *The Use of Tradition.*[9] This is the Henry Glassie of *Passing the Time in Ballymenone*, the distinguished North American folklore scholar the fruit of whose extended field research in County Fermanagh was published at the beginning of the 1980s with the subtitle *Culture and History of an Ulster Community*. In the characterful work, later reissued by Indiana University Press, the leading publisher of scholarship in folklore in the United States, Glassie had painstakingly and sympathetically outlined the ethnography of folk or vernacular history in Ballymenone as it existed, and was continually re-created and transmitted, in the recounting of historical legends by the local *seanchaí* Hugh Nolan and others. That Glassie found such a vernacular tradition of folk history to be confined to the Catholic segment of the Ballymenone community while the Protestant side had entirely entrusted its historical representation to the agencies and channels of official history as reflected in the textbooks of the state schools is, in itself, interesting and raises an interesting question in regard to the alternative, oppositional histories of other subaltern groups who today demand an official historical representation – women's groups, gay groups, black groups and so forth. If Catholic history on the ground in Ballymenone was 'folklore' by comparison with the official 'history' of Protestant neighbours, is it the case that women, gays, blacks and so on lack or have lacked 'real' history until they succeeded in emerging from the folk or vernacular level of representing their identity and their past? By this reckoning too, of course, the Protestants of Ballymenone would appear to necessarily lack a folkloristic or vernacular representation of *their* identity and *their* past, which is certainly not the case – even on the evidence of Glassie's book itself with its Mrs Ellen Cutler as the Protestant *seanchaí* equivalent of Hugh Nolan, albeit with a hugely different repertoire.

I have reflected a little on some of the issues dealt with in Glassie's Ballymenone book because I think his treatment of them makes it clear that for him, folklore and history are enmeshed in Ballymenone cultural practice and also within the unified scholarly horizon with which Glassie himself operates. In his 1988 article however we discover what amounts to an attack on history as a professional discipline. He begins with what I took at first to be an ironic expression of the received view of historical tradition from the historian's alleged perspective. Folk history constitutes, he says, an oxymoron, a false truth, absurd because it holds no meaningful relation to the historian's 'chronicle of fact'. Having next outlined again the ethnographic reality of folk history in Ballymenone as he encountered it, he proceeds to project a picture of the *seanchaí*, the 'native historian', the bearer and transmitter of historical legends, as somehow the only 'real' historian, discharging as he does a double responsibility both of truthfulness to the past and usefulness in the present. He seems to envisage a kind of self-correcting mechanism in the transmission of oral history, given its already knowledgeable local audience, and even suggests the possibility of a sort of 'infallibility factor' at work in oral tradition by contrast with academic history. Let me quote a little:

> Folk history and academic history cannot be sundered by truth, for both are as true as their practitioners can make them. Nor can they

be sundered by significance, for both are meaningful in context, absurd when shattered into fragments. Differences do remain.

A minor difference between folk and academic histories is to be found in the medium of communication. In oral history it is difficult to preserve the unmemorable; the welter of dull detail and fine webs of qualification that make written arguments seem complex and convincing do not belong in good tales. Oral history cannot be boring. Yet, in oral history it is hard to lie. Face to face with a small and knowledgeable audience, the historian is checked constantly and prevented from drifting off along lines of thought that shifting, permute into falsehood in the solitude of the study.[10]

Glassie, moreover, sees the major difference between our disciplines as residing in what he calls the culture of the historian – which I take to be something akin to the philosophy of history as Glassie perceives it. He speaks of the academic historian as operating with profane and rationalist notions of agency and causality by contrast to the sacred and supernatural metaphysic of folk history. He contrasts the rootedness of folk history in landscape (echoes of *dinnseanchas*?), a rootedness which he claims is truly *global*, with what he regards as the truly *provincial* nature of academic history in its aspiration to amount to world history when it is in reality the view from the privileged West. Finally, he contrasts the concern of *academic* history to delineate the wilful machinations of competing agencies in pursuit of selfish freedom, happiness, wealth and power – with the presumably more authentic characterisation of the human lot of *folk* history as one of eternal dilemma and paradox, one of powerlessness but also of endurance, an endurance enlivened by creativity and community. As compared with the timeless veracity of folk history's characterisation of human realities, he seems to regard academic history as an invention of modernity that will die with modernity in the deconstruction of notions of progress and development in the face of post-modern insight into global culture and culture process. Reflecting, perhaps, his earlier career as a student of material culture, and wanting, in the context of the festschrift to pay homage to the work of the Ulster Folk and Transport Museum, Glassie asserts that true history resides not in the written record of the document but in the vernacular artefacts of popular material culture, the humble implements and technology of labour, and in the oral narrative performances of such as Hugh Nolan at his fireside – entertaining his neighbours gathered in *airneán* or *céilí*. As the true source and representation of the past, Glassie here privileges what he terms 'the history that is written into the earth and that is alive at the hearth'. One wonders whether he can accept that – even on his own terms – such privileging cannot be confined to the context of traditions of the rural past but should be recognised today as also to be found written into the microchip and alive at the modem and in the surfing of the internet and the World Wide Web, as electronic cultural discourse increasingly becomes something of a plaything for the masses. Notwithstanding my admiration for the Ballymenone book, I believe that aspects of Glassie's later view of the relation of folklore and history are extreme.

Professor Elizabeth Tonkin, author of the Cambridge publication *Narrating our Pasts: The social construction of oral history*, formerly of the Centre for West African Studies at the University of Birmingham and later head of the Department of Social Anthropology at Queen's University Belfast, offers a far more balanced view while still wishing to fault historians for their frequent addiction to what she calls the myth of realism.[11] She urges instead that 'to believe in the natural veracity of any narrative form is a false faith' and argues that both historians *and* students of oral tradition are faced with a similar task of interpreting their materials in ways that make allowance for the subjective, creative, imaginative, emotional, desire-based non-realistic nature of all testimony. For Tonkin, oral historical accounts and written history too constitute, by definition, a form of verbal exchange, a process of cultural communication that originates in the memories and the imaginations and the speech behaviours of historians, native or academic, who re-create and give expression to both vernacular and specialist modes of understanding the past. As representations of 'pastness', in Tonkin's view then the forms of both written and oral history – say the historical monograph and the historical legend – should be seen as being essentially acts of speech within an ongoing discourse of broader cultural communication. Monograph and legend alike comprise what, in Tonkin's words, all histories must be: 'chains of words, ordered in patterns of discourse [and] interpreted by hearer or reader ... in accordance with conventions of interpretation'.[12] If, as a member of some native audience of tradition – at the *airneán* fireside perhaps – or as a professional student of academic history, one shares the performer's or the author's conventions of interpretation, then no gap will be perceived between oneself and the text, the 'meaning' of which seems transparent. 'Gaps,' however, 'are soon noticed when one encounters a discourse built upon unfamiliar conventions.'[13]

We can all recognise our dilemma in confronting a text whose surface meaning may be literally clear but which is full of nuances and associations and invoked contexts that will register to the full only in what I might here term the 'native ear' or the 'native eye' of the 'native speaker' of the cultural discourse in question, be it 'history' or 'folk vernacular'. As historians and as folklorists, part of our primary task is to allow such a text to speak its meaning to the fullest extent possible through our being aware of both the historical and cultural contexts of its original creation, and its contribution to the representation of those contexts both at the time of its creation and subsequently, to such as our later ears and eyes. We might here perhaps take, for example, a text which I have myself tried to confront in this way, a text that originates from the narrative performance of Peig Sayers in the Great Blasket Island. Professor Kenneth Jackson wrote down this account as, he says, 'sound for sound' from her lips in the mid 1930s and published it in the anthology *Scéalta ón mBlascaod* which originally appeared in 1938.[14] Jackson summarises the story as follows:

> Anna McCarthy (also called Ana Ní Áine) lives to an enormous age at Kenmare. Prophesied that she will never die till she is prepared for death by Seán Bráthair Ó C'nuchúir. Young priest comes to her house and finds her being rocked in cradle by her great-granddaughter; he says he is that same Seán. She tells of the greatest marvel she saw in her long life; how party sailing to the Skelligs was met by a cloud with the ghost of a woman in it, who told a priest that she had killed two people and her own unbaptized child by a priest. He said it was the third that damned her; and then exorcised her. Seán prepares Anna for death, and she dies. It is still a saying 'She is as old as Ana Ní Áine'.

What we can, I believe, discover in such a text – by an interpretation sympathetic to the 'native ear' – is the historical or quasi-historical embodiment of two of the great archetypal elements of native Irish consciousness and representation of the past. First, the enduring sense of the presence of the eternal female, the sovereign mother goddess -cum- landscape hag or *cailleach*, and secondly, the equally archetypal sense of a Christian redemption out of that physical eternity into the divine male realm of the Christian afterlife. I hasten to point out, of course, that what we have here in the story of Ana Ní Áine or in the testimony of Peig Sayers about her is not *seanchas staire*, a text of folk history, but rather *seanchas miotaseolaíoch*, a text of mythological or perhaps cosmological provenance. What I want to emphasise however is the way in which the text invokes or manifests a historical provenance also and I would suggest that all folklore testimony regarding the past – historical or quasi-historical – should be approached as comprising a similar mingling of the realistic and the symbolic. Even *seanchas* bearing directly on flesh and blood figures of 'real history' – such as that studied by Professor Ríonach Uí Ógáin in her books on Daniel O'Connell in tradition – show clear evidence of the shaping power of the dreaded 'folk-mind' – which is in fact the power and the expression of the mythologic aspect of consciousness.[15]

Another example I would like to address is the folklore record of the Great Irish Famine as compiled by the collectors of the Irish Folklore Commission in the field and, specifically, in response to a commission questionnaire on the Famine which was issued in 1945 to some 328 correspondents, of whom 141 made a completed return with the mean age of the informants being about seventy-four years. The testimony that this folk record of the memory and understanding of the Great Famine offers must be of the greatest interest to historians as well as to folklorists and offers us the opportunity of combining forces, as it were, in the common task of throwing light on what happened, what it meant to whom at the time and what it has meant to whom subsequently – including the present time when there is a widespread concern to commemorate the Great Famine from a variety of motivations. I want to suggest that our common task of interpreting the record has to contend not only with mythologic non-realism but also with factors of human psychology in regard to the construction of representations of the past. This is very pertinent, I think, to *Béaloideas an Ghorta*. The basic facts appear to be relatively simple to state. The potato harvest failed in successive years; those excessively dependent on the potato as a staple experienced starvation and disease, leading to death, social devastation and population shift. Social structure and cultural identity, the lifestyles and the worldviews of Irish communities were radically transformed in the aftermath of the disaster.

We are all interested in understanding the significance of such 'facts' in context – the contexts of history and the contexts of culture – as they are recorded in oral history and in documentary history, in visual history, in quantitative history, in folk culture, in oral tradition, in legend, in song and in story. On the folklore side of it, *Béaloideas an Ghorta* had received little enough analysis of any kind apart from the preliminary treatments given by Roger McHugh[16] over sixty years ago and by Cormac Ó Gráda in 1992[17] and Cathal Poirtéir in 1996 and 2012.[18] Any examination of these folklore records of the Famine shows how far it is from being any kind of exact or unmediated testimony. One is struck, for instance, by the motif-like recurrence of certain elements of the accounts of local distress throughout the country. The frequent claim, for instance, that 'no locals starved to death here', that those who died of hunger were strangers and travellers; the widespread assertion that the loss of the potato crop with its attendant suffering and death was a punishment from the Almighty in retribution for the abuse of previous abundant harvests; the claim that the greater part of local distress was due to the malevolence of those put in charge of the soup kitchens; the assurance that those better-off local farmers who failed to give help to poor, starving people were themselves subject to disastrous misfortune in a short time. There is also a motif-like quality in the many local accounts of pitiful and edifying attempts made by individuals to care for and nourish their relatives, *in extremis*, and when death occurred, to provide for them a decent burial, walking miles to a graveyard, perhaps, bearing the corpse on their back.

Overall one senses a certain arm's length quality in much of *Béaloideas an Ghorta*, especially the narrative record made up of personal memorate and local legend. Certain very fundamental questions suggest themselves. To what extent is *Béaloideas an Ghorta* the oral history record of Famine victims? It cannot, clearly, be the testimony of those who died or who emigrated. To what extent is the testimony of survivors of the Famine and descendants of survivors affected by that mixture of shame and guilt that President Mary Robinson has alluded to in connection with encountering the reality of contemporary African famine at first hand? Is it not the case that what we have is a highly constructed folk history of the survivors, that is bound to contain an element of self-justification – largely, perhaps, unconscious – and that has to be reinterpreted mythically and psychologically within the cultural discourse of both history and folklore if it is to be a contribution to the elucidation of what the Great Irish Famine really was. Survivors of catastrophes can be expected to possess knowledge that they would prefer to conceal – even from themselves – and they leave an ambivalent legacy of cultural and historical identity to their descendants whose folk history will be subject to shaping and re-creation in response to the demands of their own contemporary self-definition in transformed circumstances. It is unlikely that we will find in the folklore record of the Famine years' experience much acknowledgement of the degree of complicity – even unwilling complicity – in taking advantage of others' misfortune, which can be expected to have been a component of aspects of the social and cultural heritage of latter-day informants.

Nevertheless, while I am suggesting that the folklore of the Great Famine conceals as well as conveys the historical reality it purports to represent, as perhaps must always be the case with all testimony, the combined effort of the historian and the folklorist, applied with a common understanding of the created, constructed nature of tradition *and* of history, can extract a great deal of meaning from *Béaloideas an Ghorta*. What a common enterprise of interpretation like this amounts to is a kind of 'speaking with the dead'. I should like to suggest, in drawing this talk to a conclusion, that in fact all historical and folklore research aimed at representing the meaning of the past is just such a speaking with the dead – and indeed with dead historians and folklorists too as much as with dead individuals and communities and groups and classes, the records of whose social and cultural experiences and behaviours constitute the materials to which the contemporary disciplines of folklore and history must apply themselves. To 'do' history, to 'do' folklore is to engage in dialogue and discourse in a way that is the hallmark of all study in the humanities – just as it is the hallmark of the participation by all of us in social and cultural life – a participation that constitutes in a most fundamental way being human and being alive. Both as participants in the discourse of the life of our own times and as participant observers in the discourses of the present and of the past, historians and folklorists alike are required to be ethnographers of the production and the interpretation of meaning – the meaning of human experience. If this is wisdom, then it is a return, in part, to the wisdom of the earliest Greek historians who were themselves, in part, ethnographers of the lives and cultures of the non-Greek 'savages' and 'barbarians' who engaged their curiosity.

Finally, I would draw attention to two other books. One is the work of the Swedish anthropologist Ulf Hannerz, who offers a convincing and highly serviceable model of cultural complexity that will be found instructive for the interpretative purposes of both the folklorist and the historian.[19] The other is a book called *How Culture Works* by Professor Paul Bohannan, a long-time Africanist, who also sets out to clarify the fundamental principles by which cultural meaning is continually being constructed and transformed over time, and does so with examples that will be found to be very relevant to the understanding of the relationship between history and folklore or vernacular culture.[20] It was Máirtín Ó Cadhain who had one of his characters pronounce, '*Is gabhlánach an rud í an scéalaíochť* – 'narration [whether of the folkloric *or* the historical sort, may I suggest, together with literary narration] is a highly ramified business' – and, interestingly, Bohannon prefaces his book with a similar sort of epigram, as follows: 'There's no limit to how complicated things can get on account of one thing leading to another.' Folklore and history need each other as sister disciplines in the face of the ramifications of popular culture, of the writing of history and of all representations of the past.

CHAPTER 19

The Vision of Liberation in *Cúirt an Mheán Oíche*

[Published in P. de Brún, S. Ó Coileáin and P. Ó Riain (eds), *Folia Gadelica* (Cork: Cork University Press, 1983), pp. 95–104]

C*úirt an Mheán Oíche* is surely the most genuinely popular poem in Irish known to us. Among ordinary people, of perhaps no very sophisticated literary tastes, it has been, and still is, a sort of instant success. The delights of its humour and its energetic fluency account for much of its popular appeal. For a people allegedly appreciative of verbal excellence *An Chúirt* constitutes a sort of test piece. The attractiveness of its broad comedy is self-evidently not confined to Irish speakers only or indeed to the Irish people in general. The plain honesty and frankness with which Merriman deals with bodily appetite and the frustration of its satisfaction is guaranteed to have the widest appeal at the popular level where the niceties and reticences of 'respectability' are commonly regarded as humbug and hypocrisy. In my view, however, the power of Merriman's vision, the message of the poem, if you like, must also play a role here. I know that other commentators have denied the existence of any such message or personal vision on the part of Brian Merriman as expressed, at least, in *The Midnight Court*.[1] I think they are wrong and that it is possible for us to see in the poem the expression of a personal vision that is at once large and psychologically very powerful. Seán Ó Tuama has spoken of the 'leit-motif of the poem' at all main stages as being its concern that human beings must not allow their basic sexual vigour or instincts to become arid or conventionalised, and Ó Tuama sees a connection here with some kind of disturbing socio-political process in the poet's own late eighteenth-century world.[2] A main purpose of this chapter however is to show that such a concern is more than a motif in *The Midnight Court*, that it is, rather, the poet's chief assertion and the deepest strand of the poem's meaning – a meaning that strikes home in a very fundamental way to the ordinary Irish people (or that segment of them who are able to have access to it) who have been enduring the official respectability promoted by a largely English-speaking and increasing Catholic middle-class establishment since Brian Merriman's day. One recalls Seán Ó Ríordáin's characterisation of the ordinary Irish people in the nineteenth century as a people so demoralised as to be prepared to believe that their reproductive organs were, *ipso facto*, an occasion of sin. Not only in the vigour of its language and the earthiness of its themes but also in the genuine liberalism and humanity of its vision of life, *The Midnight Court* has represented a minor and, of necessity, a subterranean kind of triumph for basic qualities of human living denied practically any positive recognition in the Ireland of the nineteenth and early twentieth century.

The banning in the 1940s of a translation of *The Midnight Court* into English would seem to support the view that Merriman's poem was officially then regarded as still dangerously subversive of propriety. The academic treatment of the poem in the twentieth century also demonstrates, I think, the continuing existence of some of the attitudes of mind to which the vision of the poem itself is diametrically opposed. I will mention T.F. O'Rahilly and Daniel Corkery as two scholars for whom the poem seems to have been in some senses an unfortunate creation, best dealt with firmly once, and then left alone. While granting Merriman credit for his inventiveness, both critics deny his work any high poetic status. Corkery says that Merriman, having no contact with a school of poetry, a *cúirt éigse*, was unable to achieve greatness, confined as he was to common speech and folk models; that his verse is vigorous rather than refined and that, in general, Merriman constitutes a sort of bridge between the truly 'literary' poets of Munster and the mere 'folk' poets of Connaught.[3] He does grant Merriman occasional flashes of the devastating bleakness that he recognises as a characteristic Gaelic strain, but he finds in the poem neither music nor charm, nor, as he puts it, 'any awareness of the incommensurable'. O'Rahilly takes something of the same line.[4] The poem, he says, 'roams, but it never soars'. 'It is brilliant but its brilliancy is that of prose.' Despite its splendid rhythmicality it lacks any 'divine afflatus'. One gets the impression that Brian Merriman's poem made these critics feel uncomfortable and liable to dismiss *The Midnight Court* with hardly disguised distaste. Frank O'Connor, on the other hand, hailed the poem as a masterpiece on the grounds that it 'cut the navel-string of the new-born democracy' of late-eighteenth-century Ireland in a way very close to that of contemporary English verse.[5] For O'Connor, Merriman's work is another sort of bridge, a bridge from the aristocratic, semi-feudal, Gaelic world into the enlightened world of late-eighteenth-century English literature. For O'Connor, Merriman is a kind of intellectual Protestant writing urbane couplets regarding the civil dimensions of life – in all but language an Anglo-Irish man of letters. Piaras Béaslaí seems to me to have been the early critic who responded most acutely to *The Midnight Court*, seeing in it an attack on the suppression of nature and the consequent evils to which such suppression gives rise.[6] He saw Merriman as a moralist, encouraging 'a spirit of health and mirth and vigour' but seems, along with the other early critics, to have missed seeing Merriman's unique poetic achievement in embodying this moral in a work simultaneously employing the European motifs of the medieval love courts and the Irish motifs of an ancient Celtic sovereignty myth. The overall effect of the poem if we can see it like this is, I contend, profound both in its conception and, at least partially, in its execution. The effect of the invocation of the sovereignty myth, chiefly in the person of Aoibheall, and the relevance which Brian Merriman creates for it to the social realities of east Clare and much more of the Irish countryside in the last quarter of the eighteenth century have not been properly understood and it is to this aspect of *The Midnight Court* and of Brian Merriman's poetic achievement that I especially want to call attention.

The Midnight Court's great indebtedness to the later medieval 'court of love' tradition has been pretty obvious for a long time now, having been earlier shown by scholars like Gerard Murphy[7] and H.R. McAdoo.[8] Seán Ó Tuama has recently gone on from further demonstration of this to asking how specific elements of the poem, both thematic and structural, that are traditional medieval 'love court' elements can have suggested themselves to Merriman in east Clare in the 1770s, and I am interested in his suggestion of a submanuscript-level, popular borrowing of such elements from post-Elizabethan English literature into Irish popular tradition by Merriman's time.[9] The town of Gort, it has been suggested, is likely to have been a special location in the district for such coming together of eighteenth-century English and Irish traditional literatures, frequented as it was by sailors off ships calling to Kinvarra. And since local tradition has a gregarious Brian Merriman playing his fiddle at social gatherings of all kinds in the locality, we can see that in his case this kind of link-up is indeed possible. The other area of Merriman's indebtedness as regards *The Midnight Court* that has been generally, though not universally, conceded is in relation to the poets and writers of the Enlightenment and of eighteenth-century English letters. Corkery would dispute that Merriman had to look an inch beyond traditional folk themes to discover models for his treatment of marriage, bastardy and clerical carnality,[10] but in general we are asked to believe that the author of *The Midnight Court* was on terms of good acquaintance with authors such as Voltaire, Rousseau, Swift, Savage, Goldsmith and Burns. Oddly enough, nobody seems to have pointed out the specific elements of Merriman's poem that are derived from such writers, or identified the actual Merriman lines in question – with the exception of Frank O'Connor who has twice argued[11] that the famous passage in the first monologue where the young girl lists the wiles she has employed to obtain a partner[12] has been translated by Merriman straight from the pages of Robert Burns' poem *Hallowe'en*. There is certainly a striking similarity in the lists, and one can think of a series of intriguing possibilities, among which are the following: (a) it was Burns who translated from Merriman; (b) there was at that time an uncommonly similar folk culture – at least in regard to the business in question – in the hinterlands of Feakle and Ayr; (c) some one single account of popular tradition somewhere supplied both poets with a common model; (d) O'Connor is right and the celebration in 1980 of the *Court*'s bicentenary was at least ten years too early, since the poem *Hallowe'en* was not published before 1790. There is even a Renaissance connection for *The Midnight Court*, since James Stewart has shown that the use in late Gaelic literature of a female parliament or assembly to discuss and promote morality and moralistic views – as in An tAth. Domhnall Ó Colmáin's *Párliament na mBan* – is something essentially derived from the didactic of Erasmus, who was certainly no medievalist but who, very interestingly but no doubt entirely coincidentally, turns out to have been himself illegitimate and to have invented a romantically untrue account of the circumstances of his birth, *à la* Richard Savage, another of the authors to whom Merriman is allegedly indebted.[13] There is, obviously, plenty of scope here for the worst kind of literary scholarship on *The Midnight Court*. Basically, it seems to me that Merriman combined two models to produce the structure of his poem. One of these is undoubtedly the 'court of love', probably in the burlesque versions of the *Roman de la Rose* tradition. But he embedded all the court elements in the framework of the *aisling* tradition – in both its early native form, concerned with love and prophecy, and in its eighteenth-century allegorical form concerned with the restoration of political sovereignty. What he produced is a unique Irish poem which brings one of the deepest myths and traditions of Irish literature to bear in an extremely novel way on issues arising from the contemporary social and political scene. Though he writes in a sort of heroic couplet, Merriman is surely a mainstream Gaelic poet confronting the 'new world' with resources of language and metaphor rooted in the most ancient of Irish traditions. That we now must see him as the last of an old line rather than the first of a new is something dictated by real events in the real world. As things turned out, he brought no one with him into an educated and urban world of Gaelic letters in the 1800s, but he could have been a bridge, to use that metaphor a third time, if it were to be that the native literary tradition was to extend in other than a vestigial way into the increasingly town-orientated, commerce-dominated Ireland of the nineteenth century.

Claims made concerning the 'revolutionary' nature of *The Midnight Court* in seeming to call for the abolition of marriage, for the exaltation of bastardy and for the casting aside of clerical celibacy have been refuted on the grounds that these themes are very frequently encountered both in the learned and popular traditions of medieval Europe. It is certainly true that their occurrence in his poem is not, in itself, solid evidence of Merriman's having been imbued with the notions of the European Enlightenment. Yet the poem does seem to me to be extremely radical in another sense in regard to these matters. Merriman's concern throughout the poem is with the flowering of human sexuality and, while this in itself is not a radical departure in literature, what is startling in the Irish literary tradition is the informing of the call with the power and authority of the Gaelic sovereignty myth whose *bona fide* or writ in Ireland runs back to insular Celtic times. The use to which Merriman puts the myth in late-eighteenth-century east Clare is, to my mind, truly revolutionary, in that he invokes its characters, its images and its power not in the cause of tribal or national sovereignty but in the cause of the civil and psychological liberation of the individual at the personal level.

It has been remarked that romantic love is absent from *The Midnight Court*. So it is, just as romantic love is absent from the earliest examples of the *aisling* a thousand years previously and it is to this *aisling* tradition stretching back far beyond the eighteenth-century allegorical variety of the genre that Merriman looks for the fundamental orientation of his poem. Early Irish, Proinsias Mac Cana tells us, offers surprisingly little literature

of love in the conventional medieval European sense.[14] The 'wooings',
the 'elopements' and other forms of early Irish love literature present us
with lovers not in any personal roles but, instead, in mythological ones so
that what is expressed in the text is the course of erotic encounter rather
than the working out of personal relationship. This note, it seems to me, is
struck again and struck very definitely in *The Midnight Court*. Once more
the adjective 'revolutionary' can be used to describe what Merriman does
to the *aisling* tradition of his day. And he achieves his effect very simply.
By locating his dramatic monologues, deriving partly from the burlesque
version of the *Roman de la Rose* tradition, in a court presided over by
Aoibheall of Craig Liath, he is able by virtue of his poetic creativity of
language to transform the mythological tie between the sovereignty of
Ireland and a rightful hereditary king into a relationship between woman
and man and between both and the eighteenth-century Irish countryside
at the social and psychological level.

From time immemorial in Gaelic tradition, the mythological role of
love and sexuality was bound up with the notion of the divine mother
who personified the land and its well-being. For Irish poets from the
earliest times to the eighteenth-century allegorists, the public welfare, the
common good, of land and of people was tied to the notion of mystical
sovereignty and its embodiment in the person and authority of a rightful
leader.[15] By the eighteenth century, of course, real history had decreed that
the liberation of Ireland as still envisaged by *aisling* poets such as Aogán
Ó Rathaille and Eoghan Rua Ó Súilleabháin – the return for instance of a
Stuart king in place of a dispersed native nobility – was a hopeless dream.
The *aisling* poet Merriman also dreams of the liberation of the people
but for him it is a civil and psychological liberation of the individual, at
the carnal level first, that counts, rather than some impossible political
liberation in the terms of a bygone age. Both Ó Rathaille and Merriman
each have a vision of a restored Ireland and of a restored Irish people and
both deliver their visions with eloquence and with a profound sense of
tradition. But they do so in very different ways indeed; the one with a
backward-looking contemptuous regret, the other with a contemporary
and dynamic comic gusto. It was not to any merely mortal royal liberator
that Merriman looked for deliverance for country and people but to the
older, supernatural, 'female' sovereignty of the spirit of the land itself.
The return and perpetuation of fertility and prosperity for all, not in the
restoration of the Stuart or any other royal line but in the restoration of the
primacy of *fonn na fola agus fothrom na sláinte*, the basic, healthy, animal,

life instincts of the mature, adult, individual man and woman, free from conventional guilt or shame or repression. In effecting this transformation of the *aisling*, Merriman liberates sovereignty or love – in the person of Aoibheall of Craig Liath – from its mythological role and brings it into play on the plane of the psychological and the naturalistic. In praising the allegorical *aisling* poems, Daniel Corkery says that they are – by comparison with the Scottish Jacobite songs in English – in the heroic rather than the affectionate plane with the result that we are dazzled by the splendour of their art rather than moved by their intimacy.[16] It is my contention that Merriman deliberately chooses to move his *aisling* away from this heroic plane, not, however, to indulge the affections but to liberate the psyche in a work that is full and fierce and carnal, and that yet is free of all sentimentality or shame, so that we his readers are ourselves humbled and liberated by his vision and by the maturity of its expression.

It is highly likely that contemporary eighteenth-century ideas regarding the freedom of the individual and the proper philosophical basis of social life influenced Merriman in writing his poetry, but the important point for me is that he expresses these ideas in a way that is so much within the traditional canon of Gaelic literature. Not for him any ideological celebration of the peasantry which was eventually the case with other leading intellectual and literary figures of the European Enlightenment. He picks up one of the oldest of traditional literary themes and by the invocation of its power and by the power of his own poetic imagination working through it he gives us a vision of a peasantry emancipated in a primary way, thereby presumably empowered to achieve other kinds of emancipation too.

It is interesting to note that of the eight motifs of the earliest form of the sovereignty-kingship myth listed by R.A. Breatnach, Merriman uses four in *The Midnight Court*.[17] These are: (1) the encounter with the *puella senilis* (the *báille* of the court being the old and ugly *alter ego* of the beautiful and gracious Aoibheall); (2) coition – which surely can be said to be rampant throughout the poem; (3) metamorphosis – it is the countryside itself and the future generations who will be transformed in fruitfulness and vigour rather than the mythological Aoibheall; (4) bestowal of sovereignty – it is the sovereignty of people over themselves that will be restored, not that of any rightful or refugee king, once nature is set free and copulation flourishes in the countryside.

It is surely relevant that the *spéirbhean* of *An Macalla*, Merriman's other *aisling*-type poem, is also a personification of the countryside harping back to an older image than the *spéirbhean* of the conventional eighteenth-century allegorical *aisling*. *An Macalla* ends on a pious note with the poet appealing to the lamb, an image of the Christian God, to grant release to all from their tribulations in a heaven above. *The Midnight Court* has of course a tougher – if more immediately pleasurable – prescription for the winning of joy.

As a voice of the hidden Ireland of the eighteenth century, Brian Merriman in his life – what we know of it – and in his poetry certainly represents the less rural, the 'urbanising' end of the social spectrum, though it is obvious that I am arguing that as a Gaelic man of letters he brings into this new world a feeling for, and a sympathy with, the oldest traditions of the Gaelic world. The transformation of the Irish countryside from a pre-capitalist and largely pastoral, political economy to an urban-dominated capitalist-industrial one is a process which, having begun to gather momentum in the late seventeenth century, is, of course, not yet complete in our own day. The two great phases of this transformation that have relevance in the context of *The Midnight Court* are (1) the emergence throughout most of Ireland since the mid-seventeenth century of a new social world consisting of two great orders: a land-owning, or land-holding, ascendancy on the one hand and a vastly more numerous order of tenant farmers and cottiers on the other; (2) the emergence of class distinctions within this new world as a result of population pressures and the competition for scarce resources in the course of the eighteenth century. These developments occur against a background of increased trading activity and the growth of towns whose influence – economic, social and cultural – permeates the countryside to an ever-greater degree. Ireland was, of course, not alone in undergoing such a social transformation, though the accompanying language shift gives the transformation of Ireland a tremendous finality, in cultural and psychological terms as well as in social.

Right across Europe, however, from the Atlantic to the Urals and beyond, this transformation of society from being a hierarchy of orders – defined in terms of hereditary power or lack of it – to being a hierarchy of classes – defined in terms of accumulated wealth – is taking place throughout the eighteenth and nineteenth centuries. It is estimated that in the last quarter of the eighteenth century, 75 per cent of the European population still lived on the land, and one historian speaks of the spectrum of subservience in what he calls 'the servile lands' running from France to Russia.[18] While all the British communities and to an even greater extent Ireland are peripheral to this whole process and need to be treated separately, nevertheless the remarks of the Russian historian N.M. Karamzin regarding the absence of any civil rights in Russia at the end of the eighteenth century seem apposite to the world of Brian Merriman in east Clare at this time. Writing in 1811, Karamzin says that Russians had no 'civil rights', properly speaking. 'We have only ... the specific rights of the various estates of the realm; we have gentry, merchants, townsfolk, peasants and so forth – they all enjoy their specific rights, but they have no right in common, save for that of calling themselves Russians.'[19]

When we add the Penal Laws to some such characterisation of the powerless and dispossessed state of the majority of the ordinary Irish people in Merriman's day – there had been sixty such laws enacted between 1695 and 1780 – we can get some insight into the demoralisation that was still the lot of a majority of the Irish people in 1780. It was for these people at large that Merriman wrote, if he wrote for anyone other than himself, which is questionable, and his poem, his vision, struck some chord in them – if we are to judge by their response to it as reflected in its manuscript history – a chord that seems to have helped alleviate their distress and that provided them with a personal re-creation in the same way as Corkery rightly claims that Aogán's and Eoghan Rua's poems did also. My contention is that the chord struck was a deeper one than a simple delight in eloquence and comedy and that the popularity of *The Midnight Court* among the Irish people is a matter of their response to its author's vision, or message, as much as it is an appreciation of its humour and its fluency of expression.

Eighteenth-century Gaelic poets adapted in a wide range of ways to the transformation of Irish society as it affected them in their personal circumstances. We see someone like Aindrias Mac Cruitin, who lived until 1738, being *ollamh* to an O'Brien at the same time as he practised the trade of schoolmaster, and staying, so to speak, in the rural and less urban setting of eighteenth-century Ireland. We see other poets, especially as the eighteenth century progresses, join Brian Merriman in crossing into the world of the town and the class society: Seán Ó Tuama an Ghrinn in Limerick, Donnchadh Caoch Ó Mathghamhna and Micheál Óg Ó Longáin in Cork. The passage of time made it easier for the later-eighteenth-century writers to accommodate; slowly but surely the world about them was becoming town-orientated and commercialised, whatever they felt about it. Whereas Aogán Ó Rathaille could hardly bear to contemplate the changes that were coming to pass in the world he knew,

Tír gan eaglais chneasta ná cléirigh
tír ɾe mioscais, noch d'itheadar faolchoin
tír do cuireadh go tubaisteach traochta
fá smacht namhad is amhas is méirleach

Eoghan Rua Ó Súilleabháin and Donnchadh Rua Mac Conmara and Tomás Ó Casaide can make the best of it, as it were, can accommodate somewhat and create their word-music and their songs to win popularity in the market place and the tavern. Brian Merriman, it seems to me, manages in his poem to possess or repossess, so to speak, this new Irish or Anglo-Irish world through the medium of the Irish language and to pass it through the furnace of his poetic imagination, so that *The Midnight Court* has vignettes of social life and custom in late-eighteenth-century Clare that are startlingly alive and convincing as ethnographic description, though I think that it would be a great mistake to imagine that Merriman in any sense set out to write descriptive verse, or any kind of social documentary. Daniel Corkery accuses him of having no feeling for the literary mode and of knowing only the language of the commercial life of the market place. The implication is that Merriman compares unfavourably as a poet with the humble members of the *cúirteanna filíochta* who were, in Corkery's phrase, 'the visible blossoming of the ancient literary tradition'.[20] Corkery would also seem to approve of the latter's continued cultivation of the allegorical *aisling* tradition with its dream of restoring the rightful leader to the throne. But if the poor peasant poets of the eighteenth-century *cúirteanna* were genuinely seeking the restoration of the old orders of society, then the question arises as to whether they were in fact victims of mystification by the very tradition they sought to protect and maintain. They were themselves, historically, now members of an increasingly class-orientated society where personal freedom and social mobility was at least a theoretical possibility. Merriman, for his part, seems to have consciously inhabited that contemporary emergent world and to have sought the maturity and independence of individuals in it rather than the restoration of some bygone order of things.

The charge is sometimes made that the complaint of the young woman plaintiff at the court of Aoibheall that spouses are hard, if not impossible, to find in the Irish society of the day cannot be true, since the population of the country was burgeoning at the time, and that this somehow proves that Merriman is writing a pure fantasy with no relevance to the society of his time. The charge cannot, I think, be sustained if examination is made of the demographic facts in any detail.[21] Following the fall-off in population growth at the beginning of the eighteenth century, the rate of increase grew rapidly again from mid-century on. The overall population figures have been put at 2½ million in 1700, 4½ million in 1780 and on to 8½ million in 1841, so that in Merriman's day, there would seem to have been in theory no shortage of eligible young men and women. The fact is, however, that it was in the ranks of the landless labourers and the cottiers that evidence is found for the most frequent and earliest marriages. With the emergence of class differentiation and the competition for land and other resources, there was a tendency for farmers, tradesmen, the better-off in general to marry later, and there is a sizeable statistic of non-marriage within these groups at the time. The 'match', the arranged marriage with all its attendant dealing and bargaining and with 'every shilling brought into account', was starting to become more frequent in the relatively higher social grouping of later-eighteenth-century rural Ireland. Merriman, perhaps to be seen as rising socially, certainly moving, at least partially, in the better-off circles, would have been aware of this and would have noticed its discouraging effect on young people's marriage prospects as the increasingly market-orientated and class-stratified society developed. Such a class-defined mercenary constraint on the easy coupling of the sexes may well be the social reality that lies behind the young woman's complaint, which is after all the prime matter regarding which the court of Aoibheall sits.

It must be emphasised however that *Cúirt an Mheán Oíche* is primarily and unreservedly a work of the imagination. Its author ultimately requires no justifications other than those of his own creative impulses for any assertions in the mouths of its characters. Our perceptions today of the historical and, more importantly, the cultural realities of Brian Merriman's world are, at best, only approximations to his and it is possible that much of what we would regard as having significance in the poem's contemporary Irish and European context is hidden from us. The personal and artistic relationship of Merriman himself to that context must remain an even deeper mystery.[22]

There remains the question of the relationship of *The Midnight Court* and the relationship of Brian Merriman to what is known since the mid-nineteenth century as folklore, but which is more properly called oral tradition or, in the older native term, *seanchas*.[23] We might first look at Merriman's alleged relationship to Burns. In my view the relationship with Burns is the common circumstance of a poetic imagination exercising itself in the rapidly commercialising world of the late-eighteenth-century post-Celtic hinterland. In the case of both poets it is the common people, their plight and their prospects, that engages that imagination and gives it impetus. In Burns' case critics have spoken of 'the animating life ... the powerful outflow of genial and generous sympathies, the spirited independence and vigour of judgement, the warmth and generosity of regard for intrinsic human worth', and these sentiments surely apply in Merriman's case also.[24] On the part of both poets there is a 'natural recoil of sympathies against things that thwart the creative energies and potentialities of life and pervert the essential nature of man'.[25] Both poets employ the idiom of the people in their work, the speech of complex communities, a speech with its own very old traditional life.

> The words came skelpin' rank and file
> anainst before I ken.

Each poet's achievement in language starts from the conversational level – from small market town and village talk – and goes on to be a powerful antidote to sterility and barrenness not only in the lives, but in the minds and feelings, of men and women. If the courtly motifs which Merriman uses are, as Seán Ó Tuama claims, found in popular tradition in Ireland, then too the gusto, the earthiness, the fluency with which he sets them forth is the gusto, the earthiness, the fluency of the people's own voice, the voice of the master *seanchaí*, the voice of folklore. In terms of content or motifs there is little if any 'folklore' in *The Midnight Court* but in important ways its voice and its message are those of folklore, not the folklore of the Indo-European *märchen* but the folklore of the native tradition, the world of Aoibheall and of Munster and of Ireland. Merriman, in his literary achievement, strangely echoes the achievement of the master *seanchaí* in creating a work consisting of virtuoso linguistic performance in which the plain people are vindicated. In theme and in execution, *Cúirt an Mheán Oíche* is an example of how oral tradition in Ireland could at the end of the eighteenth century still inspire major literary artists in ways that seem impossible now.

CHAPTER 20

'The French Are on the Say'

[Lecture given at the Bantry Bay Summer School in July 1996. Published in John A. Murphy (ed.), *The French Are in the Bay: The expedition to Bantry Bay 1796* (Cork: Mercier Press, 1997), pp. 120–37]

A French invasion fleet did arrive at Bantry Bay in December 1796. The significance of this event in terms of history and politics is being thoroughly explored by other contributors. I wish to consider its symbolic and mythic significance in the context both of the popular culture of the 1790s and the folklore record of succeeding times. Two aspects of the popular culture of the 1790s that are most relevant are: 1) traditions of a heroic liberator coming to the aid of the native population and leading them in a final battle in which the old order is restored; 2) the tradition of the personification of Ireland and of Irish sovereignty as an abused and abandoned royal female figure in thrall to a foreign usurper. These traditions had found characteristic eighteenth-century expression in prophecies, in legends and in verse form and were one prominent feature of the popular worldview existing in the Ireland of the late eighteenth century within whose horizon the French invasion fleet appeared. The folklore record of succeeding times is very meagre in respect of the events at Bantry Bay of December 1796. We have, on the one hand, oral traditions of eyewitness evidence of the French presence and, on the other, folk legend narratives that recount the event within a traditional paradigm which emphasised a continuing ecclesiastical authority in the popular domain and a patriarchal repulsing by that ecclesiastical authority of outside, and possibly female, challenge.

To begin with, we can look at two pieces of eyewitness lore that remind us of how vividly oral tradition can transmit the actuality of historical events. Recalling listening to an old man in County Longford

318

describing so vividly the incidents that took place there at the time of the French invasion of 1798, Frank O'Connor once wrote, 'I had to pull myself together and remind myself that it was not this old man who had seen them, but his grandfather.'[1] Something of this emotional charge that seems to telescope time can be sensed in both pieces of eyewitness lore concerning Bantry. The first piece is recorded by C.J.F. MacCarthy, where he quotes a Cork resident whose mother, a native of the Drimoleague area, 'could recall her grandfather telling her how, when a child, his father had carried him up Deelish to see the French ships down in Bantry Bay during Christmas 1796'.[2] Deelish is the name of a district to the north-west of Drimoleague from where one can see down over the inner part of Bantry Bay and Mr MacCarthy's informant told how local people gathered to see the French in the bay between 22 December 1796 and the end of the first week of the new year of 1797. One might think that the memory of this would be prominent in the local tradition of the Deelish area in general and yet there does not appear to be any trace of it in the historical lore reported in 1937–8 to the Irish Folklore Commission from the schools of that area – or indeed of other strategic locations such as Durrus, Adrigole or Dursey – as part of the commission's Schools' Collection project. We can see here evidence of the individually and communally selective nature of oral tradition which is far more vulnerable to revision and reinterpretation by those transmitting it across the generations than is the documentary record. This point will be considered further in relation to the folk legends of Bantry '96 to be discussed below.

The second piece of eyewitness lore concerns not events in Bantry Bay itself but their repercussion in terms of military activity in the hinterland of Cork city. A Mr Eoghan Lane, a farmer of Berrings, near Inniscarra, who was aged eighty-four years in 1938, told Seán Ua Cróinín, collector for the Irish Folklore Commission, that he recalled:

> ... my grandmother, who was ninety-six years of age when she died, and she is dead now close on sixty years, telling me that she remembered going into Cork with her father when she was about twelve years of age and, as they were going along the road, the army of soldiers came along from Cork, out, and as they were told after they passed, that they were going on to Bantry – that the French invasion was in there.[3]

Seán Ua Cróinín records Eoghan Lane as reporting that his grandmother was living at Berrings at the time when she told him of her memories of seeing the troops on the move west but it is not stated where she lived at the earlier time of her actual childhood encounter with the troop movement. We can, I imagine, take it that this was also in the western hinterland of Cork city and that what we have from her, via the verbal account from her grandson, is eyewitness evidence of the marching out from Cork to Bandon of the company of fencible soldiers to which Tom Bartlett has referred from the historical record.

Both pieces of eyewitness lore, or both 'memorates' to use the technical folklore term, attest to the fact that in December of 1796 the French invasion 'was in'. What, we may ask, was, as a result of this, likely to come ashore at Bantry at that time? A variety of answers is possible in accordance with the various worldviews of those witnessing the event and hearing of it then or later. For the likes of the inhabitants of Seafield, later Bantry House, it was anarchy and revolution that were likely to come ashore; for the United Irishmen it was the forces of reason and the European Enlightenment; for many of the Irish-speaking majority of the ordinary people of the south-west coast it would have seemed the imminent fulfilment of millenarian prophecy and Jacobite poetic imaginings regarding the restoration of the true order of things, metaphysical as well as political, in the coming ashore of the messianic forces of liberation.

It is of interest to examine the origins of this last, essentially conservative popular vision of the significance of the French in the bay and to note the ironic contrast between this majority conservatism of apprehension and the radical modernity of apprehension and expectation on the part of the United Irishmen minority in their estimation of the meaning of the approach of the Hoche armada to the south-western coast. If the French invasion was, in United Irishman terms, the appreciation to the Irish body politic of a forward-looking Enlightenment ideology of liberty and equality for all citizens, it also represented, in the ideology of popular culture as expressed in the prophecies and poetry of one brand of ancestral tradition, a move towards the regressive restoration of a medieval ordering of society in accordance with archaic notions of kingship and royal sovereignty that underlay the Jacobite poetry of eighteenth-century Gaelic Munster. I want to suggest that there was (and is) a yet further way of perceiving the significance and the potential – at symbolic and mythic level – of the French forces in Bantry Bay and that this further kind of perception, while still congruent with the Enlightenment perspective on the 'invasion', connects to yet another brand of Irish ancestral tradition that is very different from that of the patriarchal mythology which envisages the liberation of a hapless Mother Ireland sovereignty queen figure by some hero from over the water. First however it is necessary to examine the nature of both the heroic liberator and the sovereignty queen paradigms.

The sovereignty queen figure is associated with the symbolism and the ritual of an archaic notion of 'sacred marriage', the *heiros gamos*, that is widespread throughout Indo-European cultures. The central motif of this conception is that a rightful king is wedded to the territory of his kingdom – in the person of the supernatural female who constitutes the total and divine personification of the territory in question. The corollary of such rightful union of mortal king and immortal divine bride is the prosperity of land and people – a state of affairs that is thought to last while the king himself remains righteous and unblemished. Should he deliver false judgement, should he become disabled physically or – worst of all – should he be displaced by some usurping stranger, in violation of the sacred marriage bond, then a blighted and wasted landscape, in which nothing thrives, will mirror the sorrowful state to which such circumstances reduce the divine female personification of the kingdom's territory. This myth of a sovereignty queen as divine spouse of the lawful king was widely used in the political propaganda with which competing Irish royal lineages pressed their claims for the recognition of their supremacy in the early medieval period.

The Uí Néill, for instance, in their northern supremacy and the Uí Bhriain in their supremacy in north Munster both invoke the figure of the sovereignty queen in stories that locate their own assumption of political legitimacy in a mythic encounter with the divine female agency on the part of their founding ancestors – encounters that saw the sovereignty goddess confer primacy on the particular lineage – O'Neill or O'Brien – and pledge it for succeeding generations. The sovereignty queen myth in early medieval Ireland is thus a device of political propaganda indulged within the cultural worlds both of the political and literary elites and of popular tradition. Later on, with the development of different conceptions of the Irish nation and of national sovereignty, the figure of the divine sovereignty queen continues to occupy a very prominent position in the (at once) literary and popular firmament constructed and cultivated by poets of ancestral disposition. By the eighteenth century, in the aftermath of the overthrow of the royal house of Stuart and its replacement by the house of Orange, the literati of Gaelic Ireland, and particularly of Munster, had developed a variety of vision or *aisling* poetry in which a forlorn female figure appears to the poet and, on questioning, identifies herself as Ireland mourning the loss of her rightful royal spouse and seeking deliverance from the thralldom in which she finds herself. Such a symbolic figure looms large in the late-eighteenth-century popular imagination on which the events of Bantry Bay 1796 impinge.

The chief potential heroic deliverer of *aisling*-type poetry is the leader of the House of Stuart who is envisaged as coming as liberator from over the water to set things to rights. As such, Bonnie Prince Charles, *An Séarlas Óg*, is but the latest in a long line of liberator/deliverers whose symbolic lineage stretches back in Irish myth and literature to as equally archaic an origin as that of the sovereignty queen. In fact it may be asserted that the divine hero *Lugh* – himself the mythic prototype of the rightful king – is the original deliverer in the role he plays in the story of the Battle of Moytura (*Cath Maige Tuired*) – the paradigmatic final showdown of ancestral myth – wherein the supremacy of the native order was recounted and asserted by the medieval literati. Just as the political contest between early medieval Irish lineages for supremacy utilised the ancient figure of the divine sovereignty queen, so too use was made of the ancient figure of the heroic deliverer in ways that associated him with the interest of specific political factions within the native order.

The figure of *Aodh Eangach* is one such mythic figure, developed in the course of ninth-century Uí Néill struggles for political supremacy. *Aodh Eangach* becomes the potential deliverer of the Uí Néill from their oppressors and it was alleged that his coming had been foretold centuries earlier by Saint Bearchán. It is, incidentally, in association with the figure of *Aodh Eangach* – the warrior saviour of the Uí Néill – that the symbolic Red Hand develops which became the talisman of northern political allegiance and identity. *Aodh Eangach* himself and the mythic potential deliverer of the Uí Néill are envisaged as having the mark of victorious slaughter visible on their bodies – the bloodied hand signifying that 'great battle', the final, showdown battle, in which the enemies and oppressors of the Uí Néill are to be overthrown and repulsed. In later Uí Néill praise poetry and vision poetry (*aisling*) the great leader who will bring them triumph over their enemies is called *Crobhdhearg* – the red-clawed or red-handed one.

While no one in the Bantry Bay area in the 1790s would have mistaken the imminent arrival of Tone and a French liberation army as the coming of a *Lugh* or an *Aodh Eangach* or a *Crobhdhearg* to provide prophesied deliverance, nevertheless the continuing availability in popular ideology of just such an expectation of overseas deliverance and its flowering in Munster Jacobite popular verse towards the end of the eighteenth century is evident. Two examples of the application of such an idea, examples from the 1590s and the 1690s, are relevant ones. Hugh O'Neill, the earl of Tyrone, in open rebellion against Elizabeth I, was said by his poet, prior to the Battle of the Yellow Ford in 1598, to be engaging in the final showdown battle prophesied by Bearchán. We cannot know for sure the influence of that poet's pronouncement on the mood of O'Neill's troops but O'Neill was, as we know, victorious in battle on that occasion.

In the 1690s an Irish-born officer of the Spanish army arrived into Ireland a few days after the Battle of the Boyne and joined the retreating Jacobite forces. This man was an O'Donnell with the rank of earl and the reputation of being marked on his body with the red sign of the messianic saviour of his people. The *Ball Dearg*, or Red Spot, a similar prophetic mark to that of the Red Hand, was an item of popular belief widely known and understood, and it was as *Ball Dearg Ó Domhnaill*, as heroic deliverer from over the water, that this O'Donnell participated prominently in what was popularly perceived to be another 'final battle' – at Singland during the Siege of Limerick. Victory did not, on this occasion, attend the efforts of *Ball Dearg* and, having avoided engagement at the subsequent and even more disastrous Battle of Aughrim, he changed sides, fought in the Williamite cause at Sligo and was the recipient, on his return to Spain, of a Williamite pension until his death in 1704.

Another century on, in the 1790s, the Stuart pretender is the figure who fills the role, in Munster popular liberation ideology, of the hero from across the sea who will come to the aid of Ireland and her stricken people. This Jacobite allegorical belief and expectation endures in Munster vernacular literature and in the popular culture of the south-west at the end of the eighteenth century despite the kind of class development in Munster society of which David Dickson speaks;[4] despite growing bilingualism, despite spreading literacy, despite increasing participant experience in the rapidly modernising world; despite, even – in poet Eoghan Rua Ó Súilleabháin's case, at least – active service in the British navy. This conviction that help would arrive from over the water to restore the old order and rout the enemy oppressor would seem, in a sense (a sense we can surmise as having a lively existence in the minds of many), to have been answered directly by the arrival of the French fleet into Bantry Bay. Such an occurrence could surely be taken to be the long-prophesied deliverance, of which, for instance, the poet Seán Clárach Mac Domhnaill had spoken:

> *Fé mar luadar seandraoithe*
> *do dhéanadh*
> *beidh flít i gcuantaibh Bhanba*
> *fá fhéile Shan Sheáin.*

[As the ancient druids mentioned
Who were wont to make prophecy and foretelling
There will come a fleet into the harbours of Ireland
By the midsummer feast of St John.]

We may wish to note, somewhat ironically, no doubt, that the original Hoche/Tone strategy was indeed for a midsummer expedition – and that French naval unreadiness was the reason why the actual date of sailing diverged so far from the one foretold by Seán Clárach and planned for in reality, by Tone, in the first instance.

Another expression of the prominence in oral tradition and folklore of the hope of aid from abroad – and specifically French aid in this instance – is the well-known if anonymous late-eighteenth-century Whiteboy song of south Tipperary, '*Sliabh na mBan*'. Reference is made in this song to the imminent arrival of a French fleet who will redress the existing state of affairs.

> *Tá an Franncach faobhrach lena loingeas gléasta*
> *Agus crannaibh géara acu ar muir le seal*
> *Isé scéal gach éinne go bhfuil a dtriall ar Éirinn*
> *Is go gcuirfid Gaeil bhocht arís ina gceart.*

[The keen French with their fleet under sail
Are standing to sea this while with their elegant masts
It is everyone's story that they are to journey to Ireland
And that they will set to rights again the plight of the poor Gaeil.]

Yet another powerful expression of such expectation is the famous '*Rosc Catha na Mumhan*', a quintessential Munster Jacobite song prophesying the return of the Stuart prince:

> *Measaim gur subhach don Mhumhain an fhuaim*
> *Is dá maireann go dubhach de chrú na mbuadh*

Torann na dtonn le sleasaibh na long
Ag tarraingt go teann 'nár gceann ar cuaird.

[I adjudge it a joyful sound for Munster
And for those yet surviving in sorrow of the bloodlines of nobility
The beating of the waves on the sides of the ships
That are drawing strongly on to visit us.]

In quoting these lines, Maureen Wall reminds us of the role of such songs in both building up and giving expression to the public opinion of the day.[5] Her remarks are worth quoting in full – given their relevance to the apparent fulfilment at Bantry Bay in 1796 of the long-held and fervent expectation of external deliverance:

> It should not be forgotten that the Gaelic poets of the eighteenth century were the pamphleteers and journalists of the Gaelic-speaking multitude. Many a song was sung at a fair or in a tavern or around the firesides … denouncing local injustice, or reminding the people of their national identity; and prophesying, rather unrealistically, a utopian future, with the Irish language and the Catholic religion high in favour again, when, with the aid of Louis of France, the Stuarts would return to the throne. Those songs helped to build up a public opinion of which the ruling class of the day, and even English-speaking, well-to-do Catholics, were largely unaware.

These country people and especially the Irish-speaking country population of those living on the shores of Bantry Bay at the end of the eighteenth century would, in Maureen Wall's view, have envisaged a revolution in the wake of a Stuart return, a revolution that would constitute 'a panacea for all their ills' in the re-establishment of the rightful king.

The actual revolution that the arrival of a French fleet into Bantry Bay seemed to presage was a revolution involving, of course, not the restoration of an old order under a rightful royal ruler but the application to the Irish body politic of the ideals and principles of radical Enlightenment ideology as mediated through the French Revolution. The apparently huge gap between the conservative hopes and expectations of the Jacobite tradition and the radically progressive ideology represented by 'the French in the Bay' should, however, be seen as itself mediated within Irish popular culture by another kind of vernacular worldview than the Jacobite one – a worldview that finds its most vigorous expression in the 1789–96 period in the reception afforded in popular cultural tradition to Brian Merriman's poem *Cúirt an Mheán Oíche* (*The Midnight Court*). In this poem the central metaphor of the Jacobite *aisling* tradition – the appearance to the poet, in a vision, of the figure of the sovereignty queen – is radically transformed in leading not to the passive hope of male deliverance but to the forcefully positive expression of female authority and female power exercised in the cause of female emancipation – and male emancipation too.

Not royal restoration but civil liberation of a democratic and proletarian order is what is imaginatively envisaged and encompassed in Merriman's poem, and the resounding oral popularity of the work from its creation in 1780, a full decade and a half before the French in the bay, is indicative of a radical, progressive, Enlightenment-like tendency in the popular culture of Munster in the 1790s that evokes for us the figure of the Marianne in French popular culture as another female personification – though not of any royal sovereignty queen but of the spirit of popular civil emancipation. The unashamed expression of sexuality in the bare-breasted figure of the Marianne and on the part of the chief female protagonists of Merriman's poem represents in either case a symbolically feminist challenge to established patriarchal authority such as can also be seen associated with political and physical subversion in later-eighteenth-century Ireland. I have in mind here the female disguises and female titles espoused in the rituals and symbols of the defender and the Whiteboy movements, whose activities were so very often carried on in the names of a *Siobhán*, or a *Sadhbh Olltach*, or a *Caitlín* – appellations of a symbolic female who is the imaginative embodiment not of the Irish nation as much as of an Irish citizenry emergent. I like to think, in this vein, of the French in the bay as potentially coming to the aid not of the *seanbhean bhocht* of Jacobite tradition, the banshee queen of a moribund and outmoded mentality, but coming rather to further the emancipation of modern men and women and in the setting free of their sexual and imaginative energies in the cause of civil liberty, equality, social and psychic justice.

It is surely relevant to note that even within the later-eighteenth-century Jacobite *aisling* tradition, the tendency is to give the figure of the female personification of Ireland more proletarian or commoner names than those previously associated with the supernatural royal queen. Rather than being *Ériú* or *Banba* or *Fodhla* or any other of the ancient royal epithets of the ascendancy sovereignty queen, Ireland or, more properly, the Irish citizenry, awaiting deliverance, is given the commoner names of *Síle Ní Ghadhra*, and *Caitlín Triail*, *Móirín Ní Chuilleanáin* and *Caitlín*

Ní Uallacháin, invoking human, flesh-and-blood women and men and their prospect of living free and equal lives in a renewed civil order freed from social and religious tyranny in line with the ideology of the United Irishman movement that looked to the land of the Marianne for support. In a Thomas Davis lecture on Irish Jacobite poetry as well as in other of his publications, Breandán Ó Buachalla has asserted that the Jacobite *aisling* tradition is not the regressive, monolithic mindset it is sometimes made out to be and that it carried into the late eighteenth century a 'powerful millennial message of individual and communal liberation'. Speaking of the popular poetic expression of Jacobite ideology – something we can safely identify as a major formant of the popular worldview of the Irish-speaking population in the hinterland of Bantry in 1796 – Ó Buachalla says:

> ... originally a conservative rhetoric imbued with the traditional values of aristocracy, hierarchy, hereditary right and social order, it was also, potentially and eventually, a radical rhetoric in that it foretold, extolled and promoted the overthrow of the existing regime. It must, accordingly, be counted among the factors that contributed to the politicization of Irish Catholics. And although Irish Jacobitism never did produce open rebellion, it did cultivate a language and a symbolism of revolt, a corrosive subversive idiom which could transcend its particular origins and through which later happenings could be mediated.[6]

It must surely be the case that the arrival of the French fleet into Bantry Bay in 1796 was an event whose meaning was mediated in a major way for the greater part of the local population by a receptivity of expectation and hope that was founded on both a sense of Jacobite deliverance and a sense of civil emancipation that we can associate equally with the female figure of Aoibheall in Brian Merriman's poem and the female figure of the Marianne in the contemporary popular cultural traditions of France.

I have referred to the comparative absence of the memory of the events of Christmas 1796 in the folklore materials collected under the auspices of the Irish Folklore Commission in the earlier part of the twentieth century. Two texts of the legend of the French in the bay do turn up in the main collection of the commission's archive. An examination of these may suggest a reason for the relative absence of any substantial memory of the powerful responses which the event of 1796 must have evoked on the lines I have outlined in the ranks of the bearers of popular culture and oral tradition of the time.

The two texts I refer to are evidence that in the course of the nineteenth century, with the extension of ecclesiastical control and the spread of the values of a conservative Catholicism into most areas of popular culture, the story of the failure of the French expeditionary force at Bantry Bay 1796 was retold as the story of the victory of the priest over the forces of evil. This story, signifying the historical displacement of the native ancestral religious sensibility by Christianity, has been a major item of both literary and oral narrative tradition in Ireland since early medieval times. The famous ninth-century 'Lament of the Old Woman of Beare' gives expression in high poetic fashion to this concept of the Christian displacement of the native religious sensibility, as does a twentieth-century legend in the oral narrative repertoire of the Blasket Islands as written down verbatim by Kenneth Jackson, from the rendition of none other than Peig Sayers. In both texts the ideology over which the Christian clerical order is seen as victorious is personified as a female of wanton libidinousness and it does not, I submit, in any way strain our legend texts concerning Bantry 1796 to interpret them as portraying in a general way a similar victory on the part of clerical and patriarchal orthodoxy over the challenge of a foreign and especially a feminist-inclined attempt to introduce emancipatory revolution.[7]

No female of any sort is mentioned in either Bantry text but the use of the motif of the priest reading prayers and manipulating the elements to dispel a threat is one that is traditionally associated with the overcoming by a Christian cleric of an evil woman not only in Irish folklore but in the example literature of medieval European Christendom. Certainly I believe that the native audience, so to speak, for these folk legends – down to the 1930s when they were collected by the Folklore Commission – would have readily intuited the female nature of the threat that is warded off by the priest, out of their familiarity with the traditional repertoire of oral narrative legends in which such clerical victories over female challenge are commonplace. That native audience would also, of course, have first-hand knowledge of other encounters in which the authority of a patriarchal Christian clergy is challenged by powerful female figures: stories about *Cailleach Bhéarra* herself; stories about wise women; stories about keening women at wakes and funerals who on occasion resisted and even fought back against the individual priests who tried to suppress their activities. With such stories of female-inspired or female-centred challenges to male clerical authority still prominent in the oral narrative repertoire of popular tradition in the earlier part of the twentieth century, we can take it for a certainty that at the end of the eighteenth century the worldview finding expression in the folk narratives and the popular culture of the south-western parts of County Cork would have contained a lively sensibility of this *cailleach*/cleric duality and competition in matters of authority at times of life crisis – at times of birth and at times of death, for example.

What I am suggesting here is that the political and cultural life crisis of the prospective French invasion at Bantry in 1796 would have triggered a reaction among the ordinary Irish population that brought together the traditional millennial idea of the deliverance of the female personification of the Irish nation with a modern, United Irishman radicalism that looked to the French model of the emancipation of men and women, and that connected also with the emergent emancipatory energies and appetites of ordinary men and women – such as those proclaimed by Aoibheall in Merriman's *Midnight Court* and represented in the popular culture of France by the figure of the Marianne.

Let us be clear that the strongest evidence I can put forward for this claim here is the reverse or indirect evidence of the transformation of the later folk memory of the coming of the French force in 1796 into accounts – in the legends of the invasion attempt that survived in the folklore record of a century and more afterwards – of how the French, and the female symbolism inherent in their coming, were repulsed by clerical power and authority.

One of these two folk legends was collected in 1936 from an eighty-seven-year-old woman in Gortluachrach, Kealkill who was born in 1849. The other was collected from a sixty-year-old man in West Muskerry who tells a far less locally grounded story of the events of 1796 than the older Kealkill informant. The texts of the legends are given here as they occur in the Irish language in the Irish Folklore Commission manuscripts.[8] The translation is my own. I give the West Muskerry text first.

> *Nuair a bhí Franncaigh ag teacht isteach go Bá Beanntruí do bhí fear áirithe sa tsráid go raibh fhios aige go rabhadar ag teacht. D'innis sé do roinnt daoine go rabhadar chucu agus d'airigh an sagart é. An chéad Domhnach eile agus an sagart ag rá an Aifrinn, d'iompaigh sé tímpeall agus do labhair sé: 'Cá bhfuil an fear a dúirt go raibh na Franncaigh ag teacht?' ar seisean.*
>
> *'Táim anso,' arsan fear ag éirí as suíochán istigh sa tséipéal.*

'An tusa a dúirt go raibh na Franncaigh ag teacht?' ar seisean.
'Is mé, cheana,' arsan fear.
'Cá bhfios duit?' ar seisean, 'go bhfuiltear ag teacht?'
'Is cuma dhuitse sin,' arsan fear eile. 'Tá an t-eolas san agam,' ar seisean,
'agus is cuma d'éinne cá bhfuaireas an t-eolas san.'
'Cathain atá na Franncaigh ag teacht?' arsan sagart.
'B'fhearra dhuit an t-Aifreann a chríochnú,' arsan fear eile, 'beifear
chugat sar mbeidh deireadh ráite agat,' ar seisean.
D'iompaigh an sagart isteach agus do chríochnaigh sé an t-Aifreann agus
díreach agus é ag rá na bhfocal bá dheireannaí, do ghluais an ráfla go
raibh na Franncaigh ag teacht isteach. D'oscail an sagart leabhar áirithe
(ní feadar arbh é leabhar an Aifrinn é nó nárbh é, ach d'oscail sé leabhar
éigin). Do léig sé cuid éigin den leabhar agus len linn sin do tháinig stoirm
mhór agus do scaipeadh loingeas na bhFranncach ar an bhfarraige. Do
scaipeadh soir siar iad agus do báthadh cuid acu. D'iompaigh tuilleadh
acu thar nais agus níor stadadar dur bhaineadar a dtír féin amach.

[When the French were coming into Bantry Bay there was a certain man in the town who had knowledge of their coming. He told several people that they were coming and the priest got to hear of it. The next Sunday while the priest was saying Mass he turned around and he spoke: 'Where is the man who said that the French were coming?' he said.

'I'm here,' said the man, standing up in his seat in the chapel.

'Is it you who said that the French were coming?' said the priest.

'I am the very man,' said he.

'How do you know,' said the priest, 'that they are coming?'

'That's all the one to you,' said the other. 'I know that much,' he said, 'and it's all the one to anyone, how I know it or where I got it.'

'When are the French to come?' said the priest.

''Twould be as well for you to finish off Mass,' said the other one, 'they'll be here before you're finished,' said he.

The priest turned back to the altar and he finished Mass and just as he was saying the last words the rumour spread that the French were on their way in.

The priest opened a certain book (I don't rightly know if it was the Mass-Book or not but he opened up some book). He read some part of the book and while he was doing that there came a great storm and the French fleet was scattered about the ocean. They were scattered hither and thither and some of them were drowned. Some more of them turned back and they did not stop until they reached their own country.]

The other version of the story, in the Kealkill text, is as follows:

Do bhí sean-fhear thiar ar an gCaol Cill fadó agus saghas seanndraoi a b'eadh é ar shligh éigin. Bhíodh sé i gcomhnuidhe ag innsinn go dtiocfadh na Franncaigh isteach go Beanntraighe. Dubhairt sé leo sa deireadh go rabhadar le teacht agus an lá a thiocfaidís agus gach aon nídh riamh.

Datha Daora a thugadh na daoine ar mo dhuine agus do bhíodh an sagart ag magadh fé agus ag tabhairt fé i gcómhnuidhe.

Lá Nodlag a bhí ann ar aon chuma agus do bhí innste age Datha go mbeadh na Franncaigh chúthu an lá san. Do bhí an sagart ar an altóir ag léigheamh an Aifrinn agus do chas sé thart ar a shálaibh agus ar seisean:

'Cá bhfuil Datha anois,' ar seisean, 'nó an ineosfadh sé dhom cá bhfuil na Franncaigh?'

'Cuir díot an t-Aifreann ar dtúis', arsa Datha.

Nuair a bhí an t-Aifreann críochnuighthe ag an sagart ní raibh duine sa tséipéal aige ná raibh in airde ar na cnocáin ag féachaint ar an gcabhlach thiar sa chuan.

Do chuir an sagart mallacht ar na Franncaigh annsan agus d'éirig an stoirm a chuir leaghadh cubhar na habhann orthu ins gach treo ach ba mhór a'luach saothair a fuair an sagart. Feircín óir a thug White (an Tighearna Talmhan) dhó agus deirtear gur istigh i dTigh Clarke i mBarrack Street i mBeanntraighe a thug sé dhó é agus dá chomhartha san féin tá rian an fhircín ann fós. Déarfadh daoine leat nár tháinig éinne des na Franncaigh i dtír an uair sin ach ní fíor san. Tá sé raidhte gur chuireadar mórán óir i bhfolach ar an dtalamh in áit éigin 'dtaobh abhfas d'Oileán Faoide.

Bhí sean-chrunucacháinín fir thall ansan ar an [?] fadó ar a thugaidís Mícheál a' Chápa. Is cuimhin liom féin é agus níorbh dheallramhthach le haon Éireannach nó Sasanach dá bhfeaca riamh é, ina chuma, 'na chaint ná'n shlighe. Duine des na Franncaigh é sin adeirtear. Agus tá fear eile ina bheathaidh thiar taobh le Beanntraighe agus sé ainm atá air na Sullivan Fach. Is minic d'airigheas go mba Fach ab'ainm dá athair agus gur thugadar Sullivans orthu féinig. Dar ndóigh bhí seó díobh ann ach do shéanadar a n-ainm agus ghleacadar sloinne Gaedheal chuchu féin.

[There was an old man west in Kealkill long ago and he was a kind of wizard, somehow. He was forever telling that the French would come into Bantry. Eventually he announced that they were coming and the day they would arrive and every other last detail. Datha Daora [Davy Daora] is what the people called this fellow and the priest used to be making fun of him and giving him a hard time always.

Anyhow it was Christmas and Davy had announced that the French would be arriving on that day. The priest was on the altar reading Mass and he wheeled about and he said, 'Where is Davy now,' he says, 'or would he tell me where are the French?'

'Finish off your Mass first,' said Davy. By the time the priest had finished Mass there wasn't one of the people that had been in the chapel that hadn't gone up onto the hillocks looking at the fleet west in the bay.

The priest cursed the French then and the storm rose that melted them in every direction like foam on a river. And it was a big reward the priest got for what he did. White (the Landlord) gave him a barrel of gold and it is said that it was inside in Clarke's Shop in Barrack Street, in Bantry, that he gave it to him and there are traces of the barrel left there still.

People will tell you that none of the French came ashore that time but that's not true. It is said that they had a lot of gold in the ground on this side of Whiddy Island.

There was a stooped shrivelled old man living over there long ago that they called Mícheál an Chápa. I remember him myself and he wasn't like any Irishman or Englishman that ever I saw, in his appearance, in his speech or in any way at all. It is said that he was one of the Frenchmen. And there's another man living west near Bantry and the name he has is Sullivan Fach. It's often I heard it said that Fach was his father's name and that they called themselves Sullivans. Of course there was a great number of others of them there, but they denied their name and they took Irish surnames.]

In a sense what we see in those two versions of an early-twentieth-century folk legend is the waters of the political status quo of post-Famine Ireland – secular and clerical – closing over the memory of the events of 1796 in Bantry Bay. The political ideologies of Jacobitism and the United Irishmen have disappeared from popular worldview. The civil and psychological radicalism of imagination that responded to the emancipatory vision of Merriman's poem has yielded to notions and standards of respectability and caution. The *giolla mear* and the *buachaill bán*, Aoibheall and the Marianne have all alike succumbed to the values and the horizons of the new world order that has established itself in the aftermath of the Great Famine, an event the memory of which in the records of oral tradition is itself distorted equally with the memory of the French in the bay. Oral tradition continually recasts the past in terms appropriate to prevailing popular values and to the prevailing popular worldview. In this, folklore and popular oral tradition are constantly revisionist to a degree way beyond anything that practitioners of history would attempt. The folklore then of an event like the French invasion at Bantry Bay 1796 is as much a record of the interpretation, the transformation, the distortion and the application and reinterpretation of historical facts as it is a record of the events themselves. Much source criticism and contextual analysis must always be brought to bear on oral tradition in this respect. The present essay merely outlines some aspects of the problems to be grappled with in such an exercise.

CHAPTER 21

Responding to the Rising

[Published in Máirín Ní Dhonnchadha and Theo Dorgan (eds),
Revising the Rising (Derry: Field Day, 1991), pp. 50–70]

WHEN WAS 1916?

An attempt to explore the reality and significance today of the 1916
Easter Rising can begin from a number of different standpoints.
These can be expressed as a series of questions: 'Where was 1916?',
'Why was 1916?', even 'When was 1916?' The apparent simplicity and the
factual nature of such questions is quickly discovered to be deceptive when
we try to answer them in a way that takes account of present-day insights
into the interplay of cultural process, history and mythology. One of the
editors of a recent work in this field speaks of our failure to recognise
the essentially rationalistic nature of the historian's claim to deal in exact
knowledge.[1] The claim of rationalistic realism is, in fact, the special myth
of our western culture, a myth to which, in our analytic commentaries,
we are prone to be naively blind. Such blindness detracts grievously from
our ability to understand and interpret the past and to perceive its true
interaction with the present and with the consciousness of present-day
society. The authority of the scholarly pronouncement on historical matter
is challenged by the realisation that the power of myth can and does shape
not only history but the lives of historians and our own lives too, whether
or not we engage in any kind of commentary on the past.

In his seminal article on '1916 [as] Myth, Fact and Mystery',
F.X. Martin, conscious of this dilemma for the professional historian,
called for the establishment of an institute for the study of the Rising, as if
to marshal the maximum amount of the historian's professional resources
for the purpose of gaining exact knowledge of the truth of the multi-

faceted, elusive, layered event that took place in Dublin during Easter Week 1916.[2] While Father Martin's splendid article, written for the half-century commemoration of the Rising, brings out very clearly indeed that event's literary-dramatic and mythic qualities, there is the sense in which – given enough of the application of the historian's resource – the form of even the myth of 1916, in Martin's view, can be expected to be fixed, thereby disengaging 1916 from contemporary consciousness by properly dissipating the sense of its mystery to which the title of his 1967 article alludes.

Writing much more recently of the uses to which myth is put in Irish society, Richard Kearney asks that we use our reason to discriminate between 'authentic' (i.e. liberating) and 'inauthentic' (i.e. perverse) ways of doing this.[3] Inauthentic use consists of regarding myth as a closed product, something that can imprison the mind – and the life – of the myth's devotee in a kind of idolatry, while authentic practice uses myth as a creative symbol in an open-ended process of cultural emancipation. This formulation places primary emphasis on rationality and personal choice on the part of the individual who contemplates the possibility of 'using' myth. But we must surely use emotion, too, in order to understand myth itself and its authentic operation in today's world. Reason alone is fated to miss out central resonances in the meaning of past events in relation to present circumstances, and vice versa. One hears Soviet commentators on television current affairs programmes referring to the old dictum that Russian history cannot be understood in the head only, but must be understood in the heart as well. This is another call – from nearer the front line than the lecture hall this time – to place a sensitivity to the operation of myth and mythic process at the centre of our attempts to follow and understand popular movements.

One can point to another recent, and perhaps more weighty, assertion of the centrality of the affective domain (and its expression in mythic form) to the task of understanding and interpreting history and culture. The distinguished Indianist Wendy Doniger O'Flaherty ends her recent work on the roles myth plays in all cultures, with the following passage:

> The historians have demonstrated that there is no such thing as an even theoretically impartial observer, and the anthropologists have cynically undermined our hopes of getting inside the heads of other cultures, relativistically or otherwise. The linguists and philosophers have, finally, hopelessly defamed the character of language as a

possible vehicle for mutual understanding. So we are stripped down to our naked myths, the bare bones of human experience. They may be our last hope for a nonlanguage that can free us from these cognitive snares, a means of flying so low that we can scuttle underneath the devastating radar of the physical and social sciences and skim close to the ground of the human heart.[4]

O'Flaherty's work, *Other People's Myths*, significantly subtitled 'The cave of echoes', illustrates ways in which mythic narrative interacts with historical reality in individual lives. One is reminded forcefully of the acute observation of Malinowski's long ago that, when it comes to understanding the significance of mythic discourse in the 'going concern' of culture, we deal 'not with a story told but with a reality lived'. One need not accept in over-literal fashion the further truth of Lévi-Strauss' later observation that it is not the men who think the myths but the myths that think the men, to want to question the kind of autonomy present in the 'choice' that Richard Kearney seems to imply a people or an individual can and indeed should make in relation to bringing myth to bear on the present day and its affairs. In some sense that we do not clearly understand, the myth will find its own channel. Whether we choose to pay much attention to it or not, the pressure of the past in mythic form bears continually on our imaginations and on our deeds and is, surely, the basis of the characteristic that Liam de Paor points to in the Irish capacity for ambiguity in the presentation of themselves to each other. The Irish, he says, maintain

> an insistence that we are not what we seem on the surface to be but something else – older, wise, truer, which is, however, to be found not here and now but in the past, or in the future.[5]

The story of the 1916 Rising is one of Ireland's national myths and, as such, cannot be made subject to any brute chronological fixation in some objective calendar. Approaching the historical commemoration of 1916 in this fashion, we open up, in the words of Raphael Samuel,[6]

> a history which refuses to be safely boxed away in card indexes of computer programmes, which, instead, pivots on an active relationship between past and present, subjective and objective, poetic and political.

So '1916', in the cognitive and affective sightings of it in my personal head and heart (as in the sightings of many readers), is not a fixed point in time, even though we justly mark the seventy-fifth anniversary of its occurrence. As well as happening seventy-five years ago, '1916' for me happened at the beginning of prehistory; never happened at all and is 'only' a story; happens regularly at intervals determined by political occurrences; is happening now; is yet to happen – and so on. For me to ponder the reality of even the seventy-five years since the calendrical year 1916 is to engage with ambiguity. In all my growing years until now, I understood 1916 to have been long, long ago. And yet when I was born in 1940, 1916 had been 'over' for only twenty-four years and I am now more than double that age, so for me it is true that, in my 'today', 1916 is really 1967 – which I regard in many ways as 'yesterday'. And since my father, who was born in 1903, lived through 1916, it must have appeared to him ever after in some sense that is akin to the sense in which the revolutionary events that led to the break-up of the Soviet Union in 1991 will appear henceforth to my thirteen-year-old daughter. When I myself was thirteen, there were another thirteen years more to go before the fiftieth anniversary of 1916. After that fiftieth anniversary, my mother framed a reproduction from the *Observer* colour supplement of a collage portrait of P.H. Pearse over a heavy revolver; she hung it above the television set in our living room. In the backyard she used the lump of Nelson's Pillar, recently blown up, which I had brought home from Dublin, as a doorstop for her bunker of the best English coal. And life went on.

So when was 1916? I can only say that, in relation to profound questions regarding my personal, social and national identity, it always has been 1916 and it is 1916 now, whatever my misgivings about violent bloodshed, the fabrication of tradition, the alienation of fellow Irish men and women, the hypocrisy of some, the disdain of others, the initial incomprehension of a majority of my fellow citizens. This is so because, in my memory/imagination of the people and events of 1916, there moves something of myself in that grotesque and violent yet dignified assertion of national and individual self-esteem, social and political emancipation and shared vision of the common good.

I realise that, in apposite parallel to 1916, it is always 1688 and the Glorious Revolution in the memory/imagination of some million other Irish people, and that it remains for us all to see our way towards some system of joining together hearts and minds for the common purpose of defending and promoting the civil and religious liberty of all the inhabitants of Ireland – whether the charter we look to is Puritan or Romantic and whether it derives from the end of the seventeenth or the beginning of the twentieth century. The aspiration to a life lived in freedom, with justice for all under the rule of law, and with the fair sharing of the produce of human labour, cannot be incompatible with the deepest desires of all who truly cherish the memory and the myth of Easter Week 1916 or of the Glorious Revolution of 1688, and we can even dare to envisage a sense in which 1916 is 1688. Perhaps our commemorative proclamation should be that 'the Spirit of 1916', much invoked in 1991 on fly-poster and public platform, is fully congruent with the spirit of the Czech Charter 77 and the British Charter 88 movements, and that we seek ways of exploring – together – how the civil and religious liberties of all who live in Ireland and Britain can be best served today.

For this task, also a task of revolutionary proportions, '1916' and the men and women of Easter Week are paradigmatic for me in ways that profoundly resist assertions of continuity between 1916 and today's provisional republican movement. Mythic discourse which allows great events to be symbolically re-enacted or to be ever-present in a timeless and mythic now, enriches every human life it touches, rather than defiling and even destroying it with the bullet and the bomb, resorted to in the profane temporal. Symbolic and mythic re-enactment can never be replicative of bloody sacrifices contained in 'original' sacred or dream-time events; claims to the contrary violently distort the values that lie, in different ways, at the hearts of the historical and the mythic processes.

WHERE WAS 1916?

In one sense it began and ended 'on the holy streets of Dublin town', *ar shráideanna naofa Bhleá Cliath*. It was 'at' Mount Street Bridge, and the South Dublin Union and Bolands Mills and North King Street and St Stephen's Green and, above all, at O'Connell Street, in the GPO, under and behind the shattered, smoking ruins of the much-photographed aftermath. But in another sense it was more widespread – not only at the places throughout Ireland that did, or did not, 'rise with Dublin' but at the places that gave to the Dublin scene the actors and the energies of Easter Week. So we can say that 1916 was in many parts of Ireland outside Dublin – for example, in Seán MacDiarmada's County Leitrim and Eamonn Ceannt's County Cork; and in other places, too, like James

Connolly's Edinburgh, Michael Collins' London, even John McBride's South Africa. What happened in Dublin in 1916 drew together the life experiences and the politico-historical visions of a diverse company of men and women into an eruption of the social and political order 'at home', while the social and political order of the greater European world was itself undergoing a violent cataclysm of suffering and transformation. Dublin experienced a dramatic and fateful starburst, whose traumatic intensity contrasted starkly with the recent Joycean characterisation of the city as a 'centre of paralysis'. Dublin's turn-of-the-century provincial and derivative courtly establishment centred on the castle, its devotion to the ways and effects of the life of a substantial military garrison, its enervating, clerical-coloured standards of social respectability, the widespread poverty and immiseration of its large underclass, its low-power, largely mercantile and service economy, had – taken together – made it a version of the pre-industrial city, of the type that is recognised in the social sciences as commonly forming the urban hub of a peasant/colonial world.

Such a world, the world of peasant society – *à la* the Redfield/Shanin anthropological perspective – developed within the Irish polity of the seventeenth century, with the establishment of a new land-owning and land-working class, who differed from the mass of their tenants and labourers in respect of ethnic origin, language, religion, social values, technology and lifestyle. The eighteenth and nineteenth centuries saw the gradual dissolving of the patterns of such a peasant/colonial world, centred as it was on the 'big house', the market town and the pre-industrial city. Political developments, such as the rise of a Catholic bourgeoisie, the disestablishment of the Anglican Church and the passing of the Land Acts, marked the transformation of Irish life in fundamental ways. Dublin life, however, retained its character as that of a community whose ruling elites still cherished the fading glory of former days when they knew themselves to live in the second city of the British Empire. Liam de Paor speaks of the revival of republicanism and radical nationalism in turn-of-the-century Dublin as being partly due to the 'sheer shamed hatred' of the shoddy provincialism of Dublin life on the part of thinking individuals.[7]

Within the framework of the conflagration of the Great War, thinkers, writers and men and women of action collaborated and conspired together in Dublin and throughout the country to break through to a new social, political and intellectual order for Ireland. In a curious sense, looking back now on the channels in which these energies ran, and conscious of doing so at a time when the peoples of central and eastern Europe were fashioning new social, political and intellectual orders, one can say that, for some of its participants, the Easter Rising was no more than an attempt to swap monarchs and empires as a minimal first step towards liberating the lives of Irish people from a system that many of them perceived as socially and culturally moribund, as well as politically unjust. Arthur Griffith's Hungarian interest and his notion of the establishment of an Irish dual monarchy, and Pearse's and Plunkett's willingness to see a German, Prince Joachim, installed in Dublin Castle as king of an independent Ireland should Germany be victorious in Europe, may appear bizarre to us today, but are evidence of how apparently different a European world from our own existed seventy-five years ago.

And yet underneath the surface changes of twentieth-century history and the apparent sweeping away during the last seventy-five years of imperial and totalitarian rule, west and east, there is a sense in which equally imperious and oppressive regimes still threaten to dominate our lives in the new Europe and the new world order. These are the regimes of practically unrestrained free market capitalism under the control of corporate multinational business. Under their shadow and in a perhaps equally bizarre but symbolically suggestive sense, it is arguably possible to envisage a contemporary equivalent to 'Prince Joachim' still proffering to hold sway in Dublin within the financial empire of the new European order. Dublin today is no longer the second city of the British Empire but is, instead – in this seventy-fifth anniversary year of 1916 – the European City of Culture, with pretensions to an eminence on the new European stage that enable its masters to disregard or dismiss the true cultural poverty of the lives of so many of its citizens. In this respect, today's Dublin – a financial freeport of European and international capital, set as a dubious jewel in a countryside that is increasingly seen as a playground for the financial barons (a kind of cold Caribbean where the musical gifts, sporting prowess and linguistic colourfulness of the native population is proverbial) – is surely not the place where the Easter Rising, the attempted resurgence of the people of Ireland, our willed republican emergence from under an imperial yoke, occurred. But occur it did, in 'Dublin town', *ar shráideanna naofa Bhleá Cliath*, wherever that was in 1916, and wherever that is today. Like the New Jerusalem, like the Moscow of the mind, like Sliabh Luachra, like Seán Ó Ríordáin's Dún Chaoin, 'Dublin town', where the Irish republic was established to give Irish people the chance to live their lives in freedom and in a form of social organisation that really does cherish all the children of the nation equally, is perhaps best regarded as a dream-location, a construct, a model to be striven for, if never realised – or realised only intermittently. 'Dublin town' is where *communitas* reigns in the sense developed by Victor Turner, a space within the structures of profane reality where the human potential for playfulness, for imagination, for self-transcendence, for creativity, both flowers and bears fruit. Whenever that happens and wherever that happens, 1916 is there present and it is there present too in the dedication of all who work the ordinary structures of the profane world with the purpose of honouring and facilitating that potential in every citizen. Those who believe in 'the values of 1916', the values that seven men proclaimed in 'Dublin town' and that were attempted to be written down in the programme of the First Dáil, also believe, of course, that these same values were not invented in Dublin seventy-five years ago, but have a timeless and universal appeal because of the way they reflect and respect the shared hopes of humanity to achieve the best life possible for the maximum world as we know it.

The Easter Rising was a particular witness to and a particular striving for the putting into effect of such values as are found to inspire all revolutionary movements that seek to release people from oppressive rulers and systems of rule. It took place in specific historical circumstances and featured particular actors and actions that can indeed be studied with a view to establishing an 'exact knowledge' of events. The fullest meaning of it all, however, is not so easily conceived or expressed, even if we try to stay close to the facts of the historical process of which 1916 is a part.

WHAT WAS 1916?

I have been trying to say how, for myself at least, there is a real and important sense in which the Easter Rising is not fixed in time or place. It can be present here and now as an element in the imagination and the subjective experience of the individual who seeks the honouring in everyday life of certain values that may be regarded as conducive to a social order in which people's lives can be lived to fulfilment within the ultimate constraints and realities of the human condition. Many other kinds of historical and quasi-historical narratives, as well as the story of 1916, equally can play such a role, and all such roles tend, in general, to become invested for the individual or the group that claims them as paradigmatic, with a sense of the sacred, the timeless, the otherworldly. In human terms, however, their central significance remains the way in which they embody and promote the values of mature self-esteem, individual and social autonomy, and a communal vision of the 'good life' as both a philosophical and a pragmatic ideal. On the self-esteem side, the great danger is that excessive preoccupation with 'our' view of ourselves, and the necessity to defend and promote it, can produce the excesses of a nationalism of the Zionist, Afrikaner or Provisional IRA variety. On the side of programmatically organising the 'good life', the danger is that of a totalitarian regime of imposition – whether of the 'right', for example Hitler's, or of the 'left', for example Stalin's.

Whatever else 1916 was, it was a proclamation by some Irish people – on behalf of all – of an independence rooted in individual and national self-esteem and seeking in the exercise of political autonomy on the part of Irish people the communal embodiment in civil society of an indigenous version of the 'good life', which an oppressive and exploitative colonial/imperial connection with our British island neighbours had hitherto made impossible. At least, with hindsight, this is a view that I myself espouse. Looked at from other angles, from say the point of view that saw/sees nothing oppressive and exploitative in Anglo-Irish relations pre-1916, the Easter Rising appears as an act of the vilest treachery and most sickening folly, a suicidal insanity on the part of a tiny self-appointed minority of criminally irresponsible leaders, fuelled by hatred of England and an infantile delusion of historical nationhood that was the creation of sick brains. Today we are all free to make our own judgements on the events of Easter Week. In truth, however, a majority of the Irish people, since immediately after 1916, have accepted that what happened then was a legitimate expression of their will as a people, leading eventually to the proper establishment of a separate state that would embody 'our' national and socio-political aspirations in all the human ambiguity of those aspirations. In 1916 – a year of colossal, sacrificial carnage in Europe – the Easter Rising was, as things turned out, an irrevocable step on the part of Irish people and, unsurprisingly, was canonised as the foundation myth of the republic that came into being as its temporal consequence. Popular and private expressions of that canonisation of 1916 were, at the time of the fiftieth anniversary, complementary to the official state celebrations that honoured the memory of the state's founding fathers and the locations in which they carried out their heroic deeds. In 1991, by contrast, there is a sea change in both the official and, to a less clear-cut degree, the private and popular perception of the events of 1916. Many Irish people appear not to be sure of the heroic quality of the events of Easter 1916 and are certainly extremely dubious about the significance of the Rising for their own times and circumstances. One gets the impression that the Irish have outgrown the nationalist dream and that their European future will cater adequately for their aspirations as a people in both the symbolic and the socio-political spheres.

The inexorable reality is that history moves on and that heroes and heroic events lose their charisma and are replaced by others. Equally, notions of nationalism and the nation-state, socialism and the forms of state welfare for citizens, alter in response to the events of the historical process, i.e. what people do and how they understand what they are doing. Equally inexorable, however, in monarchy or republic, or in any other version of the organisation of the body politic as yet undiscovered or undeveloped, are the basic human demands of individual and community self-esteem, social autonomy and a shared vision of a just society. The degree to which the Irish republic that is the legacy of 1916 has succeeded in promoting such values of the Easter Rising within its boundaries, its culture and its citizens' lives is a mark of its fitness to exult in that legacy. In my view, the fact that the Irish state has all but totally declined to exult in, or even celebrate, the seventy-fifth anniversary of the Easter Rising has as much to do with its enthralment to other sets of values than those of 1916 as it has to do with its current sensitivity to the complexities of the new order of official Anglo-Irish relationships or the murderous impasses in social and political life in Northern Ireland.

These other values to which the state and a large proportion of the Irish population are increasingly drawn derive from the recent resurgence of capitalism in the extreme forms associated with monetarism and the political rhetoric of the 'free market'. They also derive from an acceleration in the cultural convergence of Ireland with the remainder of the British Isles, a process that the cultural nationalism of the turn of the century and the establishment of the Irish Free State were intended to halt or even, in certain respects, to reverse. While the notion of a traditional Ireland maintaining itself in the face of the modern world was, to the extent that it really existed in the minds of Irish people, hopelessly unrealistic, it was envisaged that an independent Irish state with a republican constitution would offer the Irish people an opportunity to consolidate their cultural identity while building a successful economy that could deliver the means to sustain the population of Ireland at home to the extent that citizens chose to remain in the country. Instead, the intensification of free trade competition and revolutionary developments in information and communications technology have combined to bring about a situation where very high levels of unemployment and poverty coexist with a search for fresh ways of expressing new forms of identity in the face of the rejection by many people of the more traditional aspects of Irishness. On the question of culture and national identity, the acutest, if bleak, account has been that of Liam de Paor, who sees the official ideology of the twenty-six-county state made a nonsense of by unemployment, poverty and emigration and also by the profound alienation of the mass of the Irish people, whose ancestral culture has been succeeded, in his term, by a 'cultural desert' within which the new Irish elites, 'neither peasant nor bourgeois' but rather 'products of the cultural desert', lack conviction 'regarding the ideology of nationhood that gave birth to the State'. In these circumstances there is a sense in which it is the state itself which is the source of any continuing national identity in the Irish republic and, since the immediate servants of the state and wielders of state power share the pragmatic approach of the majority of the population to questions of identity and the national interest, it is not unexpected that their enthusiasm should be lacking for celebrating Irish identity and the Easter Rising foundation myth of the Irish state in terms of a seventy-fifth anniversary.

Another important consideration is that, despite the traumatic upheaval of 1916 itself, no radical overthrow of the existing social and political order took place in the establishment of the Irish state that came into being in the early 1920s. Thus there was built into the official bones of the new state a regressive, conservative element that was unlikely thereafter to exert itself in the most imaginatively pro-active ways to pursue the expression of national identity. The practical effect of this carry-over from the imperial administration – especially in a financial focus – can be traced in section after section of J.J. Lee's recent work on Irish society and politics from 1912 to 1985.[8] It is probably true to say that the most radical task with which the state apparatus allowed itself to be burdened in the aftermath of 1916–22 was the national policy concerning the Irish language. The radicalness of the Irish-language policy of the Free State, if this were to be fully and successfully implemented, is hard for us to envisage today in the disillusioned and even cynical aftermath of the effective failure of this, along with many other aspects of the republican programme of the First Dáil. Perhaps the decision effectively to turn over the implementation of language policy to the teaching profession, who in turn could pass it on to a school-going population, with little defence against its alarming ability to engender frustration (and worse) on all sides, was in fact a shrewd judgement on the part of civil servants and politicians of the time; they were, respectively, the unwilling and the naïve perpetrators of a policy that, had it succeeded, would indeed have set the Irish state and the Irish population on a road qualitatively very different to the one they have subsequently travelled.

In important ways, what 1916 was, and the sense in which its significance is at variance with the Ireland of today, is encapsulated in the case of the Irish language and its present position. For a significant portion of the Irish people at the turn of the century and for some of the leading actors in the Easter Week story, the Irish language appeared to be a chief element in the revolutionary struggle to achieve national independence. Irish was, for these, the symbol of a mentality, a culture, a worldview opposed to English mentality and British rule. The speaking of Irish was perceived as itself a kind of revolutionary behaviour at an ideological level and in other, practical, ways. When the Free State was established to serve the interest of Irish people in their democratically expressed desire to be in charge of their own society and to control for themselves matters of cultural policy, it was expected by those for whom the Irish language was the greatest symbol of Irish separatist identity that the new government would see to it that the speaking of Irish would recover numerically and territorially. The state, to an extent, did attempt to respond to this expectation, chiefly in terms of educational policy. The qualified success of this policy in achieving its aims of teaching the language to school-goers and providing education through Irish to many of them has to be balanced against the resentment and resistance on the part of those less convinced of and even opposed to the notion of 'compulsory Irish'.

What has replaced the state's initial dedication to the fostering of Irish-speaking – perhaps never as convinced or committed a dedication on the part of the majority of civil servants as the official record might indicate – is a form of management technique, whereby the demands of Irish speakers are handled by the state apparatus in line with other minority demands within a general approach that sees Irish as one consumer commodity among others. The state's commitment to the Irish language in these circumstances amounts to no more than the protection of the home product in the arena of the open market, as Hilary Tovey has described it, in order that an option to choose Irish will continue to be theoretically on offer to 'customers', who for the most part would rarely require or even imagine any educational option to be available to them other than the English-language one.

Such faint-hearted, bureaucratic calculation of the minimalist provision for Irish and Irish-speaking is part of a larger scenario that contrasts with the state's idealism and official determination in its earliest years to provide the political instruments required to allow the new-found national self-esteem and the newly won social autonomy of the Irish people to find expression in the building of a distinctive society on secure, economic and cultural foundations. Today, instead, the state is concerned to maximise the degree to which its resources further the economic and social interest of a minority sector – that of property and big business, whose wealthy magnates and whose many imitators inhabit mental and cultural worlds in which the notion of a separate Irish state for a sovereign Irish people is of little moment. The state's justification for this is the necessity, at all costs it seems, to follow current free-market capitalist fashions on the alleged road to economic prosperity. One outcome is the tendency to treat the requirements of many other social and cultural interests as 'luxuries we can ill-afford'; to be funded, if at all, out of the National Lottery, a process whereby the greed of some and the desperation of others is tapped in the cult of the 'big win' to support research institutes and artistic enterprises, among other 'luxuries'.

The meaning of 1916 in this new Ireland of 1991, and new Europe and alleged new world order of 1992 and after, is far from clear. I suggested earlier that we can approach it as something that has an active relationship to the present, and I wish, finally, to look at certain aspects of that kind of relationship to the present day of myth and tradition.

THE FUTURE OF 1916

As mythic discourse, the 'history' of the Easter Rising of 1916 is part of 'national tradition' within the wider field of Irish culture. The concept of 'tradition' per se is a complex one, not yet fully understood in a scientific sense, despite the widespread commonsense claim that 'everyone knows what tradition is'. In fact, we are only starting to investigate the true nature of tradition and its uses in society. Dr Alan Gailey of the Ulster Folk and Transport Museum has written at considerable length about the meaning of tradition; he has added to our theoretical grasp of what it involves through an analysis of the nature and operation of specific traditions in Ireland and elsewhere.[9] An important realisation has been that traditions that appear very ancient and fixed can be the products of very recent times

– developed on occasion by interested parties for their own political and other advantages, as is shown in the celebrated studies gathered together by Hobsbawm and Ranger as *The Invention of Tradition*.[10] The most penetrating investigation of the cognitive nature of traditional discourse has been provided very recently by the anthropologist Pascal Boyer, who argues that not only is there no such thing as a 'theory of tradition', but that the very term 'tradition', in both commonsense usage and as a taxonomic category, fails to be a proper theoretical concept. While, on the one hand, diverse phenomena tend to be lumped together as 'tradition' on the basis of their alleged resemblance to certain prototypical cases, it is almost certain, on the other, that any theory of tradition that can be developed will not account for all that is commonly called 'the traditional'. So there are manifold grounds for being wary regarding the genesis, the nature and the operation of 'Irish tradition' as we encounter this idea in different domains of Irish life.

Whatever else it is, 'Irish tradition' or any specific instances of it – for example, '1916 tradition', 'Irish music tradition', 'Anglo-Irish tradition', 'loyalist tradition', 'nationalist tradition', and so on – cannot be regarded as a fixed body of belief and practice whose periodic repetition in various ways conserves a certain worldview or lifestyle associated with a historic era or event. Rather than being fixed, tradition is always a *process* of selective remembering (and not remembering) that is subject to and responsive to both the creative dynamic of the individual memory and the shaping of memorisation at individual and communal levels by current circumstances and interests. So we have different versions of the Wolfe Tone commemoration at Bodenstown, which reflect different perceptions of the man, the events of his life and his 'legacy' to our times as 'handed down' in different traditions that each claim to be the true one. What each of these commemorations of tradition is doing is communicating knowledge, attitudes, values and feelings on the part of adherents to the tradition that are formed from an amalgam of memory, imagination and desire which has only a tenuous relationship to history in the strict sense. The same is true of 1916 tradition. It would be very enlightening to have as full an account as possible of the various forms of commemoration or celebration – official, public and private – that have been made of the Easter Rising in the course of its seventy-fifth anniversary year. Such a description or listing – including no doubt, this publication – would throw a limited amount of light on 1916 as 'history', but a very considerable amount of light on Irish society and Irish culture in 1991, when, as in any other year, Irish culture comprises the partly alternative, partly complementary worldviews and lifestyles of different groupings of Irish people getting on unselfconsciously with the business of life on this island.

It is in relation to Irish culture, understood in this way as continually refashioned worldview and lifestyle, that 1916 has a future. As strict history it is over, complete, but as culture, as tradition, as the ever-renewing product of the meeting of the past with the present in the memory, the imagination, the mythic discourse of the society of the present day, it is alive and psychologically salient, a characteristic that Pascal Boyer insists is an essential of any authentic tradition. Perhaps here, too, we are still dealing with history in that very broad sense inherent in the phrase 'that's a part of our history', applied by people to things and events perceived as of great national significance and thus acknowledged to have entered the mytho-historic, traditional dialogue of imagined past with imagined future that is as 'read' as any of that 'exact knowledge' that historians of the school of rationalistic realism claim to provide.

A real concern for anyone looking at Irish culture today in the light of the values of 1916, as I have tried to perceive and present them, must be the degree to which the cultural process itself, the generation of meaning, motivation, direction and that sense of belonging that is the reverse of alienation and anomie, is affected by a public disinclination or inability to confront or balance the encroachment on people's lives of values and behaviours promoted by agencies whose only motive is commercial success and expansion. People's individual creativity, and the social and institutional channels in which that creativity flows, are alike being blocked and drowned out on so many fronts by that kind of mass-produced artefact and culture that it pays the business world (corporate or self-employed) to manufacture and disseminate. At a time when the western world is relishing the downfall of the concept of the 'command economy', Irish society is increasingly subject to the similarly suffocating effect of what I can only call the command culture, whereby the production of cultural knowledge is regulated by the intervention of powerful business interests, geared to exploiting the potential of mass markets by catering primarily to an artificially stimulated demand for designer goods and services (highbrow and lowbrow) that are consumed passively at the dictate of agents of the business interest themselves, whether these agents are directly in the business interests' employ or not.

Such 'bread and circuses' – not only the fast-food, the pop music and the fashion 'industries', but so many other sectors of modern society – need to be counterbalanced by the organisation, on the part of the state or of private bodies, of cultural production (whether material goods, services, institutions, facilities, and so on) based on values other than profit and competitive efficiency. At present, even in the sectors like health, social welfare and education – where profit and competition are inappropriate and where the state itself is the major producer of sectoral culture, i.e. of worldview ('policy') and lifestyle ('implementation') – the vogue now among government ministers and senior civil servants is to bring business criteria to bear on their enterprises in a way that does considerable violence to the rich human values and aspirations to which the perpetrators of the Easter Rising strove to give witness and wished to see inscribed on the practice as well as on the rhetoric of those who would govern the Ireland of the future. Thus, there can be little prospect of any independent, culturally progressive line being taken by today's government and civil service in such fields as heritage, the environment, agriculture, fisheries, and science and technology. Moreover, such a line is not being pursued in Irish universities, whose authorities also are succumbing to the 'corporate business' model of education and of life.

Government ministers and civil servants, high and low, are Ireland's own people, however, not agents of any foreign power. That the country's levels of local cultural self-esteem and social autonomy should be so low, and that its local and national vision of the 'good life' to be shared by all should be so powerless in the face of the social and cultural forces of the present-day world, is an indictment of the use that was made of the relative 'freedom' that did follow from the Easter Rising. And since they live in a democratic republic, the Irish cannot 'blame the government' for their circumstances, though they can expect state agencies to help them think and live their way out of the present situation. For me, it all begins with the recognition of the truth – not only at the diplomatic-political level, but also at the personal, subjective and psychic level – of Michael Collins' dictum about the 'freedom to achieve freedom'. Ireland's history, mythology (ancient and modern), literature, languages, traditions, culture, society – all offer its people resources with which to build and reinforce their sense of individual freedom, personal self-esteem, and true participation in life's affairs. And this is not a task for the educated middle classes alone. A culturally healthy society will provide all its members with a sense of worth and a vision of the common good, both of which grow out of daily experiences. Irish society is patently not succeeding in doing this, and it behoves the educated middle classes, as much as others, to look for ways in which the experience of Irish people can be made more likely to provide them with that sense and that vision. Working on enriching Irish mythic discourse is one possibility, and the myth of 1916 is as good a starting point as any. Perhaps that institute that F.X. Martin called for a quarter of a century ago is still needed. Not for 'the study of the Rising', however, but for the study of how the Rising did and does and could – as mythic-historical event and as cultural resource – interact with and influence current affairs. It would be necessary to interview Gerry Adams again about this, but it would be important also to interview the ordinary people of Ireland to find out what 1916 is or is not to them, as a prelude to attempting to give them access to its mythic potential for life-enhancement. Nineteen sixteen will not go away. Unless the Irish want it to be a source of oppression and murder – as a profane stereotype for terrorist violence – they had better allow it to come to life among them as a proper myth. Elizabeth Grey[11] and Tomás Ó Cathasaigh[12] have taught Irish people how they may begin to understand how the memory/imagination of mythic events such as those reflected in textual accounts of the Battle of Moytura or the life of Cormac Mac Airt could serve paradigmatically, in medieval times, to elucidate and to valorise various aspects of the society in which it operated as mythic discourse. Today Irish people badly need to learn how to allow their own lives to be elucidated and valorised for themselves by a variety of mythological and cultural resources, of which their own Irish repertoire – including 1916, and, of course, 1688 – forms not the least part.

CHAPTER 22

The Primacy of Form: A 'folk ideology' in de Valera's politics

[Paper read at a conference at University College Cork, 1–3 October 1982. Published in J.P. O'Carroll and John A. Murphy (eds), *De Valera and His Times* (Cork: Cork University Press, 1983, pp. 47–61]

INTRODUCTION

Folklore is mentioned only once in 600 pages of Maurice Moynihan's recent edition of speeches and statements by Éamon de Valera.[1] It occurs in the course of Mr de Valera's senate speech on the Institute for Advanced Studies Bill in May 1940. In justification of the bill's intentions in regard to Celtic studies he explained that work of a similar nature had already been undertaken by, for instance, the Manuscripts Commission. He then said, 'We have also had to deal with the body of folklore which, it was obvious, we should set about collecting as quickly as possible while it was still in a fairly pure form. In a footnote to the text of the speech, Maurice Moynihan sets down that the Irish Folklore Commission was established by de Valera's government in 1935 to undertake the preservation, study, etc. of all aspects of Irish folk tradition. De Valera's relationship to that folk tradition and his stated concern for its preservation in pure form is, I suggest, an element in recent Irish history that deserves consideration.

DE VALERA AND FOLKLORE STUDIES

Speaking in April 1926 of the aims of the party he proposed to found, de Valera had restated his conviction that there lay in the heart of every

Irishman a native, undying desire to see his country not only politically free but truly Irish as well. Perhaps the clearest, and certainly the best known, statement of de Valera's vision of what that truly Irish country would actually be like is that passage in the famous radio broadcast of St Patrick's Day 1943 with its references to cosy homesteads, joyous fields and villages and fireside forums for the wisdom of serene old age. It should be remembered, I think, that de Valera presented this picture of Irish society explicitly as the formulation of a dream, a dream claimed by him for Fianna Fáil and, in retrospect, for the Volunteers of a decade previously. He acknowledged that its origin lay with Davis and the Young Irelanders in their attempts to devise a modern, national programme for the regeneration materially and spiritually of a historic nation and he saw in the ideals of the Gaelic League a continuation of the philosophy of Davis. Now the Gaelic League was very concerned with folklore and folk tradition and Douglas Hyde, who in his latter-day role as president is spoken of by one of de Valera's biographers as the 'embodiment of Ireland's spiritual emancipation', was pre-eminent in promoting its collection and study.[2] As professor of modern Irish in UCD Hyde had, in the early 1920s, played a very large role in the inspiration and academic formation of the man who was to personify much of that story of folklore studies in Ireland in the twentieth century. That man was James Hamilton Delargy, the founding father of the Folklore of Ireland Society whose planning and establishment was taking place in precisely the same period at which Fianna Fáil was founded.[3] In the first number of the society's journal, *Béaloideas*, published in June 1927, Delargy, its editor, spoke of preserving for the nation and transmitting to its future generations an authentic record of the folklore of the Irish people. He also referred to 'nonsensical rubbish which passes for Irish folklore both in Ireland and outside' at the then present day.[4] Delargy too had *his* dream, *his* vision connecting his life's vocation to Ireland and the Irish people. T.K. Whitaker has recently quoted for us – from a short autobiographical piece of Delargy's – a description of the latter's return to Dublin from Scandinavia in 1928 and his feelings as the mail-boat neared the coast:

> I went right out to the bow and I saw the Irish hills … and I said 'the tradition of Ireland is behind those hills and we've got to rescue it before it's trampled into the dirt' … because it was a jewel of great price and one had to see that it was given a refuge and an appreciation by the Irish people.[5]

This vocation was one of which de Valera would obviously approve and his government was later, in 1935, to provide an annual grant of more than £3,000 to the Folklore Commission of which Delargy was to be honorary director from its inception until the year when de Valera also finally relinquished public office – 1973. During that time, and especially up to the end of the 1950s, the Folklore Commission amassed a huge corpus of traditional lore along with a very considerable body of ethnographic description of the material culture and social organisation of those whom we might term the plain people of Ireland, those same plain people whose political aspirations and expectations de Valera and his party claimed best to represent and on whose behalf Fianna Fáil sought to wield power. It is my contention that the image of himself and of his party that de Valera offered to the Irish people in general took into account the 'folk' proclivities of a large proportion of the Irish electorate.

DE VALERA AND A NATIONAL MYTHOLOGY

Oliver MacDonagh has spoken of an ideological frigidity in Irish politics and Irish political thinking from 1870 on and suggests likely explanations.[6] I am suggesting here that a possible corollary of such a phenomenon is that it became possible over sixty years for the Gaelic League and the Volunteers and de Valera to build a national ideology on an essentially static conception of a 'truly Irish' way of life, a static conception that derives from both the eighteenth-century Romantic movement roots of Davis' vision and also older and perennial, native, Gaelic roots involving the personification of Irish sovereignty in a mother figure who must be delivered from bondage and rejuvenated by the selfless sacrifices of her children, the 'scattered children of Éire', 'our sweet, sad mother' as de Valera himself put it in 1920.[7] Such a 'truly Irish way of life', in essence both noble and loyal, was envisaged as morally superior to the way of life of the modern, cosmopolitan, commercial world and it was to the prior claim of this superior lifestyle on all Irish people that de Valera continually drew the attentions of the Irish electorate and their parliamentary representatives. Now much of the Irish electorate in the period of the twentieth century prior to the Second World War was still relatively free of the grosser effects of the transformation of social and political sensibilities that accompanies – and, in this instance, did later accompany – more or less total exposure to forces of modernisation in technology, economy, social organisation and education, and it was where some version of a traditional or pre-modern mentality still survived that de Valera and Fianna Fáil attracted the greatest measure of a fairly unreflecting allegiance. In a countryside where versions of the Barbarossa legend – of the sleeping giant who is destined one day to liberate his people – were still being collected in the 1940s and '50s,[8] de Valera wore easily the proffered mantle of 'chief'. The messianic character of an aspect of de Valera's public image has been generally, I think, acknowledged.[9] It is as anti-Christ, however, rather than as a version of the *Christus*, that he is by some remembered. The full impact of the legend that he was born with the mark of the cross on his back is, I feel, more properly ambiguous.

Denis Gwynn has written that 'de Valera's command of public confidence owed little to popular appeal but rested upon his long record of austere integrity and patriotism and his sagacity as a political leader'.[10] This seems to me to underestimate the folk proclivities of very many communities of the plain people of Ireland from whom de Valera sought and received support as a type of uncrowned king who, in the words of Oliver MacDonagh 'alone among modern Irishmen … had reached the rank of O'Connell, Parnell and – if the anti-kings be counted also, Carson'.[11] If, in the aftermath of civil war, the Irish people had turned away from the idea of romantic nationalism and had set their faces to the matter-of-fact task of building a free state, a sufficient number of them were, from 1932 on, willing to entrust the continuing political and socio-economic development of that state to a man who, while his vision of a free and truly Irish society was based on a stereotype deriving ultimately from an antiquarianism that even in the 1920s was outmoded, could still represent, in the contemporary world, a continuation of ancient cultural identity.

If it is true that to many of his countrymen and women, supporters and opponents alike, de Valera was a folk hero or anti-hero, it does not follow that he himself projected himself as such in the national and political arena. Just as the Cromwell or Swift or O'Connell of folklore are to be distinguished sharply from the historical persons, whose names these stereotypes bear, so too the flesh-and-blood de Valera can remain entirely separate from whatever version of himself could be built up from the archives of that same Folklore Commission which his government supported financially. It is not to de Valera the folk hero that we need look to find a folk connection. It is in the thoughts and actions of de Valera the man, the actual, historical, political leader, that we can find operating a model of the Irish people – or at least of a majority of them

– that is to a certain extent based on notions of the 'folk'. That model has, it appears to me, very interesting relationships both to a European perception of the life and culture of so-called folk societies that is essentially nineteenth century in character and also to a twentieth-century perception of peasant society that finds its characteristic expression in the writings of anthropologists such as Robert Redfield and George Foster.[12] Both perceptions ignore 'class' issues and it is, I believe, significant that a political model of Irish society congruent with them should find such favour among the twentieth-century Irish electorate.

IDEALISATION OF PEASANTRY

The characteristically nineteenth-century strand of de Valera's social thinking derived in large part from the philosophies of cultural nationalism developed in Germany and England under the influence of the Romantic reaction to eighteenth-century notions of social organisation. It was itself characterised as a way of thinking by an idealisation of 'the peasant' – an idealisation commonly encountered in the approach to traditional society in the European countryside of many amateur scholars and social observers throughout the nineteenth century. Such idealisation tends to lift 'the peasant' and traditional society in general out of history, regarding them both as changeless, as somehow not subject to the process of continuous transformation that is the actual lot of all societies in the real socio-economic world. Another aspect of such idealisation, has, historically, been to regard traditional society as far less 'tainted' by industrialism, by technological development and by the commercialised relationships that go with a fully monetised economy, than has actually been the case. Despite the fact that the Irish people as a whole were in the 1920s very far indeed from being simple-minded and naïve as regards transactions of an economic nature in the modern world, de Valera still chooses in July 1928 to lecture the Dáil, and the Irish electorate, on the subject of economic policy in the following terms:

> We ... had to make the sort of choice that might be open, for instance, to a servant in a big mansion. If the servant was displeased with the kicks of the young master and wanted to have his freedom ... he had to give up the ideas of having around him the cushions and all the rest that a servant in a mansion might have, and the various things that might come to him from the table of the lord.[13]

Is this the imagery of the medieval manor house of the Kiltartan countryside? Some may, perhaps, suggest that it is the imagery of Bruree, since he goes on:

> If a man makes up his mind to go out into a cottage, he must remember that he cannot have in the cottage the luxuries around him which he had when he was bearing the kicks of the master ... [but] has to make up his mind to put up with the frugal fare of the cottage.

Whatever the source of such imagery, one is struck by its artificiality in relation to the life experience of the overwhelming majority of the people to whom his remarks are ultimately addressed. The tone of the passage contrasts in the starkest manner with the hard-headedness in regard to matters economic of the first of the classic Gaeltacht autobiographies,[14] which was to be published in the following year.

And yet the historians tell us that it was due at least in part to its economic policies that Fianna Fáil came to power in the 1932 general election. The message of economic self-sufficiency – no matter how awkwardly or ahistorically illustrated – had, it seems, its own inherent attractions for a majority of the electorate. But that message in itself, however or by whom illustrated, seems to me to be peculiarly suited to a time and place where the idea prevails that a hitherto exploited and depressed peasantry is at last in the position of being able itself to appoint the individuals who will form its government. Surely, it is implied, self-sufficiency will be the lot of a people whose thrift and self-restraint had previously been cruelly traded on by a hated ascendancy, but who are now largely in control of their own destinies and who live in a society where class differences are officially non-existent. This establishment view of rural Ireland in the 1930s has, it seems to me, elements that bear some comparison with aspects of the perceptions of peasant society developed in anthropology at that period and I feel that such a comparison is relevant to my theme even though it is doubtful if de Valera himself or any members of his government were in the 1930s and '40s very conversant with the theories of 'peasant society' then being advanced by certain transatlantic scholars.[15]

There has always been a sense of controversy in Ireland surrounding the terms 'peasant' and 'peasantry' in their application to the Irish rural population. Some people have regarded them as unpleasant and hostile labels imposed for our humiliation by scholars having that ulterior motive. The title of Kenneth Connell's book *Irish Peasant Society* is still regarded by some as being consciously provocative.[16] There are obviously good grounds for caution in the use of general appellations of the type 'peasant' and it is true that the peculiar circumstances of Irish political and socio-economic history demand that certain specific qualifications be borne in mind when the term is used in the Irish context. This however is a matter of degree, and qualifications of a similar nature must equally apply in the case of every individual community to which the term is applied. Some of the main qualifications that are urged in the Irish case are that the alleged 'peasantry' includes large elements of a depressed aristocracy (thus maintaining everyone's chances of being, in reality, descended from high kings); that a literate tradition of poetry and learning survives among the people at large, if only in a vestigial way (there is the tradition of Greek- and Latin-quoting farm labourers); and that, unlike – so it is alleged – the case of Central European or Central American populations, the memory of past glory and of another order of social organisation perpetually fuels a desire to throw off the demeaning yoke of foreign oppression and to resume a very different lifestyle from that prevalent in the countryside in recent centuries. Two of de Valera's statements have direct relevance to this issue. In the course of his address at the opening of the Athlone Broadcasting Station in 1933 he spoke at some length of Ireland's history and of her contributions to European culture. In regard to the tradition of Irish learning he points out that it was never wholly lost – even during the darkest period of the English occupation. 'The "hedge schools", taught by wandering scholars, frustrated in a measure the design to reduce the people to illiteracy ...' 'Some of the finest poems ... were written ... by men who spent their lives in poverty, dependent on the hospitality of an impoverished and outcast peasantry.'[17] Here we have the term 'peasantry' itself applied in a more or less straightforward way. Five years later in 1938, however, we get clear evidence of the line of thinking already referred to which sees the Irish peasant as really a type of aristocrat-in-disguise. In his speech at the inauguration of Douglas Hyde as first president of Ireland de Valera addressed the new office-holder as follows:

> In you we greet the successor of our rightful princes and, in your accession to office, we hail the closing of the breach that has existed, since the undoing of our nation at Kinsale.[18]

Such rhetorical denial of true 'peasant' status to Irish rural society is something that seems to me to go hand in hand with a tacit acquiescence in the use of a largely 'peasant' model for thinking about and managing social and economic development in the years of de Valera's ascendency. And such a model was not wildly inappropriate to the facts of the case as they were then officially perceived. The general changeover from tenant farming to peasant proprietorship had had little effect on the nature of rural society or the structures of agriculture. With the safety valve of emigration, the kind of rural lifestyles that are so graphically depicted in the pages of Arensberg and Kimball[19] could suggest themselves as the typical lifestyles of a population living to a pattern that was unbroken from time immemorial, while a new metropolitan elite could, since the revolution, maintain a seemingly benign form of the old structural ascendency over the 'liberated' countryside.[20] Here was indeed a source of that 'truly Irish' order of things that was so important a part of the national dream. Cleared of its 'big houses' – in reality or by selective vision – the hinterland of the essentially pre-industrial Irish market towns was at once the source of economic self-sufficiency, in all but a few instances where imported frugal luxuries were not to be decried, and also the heartland of moral and social values bearing testimony to the spirituality and selflessness of the Irish people.

STEREOTYPING IN 'PEASANT' MODEL

In a sense this vision of the Irish countryside fits well enough with the notions of peasant society being developed by such as Redfield and Foster.[21] These ideas – largely the product of fieldwork, in Mexico and elsewhere – had led within anthropology to 'peasant' society being proposed as an exact term for an autonomous, stable category of social organisation rather than as a loose description of an intermediate stage in some inevitable social progression from hunting-gathering to urban living. For Redfield any list of the central elements of peasant society would include the following: being definitely rural but relating to market towns; forming a segment of a larger regional population that itself contained urban centres; lacking the isolation, political autonomy and self-sufficiency of tribal society; retaining old identity, integration and attachment to soil and cults.[22] Now, as is well known, the theory of peasant society has developed almost out of recognition since Redfield published his classic study of Tepoztlán in

1930 and his concept of 'peasantry' – that I see as matching the model implicit in de Valera's social and economic theory fifty years ago – must today to be regarded as inadequate conceptually and methodologically. One of the chief objections to it is that it lifts the society it purports to describe out of the actual, historical social and economic complexities of the real world and substitutes mechanistic abstractions for the endlessly dynamic and contingent ramifications of individual and group choice in the actual circumstances of every community at every specific trine. A similar observation can surely be made in regard to the vision of the life of the Irish people that de Valera promoted from the day he came to power. They – the Irish people – were to be largely untroubled by developments within any historical process. Their tranquil, Christian lives were to be an example to a world far gone on the paths of unprincipled and materialist excess. The bedrock of the Irish way of life that was to contrast so much with the way of the world outside our shores was of course 'the age-old certainty of our cultural identity and cultural values'.

The very first speech of de Valera the parliamentary democrat, delivered on his arrival in Ennis in June 1917 to contest the East Clare by-election, had given warning of this *leitmotif* of de Valera's social and political thought to see behind changing appearances to the timeless realities that are really worthy objects of human endeavour. Speaking of free and absolute independence for Ireland, he said of the men of 1916 that 'they went out ... because they knew it was in the bottom of the heart of every Irishman, no matter what was on the surface'.[23] This choice of the continuity of identity and value as something superior in significance to any developments on the social and economic plane continues throughout de Valera's political career in terms of his radical pursuit of and emphasis on Irish sovereignty and independence primarily at a constitutional and symbolic level. The social and economic conservatism of this constitutional radicalism cannot, of course, in any sense be attributed entirely to a single individual. Large historical and structural factors inhibited any extreme, revolutionary aftermath to the establishment the Irish Free State. Nevertheless, I contend that the conception of a folk or peasant-type society that seems to me to lie at the heart of de Valera's and Fianna Fáil's political philosophy from 1932 to 1959 made it easier for both leader and party to get on with the 'real' job of manifesting and reinforcing Irish sovereignty while leaving Irish society relatively unaltered. But it cannot be forgotten that support for this political philosophy was given again and again by the electorate who demonstrated, in their loyalty to the 'chief' in the face of dire social and economic necessity, the need for all of us to look beyond economic welfare alone in order to see the political meaning of individuals and their actions. Throughout a period of economic hardship and military threat a larger proportion of the Irish electorate responded positively to de Valera's constant emphasising of the sovereignty of the people, their superior qualities, their noble history, their glorious cultural heritage, the rightness of their national cause. This response is, to my way of thinking, evidence of the continuing political efficacy in de Valera's day of a mentality deriving not from the consciousness of 'class', in any modern sense, but rather from the consciousness of collectivities whose focus is primarily neither political nor economic.

STEREOTYPING OF FOLK TRADITIONS

In his celebrated reply to Winston Churchill, de Valera reached what I think of as the highest point of his career as a veritable personification of national identity. In this broadcast he speaks not only for the Irish people but for *Éire* herself, thanking on her behalf the Gaels who had not failed her: *'Níor chlis sibh orm, a Ghaela.'*[24] One cannot avoid feeling the pressure of mythology here and sense the looming of mythological personages.

The *Cailleach Bhéarra*, shaper and guardian of the landscape itself and goddess of sovereignty, comes to mind. She has inhabited Gaelic consciousness from pre-historic times and her legend was still in de Valera's day being recounted to the full-time collectors of the Folklore Commission. The temptation to see a mythological correspondence between de Valera and the *Cailleach Bhéarra* cannot however be easily indulged, and not simply because of gender difficulties. A major aspect of the *cailleach* tradition is her fertility and her general lasciviousness, and these qualities would surely not appear to any conspicuous degree in de Valera's public image. That public image, in fact, in its austerity, aloofness, respectability, sombre and dignified good sense, fits very badly with the tone and quality of much of the genuine folklore and traditions of the very people whose sovereignty and cultural identity de Valera took it upon himself to personify. The gaiety, the earthiness, the humanity of the Irish folk imagination sits uneasily with the stereotype of Irish folk tradition that emerges from an examination of the pronouncements on the subject by the founder-leader of Fianna Fáil and the role he chose to adopt under its inspiration. There is a correspondence in this regard between the ideas of de Valera and those of Pope Pius XII who has been quoted as follows on the subject of folklore:[25]

> Folklore takes on its true meaning in correcting the errors of a society which ignores its healthiest and most fertile traditions. It strives to make it maintain a living continuity with the past, not a continuity imposed by outside forces, but one resulting from the profound feelings of generations, which have found in folklore the expression of their special aspirations, their beliefs, desires and sorrows, their glorious memories of the past and their hope for the future ... In Christian countries when the faith is strong, religious faith and the people's lives form a unity comparable to the unity of body and soul. Where such unity is still preserved, folklore is not merely a curious survival from the past ages; it is a manifestation of present-day life, which recognises its debt to the past and attempts to maintain itself and adapt itself intelligently to new situations. It preserves the people from cultural laziness which is a sign of the degeneration of the social organism.

These sentiments could well, it seems to me, have been those of de Valera himself as, on occasion, indeed, his own pronouncements seemed appropriate to a supreme pontiff. In the Athlone broadcast to which reference has already been made, the following passage occurs:

> The Irish genius has always stressed spiritual and intellectual rather than material values. That is the characteristic that fits the Irish people in a special manner for the task, now a vital one, of helping to save western civilisation. The great material progress of recent times, coming in a world where false philosophies already reigned, has distorted men's sense of proportion; the material has usurped the sovereignty that is the right of the spiritual. Everywhere today the consequences of this perversion of the order are to be seen. Spirit and mind have ceased to rule. The riches which the world sought, and to which it sacrificed all else, have become a curse by their very abundance.

Such statements offer little evidence of any great degree of enthusiasm for the fruits of economic development. They also lack any for the mundane involvement in the matter of sustaining life on the material and corporeal level that must be the primary and sustained concern of the ordinary bearers of even the most magnificent of cultural traditions.

One may wonder as to the equivalent degree of fit between Ulster unionist folk tradition and the mind and manner of Carson who in many respects stands in relation to that tradition as de Valera does to the southern nationalist one. It is interesting to note their co-occurrence as folk characters in the repertoire of a border community in Fermanagh where the two traditions co-exist. In his recent study of the folklore and history of the small Ulster community of Ballymenone, Henry Glassie gives the following two verses joining de Valera and Carson in a frame:

> Sir Edward Carson had a cat
> it sat upon the fender;
> And every time he fed the cat,
> it cried out, No Surrender!

> De Valera had a cat,
> he fed it on a plate;
> And every time he hit the cat,
> it shouted, Up Free State!

Glassie's own commentary is as follows:

> The men make a mirrored pair. So do their cats who repeat party slogans when fed and symbolize the people who humbly and loyally surrender their human will to ideology.[26]

A folk proclivity as an element in the popular reaction to political leadership by a great public figure who touches on values commonly regarded as eternally indispensable by the plain people is not, it seems, to be regarded as the exclusive possession of the southern Irish.

SUMMING UP

Three separate aspects of the style and content of de Valera's leadership of both Fianna Fáil and Dublin governments during nearly three decades of power up to 1959 seem to be capable of being perceived together as a cluster of mutually reinforcing phenomena resistant to class consciousness and characteristic of a politics carried on at a definite remove from the pragmatic realities of the current moment. I hope that what I have been saying in this chapter until now has made it clear both what these phenomena are and how they can be seen as being related in the way I propose. Listed together they comprise:

(a) de Valera's consciously indulged role as representative, at a symbolic level, of the sovereignty and cultural identity of the Irish people;
(b) the stereotype underlying de Valera's and Fianna Fáil's vision of the nature and potential of Irish society;
(c) an actual propensity in the popular imagination of the times to run in moulds deriving from a traditional universe of discourse rich in the materials of folk narrative.

The combination of these led, it seems to me, to the establishment in most of Ireland of a style of politics in which the surface landscape of political decision-making and executive implementation was somehow of less moment than the formal way in which, beneath this landscape, the structure of political reality was reinforced.[27] Thus, in a sense, whatever *was* said and done out of the range of things that could possibly be said and done hardly mattered once the things that *were* said and done were the right things to *say* and *do*. And a majority of the Irish electorate quickly learned, from 1932 on, that they could depend entirely on de Valera and his party to say and do the *right* thing, whatever it was that, from day to day or budget to budget, they *actually* said and did.[28]

Today, three leaders later, a degree of structural rigidity and a degree of abstraction from the realities of life as encountered and experienced by people outside the party may appear to be still the lot of Fianna Fáil in the aftermath of its charismatic founder. For many kinds of reasons, saying and doing the right thing in today's politics means something altogether different from what it meant prior to 1960. For many better-off and professional-class Catholics then, of course, an adherence to Catholic social principles was a fundamental criterion of the 'rightness' in question. For many more, however, I feel, the issues of sovereignty and identity were paramount. For most Irish people at that time the leader of Fianna Fáil played the right note.[29] With the effective passing of de Valera from the political scene after 1960 the clarity of the signal faded.

Increasingly, in recent years, public debate and actual economic and social development have opened up and called into question the foundations of political ground that was *terra firma* while de Valera ruled. The Northern question has not been the least of such issues, but any list would include health, civil liberty, public morality and the national aims in relation to topics as various as language and the ownership of wealth. The very heavy weather that Irish politicians at present make of the business of deciding on and implementing constitutional and legislative reform owes, I think, some part of its explanation to the continuing influence on the Irish political system of the ideology and practical style of the great figure who towered over it for so long. In particular for the party he himself founded, difficulties persist in adapting the practice of politics to the circumstances of a world so different from that in which de Valera's vision of our destinies seemed to so many to be of universal significance.

CHAPTER 23

De Valera's Other Ireland

[Published in Gabriel Doherty and Dermot Keogh (eds), *De Valera's Irelands* (Cork: Mercier Press, 2003), pp. 155–65]

This chapter will be concerned more with culture than with history but I hope that it can be taken as a contribution to certain common issues of a theoretical nature that have loomed large in recent years in respect of both historiography (the writing of history) and ethnography (the writing and representation of culture). I want to suggest that the emphasis given in the cultural ideology of de Valera's Ireland to folk tradition, as an expression of Irish identity, served in effect to mask and to mute the actual cultural history of Ireland in the four middle decades of the century, and that another Ireland of those years has gone largely unrecorded. That other Ireland is the Ireland whose cultural expression was the popular culture of the city streets and the factories, the popular culture of town life in the urbanising countryside, the popular culture arising from the modernising aspects of village and rural life, as in the effect, for example, of rural electrification that culminated – in popular cultural terms – in the establishment of an Irish television station in 1961 when so many ordinary Dublin and east coast homes were already festooned with reception masts reaching for the popular media culture of the British stations.

De Valera's inaugural address to the new Irish television audience in 1961 reinforces, in a way, his radio message to the Irish people on St Patrick's Day 1943 regarding the nature of Irish cultural identity and the noble traditional heritage that nourished and sustained it.[1] Folklore was, still, in the official cultural perspective of de Valera's Ireland, one very important element, perhaps the chief one, in that identity and that heritage, and was a main ground for the ideological bias that disregarded contemporary and urban popular culture in the official reckoning and promotion of cultural self-perception and in its official representation. This ideological bias had its historical roots in an era much earlier than that of de Valera's Ireland but was still sufficiently current, in the de Valera years, to result in the kind of ethnographic and historical denial of actual popular cultural creativity that matches the imaginative myopia underlying the denial and suppression of literary creativity that the Censorship of Publications legislation of 1929 implied.

As regards the quality of official Irish cultural thinking then, as much was already being said in 1940 by Seán Ó Faoláin who wrote, in the first issue of *The Bell*, that the magazine would stand for 'Life before any abstraction, in whatever magnificent words it may clothe itself'.[2] In the pages of his magazine, he promoted an intellectual pluralism and a cultural internationalism that was the antithesis of the prevailing ideology regarding Irish culture and Irish cultural identity. The folk tradition aspect of that view of Irish culture which *The Bell* opposed and, specifically, of Irish popular culture is also to be found, well in the aftermath of the de Valera years, in the closing words of an article published in 1979 and written two years earlier in commemoration of the founding a half century before of the Folklore of Ireland Society in 1927. The title of this article is 'The Irish Folklore Commission: Achievement and legacy' and its author, Bo Almqvist, professor of Irish folklore at UCD, was successor in that position to Séamus Ó Duilearga, the father figure of folklore study in Ireland in the de Valera years. Bo Almqvist closed his article with this exhortation to the Irish people:

> A mhuintir na hÉireann!
> Do not neglect one of the greatest treasures you possess! I beseech you for your own sake, for the sake of your men and women, for the sake of past generations – all the humble but truly great men and women who cherished their national heritage and passed it on in trust to us – for the sake of understanding, identity and unity in this country in these troubled times, for the sake of joy and beauty in generations to come, for the sake of truth and of learning, for the sake of everything you hold dear, noble and holy, do not let us down in our work.[3]

This passage strikingly illustrates an essentialist and essentially romantic antiquarian notion of Irish identity – at least as far as popular culture is concerned – and represents the thinking, in regard to folklore and traditional culture as the expression of Irishness, that was endorsed by Irish governments of the de Valera years to the extent of their continual support for an official Irish Folklore Commission under the direction of Séamus Ó Duilearga. Ó Duilearga had been a student of, and later assistant to, Douglas Hyde at UCD. Douglas Hyde's role was paramount in promoting in Ireland the philosophy of the romantic antiquarian movement that underlay the nineteenth-century nationalism of many of the European nations striving to build their identity in terms of native language and folk tradition.

Roy Foster has noted that Hyde's 1892 address to the National Literary Society 'On the Necessity for De-Anglicising Ireland', delivered in the same year as his *Love Songs of Connacht* anthology of folk poetry was published, 'rapidly achieved legendary status', being 'credited with inspiring the foundation of the Gaelic League a year later' and becoming 'a canonical text of Irish cultural nationalism'.[4] In a review of Hyde's *Love Songs of Connacht* by W.B. Yeats, we have the expression by Yeats too of a perceived need, as Foster puts it, 'to derive inspiration from a basic energy, by knowing one's roots' that is, I submit, on a par with the message Bo Almqvist still had for the Irish people as recently as the late 1970s. In his 1893 review Yeats had written:

> As for me, I close the book with much sadness. These poor peasants lived in a beautiful if somewhat inhospitable world, where little had changed since Adam delved and Eve span. Everything was so old that it was steeped in the heart, and every powerful emotion found at once noble types and symbols for its expression. But we – we live in a world of whirling change, where nothing becomes old and sacred and our powerful emotions express themselves in vulgar types and symbols. The soul then had but to stretch out its arms to fill them with beauty, but now all manner of heterogeneous ugliness has beset us.[5]

In the face of this modern metropolitan world, Irish cultural nationalism, of the sort Hyde and Yeats espoused and that de Valera was to attempt to practise – deriving, historically, from the philosophy of J.G. von Herder in eighteenth-century Germany and flowing through the writings of Thomas Davis and the Young Irelanders – sought, in the later nineteenth and earlier twentieth centuries, to locate folk traditions at the heart of national identity. I believe that such a conviction regarding the essential nature of national identity still operated as an important element in the decision of de Valera to choose Douglas Hyde as an appropriate person to be inaugurated as first president of the Irish republic in 1938.

At the level of party politics it is suggested that Hyde was not de Valera's first choice for president, but that the risk of having a party politician such as Seán T. O'Kelly rejected by the people in the aftermath of his narrow constitution referendum victory caused de Valera to opt for someone who, in J.J. Lee's words, could safely satisfy 'sundry national self-images' while still guaranteeing a Fianna Fáil presidency.[6] The factors motivating any such potential choice are surely complex and calculated – perhaps especially so in the case of Mr de Valera – but I believe that one significant element in the choice of Douglas Hyde to fill the presidential office was that, in de Valera's perspective and that of other Irish Irelanders – within Fianna Fáil and outside it – Hyde's career and public image had given public witness to a deep allegiance to the Irish-Ireland ideal. In office as first citizen and symbolic representative of the Irish nation, Douglas Hyde would give effect to the cultural equivalent of the political policy of Sinn Féinism and the economic policy of protectionism which we can also associate with de Valera's Ireland. Such political use of Hyde as a kind of cultural icon by de Valera suggests something of a renewal in the de Valera years of the ideals of the early Gaelic League era regarding the cultural expression of national identity. In fact the more imaginative, ecumenical and potentially unifying aspects of the kind of cultural revolution that Hyde and the early Gaelic League had intended and pioneered had not survived the lurch to physical-force nationalism. Instead a narrower, more conservative and, indeed, somewhat anti-modern tendency marked the cultural nationalism of the years between 1916 and the end of the de Valera era.

Mr de Valera himself would, in due course, also fill the president's office in a manner similarly appropriate to the perception of Irish national identity as residing chiefly in matters of a conservatively defined cultural tradition. By then, however, the appeal-power of even the attenuated version of a romantic antiquarian definition of Irish cultural identity had waned. The centrality of ancient tradition in official cultural ideology was yielding ground to the influence and implications of the fresh economic and social thinking of the Lemass era. This focused on the exclusively insular concerns of an Irish government preoccupied with matters of basic political stability, economic survival or external threat in a time of war.

With hindsight, we can see that the implication of the cultural ideology that prevailed in de Valera's Ireland was to privilege the memory of traditional cultural forms that were expressive of the worldview and lifestyle of former rural, relatively unsophisticated, largely under-educated and perhaps only partly literate segments of the Irish population. This memory culture of the non-elite and non-urban tradition formed, of course, the central concern of the activities of the Irish Folklore Commission that had been established in 1935 with de Valera's approval. The sense of an essential heritage of cultural riches in danger of being lost forever in the displacement and destruction of tradition by the forces of modernity was well caught in the motto of the Folklore of Ireland Society's journal *Béaloideas*, every number of which since 1927 has carried the gospel quotation: *Colligite quae superaverunt fragmenta ne pereant*, a sacred injunction to preserve precious survivals now in danger of discard.

In Germany, we know that the implications of a similar later-nineteenth- and early-twentieth-century preoccupation in national cultural ideology, with the symbolic recovery and repossession of the past, had a more directly political and sinister outcome than was the case in Ireland. A recent study by Uli Linke of the focus of research in the history of German folklore scholarship has proposed a direct relationship between culture theory and the exercise of political power by the state, that is relevant to a consideration of the privileging of folk tradition in the cultural ideology of de Valera's Ireland. Linke's article raises issues in regard to the potentially negative side of an exclusive privileging of what Linke terms 'peasant lore' and 'commonplace culture' in showing how such a preoccupation in German folkloristics facilitated the emergence of social and political policies of a racist and totalitarian nature. In an introductory paragraph Linke writes:

> I begin with a brief discussion of the fetishism of peasant lore, and of commonplace culture in the nineteenth and early twentieth centuries. During this era of European nation-building the romanticised life-world of peasants served as a template for the political identity of an emerging German state. Contemporary folklorists equated peasant traditions with the unchanging customs of the past: peasant lore was presented as a pristine and authentic repertoire for building a common German culture. From this discussion of 'regressive modernisation' – the political journey into the future by detour through the past – I extract a nationalistic

concept of culture in which a theory of power is absent: the workings of power are ignored or perhaps even silenced. I suggest that early German folklorists, as active participants in cultural politics, were not motivated to uncover or elucidate the hidden dimensions of power they so skilfully manipulated. This non-treatment of power is even more pronounced in the context of Nazi folklore scholarship: by concealing the strategies of power, the study of folk culture becomes a means for legitimating Hitler's imperialist policies and racial concerns for 'purity of blood' and reproduction.[7]

Linke goes on to show how, in Germany, the romantic perception of the value of common cultural tradition (akin to the Davis position in the Irish case) gave rise to expressions of distress that 'large segments of the German population had abandoned their native heritage in favour of foreign models of refinement' (akin to the Hyde de-Anglicisation position). In the twentieth century in both Germany and Ireland, we know that cultural nationalism took on radically political and militaristic form. Here in Ireland Hyde had claimed that his message was essentially apolitical, holding that 'an agenda of cultural revival should be as attractive to unionists as to nationalists since it was above politics'.[8] Hyde relinquished his leadership of the Gaelic League in 1915 when he was unable to stop it from embracing an openly partisan political stance on the question of national self-determination by military means and returned to political office (albeit one allegedly above politics) only in 1938 to personify (at de Valera's wish) that partly self-determined nation as its president.

The significance of folklore studies in the newly established Irish Free State and in the later republic was, meanwhile, endorsed by official government support and accorded the symbolic importance which I have argued that de Valera's choice of Douglas Hyde as president contained. Its influence on social and political affairs, however, was largely confined to its diverting of official and scholarly attention away from the lived popular culture of Irish people in the 1930s and '40s in favour of a concern for the preservation of the record of past cultural forms. Things had, as we know, taken a grimmer turn in Germany where what matches the official Irish lack of interest in urbanised popular culture is a virulent aversion to cosmopolitanism that saw cities as the locus of decadence. Linke cites two quotations that vividly illustrate this. The first, dated 1935, is from an anthropological journal entitled *Volk und Russe*:

> Dangers threaten the population when it migrates to the cities. It withers away in a few generations, because it lacks the vital bond with the earth. The German nation must be rooted in the soil if it wants to remain alive.[9]

In the previous year, 1934, the director of the Working Group for German Folklore had asserted:

> German folklore is the study of the racial and traditional world of the German people which is purest and most alive in those communities which have experienced the most eternal contact with blood and soil.[10]

Here in Ireland the anti-urban, anti-cosmopolitan bias of earlier-twentieth-century folklore studies amounted in effect to little more than neglect of the popular culture of the contemporary urbanising world – as evidenced in the exclusion of city schools from the commission's 1937/8 Schools' Folklore Collection project (whereby the pupils of all primary schools in the state – barring the cities – were set to work to write down the folklore and traditions remembered by their elders). When, in 1938, de Valera greeted Douglas Hyde's accession to the presidency as that of a 'rightful prince' and hailed it as closing, in his (de Valera's) perspective, a symbolic breach that had existed since 'the undoing of our nation at Kinsale',[11] his words remained at the level of rhetoric and cultural ideology fuelling, not social and political hatred, but rather the antiquarian and traditional construction put officially on Irish cultural identity – surely one of the abstractions against which Seán Ó Faoláin set his sights in *The Bell*.

That continuing antiquarian/traditional construction of what constituted Irish folklore or popular culture was effected by folklorists and cultural nationalists on the basis of traditional materials gathered more from the memories than from the living behaviour of informants and culture-bearers, who were themselves of course living in a society and a culture deeply transformed by the technology and social organisation of the contemporary modern world.

Today, historians and ethnologists alike would question whether the concepts of an exclusive 'folklore' and an exclusive 'folk tradition' can be historically or ethnographically meaningful – given the artificial nature of the distinctions they imply in social reality and cultural experience. Is there any meaningful way in which 'folklore' can be separated off from the totality of a society's or an individual's production of and participation in cultural knowledge and cultural forms – material, social or symbolic? The fullest, most recent, Irish discussion relevant to this question is that of the historian Seán Connolly, who attempts to outline and analyse the history of the idea of popular culture as addressed in historical writing about Ireland in the eighteenth and nineteenth centuries.[12]

At least two separate issues arise from Connolly's treatment of the historiography of Irish pre-twentieth-century popular culture, that are relevant to a consideration of the neglect of the actual popular culture of de Valera's Ireland by folklorist and historian alike. The first of these has to do with the very idea of a popular culture that is in some way detached or detachable from the overall picture of cultural activity in the case of any society. Citing examples from the culture of the eighteenth and nineteenth centuries in Ireland – such matters as card-playing, dancing and hurling in the domain of recreation or beliefs and practices associated with the fairy faith in the domain of religion – Connolly is able to argue convincingly for a flow of cultural transmission, a sharing and a spreading out of cultural knowledge and patterns of behaviour within the social world that defies the setting of boundaries between folk and non-folk. The cultural reality of that world is, instead, best thought of in holistic terms as comprising an unbounded and unstructured flow of ideas, behaviours, institutions and material artefacts, that both shift and change in response to shifting and changing economic and political life in the framework of the general modernising tendency of the European world. In Connolly's view, any attempted rigid division of cultural reality into separate subaltern and elite cultural worlds is untenable, in a way that highlights a similar implausibility in the constructed, artificial nature of a distinctive Irish folklore world as this was officially understood in de Valera's Ireland.

Whether labelled as 'folklore' or 'popular culture' we should, in this reading, endeavour to regard the materials accumulated by the Folklore Commission as historical instances of cultural expression in particular historical contexts within the flow of a single universe of cultural discourse, without, of course, denying the very real ethnic, linguistic, economic and political diversity that existed in the social circumstances of people's lives. Viewed like this, the Folklore Commission materials retained their very considerable value as an ethnographic record. A different set of questions can, however, be brought to bear on them from the ones designed to elucidate exclusively their representative capacity in relation to some essential Irish tradition.

On this basis also, gaps in the ethnographic record can be better perceived, and the missing or largely invisible folklore and popular culture of the de Valera years themselves can be conceived of, as a target for research and elucidation by both historians and ethnologists working in partnership. Many topics quickly suggest themselves: music-hall culture; the culture of the dancehall and the whist drive; the culture of popular urban Christianity; the culture of the new slum-clearance housing estates; the culture of the factory floor. Connolly himself draws attention to our relative ignorance regarding the culture of cinema in Ireland, given its enormous popularity from the 1920s. We need, he says, to know about the cultural response to this new cultural form of different regions of the country and of different groups of people. We need to know which particular film genres most appealed to Irish audiences and to what degree the characters and the motifs of commercial cinema were assimilated into the wider culture. He reminds us that the earlier-eighteenth-century Dublin playhouse was the site for a similar hybridisation of elite and popular, or metropolitan and local, or high and low culture in the context of a then socially undifferentiated consumer demand for a commercially produced form of social recreation.

On the other hand, we can ourselves observe and experience at first hand the emergence and influence within our contemporary cultural world of similar apparently novel forms of group recreation such as comedy clubs, or of group religious practice such as charismatic healing rituals. On examination, these may well turn out to be transformations of cultural forms already present at the local or folk or popular end of the cultural spectrum of de Valera's Ireland. Rendering the specifics of the actual popular culture of the de Valera years is thus a common task for history and ethnology that is essential to any analysis of the cultural history of Ireland in the twentieth century.

A second issue raised by Connolly also has direct bearing on the question of the relative invisibility of contemporary popular culture in de Valera's Ireland. This is the dominant focus, which, Connolly alleges, exists within Irish popular culture studies on the decline and disappearance of cultural forms, together with a prevailing sense of loss and dispossession in the face of great change. Connolly suggests two reasons why such a focus should exist: one having to do with the belief that the language shift from Irish to English inevitably constituted a decline in cultural creativity; the other with a belief that 'cultural subjugation', as he puts it, the muting and suppression of cultural expression, is also an inevitable consequence of the political subjugation that Ireland has experienced since the seventeenth century. Connolly argues instead for seeing creative cultural adjustment to changing circumstances and to new possibilities in place of the view that sees continual withering away of cultural expression and cultural identity. He draws attention to examples of evidence of a capacity on the part of Irish-speaking groups in the eighteenth century to deal ably with the expanding urban and commercial sector of society.

I might mention that I have myself discussed the County Clare poet Brian Merriman, and his long poem *The Midnight Court*, as an example of this kind of hybridisation in cultural expression. It bridges native tradition and the social reality of the later-eighteenth-century north Munster world which was experiencing increasing literacy, increasing marketisation and monetarisation of the economy, and increased expansion in the operation of courts of law.[13] In that eighteenth-century cultural world, with its mixture of tradition and commercialisation, Connolly contends that what he terms the 'triumph' of the metropolitan was inevitable, whatever the language spoken and whatever the political circumstances. The demonstration of the cultural mechanism of that metropolitan 'triumph' is what is relevant to our own concerns. The National Folklore Archive, built on the dedicated labours of the Folklore of Ireland Society and the Irish Folklore Commission, comprises a huge and hugely valuable primary resource for the study of that cultural mechanism, as it actually operated within the cultural and social reality to which the testimony of the commission's contributors bears eloquent witness.

When we come to look at the popular culture of Ireland in the middle decades of the twentieth century we can see how a prevailing cultural ideology that saw cultural identity chiefly in terms of antiquarian tradition, served to divert attention away from the culturally creative nature of the adjustments to modernity that were expressing themselves in the worldview, the lifestyle and the material culture of the twentieth-century urban and urbanising world, in which Irish people actually lived increasingly metropolitan-influenced lives. Hyde had spoken in his 1892 lecture of the Gaelic past at the bottom of the Irish heart 'that prevents us becoming citizens of the empire'.[14] De Valera in his turn spoke of the wish that lay in the heart of every Irish man and woman for a country not only free but truly Irish as well.[15] The ways in which the real men and women of de Valera's Ireland could be seen to be truly Irish were, to a significant degree, circumscribed by the ideological perspective that placed little or no value on cultural forms that deviated from a kind of folk norm in official thinking.

With later developments in folklore and popular culture studies, we are able to see today how official norms and representations of cultural identity are always destined to be static and crude and out-of-date when set against the ceaseless flow of cultural creativity and cultural transmission, the transmission of ideas, values, behaviours and objects that constitute the reality of a holistic cultural world out of which new cultural forms and new expressions of cultural identity are continually being created. As Connolly rightly insists in regard to the study of cultural matters by historians, it behoves us all as students of culture to try to avoid becoming prisoners of abstractions of our own making.

The terms 'folklore' and 'popular culture' must, therefore, be used in a way that is fully conscious of the unwarranted distortion of the reality of cultural history that their use has sometimes implied. Connolly would, in theory, countenance renouncing the possibility of talking about popular culture as an historical object or a historical system of cultural activity in its own right. He envisages, however, a continued interest by historians of culture in studying local, popular cultural manifestations.

Folklore studies and ethnology have, for their part too, undergone a veritable paradigm shift since the closing years of de Valera's Ireland, that has brought their thinking on the creation and transmission of culture to a position somewhat akin to that claimed by Connolly for historians. The model of culture process that is associated with the name of the anthropologist Ulf Hannerz is one that offers the possibility of studying the local and popular production and transmission of culture and cultural identity without either a) falling into the trap of resorting to unjustified and unsustainable abstractions; or b) having to forego entirely a vernacular focus.[16] This is achieved by a continual framing of every subculture and of all local innovation within the increasingly globalised diffusion and interplay of cultural forces and forms.

Folklore and popular culture within this perspective are the cultural forms that give expression to local creativity and identity in divergent vernacular ways rather than in convergent cosmopolitan ones. Both these tendencies are, however, to be regarded as constantly at work together within the wash and flow of cultural production and transmission in the media and information age in which we live. A focus on the study of vernacular, local, popular aspects of culture and culture history within an overall frame encompassing cosmopolitan culture process offers the prospect of being able to throw light on both the history and the cultural dynamic of the means whereby groups and individuals have, in Ireland as elsewhere, continually reconciled their traditional identities and worldviews with the demands and the opportunities of prevailing economic and political circumstances, as these are created and transformed by developments in the wider world.

In mentioning, as a small example of this kind of focus, the UCC research project on the urban folklore and ethnology of Cork's northside – a project established by means of co-operation between the Department of Folklore at UCC and a number of Cork northside community organisations[17] – I want to draw attention to the considerable interest that is today being shown by communities in how best they can themselves represent (both to themselves and to others) their own traditions and their own cultural identity in the form of folklore and local history. This interest is not, of course, confined to urban communities only but, in general, it offers to folklorists and historians of culture alike the prospect of being able to collaborate with each other and with local groups in order to collect an archive of primary evidence for the operation in de Valera's Ireland, outside of the official frame of antiquarian cultural ideology, of the actual cultural process that operated in Moore Street and in Mayo, in Donnycarney and in Donegal, in Gurranabraher and in Graigue na Managh.

That actual cultural process produced – out of the reconciling of the local with the metropolitan, of the known with the new – a repertoire of cultural forms that were as valid an expression of Irish cultural identity in the de Valera years as those officially endorsed by political and educational authority in the years from 1926 to 1973. A further important consideration that arises from the collaborative nature of the kind of vernacular cultural study that the northside project involves is the reflexive, dialogical nature of both the fieldwork and the ethnographic description which it entails.[18] This raises issues of theory and methodology that were not directly addressed by students of culture in the de Valera years but they are of sufficient concern today, to the study of culture and cultural history, to merit being at least mentioned in the present context as matters that give further common cause to historians and folklorists/ethnologists alike in the pursuit of the culture and the cultural history of de Valera's other Ireland.

Notes

PART I. Introduction

1   Elizabeth Tonkin, Maryon McDonald and Malcolm Chapman (eds), *History and Ethnicity* (London and New York: Routledge, 1989), p. 16.

2   Ibid., p. 14.

3   Diarmuid Ó Giolláin (ed.), *Irish Ethnologies* (Notre Dame: University of Notre Dame Press, 2017).

4   Hastings Donnan, 'Re-Placing Ireland in Irish Anthropology', in Ó Giolláin (2017), pp. 19–35.

5   Guy Beiner, 'Locating Irish Tradition: The sociocultural construction of Irish folk history', in Ó Giolláin (2017), pp. 158–77.

6   Bronislaw Malinowski, *Argonauts of the Western Pacific* (London: Routledge & Kegan Paul, 1922), p. 517.

7   Wilhelm von Humboldt, *On Language: The diversity of human-language structure and its influence on the mental development of mankind*, trans. H. Aarsleff (Cambridge: Cambridge University Press, [1836] 1988).

8   Paul Kay and Willet Kempton, 'What is the Sapir-Whorf Hypothesis?' *American Anthropologist*, vol. 86, no. 1, 1984, pp. 65–79.

9   Séamus Ó Duilearga (ed.), *Leabhar Sheáin Í Chonaill: Sgéalta agus seanchas ó Íbh Ráthach* (Baile Átha Cliath: Comhairle Bhéaloideas Éireann, [1948] 1977).

10 Máirtín Verling (eag.), *Gort Broc: Scéalta agus seanchas ó Bhéarra* (Baile Átha Cliath: Coiscéim, 1996).

11 Ray Cashman, *Packy Jim: Folklore and worldview on the Irish border* (Madison, WI: The University of Wisconsin Press, 2016).

12 Thomas M. Wilson and Hastings Donnan, *The Anthropology of Ireland* (Oxford and New York: Berg, 2006).

13 Diarmuid Ó Giolláin, *Locating Irish Folklore* (Cork: Cork University Press, 2000).

14 Gearóid Ó Crualaoich, 'Folkloristic-Ethnological Studies in Ireland', in Ó Giolláin (2017), pp. 75–89.

15 Charles N. Kiely, 'Funerals in Ireland Today: The traditions, customs, beliefs and influences associated with death in a comparative and a historical perspective', PhD thesis, Department of Béaloideas/Folklore and Ethnology, University College Cork, 2010.

CHAPTER I – Cultural Ambivalence and Clerical Authority

1   Seán Ó Súilleabháin, *A Handbook of Irish Folklore* (Detroit: Singing Tree Press, 1970).

2   Anthony F.C. Wallace, *Religion: An anthropological view* (New York: Random House, 1966).

3   Seán Ó hEochaidh and Séamus Ó Catháin, *Síscéalta ó Thír Chonaill/Fairy Legends from Donegal*, translated to English by Máire MacNéill (Baile Átha Cliath: Comhairle Bhéaloideas Éireann, 1977).

4 Séamus Ó Catháin, _Scéalta Cois Cladaigh/Stories from the Sea and Shore_ (Baile Átha Cliath: Comhairle Béaloideas Éireann, 1983).

5 Donncha Ó Cróinín (ed.), _Seanchas Amhlaoibh Í Luínse_ (Baile Átha Cliath: Comhairle Bhéaloideas Éireann, 1980), pp. 180–1.

6 Angela Bourke, _The Burning of Bridget Cleary: A true story_ (London: Pimlico, 1999).

7 See Chapter 19.

8 Nancy Schmitz, 'An Irish Wise-Woman: Fact and legend', _Journal of the Folklore Institute_, vol. 14, 1977, pp. 169–79.

9 See Chapter 4.

10 W.G. Wood-Martin, _Traces of the Elder Faiths of Ireland_ (London: Longmans, Green & Co., 1902), p. 312.

11 Seán Ó Súilleabháin, _Irish Wake Amusements_ (Cork: Mercier Press, 1967).

12 Seán J. Connolly, _Priests and People in Pre-Famine Ireland 1780–1845_ (Dublin: Gill & Macmillan, 1982).

13 Lawrence J. Taylor, _Occasions of Faith: An anthropology of Irish Catholics_ (Dublin: Lilliput Press, 1995), pp. 145–67.

CHAPTER 2 – _An Leabhar Eoin_: The _In Principio_ charm in oral and literary tradition

1 Eamon Duffy, _The Stripping of the Altars: Traditional religion in England c.1400–c.1580_ (New Haven and London: Yale University Press, 1992), p. 215.

2 This was, for instance, the view of William Tyndale; see below.

3 F.N. Robinson, _The Works of Geoffrey Chaucer_ (Boston: Riverside Press, 1957), p. 19.

4 Don C. Skemer, _Binding Words: Textual amulets in the middle ages_ (University Park, PA: Pennsylvania State University Press, 2006), p. 63.

5 See Duffy, _The Stripping of the Altars_, pp. 215–16.

6 Pádraig Ó Héalaí, 'An Leabhar Eoin: Deabhóid agus piseogaíocht', in M. Mac Craith and P. Ó Héalaí (eds), _Diasa Díograise: Aistí i gcuimhne ar Mháirtín Ó Briain_ (Indreabhán: Cló Iar-Chonnacht, 2009), pp. 265–85.

7 On the potential reference in _Aislinge Meic Conglinne_, see Kuno Meyer, _Aislinge Meic Conglinne: The vision of Mac Conglinne, a middle-Irish wonder tale_ (London: David Nutt, 1892), p. 195.

8 Ó Héalaí, 'An Leabhar Eoin', pp. 371–4.

9 National Folklore Collection (NFC) 5: 227–8. Here and below, material from the NFC is published with kind permission from the director of the National Folklore Collection.

10 NFC 214: 494–542.

11 For more on this figure, see Gearóid Ó Crualaoich, _The Book of the Cailleach: Stories of the wise-woman healer_ (Cork: Cork University Press, 2003).

12 NFC 1797: 2–3.

13 NFC 164: 394–400.

14 Charles Plummer, 'Some Passages in the Brehon Laws III', _Ériu_, vol. 9, 1921–3, p. 115; see numbers 5: 11–28.

15 NFC 8: 174–6.

16 The Irish Folklore Commission's collector glosses _leabhrán_ here as _Leabhar Eoin_. I have made no attempts to standardise or correct the orthography of the Irish.

17 Kenneth H. Jackson, _Aislinge Meic Con Glinne_ (Dublin: Dublin Institute for Advanced Studies, 1990), p. 32; see note 7 above.

18 Diarmuid Ó Muirithe, _Tomás Ó Míocháin: Filíocht_ (Dublin: An Clóchomlar, 1988), pp. 67–70.

19 Tadhg Ó Donnchadha, 'Uiliog Ó Céirín', *Lia Fáil*, vol. 4, 1932, pp. 176–87. All translations from the Irish, where not otherwise noted, are by the author.

20 Once more, I am grateful to Professor Seán Ó Coileáin for kindly bringing this item to my attention.

21 NFC 5: 273–308.

22 I am reminded of the passage in Merriman's *Midnight Court* where the fairy queen Aoibheall sends a message *in writing*, bringing the traditional world of fairy belief into the increasingly literate reality of eighteenth-century Ireland: Ludwig Christian Stern, 'Brian Merriman's *Cúirt an Mheadhóin Oidhche*', *Zeitschrift für celtische Philologie*, vol. 5, 1905, pp. 230–1, 317–18.

23 Máirtín Ó Cadhain, *Cré na Cille* (Dublin: Sáirséal & Dill, 1949). The English translations are *The Dirty Dust*, trans. Alan Titley (New Haven and London: Yale University Press, 2015), and *Graveyard Clay*, trans. Liam Mac Con Iomaire and Tim Robinson (New Haven and London: Yale University Press, 2016). There are also translations into Norwegian: *Kirkegårdsjord*, trans. Jan Erik Rekdal (Oslo: Gyldendal Norsk Forlag, 1995); and Danish: *Kirkegårdsjord*, trans. Ole Munch-Pedersen (Aarhus: Husets Forlag, 2000).

24 Ó Héalaí, 'An Leabhar Eoin', p. 380. The expression which Ó Héalaí uses is *maitheas teoranta*, corresponding to the phrase 'limited good' employed by the anthropologist G.M. Foster.

25 Ó Cadhain, *Cré na Cille*, pp. 228, 301.

26 Ibid., p. 117. All translations from the novel are by the present author.

27 E.E. Evans-Pritchard, *Witchcraft, Oracles and Magic among the Azande* (Oxford: Oxford University Press, 1937).

28 Ó Héalaí, 'An Leabhar Eoin', pp. 377–9.

CHAPTER 3 – **Reading the *Bean Feasa***

1 A collector of the former Irish Folklore Commission (1935–71), Seán Standún, wrote down this item of lore from Mrs Eibhlín Uí Cheadagáin, aged seventy years, of Baile Iartach in Cape Clear, County Cork in December 1933. It is reproduced here – in my own translation – by permission of the head of the Department of Irish Folklore, University College Dublin, in whose archive the former Irish Folklore Commission's manuscripts are housed. An analytic commentary on this and other legends featuring the wise-woman will be found in Gearóid Ó Crualaoich, *The Book of the Cailleach: Stories of the wise-woman healer* (Cork: Cork University Press, 2003).

2 Bo Almqvist, 'Irish Migratory Legends on the Supernatural: Sources, studies and problems', in Pádraig Ó hÉalaí (ed.), *The Fairy Hill is on Fire!* (Baile Átha Cliath: An Cumann le Béaloideas Éireann, 1991), pp. 1–43.

3 Pádraig Ó hÉalaí (ed.), *Finscéalta agus Litríocht/Folk Legends and Fiction* (Baile Átha Cliath: An Cumann le Béaloideas Éireann, 1993); Pádraig Ó hÉalaí (ed.), *Glórtha ón Osnádúr/Sounds from the Supernatural* (Baile Átha Cliath: An Cumann le Béaloideas Éireann, 1995).

4 Lady Augusta Gregory, *Visions and Beliefs in the West of Ireland* (Gerrards Cross: Colin Smythe, 1970), pp. 31–50.

5 Patricia Lysaght, 'Lady Gregory (1852–1932)', in Angela Bourke et al. (eds), *The Field Day Anthology of Irish Writing. Vol. IV: Irish Women's Writing and Traditions* (Cork: Cork University Press, 2002), pp. 1435–45.

6 Schmitz, 'An Irish Wise-Woman'.

7 Verling (ed.), *Gort Broc*, pp. 297–8.

8   C.W. von Sydow, 'Om Folkets Sägner', *Nordisk Kultur*, vol. 9, 1931, p. 106.

9   Séamas MacPhilib, 'The Changeling (ML 5058): Irish versions of a migratory legend in their international context', *Béaloideas*, vol. 59, 1991, pp. 121–32.

10 Patricia Lysaght, *The Banshee: The Irish supernatural death-messenger*, 2nd edn (Dublin: Glendale Press, 1996).

11 Diarmaid Ó Giolláin, 'The Leipreachán and Fairies, Dwarfs and the Household Familiar: A comparative study', *Béaloideas*, vol. 52, 1984, pp. 75–150; Diarmaid Ó Giolláin, 'Capturer of Fairy Shoemaker Outwitted: The multiple marker versions (MLSIT 6011)', *Béaloideas*, vol. 59, 1991, pp. 161–6.

12 Criostóir MacCárthaigh, 'Midwife to the Fairies (ML5070): The Irish variants in their Scottish and Scandinavian perspective', *Béaloideas*, vol. 59, 1991, pp. 133–43.

13 Anne O'Connor, *Child Murderess and Dead Child Traditions* (Folklore Fellows Communications 249) (Helsinki: Academia Scientarum Fennica, 1991).

14 Éilís Ní Dhuibhne, '"The Old Woman as Hare": Structure and meaning in an Irish legend', *Folklore*, vol. 104, 1993, pp. 77–85.

15 Lysaght, *The Banshee*, pp. 29, 32–4, 145–6, 210, 368, 378; Patricia Lysaght, 'Caoineadh na Marbh: Die totenklage in Irland', *Rheinisch-Westfälische Zeitschrift für Volkskunde*, vol. 40, 1995, pp. 163–213; Patricia Lysaght, 'Caoineadh os Cionn Coirp: The lament for the dead in Ireland', *Folklore*, vol. 108, 1997, pp. 65–82; Évelyn Sorlin, *Crie De Vie, Cri De Mort: Les fées du destin dans les pays Celtiques* (Folklore Fellows Communications 248) (Helsinki: Academia Scientarum Fennica, 1991).

16 Almqvist, 'Irish Migratory Legends', pp. 1–2.

17 Máirtín Verling (ed.), *Béarach Mná ag Caint* (Indreabhán: Cló Iar-Chonnachta, 1999); Máirtín Verling (ed.), Beara Woman Talking: Folklore from the Beara Peninsula, Co. Cork (Cork: Mercier Press, 2003).

18 Ó Crualaoich, *The Book of the Cailleach*, pp. 100–73.

19 Bourke, *The Burning of Bridget Cleary*.

20 Ní Dhuibhne, '"The Old Woman as Hare"', p. 80.

21 Máirtín Ó Direáin, *Ón Ulán Ramhar Siar*, ed. Eoghan Ó hÁnluain (Baile Átha Cliath: An Clóchamhar, 2002), pp. 62–3.

CHAPTER 4 – The 'Merry Wake' and Popular Resistance to Domination

1   J.L. McCracken, 'The Ecclesiastical Structure, 1714–60', in T.W. Moody and W.E. Vaughan (eds), *A New History of Ireland. Vol. IV: Eighteenth-Century Ireland, 1691–1800* (Oxford: Clarendon Press, 1986), pp. 98–9.

2   Ó Súilleabháin, *Irish Wake Amusements*. This work was originally published in Irish in Dublin in 1961 by *Án Clóchomhar* under the title *Caitheamh Aimsire ar Thorraimh*.

3   Ibid., pp. 146–7.

4   Thomas Crofton Croker, *Researches in the South of Ireland* (London: John Murray, 1824), pp. 166–7.

5   Ibid., p. 167.

6   Ibid., p. 166.

7   Ó Súilleabháin, *Irish Wake Amusements*, p. 146.

8   Ibid., p. 154.

9   Ibid., p. 147.

10 Ibid., pp. 146–54.

11 Ibid., p. 150.

12 Ibid., pp. 152–3.

13 Ibid., pp. 138–41.

14 Arnold Van Gennep, *The Rites of Passage*, trans. Monika B. Vizedom and Gabrielle L. Caffee (Chicago: Psychology Press, 1960), p. 146.

15 Permission from Professor Bo Almqvist to consult, copy and take extracts from the Irish Folklore Commission manuscripts now in the custody of the Department of Irish Folklore, University College Dublin is gratefully acknowledged.

16 Liam de Paor, *Portrait of Ireland* (Bray: St Martin's Press, 1985), pp. 145–55.

17 The term 'borekeen' as used by John Prim (1852) may be assumed to be a transliteration of the diminutive form of the Irish *bórachán*, 'a bow-legged person', 'a person with crooked feet'. This term is applied to the 'joker' in card-playing, and its use in relation to the 'joker' or 'master of revels' at wakes is an extension of this meaning.

18 J.G.A. Prim, 'Olden Popular Pastimes in Kilkenny', *JRSAI*, vol. ii, 1852–3, pp. 333–4.

19 R.A. Breatnach, 'The Lady and the King: A theme of Irish literature', *Studies*, vol. xlii, 1953, pp. 321–36.

20 Máire Bhreathnach, 'The Sovereignty Goddess as Goddess of Death?', *Zeitschrift fur Celtische Philologie*, vol. 39, no. 1, 2009, pp. 243–60.

21 Lysaght, *The Banshee*.

22 Ó Súilleabháin, *Irish Wake Amusements*, chapters 4–5.

23 See Peter McPhee, 'Popular Culture, Symbolism and Rural Radicalism in Nineteenth-Century France', *Journal of Peasant Studies*, vol. v, no. 2, 1978; Norman Simms, 'Ned Ludd's Mummers Play', *Folklore*, vol. lxxxix, no. 2, 1978, pp. 166–78.

24 Prim, 'Olden Popular Pastimes', pp. 333–4.

25 Ó Súilleabháin, *Irish Wake Amusements*, p. 161.

26 Ibid., pp. 171–2.

27 Connolly, *Priests and People in pre-Famine Ireland*, p. 152.

28 Ó hEochaidh and Ó Catháin, *Síscéalta ó Thír Chonaill*.

29 Richard P. Jenkins, 'Witches and Fairies: Supernatural aggression and deviance among the Irish peasantry', *Ulster Folklife*, vol. xxii, 1977, pp. 33–56.

30 Ó Cróinín (ed.), *Seanachas Amhlaoibh í Luínse*.

31 See note 27 above.

32 Jacques-Louis de Bougrenet de La Tocnaye, *A Frenchman's Walk through Ireland, 1796–7*, trans. John Stevenson (Belfast: Blackstaff Press, 1984 [originally published 1917]), pp. 105–6.

CHAPTER 5 – **The Production and Consumption of Sacred Substances in Irish Funerary Tradition**

1 Irish Folklore Commission Manuscript no. 548, pp. 22–3 collected in 1938. The collection year is included in subsequent references also and acknowledgement is hereby made to Professor Bo Almqvist of the Department of Folklore at University College Dublin, for permission to quote from the Irish Folklore Commission Manuscripts. The letters F and M and the accompanying numbers in the reference indicate the sex and age of the informants, where this information is available.

2 IFC 1399: 65. F82. 1954; IFC 435: 39. F53. 1937; IFC 107: 496. F68. 1935.

3 IFC 641: 487. F77. 1939.

4 IFC 667: 689/9.

5 IFC 107: 487. F68. 1935.

6 IFC 565: 291. F71. 1938.

7 IFC 42: 186. F20. 1929.

8 IFC 655: 591/2. M66. 1939; IFC 1191: 21. F76. 1950; IFC 1314: 206. F65. 1952.

9 IFC 655: 592. M66. 1939.

10 IFC 1191: 21. F76. 1950; IFC 1314: 206. F65. 1952.
11 IFC 289: 364. F61. 1934.
12 IFC 1314: 195. F91. 1952.
13 IFC 300: 85/6. F65. 1937.
14 IFC 300: 85/6. F65. 1937.
15 IFC 435: 37. F53. 1937.
16 IFC 548: 25. 1938; IFC 65: 190. 1931.
17 Pádraig Ó Siocfhradha (An Seabhac), 'Nósa a bhaineas le Bas agus Adhlacadh', *Béaloideas*, vol. 1, no. 1, 1927, pp. 49–53.
18 IFC 203: 98. M. 1938; IFC 203: M78. 1938.
19 IFC 782: 247. M. *c.* 1940.
20 IFC 1191: 22. F76. 1950.
21 IFC 1191: 22. F76. 1950.
22 IFC 408: 308/9. M55. 1937; IFC 548: 27. 1938; IFC 619: 410/11. M61. 1938; IFC 641: 312/13. M. 1939
23 IFC 641: 312/13. M. 1939.
24 IFC 641: 485/6. F77. 1939.
25 IFC 782: 247. M *c.* 1940.
26 IFC 641: 487. F77. 1939.
27 IFC 1191: 22. F76. 1950.
28 IFC 96: 340. F. 1928.
29 IFC 846: 18. M76. 1942.
30 IFC 107: 493. F68. 1935.
31 IFC 619: M62. 1938.
32 IFC 655: 601. M66. 1939.
33 Jörg Biel, 'Treasure from a Celtic Tomb', *National Geographic Magazine*, no. 157.3, March 1980, pp. 429–38.
34 Ó Súilleabháin, *Irish Wake Amusements*.
35 IFC 1101: 206. 1948.
36 IFC 1399: 645. F82. 1955.
37 IFC 1161: 382. M82. 1949.
38 IFC 1457: 2184/5. M54. 1955.
39 IFC 33: 107. M70. 1932.
40 IFC 435: 391. F53. 1937.
41 IFC 1364: 262. M. 1954.
42 IFC 434: 31. M84. 1937.
43 IFC 196: 113/14. M. *c.* 1935.
44 IFC 1457: 6. M80. 1856.
45 IFC 203: 97. M. 1935.
46 IFC 7: 212. 1932.
47 IFC 408: 70. M90. 1937.
48 IFC 846: 13/14. M76. 1942.
49 IFC 323: 12. M. *c.* 1937.
50 Ó Siochfhrada (1926), p. 50.
51 IFC 1457: 185/6. M54. 1955.
52 IFC 1399: 39/40. M84. 1954.
53 IFC 1399: 645. F82. 1955.
54 IFC 488: F68. 1935.
55 IFC 408: 72/3. M90. 1937.

56 IFC 688: 419. M. 1938.
57 IFC 408: 71. M90. 1937.
58 IFC 1052: 360/1. M. *c.* 1945.
59 IFC 1314: 136. F91. 1952.

PART 2: **Introduction**

1 Hans-Jorg Uther, *The Types of International Folktales: A classification and bibliography*, 3 vols (Helsinki: Folklore Fellows Communications, 2004); Stith Thompson, *Motif-Index of Folk Literature*, 6 vols (Bloomington: Indiana University Press, 1955–8).

2 Vladimir Propp, *The Morphology of the Folktale*, English translation, 2nd edn (Austin: University of Texas Press, 1968); Claude Lévi-Strauss, 'The Structural Study of Myth', in *Structural Anthropology* (New York: Basic Books, 1963); Claude Lévi-Strauss, 'The Story of Asdival', in Edmond Leach, *The Structural Study of Myth of Totemism* (London: Tavistock, 1967).

3 Marie-Louise von Franz, *An Introduction to the Interpretation of Fairytales* (New York: Analytic Psychology Club of New York, 1970); Max Luthi, *The European Folktale: Form and nature*, English translation (Philadelphia: Institute for the Study of Human Issues, 1982).

4 Ruth Finnegan, *Oral Literature in Africa* (Oxford: Clarendon Press, 1970); Jack Zipes, *Breaking the Magic Spell: Radical theories of folk and fairy tales* (Austin: University of Texas Press, 1979).

5 Dell Hymes, *In Vain I Tried To Tell You: Essays in Native American ethnopoetics* (Philadelphia: University of Pennsylvania Press, 1981); Roger Bauman and Joel Sherzer, *Explorations in the Ethnography of Speaking*, 2nd edn (London: Cambridge University Press, 1989).

6 Roman Jakobson, 'Closing Statement: Linguistics and poetics', in Thomas Sebeok, *Style in Language* (Cambridge, MA: MIT Press, 1960); Roger Bauman, *Verbal Art as Performance* (Rowley, MA: Newbury House Publishers, 1977).

7 Dell Hymes, *Language in Education* (Washington, DC: Centre for Applied Linguistics, 1980).

CHAPTER 6 – **The Concept of Discourse in Relation to Narrative Literary Tradition**

1 Ruth Finnegan, *Oral Traditions and the Verbal Arts* (London: Routledge, 1992), p. 14.

2 J.E. Caerwyn Williams and Máirín Ní Mhuiríos, *Traidisiún Liteartha na nGael* (Baile Átha Cliath: An Clochamhar, 1979), p. 244.

3 C. Ó Huallacháin, OFM, *Foclóir Fealsamh* (Baile Átha Cliath: An Gúm, 1958), p. 25.

4 Finnegan, *Oral Tradition.* p. 15.

5 Lamont Lindstrom, 'Discourse', in A. Barnard and J. Spenser (eds), *Encyclopedia of Social and Cultural Anthropology* (London: Routledge, 1996), p. 162.

6 N. Rapport and J. Overing (eds), *Social and Cultural Anthropology: The key concepts* (London: Routledge, 2000), p. 117.

7 Dell Hymes, 'Towards Ethnographies of Communication: The analysis of communicative events', in Paulo Giglioli (ed.), *Language and Social Context* (Baltimore and Middlesex: Penguin, 1973); Dell Hymes, 'An Ethnographic Perspective on "What is Literature"', *New Literary History*, vol. v, no. 1 (Maryland: Johns Hopkins University Press, 1973), pp. 431–57.

8 Tomás Ó Criomhthainn (ed. Seán Ó Coileáin), *An tOileánach* (Baile Átha Cliath: Cló Talbóid, 2002), p. 133.

9 Henry Glassie, *Passing the Time: Culture and History of an Ulster community* (Dublin: O'Brien Press, 1982), pp. 36–7.

10 J.H. Delargy, 'The Gaelic Storyteller: With some notes on Gaelic folktales', *Proceedings of the British Academy*, vol. 31, 1945, pp. 177–221.

11 Michelle O'Riordan, *Irish Bardic Poetry and Rhetorical Reality* (Cork: Cork University Press, 2007).

12 Walter Ong, *Orality and Literacy: The technologizing of the world* (London: Psychology Press, 1982), p. 8.

13 Terry Eagleton, *How to Read a Poem* (Oxford: John Wiley & Sons, 2006).

14 Alan Dundes, 'Texture, Text and Context', *Southern Folklore Quarterly*, vol. 28, 1964, pp. 251–65.

15 A.A. Aarne and S. Thompson, *The Types of the Folk-Tale: A classification and bibliography*, 2nd revision (Helsinki: Academia Scientarum Fennica, 1961).

16 Ó Duilearga (ed.), *Leabhar Sheáin Í Chonaill*, pp. 94–100.

17 Séamus Ó Duilearga, *Seán Ó Conaill's Book*, trans. Máire MacNéill (Baile Átha Cliath/ Dublin: An Cumann le Béaloideas Éireann, 1981).

18 Kenneth Jackson (ed.), *Scéalta ón mBlascaod* (Baile Áth Cliath: An Cumann le Béaloideas Éireann, 1938), p. 43.

19 Ó Duilearga (ed.), *Leabhar Sheáin Í Chonaill*, pp. 100–20.

20 Dúbhghlás de hÍde, *An Sgéulaidhe Gaedhealach* (Baile Átha Cliath: An Cumann le Béaloideas Éireann, 1933), pp. 227–36.

21 Seán Ó Súilleabháin and R. Th. Christiansen, *The Types of the Irish Folktale* (Helsinki: Suomalinan Tiedakatemia Academia Scientiarum Fennica, 1963).

22 J.O. Swahn, *The Tale of Cupid and Psyche* (Lund: CWK Gleerup, 1955).

23 Daniel Corkery, *The Hidden Ireland* (Dublin: Gill & Son, 1925).

24 Ó Duilearga, *Seán Ó Conaill's Book*, pp. 101–2.

25 L.P. Ó Murchú (eag.), *Cúirt an Mheon-Oíche* (Baile Átha Cliath: An Clóchomhar, 1982).

26 P. Ua Duinnín, *Amhráin Eoghain Uí Shúilleabháin: Maille le beathaidh an fhilidh agus foclóir* (Baile Átha Cliath: Conradh na Gaeilge, 1901).

27 Ó Duilearga (ed.), *Leabhar Sheáin Í Chonaill*.

28 S.D. O'Grady, *Silva Gadelica* (London: Williams & Norgate, 1892).

29 Láimhbheartach MacCionnaith, SJ (ed.), *Dioghluim Dána* (Baile Átha Cliath: Oifig an tSoláthair, 1938).

30 Bláthnaid Uí Chatháin, *Éigse Chairbre* (Baile Átha Cliath: An Clóchomhar, 2006).

31 Donncha Ó Cróinín (ed.), *Scéalaíocht Amhlaoibh Í Luínse* (Baile Átha Cliath: Comhairle Bhealoideas Éireann, 1938).

32 Bourke, *The Burning of Bridget Cleary*, pp. 24–38; Angela Bourke and Patricia Lysagh (eds), 'Legends of the Supernatural', in Bourke et al. (eds), *The Field Day Anthology of Irish Writing*, vol. IV, pp. 1284–1311.

33 Ó Crualaoich, *The Book of the Cailleach*, pp. 81–99.

34 Seamus Heaney, *The Midnight Verdict* (Oldcastle, Co. Meath: Gallery Press, 1993).

CHAPTER 7 – **Irish Storytelling in Heritage Context**

1 Sources:
   Alan Bruford and Donald A. MacDonald, *Scottish Traditional Tales* (Edinburgh: Birlinn, 1994).
   Kevin Danaher, *Folktales of the Irish Countryside* (Cork: Mercier Press, 1967).
   Kevin Danaher, *The Year in Ireland* (Cork: Mercier Press, 1972).

Kevin Danaher, *A Bibliography of Irish Ethnography and Folk Tradition* (Cork: Mercier Press, 1972).

J.H. Delargy, 'The Gaelic Storyteller', *Proceedings of the British Academy*, vol. 31, pp. 3–47.

Finnegan, *Oral Traditions and the Verbal Arts*.

Alan Gailey (ed.), *The Use of Tradition* (Cultra: Ulster Folk and Transport Museum, 1988).

Glassie, *Passing the Time* (1982).

Henry Glassie, *Irish Folktales* (Harmondsworth: Penguin, 1985).

Ulf Hannerz, *Cultural Complexity: Studies in the social organization of meaning* (New York: Columbia University Press, 1992).

C.B. Harvey, *Contemporary Irish Traditional Narrative* (Berkeley: University of California Press, 1992).

Lauri Honko, 'The Folklore Process', in *Folklore Fellows Summer School Programme* (Turku: FFSS, 1991), pp. 25–47.

David Lowenthal, *The Past is a Foreign Country* (Cambridge: Cambridge University Press, 1985).

David Lowenthal, *The Heritage Crusade and the Spoils of History* (London: Cambridge University Press, 1997).

Gearóid Ó Crualaoich, 'The Merry Wake', in James S. Donnelly and Kerby A. Miller (eds), *Irish Popular Culture 1650–1850* (Dublin: Irish Academic Press, 1998), pp. 173–200.

Ó Duilearga, *Seán Ó Conaill's Book*.

Diarmuid Ó Giolláin, 'The Pattern', in Donnelly and Miller (eds), *Irish Popular Culture*.

Seán Ó Súilleabháin, *Irish Folk Custom and Belief* (Dublin: The Three Candles, 1967).

Seán Ó Súilleabháin, *Storytelling in Irish Tradition* (Cork: Mercier Press, 1973).

Seán O'Sullivan, *Folktales from Ireland* (Chicago: University of Chicago Press, 1966).

Ó Súilleabháin, *Irish Wake Amusements*.

Seán O'Sullivan, *Legends from Ireland* (London: B.T. Batsford, 1977).

Patrick Ryan, *Storytelling in Ireland: A re-awakening* (Londonderry: The Verbal Arts Centre, 1995).

Verling, *Gort Broc*.

CHAPTER 8 – Orality and Modern Irish Culture

1 E.O. Lorimer, *Tales from the Arabian Nights*, illus. Guy Nicoll (London: Oxford University Press, 1946).

2 Kenneth Goldstein, *A Guide for Fieldworkers in Folklore* (Hatboro, PA: Folklore Associates, 1974).

3 Ong, *Orality and Literacy*.

4 Jackson (ed.), *Scéalta ón mBlascaod*, pp. 79–81.

5 See chapters 15 and 16.

CHAPTER 9 – Otherworld Harmonies and Heroic Utterance: The fruits of the literary act amongst us

1 This is an unvarnished translation of a talk given on 1 February 1992 at Lisdoonvarna, County Clare to the Cumann Merriman Winter School. The character of the piece as oral performance is all too evident in the infelicities of style and structure that many readers will discern. A version of the talk was published in *Comhar*, no. 51, May/Bealtaine 1992, pp. 94–9.

2 Seán Ó Tuama, *Nuabhéarsaíocht 1939–1949* (Baile Átha Cliath: Sáirséal & Dill, 1950).

3 Tomás de Bhaldraithe, *Nuascéalaíocht 1940–1950* (Baile Átha Cliath: Sáirséal & Dill, 1952).

4 Séamus Deane (ed.), *Field Day Anthology of Irish Writing*, vols I–III (London: Field Day Publications, 1991); Bourke et al. (eds), *Field Day Anthology of Irish Writing*, vols IV–V (Cork: Cork University Press, 2002).

5 Ó Criomhthainn (ed. Seán Ó Coileáin), *An tOileánach*, p. 133.

6 Henry Glassie, *Passing the Time in Ballymenone: Culture and History of an Ulster Community* (Bloomington: Indiana University Press, 1995).

7 Glassie, *Irish Folktales*.

8 Ó Duilearga (ed.), *Leabhar Sheáin Í Chonaill*.

CHAPTER 10 – *An Bhean Mhíreáireach*: An ethnopoetic analysis of a folklore text

1 Nigel Fabb, *Linguistics and Literature* (Oxford: Blackwell, 1997), pp. 208–12.

2 Katharine Briggs, *Dictionary of British Folktales in the English Language* (London: Routledge, 1970), p. 137.

3 Ó Duilearga (ed.), *Leabhar Sheáin Í Chonaill*, pp. 153–6.

4 Propp, *Morphology of the Folktale*.

5 Jakobson, 'Closing Statement', pp. 350–77.

6 Dennis Tedlock, *The Spoken Word and the Work of Interpretation* (Philadelphia: University of Pennsylvania Press, 1983); 'Ethnopoetics' in Richard Bauman (ed.), *Folklore, Cultural Performances and Popular Entertainments* (New York/Oxford, 1992), pp. 81–5.

7 Hymes, *'In Vain I Tried to Tell You'*; Dell Hymes, *Now I Know Only So Far: Essays in ethnopoetics* (Lincoln: University of Nebraska Press, 2003).

8 Glassie, *Passing the Time* (1982), pp. 732–3.

9 Ray Cashman, *Storytelling on the Northern Irish Border: Characters and community* (Bloomington: Indiana University Press, 2008); Cashman, *Packy Jim*.

10 Jonathan Galassi, 'Updike's Violin', *New York Review of Books*, vol. lxii, no. 20, 2015.

11 Ibid., p. 209.

12 Stanley van der Ziel, *John McGahern and the Imagination of Tradition* (Cork: Cork University Press, 2016), p. 7.

13 Séamus Ó Duilearga, 'An Bhean Mhíreáireach', in *Leabhar Sheáin Í Chonaill*, pp. 153–6.

14 Donncha Ó Cróinín, 'Mar do Míníog Dro-Bhean', in *Scéalaíocht Amhlaoibh Í Luínse*, pp. 179–83.

15 Kenneth Jackson, 'An Cailín Ceann-Dáine', in Jackson (ed.), *Scéalta ón mBlascaod*, pp. 23–5.

16 Ó Duilearga, *Seán Ó Conaill's Book*, p. i. All translations are from this publication unless otherwise stated.

17 Ibid., p. ix.

18 Ibid.

19 Ó Duilearga (ed.), *Leabhar Sheáin Í Chonaill*, pp. 153–6.

20 Jakobson, 'Closing Statement', pp. 357–9.

21 Author's translation. Ni Néill translates *Cad ab áil leat díom?* as 'What do you want of me?'

22 Author's translation. Ni Néill translates *Bailig chút é sin* as 'Gather up to yourself'.

CHAPTER 11 – Language Teaching, Sociolinguistics and the Irish Folklore Text

1 Peter B. Hammond, *An Introduction to Social and Cultural Anthropology* (London: Collier Macmillan, 1978), pp. 412–13.

2 Glassie, *Passing the Time* (1982), p. 489.

3 Ó Cróinín (ed.), *Scéalaíocht Amhlaoibh Ó Luínse*, p. xvi.

4 Ibid., p. xxi.

5 G.L. Permyakov, *From Proverb to Folktale: Notes on the general theory of cliché* (Moscow: USSR Academy of Sciences, 1979), p. 8.

6 Kallen's own work on the structural study of the riddle is, in itself, a step in this direction. Jeffrey L. Kallen, 'Linguistics and Oral Tradition: The structural study of the riddle', *Occasional paper 2* (Dublin: Centre for Language and Communication Studies, 1981).

7 Dell Hymes, 'The Contribution of Folklore to Sociolinguistic Research', *Journal of American Folklore*, vol. 84, 1971, p. 42.

PART 3: **Introduction**

1 Lotte Motz, *The Faces of the Goddess* (Oxford: Oxford University Press, 1997), quoted in Ó Crualaoich, *The Book of the Cailleach*, p. 26.

2 John Carey, 'The Baptism of the Gods', in John Carey, *A Single Ray of the Sun: Religious speculation in early Ireland* (Andover and Aberystwyth: Celtic Studies Publications, 1999), pp. 1–38; John Carey, 'The Old Gods of Ireland', in Katja Ritari and Alexandra Bergholm (eds), *Understanding Celtic Religion: Revisiting the pagan past* (Cardiff: University of Wales Press, 2015), pp. 51–68.

3 Joseph F. Nagy, 'Staging the Otherworld in Medieval Irish Tradition', in Ritari and Bergholm (eds), *Understanding Celtic Religion*, pp. 69–82.

4 Máire Herbert, 'Goddess and King: The sacred marriage in early Ireland', in L.O. Fradenburg (ed.), *Women and Sovereignty* (Edinburgh: Edinburgh University Press, 1992), pp. 264–75.

CHAPTER 12 – *Cailleach agus Céile*: **The Gaelic personification of sovereignty in nature and culture**

1 Máirín Ní Dhonnchadha, 'Cailleach and other Terms for Veiled Women in Medieval Irish Texts', *Éigse*, vol. 28, 1994, pp. 71–96.

2 In the *Leabhar na hUidhre* text of *Táin Bó Cuailnge* at line 6248 of the manuscript. Vide *caillech(c)* in E.G. Quinn (ed.), *Contrib. To a Dict of the Irish Language: C Fasciculus I*, arranged by P. Ní Chatháin et al. (Dublin: Royal Irish Academy, 1968).

3 Paper read at initial conference of the Anthropology Association of Ireland, Dublin, 16 May 1987. See also Simon Harrison, 'Magical Exchange of the Preconditions of Production in a Sepik River Village', *MAN*, vol. 23, no. 2, 1988.

4 Gearóid Ó Crualaoich, 'Continuity and Adaptation in Legends of *Cailleach Bhéarra*', *Béaloideas*, vol. 56, 1988.

5 Donncha Ó Cróinín, 'Bean ón Saol Eile', in *Seanchas Amhlaoibh Í Luínse*, pp. 180–2.

6 Joseph Nagy, *The Wisdom of the Outlaw* (Berkley/London: University of California Press, 1985), chapters 1 and 2.

7 John Carey, 'Notes on the Irish War-Goddess', *Éigse*, vol. 19, 1983, pp. 263–75.

8 Vide the section on 'Cernunnos', in Proinsias Mac Cana, *Celtic Mythology* (Feltham: Newnes Books, 1983), pp. 39–42.

9 Bhreathnach, 'The Sovereignty Goddess as Goddess of Death?'.

10 de hÍde, *An Sgéulaidhe Gaedhealach*: No. 18, 'Cailleach Ghleann-na-mBiorach agus an Tarbh Dubh', pp. 132–6, and No. 21, 'An Chailleach Bhéarach agus Donnchadh Mór Mac Mánuis', pp. 227–36.

11 Ó Crualaoich, 'Continuity and Adaptation'.

12 Michael J. Enright, 'King James and His Island: An archaic kingship belief?', *The Scottish Historical Review*, vol. 55, no. 159, 1976, pp. 29–40.

13 See note 6 above.

14 Christa Maria Löffler, *The Voyage to the Otherworld Island in Early Irish Literature* (Salzburg: Universität Salzburg, Institut für Anglistik und Amerikanistik, 1983).

CHAPTER 13 – The Inner-Outer Otherworld of Hyde and Yeats: Translation and worldview in the Irish literary revival

1 Roy Foster, *W.B. Yeats: A life, 1: The Apprentice Mage, 1865–1914* (Oxford: Oxford University Press, 1997), pp. 162–200.
2 Lady Augusta Gregory, *Cuchulain of Muirthemne* (London: John Murray, 1902), preface by W.B. Yeats.
3 T.F. Ó Rathile, *Búrdúin Bheaga* (Dublin: Brown & Nolan, 1925), p. 12.
4 I am grateful to my former colleague Professor Diarmuid Ó Giolláin for informing me of Professor Caomhánach's opinion.
5 Tomás Ó Cathasaigh, 'The Eponym of Cnogha', *Éigse*, vol. 23, 1989, pp. 27–38.
6 John Carey, 'Time, Space and the Otherworld', *Proceedings of the Harvard Celtic Colloquium*, vol. 7, 1987, pp. 1–27.
7 Patrick Sims-Williams, 'Some Celtic Otherworld Terms', in A.T.E. Matonis and D.F. Melia (eds), *Celtic Language, Celtic Culture: A festschrift for Eric P. Hamp* (Van Nuys: Ford & Bailie, 1990).
8 Joan Radnor, 'Poets, Harpers and Women in Early Irish Literature', in Matonis and Melia (eds), *Celtic Language, Celtic Culture*.
9 Herbert, 'Goddess and King'.
10 Breatnach, 'The Lady and the King'.
11 Made in the course of a televised interview some years ago.

CHAPTER 14 – The *Bean Sí* in the Flesh: A rethink about goddess mythology and Irish tradition

1 See Chapter 19.
2 Herbert, 'Goddess and King'.
3 Ó Crualaoich, *The Book of the Cailleach*, pp. 113–43.
4 See Chapter 16.
5 Ó Cathasaigh, 'The Eponym of Cnogba'.
6 Ó Crualaoich, *The Book of the Cailleach*, pp. 174–224.
7 Breandán Ó Madagáin, 'Gaelic Lullaby: A charm to protect the baby', *Scottish Studies*, vol. 29, 1989, pp. 29–38.
8 Schmitz, 'An Irish Wise-Woman'.
9 Ó hEochaidh and Ó Catháin, *Síscéalta ó Thír Chonaill*, texts 14 and 16, pp. 60–1, 64–5.
10 See Chapter 5, 'Sacred Substances'.
11 See Chapter 4, 'Popular Resistance'.
12 Darach Ó Catháin, 'Liam Ó Raghallaigh', Track 5 on Seán Ó Riada, *Pléarácha an Riadaigh* (Baile Átha Claith: Gael Linn, 2008).
13 Ó hEochaidh and Ó Catháin, *Síscéalta ó Thír Chonaill*, Introduction, pp. 17–28.
14 Bhreathnach, 'The Sovereignty Goddess as Goddess of Death?'.
15 Patricia Lysaght, *The Banshee: The Irish supernatural death messenger*, 2nd edn (Dublin: O'Brien Press, 1996).
16 Proinsias Mac Cana, *Celtic Mythology* (London: Hamlyn, 1970).
17 Ó Súilleabháin, *Irish Wake Amusements*, pp. 142–3.
18 Donncha Ó Cróinín (ed.), *Seanchas ó Chairbre* (Baile Átha Cliath: Comhairle Bhéaloideas Éireann, 1985), pp. 80–1, 452.

19 Gearóid Ó Crualaoich, 'The Production and Consumption of Sacred Substances in Irish Funerary Tradition', in Hannu-Pekka Huttunen and Ritta Latvio (eds), *Entering the Arena: Presenting Celtic studies in Finland* (*Etiainen* series, no. 2) (Turku: Finnish Society for Celtic Studies, 1993), p. 49.

20 Angela Partridge (Bourke), *Caoineadh na dTrí Muire: Caoineadh na Páise i bhfilíocht bhéil na Gaeilge* (Baile Átha Cliath: An Clóchamahar, 2000), pp. 88–98.

21 Angela Bourke et al. (eds), 'Lamenting the Dead', *The Field Day Anthology of Irish Writing*, vol. IV (Cork: Cork University Press, 2002), pp. 1365–98.

22 Alwyn Rees and Brinley Rees, *Celtic Heritage: Ancient tradition in Ireland and Wales* (London: Thames & Hudson, 1961), p. 91.

23 Elizabeth Gray, 'Cath Maige Tuired: Myth and structure', Structure (1–24), *Éigse*, vol. 19, 1983, pp. 230–62.

24 Ó Cróinín (ed.), *Seanchas ó Chairbre*, p. 453.

25 Gearóid Ó Crualaoich, 'County Cork Folklore and Its Collection', in Patrick O'Flanagan and Cornelius Buttimer (eds), *Cork History & Society* (Cork: Geography Publications, 1993), p. 934; IFC, MS 550, pp. 4–6, 9–11.

CHAPTER 15 – **Continuity and Adaptation in Legends of *Cailleach Bhéarra***

1   P. Mac Cana, *Celtic Mythology* (Middlesex: Hamlyn, 1970), pp. 92–3.

2   J.G. Mackay, *More West Highland Tales*, vols I–II (Edinburgh: Oliver & Boyd, 1940), vol. I, p. xvii.

3   H. Wagner, 'Origins of Pagan Irish Religion', *Zeitschrift für celtische Philologie*, vol. 38, 1981, pp. 1–28.

4   A. Ross, *Pagan Celtic Britain* (London: Routledge, 1967); V. Newall (ed.), 'The Divine Hag of the Pagan Celts', in *The Witch Figure* (London: Routledge, 1973), pp. 139–64.

5   Eleanor Hull, 'Legends and Traditions of the *Cailleach Bhéarra* or Old Woman (Hag) of Beara', *Folklore*, vol. 38, 1927, pp. 225–54.

6   A.H. Krappe, 'La Cailleach Bhéara: Notes de mythologie gaelique', *Études Celtiques*, vol. 1, 1936, pp. 292–302.

7   Ibid., p. 302.

8   de hÍde, *An Sgéulaidhe Gaedhealach*, pp. 227–36.

9   Th. H. Gaster, *The New Golden Bough* (New York: Criterion, 1959), pp. 499–500.

10 G. Murphy, review of J. Szöverffy, *Irisches Erzählgut im Abendland*, *Éigse*, vol. 9, 1961, pp. 133–4.

11 J. Filip, *Celtic Civilisation and Its Heritage* (Wellingborough and Prague: Colet's Academia, 1977), pp. 172–9.

12 Tomás Ó Cathasaigh, *The Heroic Biography of Cormac Mac Airt* (Dublin: Institute of Advanced Studies, 1977).

13 Máire MacNeill, *The Festival of Lughnasa* (Oxford: Oxford University Press, 1962), pp. 412–13.

14 Gearóid Ó Crualaoich, 'The Vision of Liberation in *Cúirt an Mheán Oíche*', in P. de Brún, S. Ó Coileáin and P. Ó Riain (eds), *Folia Gadelica* (Cork: Cork University Press, 1983), pp. 95–104.

15 K. Myer, 'Stories and Songs from Irish MSS.', *Otia Merseiana*, vol. 1, 1899, pp. 119–28.

16 G. Murphy, 'The Lament of the Old Woman of Beare', *Proceedings of the Royal Irish Academy*, vol. 55, 1953, p. 84.

17 Ibid.

18 Ibid., pp. 84–5.

19 Ibid.

20 P. Friedrich, *The Meaning of Aphrodite* (Chicago: University of Chicago Press, 1978).
21 G. Broderick, 'Berrey Dhone: A Manx *Caillech Bérri?*', *Zeitschrift für celtische Philologie*, vol. 40, 1984, pp. 193–210.
22 Jackson (ed.), *Scéalta ón mBlascaod*, pp. 79–81.
23 Ibid., p. 213
24 Murphy, 'The Lament of the Old Woman of Beare'.
25 Ó Duilearga (ed.), *Leabhar Sheáin Í Chonaill*, pp. 144–6, 421–2, 469.
26 J. Strange (ed.), *Caesarius of Heisterbach: Dialogus Miraculorum* (Coblenz, 1850), dist. xii, cap. 20, trans. H. Von E. Scott and C.C.S. Bland, *The Dialogue on Miracles: Caesarius of Heisterbach (1220–1235)*, vols I–II (London, 1929).
27 J. Gantz, *Early Irish Myths and Sagas* (Harmondsworth: Penguin, 1981), p. 23.
28 R.I. Black, 'The Gaelic Calendar Months: Some meanings and derivations', *Shadow*, vol. 2, 1985, pp. 3–13.
29 de hÍde, *An Sgéulaidhe Gaedhealach*.
30 T. Jones-Hughes, 'The Large Farm in Nineteenth-Century Ireland', in A. Gailey et al. (eds), *Gold Under the Furze* (Dublin: The Glendale Press, 1982).
31 Breatnach, 'The Lady and the King'.

CHAPTER 16 – Non-Sovereignty Queen Aspects of the Otherworld Female in Irish Hag Legends: The case of *Cailleach Bhéarra*

1 Hilda R. Ellis Davidson, *Myths and Symbols in Pagan Europe* (Manchester: Manchester University Press, 1988), pp. 86–7; Anne Ross, *The Pagan Celts* (London: B.T. Batsford, 1986), pp. 128–30.
2 Carey, 'Notes on the Irish War-Goddess'; Bhreathnach, 'The Sovereignty Goddess as Goddess of Death?'; Marie Louise Sjoestedt, *Gods and Heroes of the Celts*, translated by M. Dillon (London: Methuen, 1949).
3 R. Th. Christiansen, *Studies in Irish and Scandinavian Folktales* (Copenhagen: Rosenkilde & Bagger, 1959), p. 4.
4 Ibid., pp. 230–1.
5 Ó Crualaoich, 'Continuity and Adaptation'.
6 Ó Cathasaigh, 'The Eponym of Cnogba'.
7 Delargy, 'The Gaelic Storyteller'.
8 Breatnach, 'The Lady and the King'.
9 See the story 'An Chailleach Bhéarach agus Donnchadh Mór Mac Mánais', in de hÍde, *An Sgéulaidhe Gaedhealach*, pp. 227–36.
10 See the story 'Cailleach Ghleanna-na-mBiorach agus an Tarbh Dubh', in de hÍde, *An Sgéulaidhe Gaedhealach*, pp. 132–6; J.G. McKay, 'The Deer Cult and the Deer-Goddess Cult of the Ancient Caledonians', *Folklore*, vol. 43, 1932, pp. 144–74.
11 Manuscripts in the Department of Irish Folklore (IFC), University College Dublin; IFC 17: 12–15; IFC 74: 22–4; IFC 227: 89–91; IFC 321: 426; IFC 321: 531–3.
12 IFC 662: 97; IFC 662: 104–5; IFC 788: 130–1; IFC 1242: 563–4; IFC 1797: 324.
13 School of Scottish Studies archive, University of Edinburgh, SA 1971/23/A2 June.
14 Emily Lyle, *Archaic Cosmos* (Edinburgh: Edinburgh University Press, 1991), pp. 6–25, 86–91.
15 IFC 1242: 564.
16 Lévi-Strauss, 'The Structural Study of Myth', pp. 215–16.
17 E. Leach, *Lévi-Strauss* (London: Fontana, 1974), p. 64.
18 T. Ó Broin, 'Lia Fáil: Fact and fiction in the tradition', *Celtica*, vol. 21, 1990, pp. 393–401.

19 P.S. Dinneen, *An Irish–English Dictionary* (Dublin: Educational Company of Ireland, 1927), p. 1067; M. Maclennan, *Gaelic Dictionary* (Edinburgh: John Grant, 1925), p. 306.

20 Neasa Ní Shéaghdha (ed.), *Agallamh na Seanórach*, vols I–III (Baile Átha Cliath: Oifig an tSoláthair, 1942–5); O'Grady, *Silva Gadelica*, p. 110.

21 SA 1968/21/B9a Tiree.

22 See IFC 1230: 240–2.

23 IFC 85: 347.

24 IFC 74: 261.

25 IFC 63: 283.

26 IFC 159: 473–8; IFC 1230: 240–51.

27 R.A.S. Macalister (ed.), *Lebar Gabála Érenn*, vols 1–4 (Dublin: Irish Texts Society, 1938–41).

28 National Library of Scotland, Royal Celtic Society MSS., AM 35.8 Mull.

29 See IFC 17: 31–4; IFC 217: 453–4.

30 IFC 74: 14.

31 P. Mac Cana, 'Placenames and Mythology in Irish Tradition: Places, pilgrimages and things', *Proceedings of the First North American Congress of Celtic Studies*, University of Ottawa, 1986, pp. 319–41.

32 G. Ó Crualaoich, 'Contest in the Cosmology and the Ritual of the Irish Merry Wake', *Cosmos*, vol. 6, 1990, pp. 145–60.

33 Some discussion of the persona and legends of the County Clare *bean feasa* ('wise woman') Biddy Early may be found in Schmitz, 'An Irish Wise-Woman' and in E. Lenihan, *In Search of Biddy Early* (Cork: Mercier Press, 1987).

PART 4: **Introduction**

1 Guy Beiner, *Remembering the Year of the French: Irish folk history and social history* (Madison: University of Wisconsin Press, 2006); Guy Beiner, 'Locating Local Tradition: The sociocultural construction of Irish folk memory', in Diarmuid Ó Giolláin (ed.), *Irish Ethnologies* (Notre Dame, IN: University of Notre Dame Press, 2017), pp. 158–77.

2 Vincent Morley, *The Popular Mind in Eighteenth-Century Ireland* (Cork: Cork University Press, 2017).

3 Richard Kearney, 'Myth and Motherland', in Field Day Theatre Company, *Ireland's Field Day* (London: Hutchinson, 1985), pp. 61–82.

4 Cliona O'Carroll, 'Public Folklore Operating between Aspiration and Expediency', *Irish Journal of Anthropology*, vol. 16, no. 1, 2013, pp. 23–9.

5 Marie-Annick Desplanques, 'Reflections on the Poetics of Fieldwork in a Living Archive', *Béascna*, vol. 9, 2015, pp. 20–43.

6 Gearóid Ó Crualaoich, 'President's Research Fund Application Document', unpublished document, University College Cork. See passage quoted in Desplanques, note 5, above.

CHAPTER 17 – **The Hidden Ireland: Myth and reality**

1 Daniel Corkery, *The Hidden Ireland* (Dublin: Gill & Macmillan, 1924 [1967]).

2 Ibid., p. 16.

3 Louis Cullen, 'The Hidden Ireland: Re-assessment of a concept', *Studia Hibernica*, vol. 9, pp. 7–47.

4 Seán Ó Tuama, 'Dónall Ó Corcora', *Scríobh*, vol. 4, 1979, pp. 94–108.

5 Jerome Blum, *The End of the Old Order in Europe* (New Jersey: Princeton University Press, 1978).

6 See for example Chapter 2 of Louis Cullen, *The Emergence of Modern Ireland: 1600–1900* (London: Batsford, 1981).

7 Gerard Murphy, 'The Gaelic Background', in Michael Tierney (ed.), *Daniel O'Connell: Nine centenary essays* (Dublin: Browne & Nolan, 1949).

8 Brian Manning, 'The English Revolution and Ireland, 1640–60', *Retrospect*, new series, no. 2, 1982, pp. 7–16.

9 Ibid., p. 11.

10 See my own piece on this aspect of Merriman's poem: Ó Crualaoich, 'The Vision of Liberation in *Cúirt an Mheán Oíche*'.

11 Cullen, *The Emergence of Modern Ireland*, pp. 32–3.

12 Victor Edward Durkacz, *The Decline of the Celic Languages* (Edinburgh: John Donald, 1983).

13 McPhee, 'Popular Culture, Symbolism and Rural Radicalism'.

14 Breandán Ó Buachalla, 'An Mheisiasacht agus an Aisling', in de Brún et al. (eds), *Folia Gadelica*, pp. 72–87; Breandán Ó Buachalla, *Aisling Ghéar: Na Stiobhartaigh agus an taos léinn, 1603–1788* (Dublin: An Clochomhar Tta, 1996).

15 Dáithí Ó hÓgáin, 'An É an tAm Fós E?', *Béaloideas*, vols 42–4, 1974–6, pp. 213–308.

16 Quoted in Seán Ó Coileáin, 'Some Problems of Story and History', *Ériu*, vol. xxxii, 1981, pp. 115–36.

CHAPTER 18 – **History or Folklore: *Cé acu an cuntas cam?***

1 Ó Duilearga, *Leabhar Sheán Í Chonaill*.

2 John's Gospel, Vl. 12.

3 Stith Thompson (ed.), *Four Symposia on Folklore* (Bloomington: Indiana University Press, 1953).

4 Jan Vansina, *Oral Tradition: A study in historical methodology* (London: Routledge, 1965); Jan Vansina, *Oral Tradition as History* (London: Heinemann, 1985).

5 David Henige, *Oral Historiography* (Harlow: Longman, 1982).

6 Elizabeth Tonkin, *Narrating on Pasts: The social construction of oral history* (Cambridge: Cambridge University Press, 1991).

7 J.J. Gumperz and Dell Hymes (eds), *Direction in Sociolinguistics: The ethnography of communication* (New York: Holt, Rinehart & Winston, 1972).

8 Dáithí Ó hÓgáin, *The Hero in Irish Folk History* (Dublin: Gill & Macmillan, 1985).

9 Henry Glassie, 'Folklore and History', in Gailey (ed.), *The Use of Tradition*, pp. 68–72.

10 Ibid.

11 Elizabeth Tonkin, 'History and the Myth of Realism', in R. Samuel and P.R. Thompson (eds), *The Myth We Live By* (London and New York: Routledge, 1990), pp. 25–35.

12 Ibid.

13 Ibid.

14 Jackson (ed.), *Scéalta ón mBlascaod*, pp. 79–81.

15 Ríonach Uí Ógáin, *An Rí gan Choróin: Dónal Ó Conaill sa bhéaloideas* (Baile Átha Cliath: An Clochomhar, 1984); Ríonach Uí Ógáin, *Immortal Dan: Daniel O'Connell in Irish folk tradition* (Dublin: Geography Publications, 1995).

16 Roger McHugh, 'The Famine in Irish Oral Tradition', in R.D. Edwards and T.D. Williams (eds), *The Great Famine: Studies in Irish history 1845–52* (Dublin: Lilliput Press, 1994 [reprint]), pp. 391–436.

17 Cormac Ó Gráda, *An Drochshaol: Béaloideas agus amhráin* (Baile Átha Cliath: Coiscéim, 1994).

18 Cathal Poirtéir, *Glórtha ón nGorta: Béaloideas na Gaeilge agus an Gorta Mór* (Baile Átha Cliath: Coiscéim, 1996); Cathal Poirtéir, 'The Folklore of the Famine: *Seanchas an drochshaoil'*, in John Crowley, W.J. Smyth and Mike Murphy (eds), *Atlas of the Great Irish Famine 1845–52* (Cork: Cork University Press, 2012), pp. 602–13.

19 Hannerz, *Cultural Complexity*.

20 Paul Bohannan, *How Culture Works* (New York: The Free Press, 1995).

CHAPTER 19 – The Vision of Liberation in *Cúirt an Mheán Oíche*

1 Seán Ó Tuama, 'Cúirt an Mheán Oíche', *Studia Hibernica*, vol. 4, 1964, pp. 7–27.

2 Seán Ó Tuama, 'Brian Merriman and His Court', *Irish Times*, 23 August 1980.

3 Daniel Corkery, *The Hidden Ireland* (Dublin: Gill & Son, 1925), pp. 237–56.

4 See review of R. Ó Fodhludha's edition of the poem in *Gadelica*, vol. 1, 1912–13, pp. 190–204.

5 Frank O'Connor, *Leinster, Munster and Connaught* (London: Robert Hale, n.d.), pp. 219–33.

6 R. Ó Fodhludha (ed.), *Cúirt an Mheádhon Oídhche* (Baile Átha Cliath: Hodges Figgis, 1912).

7 Gerard Murphy, 'Notes on Aisling Poetry', *Éigse*, vol. 1, 1939, pp. 40–50.

8 H.R. McAdoo, 'Notes on the "Midnight Court" (Merryman)', ibid., pp. 167–72.

9 Ó Tuama, 'Brian Merriman and His Court'.

10 Corkery, *The Hidden Ireland*.

11 O'Connor, *Leinster, Munster and Connaught*.

12 D. Ó hUaithne (ed.), *Cúirt an Mheán Oíche* (Baile Átha Cliath: Dolmen Press, 1968), lines 287–306.

13 'Párliment na mBan', *Celtica*, vol. 7, 1996, pp. 135–41.

14 See P. Mac Cana, *Celtic Mythology* (London: Hamlyn, 1970), pp. 85–96.

15 See ibid., p. 117.

16 Corkery, *The Hidden Ireland*, p. 133.

17 Breatnach, 'The Lady and the King'. Another publication of Professor Breatnach's relating directly to Merriman's poem is 'Ad "Cúirt and Mheadhoin Oidhche" ll. 598–8', *Éigse*, vol. 8, no. 2, 1956, pp. 140–3.

18 Blum, *The End of the Old Order in Europe*, Introduction.

19 Ibid.

20 Corkery, *The Hidden Ireland*, p. 104.

21 See K.H. Connell, 'The Population of Ireland in the Eighteenth Century', *Economic History Review*, vol. 16, 1946, pp. 111–24; K.H. Connell, 'Land and Population in Ireland, 1780-1845', ibid., 2nd series, vol. 2, 1950, pp. 278–89; K.H. Connell, 'Peasant Marriage in Ireland: Its structure and development since the Famine', ibid., vol. 14, 1962, pp. 502–23; M. Drake, 'Marriage and Population Growth in Ireland, 1750–1845', ibid., vol. 16, 1963, pp. 301–12; J. Lee, 'Marriage and Population in Pre-Famine Ireland', ibid., vol. 21, 1968, pp. 283–95.

22 See Murphy, 'Notes on Aisling Poetry'.

23 For a recent discussion of the central importance of oral tradition in the transmission of Irish learning from the earliest times see P. Mac Cana, *The Learned Tales of Medieval Ireland* (Dublin: DIAS, 1980). The term *coimcne* would appear to be the one embracing most widely the various aspects of the tradition in question.

24 See 'Burns and English Literature', in B. Forde (ed.), *From Blake to Byron* (Pelican Guide to English Literature) (Harmondsworth: Penguin, 1957), p. 94.

25 Ibid.

CHAPTER 20 – 'The French Are on the Say'

1 O'Connor, *Leinster, Munster and Connaught*, p. 286.
2 C.J.F. MacCarthy, 'An Antiquary's Notebook 17', *Journal of Cork Historical and Archaeological Society*, vol. 101, 1996, p. 169.
3 IFC MSS., vol. 573, pp. 102–3. See note 8 below.
4 David Dickson, *Old World Colony: Cork and south Munster 1630–1830* (Cork: Cork University Press, 2005).
5 Quoted by Ó Buachalla, 'An Mheisiasacht agus an Aisling'.
6 Irish Jacobite Poetry, Thomas Davis Lecture delivered on Radio Éireann, 22 March 1992 and published in *The Irish Review*, vol. 12, spring–summer 1992, pp. 40–9 (quoted with permission of the editors of *The Irish Review*).
7 The chief female character in the Blasket legend recounts the following incident (author's own translation):

> When I was a young woman, lots of strangers used to come to our house. My father had a pleasure boat and they would often sail in her to one place or another. One fine autumn day, myself and another girl got ourselves ready to go with them. There was a young priest in the boat along with us. We had a try at sailing to the Skellig but before we made a landfall there, a terrible darkness gathered in the west. My father said it would be best to turn the boat around, but the others wouldn't be satisfied. This dark, black cloud was heading for us together with a gust of wind. The priest looked towards it. 'There is some sort of opening in that cloud,' he said. It was heading for us until it was very close to the boat. As soon as it had come alongside the boat what was [to be seen] in the cloud only a woman! The priest stood up quickly, put the stole around his neck and reached for his missal. Then he spoke and he asked her what had made an evil spirit of her.
> 'I killed someone,' she said.
> 'That is not what caused your damnation,' said the priest.
> 'I killed two people.'
> 'Not that neither,' said the priest.
> 'I killed a child that wasn't baptised in my desire to become a priest's spouse.'
> 'That is precisely what damned you,' said the priest.
> Then he began to read his missal and after a short time she rose up out of the water in a flash of matter and she left our sight.
> We didn't go to the Skellig that day. We returned home; and that's the greatest wonder that I ever saw during my life.

Taken from 'Ana Ní Áine' as published in Jackson (ed.), *Scéalta ón mBlascaod*, pp. 79–81 [published here with the permission of the head of department].
8 IFC MSS vol. 536, pp. 100–2; IFC MSS vol. 219, pp. 245–6. These extracts from the main collection of manuscripts at the Department of Irish Folklore, UCD are published here with the permission of the head of department. In the case of the West Muskerry Irish text the phonetic spelling and orthography of the original manuscript have been normalised in places.

CHAPTER 21 – Responding to the Rising

1 Raphael Samuel and Paul Thompson (eds), *The Myths We Live By* (London: Routledge, 1990).
2 F.X. Martin, '1916 [as] Myth, Fact and Mystery', *Studia Hibernica*, vol. 7, 1967, pp. 7–127.
3 Kearney, 'Myth and Motherland'.

4 Wendy Doniger O'Flaherty, *Other People's Myths* (New York: Macmillan, 1988).
5 Liam de Paor, 'Ireland's Identities', *The Crane Bag*, vol. 3, no. 1, 1979, pp. 22–9.
6 Samuel and Thompson (eds), *The Myths We Live By*.
7 De Paor, 'The Rebel Mind: Republican and loyalist', in Richard Kearney (ed.), *The Irish Mind* (Dublin: Wolfhound Press, 1985), pp. 157–87.
8 J.J. Lee, *Ireland 1912–1985: Politics and society* (Cambridge: Cambridge University Press, 1989).
9 Alan Gailey, 'The Nature of Tradition', *Folklore*, vol. 100, no. 2, 1989, pp. 143–61; Gailey (ed.), *The Use of Tradition*.
10 Eric Hobsbawm and Terence Ranger (eds), *The Invention of Tradition* (Cambridge: Cambridge University Press, 1983).
11 Elizabeth Gray, 'Cath Maige Tuired: Myth and structure', Structure (1–24), *Éigse*, vol. 18, 1981, pp. 183–209; Gray, 'Cath Maige Tuired', vol. 19, 1983, pp. 1–25.
12 Ó Cathasaigh, *The Heroic Biography of Cormac Mac Airt*; Tomás Ó Cathasaigh, 'Cath Maige Tuired as Exemplary Myth', in de Brún et al (eds), *Folia Gadelica*.

CHAPTER 22 – The Primacy of Form: A 'folk ideology' in de Valera's politics

1 Maurice Moynihan (ed.), *Speeches and Statements by Éamon de Valera 1917–1973* (Dublin: Gill & Macmillan, 1980), p. 438.
2 Mary C. Bromage, *De Valera and the March of a Nation* (London: Hutchinson, 1956), p. 266.
3 An interesting piece of evidence for de Valera's early closeness to those in Gaelic League circles who were most involved with folklore is provided by Ernest Blythe in the second volume of his memoirs (de Blaghd, 1970, pp. 8–9). Blythe met de Valera for the first time in 1914 in Dublin while he himself was in the course of a journey to County Kerry. De Valera was just then presenting himself as a candidate for a position in the Department of Mathematics at University College Cork, and asked Blythe to take with him to Kerry a letter to An Seabhac (Pádraig Ó Siocfhradha) in which de Valera sought that Ó Siocfhradha should canvass on his behalf the chairman of Kerry County Council, a member of the governing body of UCC. Ó Siocfhradha was, of course, to be president of the Folklore of Ireland Society at its inception in 1927 and for many years afterwards. It is interesting also to record Blythe's impression of Ó Siocfhradha's dubiousness that the chairman of the county council could be induced to vote for the awarding of the position in question to an Irish speaker or, in Blythe's own term, a *Gaeilgeoir*.
4 Séamus Ó Duilearga (ed.), *Béaloideas*, vol. 1, 1927, p. 5.
5 T.K. Whitaker, 'James Hamilton Delargy, 1899–1980', *Folklife*, vol. 20, 1982, pp. 101–6.
6 Oliver MacDonagh, *Ireland: The union and its aftermath* (London: George Allen & Unwin, 1977), pp. 158–60.
7 Moynihan (ed.), *Speeches and Statements*, p. 35.
8 Ó hÓgáin, 'An É an tAm Fós É?', p. 213 ff.
9 For a very full account of messianism in Irish tradition see Ó Buachalla, 'An Mheisiasacht agus an Aisling'.
10 Denis R. Gwynn, 'De Valera, Éamon', in *Encyclopaedia Britannica*, 15th edn, p. 624.
11 MacDonagh, *Ireland*, p. 113.
12 The use of the term 'folk society' in anthropology has to be distinguished from what folklore scholars might mean by the term. For anthropologists 'folk society' had come to mean 'peasant society' by the mid 1950s. Various implications and applications of the use of these terms in the social sciences are pursued in Potter et al. after a fashion that

adheres fairly closely to the basic positions of Robert Redfield and George M. Foster, *Peasant Society: A reader* (Boston: Little, Brown & Co., 1967).

13 Moynihan (ed.), *Speeches and Statements*, p. 154.

14 Ó Criomhthainn (ed. Seán Ó Coileáin), *An tOileánach.*

15 In relation to folk models it should be noted that there is, in anthropology, a more technical sense of the term than is intended in my use of it in relation to de Valera's thinking on the nature and potential of Irish rural society. In that technical sense 'folk model' means a model deriving from the native, practitioner point of view rather than the point of view of the outside observer. It is as descriptions of social reality based on the perceptions of participants that Redfield originally presented his Yucatan studies. Lévi-Strauss similarly distinguishes the 'statistical model' of the analyst of social structure from the 'mechancial model' of the participant. See Claude Lévi-Strauss, 'Social Structure', in Sol Tax (ed.), *Anthropology Today: Selections* (Chicago: University of Chicago Press, 1962), p. 325. It could perhaps be argued that the model of Irish rural society dominating Fianna Fáil planning of the political economy during the years of de Valera's ascendancy was, by virtue of falling between these two stools, necessarily a poor instrument. Tom Garvin, 'Theory, Culture and Fianna Fáil: A review', in Mary Kelly, Liam O'Dowd and James Wickham (eds), *Power, Conflict and Inequality* (Dublin: Turoe Press, 1982), p. 177, points out that parallels between Fianna Fáil ideology and the arguments of functionalist anthropologists can suggest an 'organic' relationship between society and political formations that contrasts with the 'manipulative' relationship suggested, in the case of Fianna Fáil itself, by Peter Mair, 'The Autonomy of the Political: The development of the Irish party system, *Comparative Politics*, vol. 11, 1979, pp. 445–65.

16 Kenneth Connell, *Irish Peasant Society* (Oxford: Oxford University Press, 1968).

17 Moynihan (ed.), *Speeches and Statements*, p. 232.

18 Ibid., p. 354.

19 Conrad Arensberg, *The Irish Countryman* (New York: Macmillan, 1937); Conrad Arensburg and Solon T. Kimball, *Family and Community in Ireland* (Cambridge MA: Harvard University Press, 1940).

20 While the term 'Peasants' does occur in the index to Arensburg and Kimball's work, the full entry there against it reads: 'See "Farmers"'.

21 George M. Foster, 'What is Folk Culture?', *American Anthropologist*, vol. 55, 1953, pp. 159–73; George M. Foster, 'Peasant Society and the Image of the Limited Good', *American Anthroplogist*, vol. 67, 1965, pp. 293–315; Robert Redfield, *Tepoztlán: A Mexican village. A study of folk life* (Chicago: University of Chicago Press, 1930); Robert Redfield, 'The Folk Society', *The American Journal of Sociology*, vol. 52, 1947, pp. 293–308; Robert Redfield, *Peasant Society and Culture: An anthropological approach to civilisation* (Chicago: University of Chicago Press, 1956).

22 A.L. Kroeber, *Anthropology* (New York: Harcourt, Brace & Co., 1948), p. 284.

23 Moynihan (ed.), *Speeches and Statements*, p. 1.

24 Ibid., p. 471.

25 Seán Ó Súilleabháin, 'Irish Oral Tradition', in Brian Ó Cuív (ed.), *A View of the Irish Language* (Dublin: Stationery Office, 1969), p. 56.

26 Glassie, *Passing the Time* (1982), p. 297.

27 It is, presumably, at least partly for its efficacy as reinforcement of this kind that folklore is taken as seriously as it is in most eastern bloc countries. As Vitányi makes clear, there is, in Hungary at least, much cultural policy directed towards the preservation of authentic folk art – not in museums but as a catalyst among the youth of contemporary

society who seek outlets for their own creativity. Folklore, with its content of humanism, its anonymous universality and its creativity is, in this light, to be regarded as existing in its own right as an aspect of contemporary urban culture that yields, in the view of the Hungarian establishment at least, an autonomous reinforcement for the value of collectivisation. See Ivan Vitányi, 'The Function of Folklore in Modern Society', Typescript of contribution to the UNESCO Seminar on the 'Impact of Industrially Developed Societies on Traditional Culture and Popular Arts' held at the Institute for Culture, Budapest, 11–13 December 1978.

28 The continued existence of this style of thinking about political problems is provided by very recent press reports (*Irish Times*, 27 September 1982, pp. 1–2) of a government minister having berated the leader of the opposition for allegedly withdrawing, in relation to a certain subject of current debate, from 'his solemn undertaking to support an amendment to the Constitution'. The minister is quoted as having said that this alleged withdrawal not only indicated 'a tacit acceptance to provide a legislative framework which would allow legalised abortion in certain circumstance; but *worse still* (my italics) 'it indicates that the party has no feeling for the traditional values of the Irish people and is more concerned with being *fashionable*.

29 This is true of the Irish living in Ireland. The degree to which de Valera had ever spoken for the Irish diaspora after 1922 is problematic. Whatever of the transient plausibility of the 'peasant' model at home there was surely an every-increasing gap between the de Valera/Fianna Fáil vision of a free, Catholic and Gaelic-speaking Ireland – especially as regards the nature and quality of its social relationships – and the life experience of the vast majority of the overseas Irish. For the overseas Irish it is perhaps also the case that both de Valera's penchant for playing a mythological role and their own folk proclivities were of considerably less sigificance, and there was, of course, no genetic inperviousness to class consciousness on the part of 'the Irish race'. At home, however, Irish society and its intellectual and political leaders were still, in de Valera's day, prone to be resistant to the class realities of social structure in ways that certain very famous social thinkers have regarded as a deplorable form of mystification.

CHAPTER 23 – De Valera's Other Ireland

1 Moynihan (ed.), *Speeches and Statements*, p. 454.
2 Seán Ó Faoláin, 'This is Your Magazine', *The Bell*, vol. 1, no 1, 1940, p. 8.
3 Bo Almqvist, 'The Irish Folklore Commission: Achievement and legacy', *Béaloideas*, vols 45–7, 1977–9, p. 25.
4 Foster, *The Apprentice Mage*, p. 126.
5 Ibid., p. 136.
6 Lee, *Ireland 1912–1985*, p. 211.
7 Uli Linke, 'Power and Culture Theory: Problematising the Focus of Research in German Folklore Scholarship', in R. Bendix and R.L. Zumwolt (eds), *Folklore Interpreted: Essays in honour of Alan Dundes* (New York: Garland, 1995), pp. 417–18.
8 Quoted in Foster, *The Apprentice Mage*, p. 126.
9 H. Rechnenbachk, untitled article in *Volt und Russe*, vol. 10, 1935, p. 376.
10 M. Ziegler, 'Vollskunde auf Rassischer Grundlage: Voranssetzunden und aufgaben', *Nationalsozialis ische Monatshefte*, vol. 4, 1936, pp. 711–17.
11 Moynihan (ed.), *Speeches and Statements*, p. 354.
12 S. Connolly, 'Approaches to the History of Irish Popular Culture', *Bullán*, vol. 2, no. 2, 1996, pp. 83–100.
13 Ó Crualaoich, 'The Vision of Liberation in *Cúirt an Mheán Oíche*'.

14 D. Hyde, 'The Necessity of De-Anglicising Ireland', in B. Ó Conaire (ed.), *Language, Lore and Lyrics: Essays and lectures – Douglas Hyde* (Dublin: Irish Academic Press, 1986), p. 154.
15 Moynihan (ed.), *Speeches and Statements*, p. 131.
16 Hannerz, *Cultural Complexity*.
17 G. Ó Crualaoich, D. Ó Giolláin and H. Huttunen, 'Irish–Finnish Research Collaboration: The Cork Northside Folklore Project', *NIF Newsletter*, vol. 21, 1993, pp. 17–18.
18 A seminal statement of these issues is J. Clifford and G. Marcus (eds), *Writing Culture: The poetics and politics of ethnography* (Berkeley: University of California Press, 1985). Their importance in relation to folklore is reflected in B. Jackson and E. Ives (eds), *The World Observed: Reflections on the fieldwork process* (Urbana: University of Illinois Press, 1996).

Bibliography

Aarne, A.A. and S. Thompson, *The Types of the Folk-Tale: A classification and bibliography*, 2nd revision (Helsinki: Academia Scientarum Fennica, 1961)

Almqvist, Bo, 'Irish Migratory Legends on the Supernatural: Sources, studies and problems', in Pádraig Ó hÉalaí (ed.), *The Fairy Hill is on Fire!* (Baile Átha Cliath: An Cumann le Béaloideas Éireann, 1991)

Arensberg, Conrad, *The Irish Countryman* (New York: Macmillan, 1937)

— and Solon T. Kimball, *Family and Community in Ireland* (Cambridge MA: Harvard University Press, 1940)

Bauman, Richard (ed.), *Folklore, Cultural Performances and Popular Entertainments* (New York/Oxford, 1992)

—, *Verbal Art as Performance* (Rowley, MA: Newbury House Publishers, 1977)

— and Joel Sherzer, *Explorations in the Ethnography of Speaking*, 2nd edn (London: Cambridge University Press, 1989)

Beiner, Guy, 'Locating Local Tradition: The sociocultural construction of Irish folk memory', in Diarmuid Ó Giolláin (ed.), *Irish Ethnologies* (Notre Dame, IN: University of Notre Dame Press, 2017)

—, *Remembering the Year of the French: Irish folk history and social history* (Madison: University of Wisconsin Press, 2006)

Bhreathnach, Máire, 'The Sovereignty Goddess as Goddess of Death?', *Zeitschrift fur Celtische Philologie*, vol. 39, no. 1, 2009

Black, R.I., 'The Gaelic Calendar Months: Some meanings and derivations', *Shadow*, vol. 2, 1985

Blum, Jerome, *The End of the Old Order in Europe* (New Jersey: Princeton University Press, 1978)

Bohannan, Paul, *How Culture Works* (New York: The Free Press, 1995)

Bourke, Angela, *The Burning of Bridget Cleary: A true story* (London: Pimlico, 1999)

— et al. (eds), *Field Day Anthology of Irish Writing*, vols IV–V (Cork: Cork University Press, 2002)

Breathnach, R.A., 'The Lady and the King: A theme of Irish literature', *Studies*, vol. xlii, 1953

Briggs, Katharine, *Dictionary of British Folktales in the English Language* (London: Routledge, 1970)

Broderick, G., 'Berrey Dhone: A Manx *Caillech Bérri*?', *Zeitschrift für celtische Philologie*, vol. 40, 1984

Bruford, Alan and Donald A. MacDonald, *Scottish Traditional Tales* (Edinburgh: Birlinn, 1994)

Caerwyn Williams, J.E. and Máirín Ní Mhuiríos, *Traidisiún Liteartha na nGael* (Baile Átha Cliath: An Clochamhar, 1979)

Carey, John, 'The Old Gods of Ireland', in Katja Ritari and Alexandra Bergholm (eds), *Understanding Celtic Religion: Revisiting the pagan past* (Cardiff: University of Wales Press, 2015)

—, 'The Baptism of the Gods', in John Carey, *A Single Ray of the Sun: Religious speculation in early Ireland* (Andover and Aberystwyth: Celtic Studies Publications, 1999)

—, 'Time, Space and the Otherworld', *Proceedings of the Harvard Celtic Colloquium*, vol. 7, 1987

—, 'Notes on the Irish War-Goddess', Éigse, vol. 19, 1983

Cashman, Ray, *Packy Jim: Folklore and worldview on the Irish border* (Madison, WI: The University of Wisconsin Press, 2016)

—, *Storytelling on the Northern Irish Border: Characters and community* (Bloomington: Indiana University Press, 2008)

Christiansen, R. Th., *Studies in Irish and Scandinavian Folktales* (Copenhagen: Rosenkilde & Bagger, 1959)

Clifford, James and George Marcus (eds), *Writing Culture: The poetics and politics of ethnography* (Berkeley: University of California Press, 1985)

Connell, Kenneth, *Irish Peasant Society* (Oxford: Oxford University Press, 1968)

—, 'The Population of Ireland in the Eighteenth Century', *Economic History Review*, vol. 16, 1946

Connolly, Seán, 'Approaches to the History of Irish Popular Culture', *Bullán*, vol. 2, no. 2, 1996

—, *Priests and People in Pre-Famine Ireland 1780–1845* (Dublin: Gill & Macmillan, 1982)

Corkery, Daniel, *The Hidden Ireland* (Dublin: Gill & Macmillan, 1924 [1967])

Croker, Thomas Crofton, *Researches in the South of Ireland* (London: John Murray, 1824)

Cullen, Louis, 'The Hidden Ireland: Re-assessment of a concept', *Studia Hibernica*, vol. 9

Danaher, Kevin, *A Bibliography of Irish Ethnography and Folk Tradition* (Cork: Mercier Press, 1972)

—, *The Year in Ireland* (Cork: Mercier Press, 1972)

—, *Folktales of the Irish Countryside* (Cork: Mercier Press, 1967)

Deane, Séamus (ed.), *Field Day Anthology of Irish Writing*, vols I–III (London: Field Day Publications, 1991)

de Bhaldraithe, Tomás, *Nuascéalaíocht 1940–1950* (Baile Átha Cliath: Sáirséal & Dill, 1952)

de Bougrenet de La Tocnaye, Jacques-Louis, *A Frenchman's Walk through Ireland, 1796–7*, trans. John Stevenson (Belfast: Blackstaff Press, 1984 [originally published 1917])

de hÍde, Dúbhghlás, *An Sgéulaidhe Gaedhealach* (Baile Átha Cliath: An Cumann le Béaloideas Éireann, 1933)

Delargy, J.H., 'The Gaelic Storyteller: With some notes on Gaelic folktales', *Proceedings of the British Academy*, vol. 31, 1945

de Paor, Liam, *Portrait of Ireland* (Bray: St Martin's Press, 1985)

—, 'Ireland's Identities', *The Crane Bag*, vol. 3, no. 1, 1979

Desplanques, Marie-Annick, 'Reflections on the Poetics of Fieldwork in a Living Archive', *Béascna*, vol. 9, 2015

Dickson, David, *Old World Colony: Cork and south Munster 1630–1830* (Cork: Cork University Press, 2005)

Doniger O'Flaherty, Wendy, *Other People's Myths* (New York: Macmillan, 1988)

Donnan, Hastings, 'Re-Placing Ireland in Irish Anthropology', in Diarmuid Ó Giolláin (ed.), *Irish Ethnologies* (Notre Dame: University of Notre Dame Press, 2017)

Donnelly, James S. and Kerby A. Miller (eds), *Irish Popular Culture 1650–1850* (Dublin: Irish Academic Press, 1998)

Duffy, Eamon, *The Stripping of the Altars: Traditional religion in England* c. *1400 – c. 1580* (New Haven and London: Yale University Press, 1992)

Dundes, Alan, 'Texture, Text and Context', *Southern Folklore Quarterly*, vol. 28, 1964

Durkacz, Victor Edward, *The Decline of the Celic Languages* (Edinburgh: John Donald, 1983)

Eagleton, Terry, *How to Read a Poem* (Oxford: John Wiley & Sons, 2006)

Ellis Davidson, Hilda R., *Myths and Symbols in Pagan Europe* (Manchester: Manchester University Press, 1988)

Enright, Michael J., 'King James and His Island: An archaic kingship belief?', *The Scottish Historical Review*, vol. 55, no. 159, 1976

Evans-Pritchard, E.E., *Witchcraft, Oracles and Magic among the Azande* (Oxford: Oxford University Press, 1937)

Fabb, Nigel, *Linguistics and Literature* (Oxford: Blackwell, 1997)

Filip, J., *Celtic Civilisation and Its Heritage* (Wellingborough and Prague: Colet's Academia, 1977)

Finnegan, Ruth, *Oral Traditions and the Verbal Arts* (London: Routledge, 1992)

—, *Oral Literature in Africa* (Oxford: Clarendon Press, 1970)

Foster, Roy, *W.B. Yeats: A life, 1: The Apprentice Mage, 1865–1914* (Oxford: Oxford University Press, 1997)

Friedrich, P., *The Meaning of Aphrodite* (Chicago: University of Chicago Press, 1978)

Gailey, Alan, 'The Nature of Tradition', *Folklore*, vol. 100, no. 2, 1989

— (ed.), *The Use of Tradition* (Cultra: Ulster Folk and Transport Museum, 1988)

Galassi, Jonathan, 'Updike's Violin', *New York Review of Books*, vol. lxii, no. 20, 2015

Gantz, J., *Early Irish Myths and Sagas* (Harmondsworth: Penguin, 1981)

Gaster, Th. H., *The New Golden Bough* (New York: Criterion, 1959)

Glassie, Henry, *Passing the Time in Ballymenone: Culture and History of an Ulster Community* (Dublin: The O'Brien Press, 1982 / Bloomington: Indiana University Press, 1995)

—, *Irish Folktales* (Harmondsworth: Penguin, 1985)

Goldstein, Kenneth, *A Guide for Fieldworkers in Folklore* (Hatboro, PA: Folklore Associates, 1974)

Gray, Elizabeth, 'Cath Maige Tuired: Myth and structure', Structure (1–24), Éigse, vol. 18, 1981; and Éigse, vol. 19, 1983

Gregory, Lady Augusta, *Visions and Beliefs in the West of Ireland* (Gerrards Cross: Colin Smythe, 1970)

—, *Cuchulain of Muirthemne* (London: John Murray, 1902), preface by W.B. Yeats

Gumperz, J.J. and Dell Hymes (eds), *Direction in Sociolinguistics: The ethnography of communication* (New York: Holt, Rinehart & Winston, 1972)

Hammond, Peter B., *An Introduction to Social and Cultural Anthropology* (London: Collier Macmillan, 1978)

Hannerz, Ulf, *Cultural Complexity: Studies in the social organization of meaning* (New York: Columbia University Press, 1992)

Harrison, Simon, 'Magical Exchange of the Preconditions of Production in a Sepik River Village', *MAN*, vol. 23, no. 2, 1988

Harvey, C.B., *Contemporary Irish Traditional Narrative* (Berkeley: University of California Press, 1992)

Heaney, Seamus, *The Midnight Verdict* (Oldcastle, Co. Meath: Gallery Press, 1993)

Henige, David, *Oral Historiography* (Harlow: Longman, 1982)

Herbert, Máire, 'Goddess and King: The sacred marriage in early Ireland', in L.O. Fradenburg (ed.), *Women and Sovereignty* (Edinburgh: Edinburgh University Press, 1992)

Hobsbawm, Eric and Terence Ranger (eds), *The Invention of Tradition* (Cambridge: Cambridge University Press, 1983)

Honko, Lauri, 'The Folklore Process', in *Folklore Fellows Summer School Programme* (Turku: FFSS, 1991)

Hull, Eleanor, 'Legends and Traditions of the *Cailleach Bhéarra* or Old Woman (Hag) of Beara', *Folklore*, vol. 38, 1927

Hyde, D., 'The Necessity of De-Anglicising Ireland', in B. Ó Conaire (ed.), *Language, Lore and Lyrics: Essays and lectures – Douglas Hyde* (Dublin: Irish Academic Press, 1986)

Hymes, Dell, *Now I Know Only So Far: Essays in ethnopoetics* (Lincoln: University of Nebraska Press, 2003)

—, *'In Vain I Tried to Tell You': Essays in Native American ethnopoetics* (Philadelphia: University of Pennsylvania Press, 1981)

—, *Language in Education* (Washington, DC: Centre for Applied Linguistics, 1980)

—, 'An Ethnographic Perspective on "What is Literature"', *New Literary History*, vol. v, no. 1 (Maryland: Johns Hopkins University Press, 1973)

—, 'Towards Ethnographies of Communication: The analysis of communicative events', in Paulo Giglioli (ed.), *Language and Social Context* (Baltimore and Middlesex: Penguin, 1973)

—, 'The Contribution of Folklore to Sociolinguistic Research', *Journal of American Folklore*, vol. 84, 1971

Jackson, Kenneth H., *Aislinge Meic Con Glinne* (Dublin: Dublin Institute for Advanced Studies, 1990)

— (ed.), *Scéalta ón mBlascaod* (Baile Átha Cliath: An Cumann le Béaloideas Éireann, 1938)

Jakobson, R., 'Closing Statement: Linguistics and poetics', in Thomas Sebeok (ed.), *Style in Language* (Cambridge, MA: MIT Press, 1960)

Jenkins, Richard P., 'Witches and Fairies: Supernatural aggression and deviance among the Irish peasantry', *Ulster Folklife*, vol. xxii, 1977

Jones-Hughes, T., 'The Large Farm in Nineteenth-Century Ireland', in A. Gailey et al. (eds), *Gold Under the Furze* (Dublin: The Glendale Press, 1982)

Kallen, Jeffrey L., 'Linguistics and Oral Tradition: The structural study of the riddle', *Occasional paper 2* (Dublin: Centre for Language and Communication Studies, 1981)

Kay, Paul and Willet Kempton, 'What is the Sapir-Whorf Hypothesis?' *American Anthropologist*, vol. 86, no. 1, 1984

Kearney, Richard, 'Myth and Motherland', in Field Day Theatre Company, *Ireland's Field Day* (London: Hutchinson, 1985)

Kiely, Charles N. 'Funerals in Ireland Today: The traditions, customs, beliefs and influences associated with death in a comparative and a historical perspective', PhD thesis, Department of Béaloideas/Folklore and Ethnology, University College Cork, 2010

Krappe, A.H., 'La Cailleach Bhéara: Notes de mythologie gaelique', *Études Celtiques*, vol. 1, 1936

Leach, E., *Lévi-Strauss* (London: Fontana, 1974)

Lee, J.J., *Ireland 1912–1985: Politics and society* (Cambridge: Cambridge University Press, 1989)

Lenihan, Edmund, *In Search of Biddy Early* (Cork: Mercier Press, 1987)

Lévi-Strauss, Claude, 'The Story of Asdival', in Edmond Leach, *The Structural Study of Myth of Totemism* (London: Tavistock, 1967)

—, 'The Structural Study of Myth', in *Structural Anthropology* (New York: Basic Books, 1963)

Lindstrom, Lamont, 'Discourse', in A. Barnard and J. Spenser (eds), *Encyclopedia of Social and Cultural Anthropology* (London: Routledge, 1996)

Löffler, Christa Maria, *The Voyage to the Otherworld Island in Early Irish Literature* (Salzburg: Universität Salzburg, Institut für Anglistik und Amerikanistik, 1983)

Lorimer, E.O., *Tales from the Arabian Nights*, illus. Guy Nicoll (London: Oxford University Press, 1946)

Lowenthal, David, *The Heritage Crusade and the Spoils of History* (London: Cambridge University Press, 1997)

—, *The Past is a Foreign Country* (Cambridge: Cambridge University Press, 1985)

Luthi, Max, *The European Folktale: Form and nature*, English translation (Philadelphia: Institute for the Study of Human Issues, 1982)

Lyle, Emily, *Archaic Cosmos* (Edinburgh: Edinburgh University Press, 1991)

Lysaght, Patricia, 'Lady Gregory (1852–1932)', in Angela Bourke et al. (eds), *The Field Day Anthology of Irish Writing. Vol. IV: Irish Women's Writing and Traditions* (Cork: Cork University Press, 2002)

—, 'Caoineadh os Cionn Coirp: The lament for the dead in Ireland', *Folklore*, vol. 108, 1997

—, *The Banshee: The Irish supernatural death-messenger*, 2nd edn (Dublin: Glendale Press, 1996)

—, 'Caoineadh na Marbh: Die totenklage in Irland', *Rheinisch-Westfälische Zeitschrift für Volkskunde*, vol. 40, 1995

Macalister, R.A.S. (ed.), *Lebar Gabála Érenn*, vols 1–4 (Dublin: Irish Texts Society, 1938–41)

Mac Cana, Proinsias, 'Placenames and Mythology in Irish Tradition: Places, pilgrimages and things', *Proceedings of the First North American Congress of Celtic Studies*, University of Ottawa, 1986

—, *The Learned Tales of Medieval Ireland* (Dublin: DIAS, 1980)

—, *Celtic Mythology* (London: Hamlyn, 1970)

MacCárthaigh, Criostóir, 'Midwife to the Fairies (ML5070): The Irish variants in their Scottish and Scandinavian perspective', *Béaloideas*, vol. 59, 1991

MacCionnaith, Láimhbheartach, SJ (ed.), *Dioghluim Dána* (Baile Átha Cliath: Oifig an tSoláthair, 1938)

MacCormack, Carol and Marilyn Strathern, *Nature, Culture and Gender* (London: Cambridge University Press, 1980)

MacDonagh, Oliver, *Ireland: The union and its aftermath* (London: George Allen & Unwin, 1977)

Mackay, J.G., *More West Highland Tales*, vols I–II (Edinburgh: Oliver & Boyd, 1940)

MacNeill, Máire, *The Festival of Lughnasa* (Oxford: Oxford University Press, 1962)

MacPhilib, Séamas, 'The Changeling (ML 5058): Irish versions of a migratory legend in their international context', *Béaloideas*, vol. 59, 1991

Malinowski, Bronislaw, *Argonauts of the Western Pacific* (London: Routledge & Kegan Paul, 1922)

Manning, Brian, 'The English Revolution and Ireland, 1640–60', *Retrospect*, new series, no. 2, 1982

Martin, F.X., '1916 [as] Myth, Fact and Mystery', *Studia Hibernica*, vol. 7, 1967

McCracken, J.L., 'The Ecclesiastical Structure, 1714–60', in T.W. Moody and W.E. Vaughan (eds), *A New History of Ireland. Vol. IV: Eighteenth-Century Ireland, 1691–1800* (Oxford: Clarendon Press, 1986)

McHugh, Roger, 'The Famine in Irish Oral Tradition', in R.D. Edwards and T.D. Williams (eds), *The Great Famine: Studies in Irish history 1845–52* (Dublin: Lilliput Press, 1994 [reprint])

McKay, J.G., 'The Deer Cult and the Deer-Goddess Cult of the Ancient Caledonians', *Folklore*, vol. 43, 1932

McPhee, Peter, 'Popular Culture, Symbolism, and Rural Radicalism in Nineteenth-Century France', *Journal of Peasant Studies*, vol. v, no. 2, 1978

Meyer, Kuno, *Aislinge Meic Conglinne: The vision of Mac Conglinne, a middle-Irish wonder tale* (London: David Nutt, 1892)

Morley, Vincent, *The Popular Mind in Eighteenth-Century Ireland* (Cork: Cork University Press, 2017)

Motz, Lotte, *The Faces of the Goddess* (Oxford: Oxford University Press, 1997)

Murphy, Gerard, review of J. Szöverffy, *Irisches Erzählgut im Abendland*, Éigse, vol. 9, 1961

—, 'The Lament of the Old Woman of Beare', *Proceedings of the Royal Irish Academy*, vol. 55, 1953

—, 'The Gaelic Background', in Michael Tierney (ed.), *Daniel O'Connell: Nine centenary essays* (Dublin: Browne & Nolan, 1949)

Myer, K., 'Stories and Songs from Irish MSS.', *Otia Merseiana*, vol. 1, 1899

Nagy, Joseph F., 'Staging the Otherworld in Medieval Irish Tradition', in Katja Ritari and Alexandra Bergholm (eds), *Understanding Celtic Religion: Revisiting the pagan past* (Cardiff: University of Wales Press, 2015)

—, *The Wisdom of the Outlaw* (Berkley/London: University of California Press, 1985), chapters 1 and 2

Newall, V. (ed.), 'The Divine Hag of the Pagan Celts', in *The Witch Figure* (London: Routledge, 1973)

Ní Dhonnchadha, Máirín, 'Cailleach and other Terms for Veiled Women in Medieval Irish Texts', Éigse, vol. 28, 1994

Ní Dhuibhne, Éilís, '"The Old Woman as Hare": Structure and meaning in an Irish legend', *Folklore*, vol. 104, 1993

Ní Shéaghdha, Neasa (ed.), *Agallamh na Seanórach*, vols I–III (Baile Átha Cliath: Oifig an tSoláthair, 1942–5)

Ó Broin, T., 'Lia Fáil: Fact and fiction in the tradition', *Celtica*, vol. 21, 1990

Ó Buachalla, Breandán, *Aisling Ghéar: Na Stiobhartaigh agus an taos léinn, 1603–1788* (Dublin: An Clochomhar Tta, 1996)

—, 'An Mheisiasacht agus an Aisling', in P. de Brún, S. Ó Coileáin and P. Ó Riain (eds), *Folia Gadelica* (Cork: Cork University Press, 1983)

Ó Cadhain, Máirtín, *Cré na Cille* (Dublin: Sáirséal & Dill, 1949)

O'Carroll, Cliona, 'Public Folklore Operating between Aspiration and Expediency', *Irish Journal of Anthropology*, vol. 16, no. 1, 2013

Ó Catháin, Séamus, *Scéalta Cois Cladaigh/Stories from the Sea and Shore* (Baile Átha Cliath: Comhairle Béaloideas Éireann, 1983)

Ó Cathasaigh, Tomás, 'The Eponym of Cnogha', *Éigse*, vol. 23, 1989

—, 'Cath Maige Tuired as Exemplary Myth', in P. de Brún, S. Ó Coileáin and P. Ó Riain (eds), *Folia Gadelica* (Cork: Cork University Press, 1983)

—, *The Heroic Biography of Cormac Mac Airt* (Dublin: Institute of Advanced Studies, 1977)

Ó Coileáin, Seán, 'Some Problems of Story and History', *Ériu*, vol. xxxii, 1981, pp. 115–36

O'Connor, Anne, *Child Murderess and Dead Child Traditions* (Folklore Fellows Communications 249) (Helsinki: Academia Scientarum Fennica, 1991)

O'Connor, Frank, *Leinster, Munster and Connaught* (London: Robert Hale, n.d.)

Ó Criomhthainn, Tomás (ed. Seán Ó Coileáin), *An tOileánach* (Baile Átha Cliath: Cló Talbóid, 2002)

Ó Cróinín, Donncha (ed.), *Seanchas ó Chairbre* (Baile Átha Cliath: Comhairle Bhéaloideas Éireann, 1985)

— (ed.), *Seanchas Amhlaoibh Í Luínse* (Baile Átha Cliath: Comhairle Bhéaloideas Éireann, 1980)

— (ed.), *Scéalaíocht Amhlaoibh Í Luínse* (Baile Átha Cliath: Comhairle Bhéaloideas Éireann, 1938)

Ó Crualaoich, Gearóid, 'Folkloristic-Ethnological Studies in Ireland', in Diarmuid Ó Giolláin (ed.), *Irish Ethnologies* (Notre Dame: University of Notre Dame Press, 2017)

—, *The Book of the Cailleach: Stories of the wise-woman healer* (Cork: Cork University Press, 2003)

—, 'County Cork Folklore and Its Collection', in Patrick O'Flanagan and Cornelius Buttimer (eds), *Cork History & Society* (Cork: Geography Publications, 1993)

—, D. Ó Giolláin and H. Huttunen, 'Irish–Finnish Research Collaboration: The Cork Northside Folklore Project', *NIF Newsletter*, vol. 21, 1993

—, 'Contest in the Cosmology and the Ritual of the Irish Merry Wake', *Cosmos*, vol. 6, 1990

—, 'Continuity and Adaptation in Legends of *Cailleach Bhéarra*', *Béaloideas*, vol. 56, 1988

—, 'The Vision of Liberation in *Cúirt an Mheán Oíche*', in P. de Brún, S. Ó Coileáin and P. Ó Riain (eds), *Folia Gadelica* (Cork: Cork University Press, 1983)

Ó Direáin, Máirtín, *Ón Ulán Ramhar Siar*, ed. Eoghan Ó hÁnluain (Baile Átha Cliath: An Clóchamhar, 2002)

Ó Donnchadha, Tadhg, 'Uiliog Ó Céirín', *Lia Fáil*, vol. 4, 1932

Ó Duilearga, Séamus (ed.), *Leabhar Sheáin Í Chonaill: Sgéalta agus seanchas ó Íbh Ráthach* (Baile Átha Cliath: Comhairle Bhéaloideas Éireann, [1948] 1977); *Seán*

Ó Conaill's Book, trans. Máire MacNéill (Baile Átha Cliath/Dublin: An Cumann le Béaloideas Éireann, 1981)

Ó Giolláin, Diarmuid (ed.), *Irish Ethnologies* (Notre Dame: University of Notre Dame Press, 2017)

—, *Locating Irish Folklore* (Cork: Cork University Press, 2000)

—, 'Capturer of Fairy Shoemaker Outwitted: The multiple marker versions (MLSIT 6011)', *Béaloideas*, vol. 59, 1991

—, 'The Leipreachán and Fairies, Dwarfs and the Household Familiar: A comparative study', *Béaloideas*, vol. 52, 1984

Ó Gráda, Cormac, *An Drochshaol: Béaloideas agus amhráin* (Baile Átha Cliath: Coiscéim, 1994)

O'Grady, S.D., *Silva Gadelica* (London: Williams & Norgate, 1892)

Ó Héalaí, Pádraig, 'An Leabhar Eoin: Deabhóid agus piseogaíocht', in M. Mac Craith and P. Ó Héalaí (eds), *Diasa Díograise: Aistí i gcuimhne ar Mháirtín Ó Briain* (Indreabhán: Cló Iar-Chonnacht, 2009)

— (ed.), *Glórtha ón Osnádúr/Sounds from the Supernatural* (Baile Átha Cliath: An Cumann le Béaloideas Éireann, 1995)

— (ed.), *Finscéalta agus Litríocht/Folk Legends and Fiction* (Baile Átha Cliath: An Cumann le Béaloideas Éireann, 1993)

Ó hEochaidh, Seán and Séamus Ó Catháin, *Síscéalta ó Thír Chonaill/Fairy Legends from Donegal*, translated to English by Máire MacNéill (Baile Átha Cliath: Comhairle Bhéaloideas Éireann, 1977)

Ó hÓgáin, Dáithí, 'An É an tAm Fós E?', *Béaloideas*, vols 42–4, 1974–6

Ó hUaithne, D. (ed.), *Cúirt an Mheán Oíche* (Baile Átha Cliath: Dolmen Press, 1968)

Ó Huallacháin, Colmán, OFM, *Foclóir Fealsamh* (Baile Átha Cliath: An Gúm, 1958)

Ó Madagáin, Breandán, 'Gaelic Lullaby: A charm to protect the baby', *Scottish Studies*, vol. 29, 1989

Ó Muirithe, Diarmuid, *Tomás Ó Míocháin: Filíocht* (Dublin: An Clóchomhar, 1988)

Ó Murchú, L.P. (eag.), *Cúirt an Mheon-Oíche* (Baile Átha Cliath: An Clóchomhar, 1982)

Ong, Walter, *Orality and Literacy: The technologizing of the world* (London: Psychology Press, 1982)

Ó Rathile, T.F., *Búrdúin Bheaga* (Dublin: Brown & Nolan, 1925)

O'Riordan, Michelle, *Irish Bardic Poetry and Rhetorical Reality* (Cork: Cork University Press, 2007)

Ó Súilleabháin, Seán, *Storytelling in Irish Tradition* (Cork: Mercier Press, 1973)

—, *A Handbook of Irish Folklore* (Detroit: Singing Tree Press, 1970)

—, *Irish Folk Custom and Belief* (Dublin: The Three Candles, 1967)

—, *Irish Wake Amusements* (Cork: Mercier Press, 1967)

— and R. Th. Christiansen, *The Types of the Irish Folktale* (Helsinki: Suomalinan Tiedakatemia Academia Scientiarum Fennica, 1963)

O'Sullivan, Seán, *Legends from Ireland* (London: B.T. Batsford, 1977)

—, *Folktales from Ireland* (Chicago: University of Chicago Press, 1966)

Ó Tuama, Seán, 'Dónall Ó Corcora', *Scríobh*, vol. 4, 1979

—, 'Cúirt an Mheán Oíche', *Studia Hibernica*, vol. 4, 1964

—, *Nuabhéarsaíocht 1939–1949* (Baile Átha Cliath: Sáirséal & Dill, 1950)

Permyakov, G.L., *From Proverb to Folktale: Notes on the general theory of cliché* (Moscow: USSR Academy of Sciences, 1979)

Plummer, Charles, 'Some Passages in the Brehon Laws III', *Ériu*, vol. 9, 1921–3

Poirtéir, Cathal, 'The Folklore of the Famine: *Seanchas an drochshaoil*', in John Crowley, W.J. Smyth and Mike Murphy (eds), *Atlas of the Great Irish Famine 1845–52* (Cork: Cork University Press, 2012)

—, *Glórtha ón nGorta: Béaloideas na Gaeilge agus an Gorta Mór* (Baile Átha Cliath: Coiscéim, 1996)

Prim, J.G.A., 'Olden Popular Pastimes in Kilkenny', *JRSAI*, vol. ii, 1852–3

Propp, Vladimir, *The Morphology of the Folktale*, English translation, 2nd edn (Austin: University of Texas Press, 1968)

Radnor, Joan, 'Poets, Harpers and Women in Early Irish Literature', in A.T.E. Matonis and D.F. Melia (eds), *Celtic Language, Celtic Culture: A festschrift for Eric P. Hamp* (Van Nuys: Ford & Bailie, 1990)

Rapport, N. and J. Overing (eds), *Social and Cultural Anthropology: The key concepts* (London: Routledge, 2000)

Redfield, Robert and George M. Foster, *Peasant Society: A reader* (Boston: Little, Brown & Co., 1967)

Rees, Alwyn and Brinley Rees, *Celtic Heritage: Ancient tradition in Ireland and Wales* (London: Thames & Hudson, 1961)

Robinson, F.N., *The Works of Geoffrey Chaucer* (Boston: Riverside Press, 1957)

Ross, Anne, *The Pagan Celts* (London: B.T. Batsford, 1986)

—, *Pagan Celtic Britain* (London: Routledge, 1967)

Ryan, Patrick, *Storytelling in Ireland: A re-awakening* (Londonderry: The Verbal Arts Centre, 1995)

Samuel, Raphael and Paul Thompson (eds), *The Myths We Live By* (London: Routledge, 1990)

Schmitz, Nancy, 'An Irish Wise-Woman: Fact and legend', *Journal of the Folklore Institute*, vol. 14, 1977

Simms, Norman, 'Ned Ludd's Mummers Play', *Folklore*, vol. lxxxix, no. 2, 1978

Sims-Williams, Patrick, 'Some Celtic Otherworld Terms', in A.T.E. Matonis and D.F. Melia (eds), *Celtic Language, Celtic Culture: A festschrift for Eric P. Hamp* (Van Nuys: Ford & Bailie, 1990)

Sjoestedt, Marie Louise, *Gods and Heroes of the Celts*, translated by M. Dillon (London: Methuen, 1949)

Skemer, Don C., *Binding Words: Textual amulets in the middle ages* (University Park, PA: Pennsylvania State University Press, 2006)

Sorlin, Évelyn, *Crie De Vie, Cri De Mort: Les fées du destin dans les pays Celtiques* (Folklore Fellows Communications 248) (Helsinki: Academia Scientiarum Fennica, 1991)

Stern, Ludwig Christian, 'Brian Merriman's *Cúirt an Mheadhóin Oidhche*', *Zeitschrift für celtische Philologie*, vol. 5, 1905

Strange, J. (ed.), *Caesarius of Heisterbach: Dialogus Miraculorum* (Coblenz, 1850), dist. XII, cap. 20, trans. H. Von E. Scott and C.C.S. Bland, *The Dialogue on Miracles: Caesarius of Heisterbach (1220–1235)*, vols I–II (London, 1929)

Swahn, J.O., *The Tale of Cupid and Psyche* (Lund: CWK Gleerup, 1955)

Taylor, Lawrence J., *Occasions of Faith: An anthropology of Irish Catholics* (Dublin: Lilliput Press, 1995)

Tedlock, Dennis, *The Spoken Word and the Work of Interpretation* (Philadelphia: University of Pennsylvania Press, 1983)

Thompson, Stith, *Motif-Index of Folk Literature*, 6 vols (Bloomington: Indiana University Press, 1955–8)

— (ed.), *Four Symposia on Folklore* (Bloomington: Indiana University Press, 1953)

Tonkin, Elizabeth, *Narrating on Pasts: The social construction of oral history* (Cambridge: Cambridge University Press, 1991)

—, 'History and the Myth of Realism', in R. Samuel and P.R. Thompson (eds), *The Myth We Live By* (London and New York: Routledge, 1990)

—, Maryon McDonald and Malcolm Chapman (eds), *History and Ethnicity* (London and New York: Routledge, 1989)

Ua Duinnín, P., *Amhráin Eoghain Uí Shúilleabháin: Maille le beathaidh an fhilidh agus foclóir* (Baile Átha Cliath: Conradh na Gaeilge, 1901)

Uí Chatháin, Bláthnaid, Éigse Chairbre (Baile Átha Cliath: An Clóchomhar, 2006)

Uí Ógáin, Ríonach, *Immortal Dan: Daniel O'Connell in Irish folk tradition* (Dublin: Geography Publications, 1995)

—, *An Rí gan Choróin: Dónal Ó Conaill sa bhéaloideas* (Baile Átha Cliath: An Clochomhar, 1984)

Uther, Hans-Jorg, *The Types of International Folktales: A classification and bibliography*, 3 vols (Helsinki: Folklore Fellows Communications, 2004)

Van der Ziel, Stanley, *John McGahern and the Imagination of Tradition* (Cork: Cork University Press, 2016)

Vansina, Jan, *Oral Tradition as History* (London: Heinemann, 1985)

—, *Oral Tradition: A study in historical methodology* (London: Routledge, 1965)

Verling, Máirtín (eag.), *Béarach Mná ag Caint* (Indreabhán: Cló Iar-Chonnachta, 1999)

— (eag.), *Gort Broc: Scéalta agus seanchas ó Bhéarra* (Baile Átha Cliath: Coiscéim, 1996)

von Franz, Marie-Louise, *An Introduction to the Interpretation of Fairytales* (New York: Analytic Psychology Club of New York, 1970)

von Humboldt, Wilhelm, *On Language: The diversity of human-language structure and its influence on the mental development of mankind*, trans. H. Aarsleff (Cambridge: Cambridge University Press, [1836] 1988)

von Sydow, C.W., 'Om Folkets Sägner', *Nordisk Kultur*, vol. 9, 1931

Wagner, H., 'Origins of Pagan Irish Religion', *Zeitschrift für celtische Philologie*, vol. 38, 1981

Wallace, Anthony F.C., *Religion: An anthropological view* (New York: Random House, 1966)

Wilson, Thomas M. and Hastings Donnan, *The Anthropology of Ireland* (Oxford and New York: Berg, 2006)

Wood-Martin, W.G., *Traces of the Elder Faiths of Ireland* (London: Longmans, Green & Co., 1902)

Zipes, Jack, *Breaking the Magic Spell: Radical theories of folk and fairy tales* (Austin: University of Texas Press, 1979)

Index

Note: Page locators in **bold** refer to figures.